Encyclopaedia of
CRICKET

Sports Encyclopaedias published by Robert Hale Limited

ASSOCIATION FOOTBALL
Maurice Golesworthy

ATHLETICS
Melvyn Watman

BOWLS
Ken Hawkes and Gerard Lindley

BOXING
Maurice Golesworthy

CHESS
Anne Sunnucks

CRICKET
Maurice Golesworthy

FLAT RACING
Roger Mortimer

GOLF
Webster Evans

MOTOR RACING
Anthony Pritchard

RUGBY UNION FOOTBALL
J. R. Jones
(Third edition by Maurice Golesworthy)

RUGBY LEAGUE FOOTBALL
A. N. Gaulton

MOUNTAINEERING
Walt Unsworth

SHOW JUMPING
Charles Stratton

SWIMMING
Pat Besford

Encyclopaedia of
CRICKET

Compiled by
Maurice Golesworthy

SIXTH EDITION

ROBERT HALE · LONDON

ISBN 0 7091 6020 8 (Hardcover)
ISBN 0 7091 6034 8 (Paperback)

Robert Hale Limited
Clerkenwell House
Clerkenwell Green
London EC1R 0HT

*Printed in Great Britain by
Billing & Sons Limited
Guildford, London and Worcester*

FOREWORD

by

Sir Leonard Hutton

Some say that too much attention is paid to statistics in connection with our national game of Cricket and that all the piles of figures each season accumulates are merely incidental. Of course, the game's the thing, and anyone who loves cricket as much as I do will want to emphasise that, but it seems that figures and records have become as much a part of first-class cricket as the bat and the ball. Even the strongest critics of the prominence that is nowadays given to those innumerable numerals (if you will pardon the expression) will be bound to admit that the progress of many an important innings or many an important game has been influenced by the thought of averages or figures compiled by some diligent statistician.

Thousands play the game for the love of it and that includes the vast majority of the first-class professionals—it's great to be paid for doing something that gives you so much real pleasure—but while those on the village green do not heed records, the first-class game owes a lot to those cricketing historians and statisticians who delve into score-books and come up with so many intriguing and exciting records.

It was, therefore, with real interest that I spent so much time reading *The Encyclopaedia of Cricket*. All the important figures are here, but what I like most is that they have been strung together in such a readable fashion and I am sure that in the years to come I will find much to entertain me in this most informative book by Maurice Golesworthy.

It is difficult to imagine how much time and concentration Mr. Golesworthy has given to the accumulation of so many facts and figures. But certainly much careful research has been involved, and I am sure this publication will be of immense value, particularly when arguments are to be settled.

As an old player I have already been able to recapture happy days of the past within the pages of this book, and along with the young cricketer of the future, I will be able to increase my knowledge of the game.

A most interesting cricket book for young and old, and one that is sure to while away many of those long winter evenings and keep the sound of bat on ball ringing in their ears.

INTRODUCTION

THERE have probably been more books written about cricket than any other sport and some excuse may be needed for adding to that number. Mine lays in the belief that I am fulfilling a need by re-examining the figures and records with which the game abounds and setting them out in a style which makes for easy reference.

The style is one which has already proved so popular in my earlier Encyclopædias of Association Football and of Boxing and which I do not think has been previously attempted in the sport of cricket.

It was not without a feeling of trepidation that I embarked upon the task of compiling this volume for it is obvious that cricket includes more figures and records than any other popular sport, and it also includes among its followers many of the most expert, painstaking and devoted chroniclers, not to mention literary giants whose writings on the subject are ranked among the finest English literature.

Readers who prefer picturesque prose will look elsewhere, for there is no scarcity of that in a game which brings out the best in many devoted writers. This, however, is a record book based on the facts and figures of outstanding achievements.

Many of the cricketers who play the game for the game's sake abhor figures and records and believe that they are purely incidental, but there is really no doubt that records as such maintain the interest of the majority of the cricketing public.

As with any single volume of this size the greatest difficulty is knowing what to include and what to leave out, and this applies particularly to biographies. Indeed one wonders whether or not to include any biographies at all, for no matter how many are put in one is certain to be criticised for leaving so and so out. Criticism of these omissions, however, means very little, for, in many cases, the reasons for choosing one player or another are based only on matters of personal opinion.

I should point out that in compiling these biographies I have written from a statistician's point of view, and they are largely based on figures of outstanding achievements in the highest class of cricket, i.e. Tests. However, not all great players have been Test stars, and many others, both before and since Test cricket commenced, have been included.

Under the county headings I have included the various record scores both for and against. Where these records were not created in either the County Championship or, in the case of Minor Counties, in their competition, then records both inside and outside the championships are mentioned.

One of the major difficulties when dealing with cricket records is the fact that chroniclers have never come to a general agreement as to when first-class cricket really began in England. However, I have not been too strict about this in so far as I have not been afraid to mention both 18th and 19th century records where these are still of interest. The reader may judge the quality of such achievements when compared with the modern game.

However, generally speaking the records under the various headings concern only first-class cricket, while the records of the modern one-day game are grouped under the titles of the various competitions.

Throughout this book an asterisk (*) indicates a "not out" innings.

For many years before the abolition of the amateur in 1963 it was the practice in record books to distinguish between amateur and professional cricketers by using the prefix "Mr." I have entirely disregarded this for as A. E. Knight wrote more than 70 years ago in his *Complete Cricketer*, "One may be sure that the real gentleman player has no love for these miserable and most hateful labels and distinctions."

One more important point I would like to make is that not all the outstanding achievements mentioned in this book under the various headings are necessarily records. Where the figures are records then that fact is quite clearly stated.

Records in this edition are based on games played up to the end of the 1976 season, but Test figures nowhere include England v. Rest of World or Australia v. World XI.

May I dedicate this work to the most industrious but least publicised cricketing enthusiasts, the Scorers. Without them our bookshelves would be very bare of cricket publications.

MAURICE GOLESWORTHY

ACKNOWLEDGEMENTS

So many cricket enthusiasts have assisted in the compilation of this book that it would be difficult to include every name, but I am most grateful to all those secretaries, journalists, players and other cricket supporters who have so willingly answered my queries.

The prompt manner in which busy club secretaries responded to my requests for information was most encouraging. With a dearth of Minor Counties records I had to call particularly on their secretaries, and while, of course, there were one or two from whom I could not elicit a reply the majority were most helpful and those reluctant ones would blush to see how experienced club secretaries like Messers. H. Lewis of Berkshire, L. W. Hancock of Staffordshire, R. J. Charlton of Lincolnshire, and the late F. Crompton of Bedfordshire went out of their way to supply me with more information than I had requested.

Special thanks are due to the secretaries of the M.C.C., the New Zealand Cricket Council, the Board of Control for Cricket in Pakistan, and the Club Cricket Conference, for providing me with valuable facts.

I am also grateful to Miss N. Rheinberg for details of women's cricket, Mr. Roger Page of Tasmania for some records from Australia, Mr. A. M. C. Thorburn of Edinburgh for valuable information about early Scottish cricket, Mr. R. M. Crichton of Jamaica for clearing up a number of queries concerning the game in his part of the world, and to two such knowledgeable cricket enthusiasts as the late Mr. G. D. Martineau and the late Mr. John E. Price. I was particularly indebted to former B.B.C. cricket statistician John Price for the painstaking work he did in checking the first edition of this book. He certainly helped me avoid errors and omissions which can so easily plague any writer who delves into the fantastic abundance of cricket records.

In compiling a record book such as this I have had to cross check with many publications. In this connection I am especially indebted to Wisden's, without reference to which the majority of cricket books would have been much less informative. The publishers of Wisden's, Sporting Handbooks Limited, have kindly allowed me to quote their figures for the career aggregates and averages of the leading players.

I also owe a great deal to my collection of cricket annuals published by the old *Daily News* and subsequently the *News Chronicle*, now alas no more.† These little books were especially helpful in the compilation of biographies.

Thanks also to Wm. Blackwood & Sons, Ltd., for permission to include brief quotations from *The Jubilee Book of Cricket* by K. S. Ranjitsinhji.

The number of publications which have proved helpful are so numerous that I have thought it fairest to list all of these in a separate bibliography as any cricket enthusiast who does not already have these in his collection would find them well worth buying.

M.G.

ILLUSTRATIONS

BIBLIOGRAPHY

A BRIEF bibliography to be read in conjunction with the acknowledgments.

Annals of Cricket, by W. W. Read (Sampson Low, Marston & Co.) 1896.

The Australians in England, by Roy Webber (Hodder & Stoughton) 1953.

Bat, Ball, Wicket and All, by G. D. Martineau (Sporting Handbooks) 1950.

A Century of Cricketers, by A. G. Moyes (Harrap) 1950.

The Charm of Cricket Past and Present, by Major C. H. B. Pridham (Herbert Jenkins) 1949.

The Complete Cricketer, by Albert E. Knight (Methuen) 1906.

The Cricket Field, by Rev. James Pycroft (Virtue) 1873.

Cricket Records, by Roy Webber (Playfair) 1951.

The Cricketers' Who's Who, by S. Canynge Caple (Lincoln Williams) 1934.

The County Cricket Championship, by Roy Webber (Sportsman's Book Club) 1958.

Famous Cricket Grounds, by Laurence Meynell (Phoenix) 1951.

A History of Cricket, by H. S. Altham and E. W. Swanton (Allen and Unwin) 4th edition, 1948.

History of the Tests, by Sydney Smith (Australasian) 1946.

The Jubilee Book of Cricket, by K. S. Ranjitsinhji (Blackwood) 1897.

The Language of Cricket, by W. J. Lewis (Oxford University Press) 1934.

The Laws of Cricket, by R. S. Rait Kerr (Longmans, Green) 1950.

League Cricket in England, by Roy Genders (Werner Laurie) 1952.

Lord's, 1787–1945, by Sir Pelham Warner (Harrap) 1946.

Maiden Over, by Nancy Joy (Sporting Handbooks) 1950.

Scores and Biographies (Longmans) various issues 1862–1925.

They Made Cricket, by G. D. Martineau (Museum Press) 1956.

West Indian Cricket, by Christopher Nicole (Phoenix) 1956.

"W.G." Cricketing Reminiscences and Personal Recollections, by W. G. Grace (James Bowden) 1899.

Who's Won the Toss? by E. H. D. Sewell (Stanley Paul) 1943.

Also various issues of *Wisden Cricketers' Almanack, News Chronicle Cricket Annual, Indian Cricket, The Indian Cricket-Feld Annual, South African Cricket Annual, The Cricket Almanack of New Zealand*, and *The Cricketer*.

A

ABANDONED

At Lord's, in 1907, the Middlesex v. Lancashire match was abandoned after the Lancashire captain, A. C. MacLaren, had refused to continue because of the state of the pitch.

Following rain on the first day spectators had invaded the pitch to protest at the decision to give up play. Police had to clear them off but not before the pitch was cut up.

The first important county game to be abandoned without a ball being played was that between Middlesex and Kent, at Lord's in 1889.

In June 1969, after Hampshire had left the Bournemouth ground believing that their game with Glamorgan had been abandoned because of rain, Glamorgan took the field for two minutes and were declared winners. However, this decision was subsequently reversed by the M.C.C. on appeal and the result declared a draw.

Only three England—Australia Tests have been abandoned without a ball being bowled. The first two were at Old Trafford, Manchester, one in August, 1890, and the other in July, 1938. Rain prevented play.

On the third occassion, which was at Melbourne in December–January, 1970–71, the Test was abandoned after three days of rain and a one-day limited-over match was played on what would have been the fifth day.

The England–Australia Test at Leeds in August 1975 was abandoned as a draw on the fifth day after vandals had damaged the pitch during the night.

ABEL, Robert (1857–1936)

One of only three England opening batsmen to have carried their bat through a completed innings of a Test match, "the Guvnor", as this Surrey player was known, did so against Australia at Sydney in 1892 when he made 132*.

The most astonishing innings of this master batsman's career was that against Somerset at The Oval in 1899 when he made 357*. It is still a record individual score for Surrey and the highest score ever made by a player carrying his bat through a completed innings. On that occasion Abel was at the wicket for just over 8½ hours while 811 runs were scored—the highest aggregate at The Oval in County cricket.

When failing eyesight forced the Surrey midget's retirement in 1904 he had scored 32,669 runs (av. 35.47) including 13 Tests in which he scored 744 runs (av. 37.20).

ABORIGINES

The Aborigines were the first cricket team from Australia to visit England. They were brought over by Charles Lawrence in 1868.

Lawrence, who was born in Middlesex but resided for the most part in Sussex, had gone out to Australia in 1861 and had remained there to coach the Albert Cricket Club of Sydney.

There were 13 Aborigines in the party, all members of the now extinct Werrumbrook tribe of Victoria, and the names by which they became known to the cricketing public are well worth recording here:

Dick-a-Dick, Tiger, Mosquito, Johnny Mullagh, Johnny Cuzens, Red Cap, Bullocky, Sundown, Twopenny, Jim Crow, Charlie Dumas and King Cole. The last named player was taken ill and died during his stay in England.

Their tour extended from May to October and they played 47 matches. Of these the Aborigines won 14, lost 14 and drew 19.

Large crowds were attracted to many of these games and in addition to cricket they gave the spectators some remarkable demonstrations with the stockwhip as well as throwing the spear and the boomerang.

ADCOCK, Neil Amwin Treharne (1931-   )

One of South Africa's most successful Test bowlers, Adcock, who hails from Cape Town, and bowled fast right-arm, enjoyed his best series when he toured England in 1960.

In the five Tests that summer he equalled H. J. Tayfield's 1955 South African record of 26 wickets in a rubber in England. Adcock's average was 22.57, Tayfield's 21.84.

Adcock made his debut for Transvaal in 1952–53 and quickly gained recognition, playing in all five Tests against New Zealand in his second season and taking 24 wickets.

In the third Test v. Australia, at Durban, in 1957–58, he took 6 for 43 and 1 for 34.

His best match figures were 13 for 65 for Transvaal v. Orange Free State, in a friendly match at Johannesburg, 1953–54.

AGE

Oldest

Listed below are some of the oldest men ever to appear in first-class cricket:

Raja Maharaj Singh captained the Bombay Governor's XI v. Commonwealth team in November, 1950, at Bombay. He was then aged 72.

C. K. Nayudu of Holkar, India, was 62 when he made his last appearance in 1958.

60—Lord Harris (60 years 5 months).

59—W. G. Grace (59 years 10 months), Rev. A. E. Green-Price (59 years 6 months).

58—E. Smith (Yorkshire).

57—Rev. R. H. Moss (Worcestershire), A. D. Nourse (South Africa), S. F. Barnes (Wales), A. F. Somerset (Sussex).

56—C. E. de Trafford (Leicestershire), W. G. Quaife (Warwickshire), J. T. Hearne (Middlesex).

55—E. M. Grace (Gloucestershire), A. Shaw (Sussex), R. Daft (Nottinghamshire).

54—G. Cox (Sussex), J. H. King (Leicestershire).

53—G. Gunn (Nottinghamshire).

52—A. E. Newton (Somerset), W. Rhodes (Yorkshire), E. Robson (Somerset), J. C. Clay (Glamorgan), Sir T. C. O'Brien (Ireland).

51—J. Southerton (Surrey), J. B. Hobbs (Surrey), F. E. Woolley (Kent), T. W. Goddard (Gloucestershire), A. N. Hornby (Lancashire), Rev. A. P. Wickham (Somerset), H. Elliott (Derbyshire).

Note: The names given in brackets are not necessarily the sides played for in their final first-class games.

Among the old-time players it should be noted that J. Small appeared for Hampshire v. M.C.C., at Lord's in 1798 when he was 61, and W. Clarke of Nottinghamshire, the famous lob bowler, was 57 when he made his last appearance for The England XI in June 1856.

Ernest Smith of Oxford University and Yorkshire was 58 when he appeared for H. D. G. Leveson-Gower's XI v. The Universities at Eastbourne in 1928.

W. G. Quaife scored 115 v. Derbyshire, at Birmingham, in his last appearance for Warwickshire at the age of 56.

In Test cricket between England and Australia the oldest player was W. G. Grace who was a month short of his 51st birthday when he captained England, at Nottingham, in June 1899.

The English record in all Test cricket was set up by W. Rhodes. He made four appearances for England v. West Indies in 1930 when aged 52.

G. Gunn appeared in the same series of four Tests. His age was 50.

James Southerton was 49 years 4 months when he appeared for England v. Australia, at Melbourne, in March 1877. This game has since become recognised as the first Test, and Southerton is still the oldest man ever to make his debut in Test cricket.

The oldest man ever selected to make his debut in a Test match other than Southerton is Miran Bux who was 47 years 8 months when he first appeared for Pakistan v. India, at Jahore, January 1955. He made only one other Test appearance, that in the same series a fortnight later.

A. C. MacLaren came out of retirement in 1921 to captain a team against Australia, and, in the following year, he led an M.C.C. team to the Antipodes. During this tour, in the first unofficial Test against New Zealand, at Wellington, he made 200*. He was then in his 52nd year.

Lord Harris was 79 when he played in a one-day match for the M.C.C. v. Indian Gymkhana, at Lord's, August 1929.

S. F. Barnes was 62 when he made his final appearance for Staffordshire in 1935.

Youngest

The youngest player ever to appear in first-class cricket is Qasim Feroze who was only 12 years 363 days of age when he made his debut for Bahawalpur in January 1971.

C. C. Dacre was 14 years 5 months when he made his debut for Auckland v. Wellington, at Auckland, in October 1914. Dacre qualified for Gloucestershire in 1930.

One of the youngest players ever to appear in a first-class game in England was W. H. Ashdown who made his debut for G. J. V. Weigall's XI v. Oxford University in 1914 when he was only 15½.

Another 15-year-old to make his debut was W. W. F. Pullen. When he first appeared for Gloucestershire v. Middlesex, at Lord's, June 5, 1882, he was 19 days short of his 16th birthday.

B. H. Pairaudeau (British Guiana) was 15 years 11 months when he made his debut in March 1947.

16-year-old players in first-class county cricket include C. J. Barnett (Gloucestershire) 1927, A. W. Carr (Nottinghamshire) 1910, H. T. W. Hardinge (Kent) 1906, R. Harvey (Essex) 1951, and A. Kennedy (Hampshire) 1907.

The youngest player to take part in first-class cricket in Australia is C. L. Badcock. He was not yet 16 when he first played for Tasmania v. Victoria, at Melbourne in 1929.

I. D. Craig was 16 years 8 months when he scored 91 on his first appearance for New South Wales v. South Australia, at Sydney, February 1952.

The Grace family have a remarkable record among young cricketers. W.G. made his first appearance for the West Gloucestershire C.C. when he was only nine years of age. He first played in matches at the Oval and at Lord's in 1864 when he was 16.

E. M. Grace was only 13 when he played against William Clarke's All England XI in 1854, and brother G.F. was 15 years 5 months when he appeared for the Gentlemen of England v. Oxford University, at Oxford, in 1866.

Tests

The youngest player ever to appear in Test cricket is Mushtaq Mohammad who played for Pakistan v. West Indies, at Lahore, March 1959, when he was 15 years 124 days.

Next to Mushtaq Mohammad come two other Pakistanis, Aftab Baloch, who was 16 years 191 days when he played against New Zealand, at Dacca, in November 1969, and Nasim-ul-Ghani, who was 16 years 248 days when he made his Test debut against the West Indies, at Bridgetown, in January 1958.

The youngest player ever to appear in Test cricket in England completes this trio of youthful Pakistanis. When taking his place at Trent Bridge in the Second Test of 1954, Khalid Hassan was 16 years 352 days.

The youngest Test cricketers for each of the other countries are:

England—D. B. Close, 18 years 149 days, v. New Zealand, at Old Trafford, July 1949.

Australia—I. D. Craig, 17 years 239 days, v. South Africa, at Melbourne, February 1953.

South Africa—W. A. Shalders, 19 years 19 days, v. England, at Cape Town, April 1899.

West Indies—J. E. D. Sealy, 17 years 122 days, v. England, at Barbados, January 1930.

New Zealand—D. L. Freeman, 18 years 197 days, v. England, at Christchurch, March 1933.

India—V. L. Mehra, 17 years 265 days, v. New Zealand, at Bombay, December 1955.

Captains

The youngest Test captains for each country have been:

England—M. P. Bowden, 23 years 144 days, v. South Africa, at Cape Town, March 1889.

Australia—I. D. Craig, 22 years 194 days, v. South Africa, at Johannesburg, December 1957.

South Africa—M. Bisset, 22 years 306 days, v. England, Johannesburg, February 1899.

West Indies—G. C. Grant, 23 years 217 days, v. Australia, Adelaide, December 1930,

New Zealand—J. R. Reid, 27 years 260 days, v. West Indies, at Christchurch, February 1956.

India—Nawab of Pataudi, 21 years 77 days, v. West Indies, at Bridgetown, March 1962.

Pakistan—Javed Burki, 24 years 23 days, v. England, at Edgbaston, May 1962.

Century makers

The youngest player to make a century in first-class cricket is B. H. Pairaudeau who scored 130 for British Guiana v. Jamaica, at Georgetown, in October 1947. He was then 16 years 6 months.

The youngest player to make a double century in first-class cricket is I. D. Craig who scored 213* for New South Wales v. South Africans, at Sydney, January 3, 1953. He was then 17 years 7 months.

The youngest player ever to make a double century in Test cricket—G. A. Headley, 20 years 10 months when he scored 223 for the West Indies v. England, Kingston, April 1930.

AGGREGATE OF RUNS

See under HIGHEST SCORES and LOWEST SCORES.

ALEXANDER, Franz C. M. ("Gerry") (1928–   )

On his form in Australia in 1960–61 this West Indian must be rated as one of the finest wicket-keeper-batsmen in post-war cricket, and it was a blow to the West Indies when soon after the completion of that tour, he announced his retirement from first-class cricket.

In that tour he not only topped his side's Test batting averages with 60.50 (highest score 108) but also held 16 catches.

Alexander was an aggressive batsman who won his "Blue" at Cambridge in 1952 and 1953, and figured in his university's record fifth wicket stand of 220 with R. Subba Row v. Nottinghamshire.

While at Cambridge he also gained his "Blue" for Soccer as well as playing in Amateur Internationals for England and collecting an F.A. Amateur Cup winners' medal with Pegasus.

When the M.C.C. toured the West Indies in 1959–60 he appeared in all five Tests and dismissed 23 batsmen.

In the Barbados Test of that rubber Alexander caught five England batsmen in one innings.

He captained the West Indies in 18 Tests.

ALLEN, George Oswald ("Gubby") (1902–   )

G. O. Allen was born in Australia but developed his cricket at Eton and Cambridge and became captain of England and one of the most popular players in the game between the two World Wars.

He figured in the body-line controversy of 1932–33 but on returning to Australia as captain in 1936–37 it was his amiable disposition and sportsmanship which did so much to repair the gap in Anglo-Australian cricket relations.

G. O. Allen is probably remembered best as a fast right-arm bowler, he took 81 Test wickets (av. 29.37), but he was also a hard-hitting batsman who scored 750 Test runs with an average of 24.19, and made his highest score at the age of 46—180 for Free Foresters v. Cambridge University in 1948.

His first-class debut was in 1922 when he got his Cambridge "Blue" and qualified for Middlesex. His best bowling feat for his county was 10 for 40 v. Lancashire, at Lord's in 1929.

In creating this Middlesex record Allen hit the stumps eight times. Thereafter he was noted for his aggressive fast bowling with a 12-yard run-up.

One of his finest spells of bowling in Test cricket was that against New Zealand, at the Oval in 1931. Then he took 5 for 14 in 13 overs. At Brisbane, in 1936–37, he and Voce combined to dismiss Australia for 58 runs. Allen took 5 for 36.

Altogether G. O. Allen played in 25 Tests and captained England in 11 of them.

After retiring in 1953 he became a member of the Committee of the M.C.C., was Chairman of the Test Selectors for seven seasons, President of the M.C.C. in 1963–64, and Treasurer 1964–76.

ALL-ENGLAND XI

This was a team of professionals[1] which toured the length and breadth of the country in the middle of the 19th century and did so much to increase interest in the game in so many out of the way places.

Founded and captained by England's finest under-arm slow bowler of the day, William Clarke of Nottingham, they played their first game in August 1846, against Twenty-two of Sheffield, on the Hyde Park Ground, Sheffield.

Despite the strain of long distance travel in those days William Clarke's team

[1] Although really a professional combination run for profit, the side did subsequently include three famous amateurs, Alfred Mynn, Nicholas Felix, and V. C. Smith.

undertook an arduous programme of matches in different parts of the country, and, wherever they played, they were a great attraction.

William Clarke was succeeded as captain by George Parr, another Nottinghamshire man, who became one of the country's most accomplished batsmen. When Parr retired Richard Daft took up the reins.

All the country's leading professionals played for the All-England XI at one time or another. To be invited to appear for this side was the greatest honour of the day and considered far more important than playing for one's county. Big names of the team included Fuller Pilch, William Caffyn, Alfred Mynn, Thomas Box, and John Wisden.

Eventually, a feeling of dissatisfaction against William Clarke's running of the club's affairs swept through the team. Not only did the players take exception to Clarke's blunt manner but they considered him too tight with his money. For the most part the players received between £4 and £6 per match but had to pay all their own expenses.

In 1852 John Wisden and Jem Dean broke away from Clarke and formed another professional touring team, the United England XI (q.v.).

Following the death of Clarke the annual match between these two teams became one of the most important events in the cricket calendar.

The All-England XI continued until about 1870 when it faded from the scene, swept away by the increasing popularity and strength of county cricket.

ALL ROUNDERS

See also under DOUBLE, THE.

The greatest all-rounder of all time was W. G. Grace. His record of scoring 100 runs and taking 10 wickets in a match 16 times in his career is unapproached by any other player.

The Doctor was the first player to score 1,000 runs and take 100 wickets in a single season. He did this in 1873 and in each of the next five seasons, as well as in 1885 and 1886.

One of his finest performances in a single game was to score 261 and take 11 wickets for 139 runs for the South v. North at Prince's in 1877.

When playing for Gloucestershire v. Yorkshire, at Sheffield, in 1872, the Champion scored 150 runs and took 15 wickets for 79.

In 1886 at Oxford, he captured all 10 Oxford University wickets and also scored 104 in one innings for the M.C.C. This feat has also been performed by his brother, E. M., who took all 10 wickets (one man absent in a twelve-a-side match) and scored 192* for M.C.C. v. Gentlemen of Kent, at Canterbury, in 1862.

In 1859, at the Oval, V. E. Walker (Harrow and Middlesex) took all 10 Surrey wickets for England (10 for 74) and also played an innings of 108.

F. A. Tarrant also scored a century and took all 10 wickets in one innings—10 for 90 and 182* for Maharajah of Cooch Behar's XI v. Lord Willingdon's XI, Poona, 1918.

The double of 1,000 runs and 100 wickets in a season has been achieved most times by W. Rhodes (Yorkshire). He recorded the double in 16 seasons between 1902 and 1927.

Another Yorkshireman, G. H. Hirst, achieved the greatest double in a single season when, in 1906, he scored 2,385 runs (average 45.86) and took 208 wickets (average 16.50).

Australia's greatest all-rounder was probably G. Giffen. This player's finest performance in a single match was to take 16 wickets for 166 runs and score 271 for South Australia v. Victoria, at Adelaide, in 1891–92.

At Cheltenham, in 1928, W. R. Hammond scored a century in each innings and also held 10 catches for Gloucestershire v. Surrey.

AMES, Leslie Egbert George
(1905–   )

Considered by many critics to have been the best wicket-keeper-batsman of all times, L. E. G. Ames made his debut for Kent in 1926.

Unfortunately he had to give up the game sooner than he had expected when afflicted by lumbago, but when he retired, in 1951 at the age of 45, he had amassed 37,245 runs (average 43.56), scoring 1,000 runs in a season 17 times.

His wicket-keeping record, however, is even more remarkable, for although he gave up regular wicket-keeping at the end of the 1938 season his career aggregate of 415 stumpings is still a world record. In Tests alone he dismissed 96 batsmen from behind the wicket, 23 stumped and 73 caught.

Ames appeared in 47 Tests, the first in 1929–30 against the West Indies, and the last against South Africa in 1938–39. In these matches he scored 2,438 runs (average 40.63).

Three times in his career he achieved the wicket-keepers' double with 1,000 runs and 100 dismissals. In 1928 he scored 1,919 runs and captured 121 wickets. The following season his figures were 1,795 runs and 127 wickets, and in 1932 he increased his batting figure to 2,482 runs and still took 100 wickets.

Ames actually topped the 2,000-run mark in five seasons and in his best scoring season, 1933, notched 3,058 runs, including nine centuries, for an average of 58.80. In that particular season his wicket-keeping bag was 66.

It was during 1933 that he equalled a Test record (since beaten) by dismissing eight West Indian batsmen in the third Test at the Oval.

Ames scored two separate hundreds in a match on three occasions and his highest score was 295 for Kent v. Gloucestershire, at Folkestone, in 1933.

In 1950 he was appointed a Test selector, the first professional ever to receive this honour, and he was secretary or secretary-manager of Kent C.C.C. 1960–1974.

ANALYSIS

See under AVERAGES (BOWLING)

ANIMALS

In the Leicestershire v. Lancashire match in May 1889 T. H. Warren was awarded four runs when his hit was carried off by a dog before the ball had crossed the boundary.

A sparrow is preserved in the Long Room at Lord's. It was killed in flight by a ball from M. Jahangir Khan at Lord's in 1936. He was bowling to T. N. Pearce in the Cambridge University v. M.C.C. game.

A similar incident occurred at Cambridge on August 12, 1885. Then a swallow was hit and killed by a ball from Mr. Cordeaux in a game between Caius and Trinity Hall.

At Lord's, a dog was killed when hit by a ball delivered by G. Brown of Brighton (1783–1857) one of the fastest bowlers of his day.

The appearance of a mouse on the field held up the England—Pakistan Test for a few minutes at Birmingham in 1962.

When a dog carried the ball over the boundary N. I. Thompson was awarded four runs for Sussex against West Indies at Hove, June 1963.

APPEARANCES
Consecutive (County Cricket)

K. G. Suttle made a record total of 423 consecutive appearances in Championship matches for Sussex, August 1954–July 1969.

J. Vine made 422 consecutive appearances in all matches for Sussex in the early 1900's.

E. H. Killick played in 389 consecutive matches for Sussex around the turn of the century.

J. G. Binks played in 412 consecutive Championship games for Yorkshire, June 1955 to September 1969.

C. N. Woolley played in 326 consecutive Championship matches for Northamptonshire 1913–1931.

A. H. Dyson played in 305 consecutive County Championship matches for Glamorgan 1930–1947.

Consecutive (Tests)

The record is held by G. S. Sobers with 85 consecutive Test Appearances for the West Indies. This run began with the second Test against Australia in April 1955 and ended with the fifth Test against New Zealand in April 1972.

Next to Sobers comes R. B. Kanhai with 61 consecutive Test appearances for the West Indies beginning with his debut v. England at Birmingham in 1957 and ending 1968–69 tour of Australia.

The England record is shared by P. B. H. May and F. E. Woolley who each enjoyed runs of 52 consecutive Test appearances. May's sequence began in August 1953 and ended in July 1959, while Woolley's extended from August 1909 to July 1926.

Most (Tests)

Listed below are the players who have made most Test appearances for each country. This list is correct to September 1976.

England—

M. C. Cowdrey (Kent) 114, T. G. Evans (Kent) 91, W. R. Hammond

(Gloucestershire) 85, K. F. Barrington (Surrey) 82, L. Hutton (Yorkshire) 79, T. W. Graveney (Glos. and Worc.) 79, D. C. S. Compton (Middlesex) 78, A. P. E. Knott (Kent) 78, J. H. Edrich (Surrey) 77.

Australia—
R. N. Harvey (New South Wales) 79, I. M. Chappell (S. Australia) 72, W. M. Lawry (Victoria) 67, I. R. Redpath (Victoria) 66, R. Benaud (New South Wales) 63, R. R. Lindwall (New South Wales) 61, G. D. McKenzie (W. Australia) 60, S. E. Gregory (New South Wales) 58.

South Africa—
J. H. B. Waite (Transvaal) 50, A. D. Nourse, sen. (Natal) 45, B. Mitchell (Transvaal) 42, H. W. Taylor (Natal and Transvaal) 42, T. L. Goddard (Natal) 41, R. A. McLean (Natal) 40.

West Indies—
G. S. Sobers (Barbados) 93, R. B. Kanhai (Trinidad) 79, L. R. Gibbs (Guyana) 79, C. H. Lloyd (Guyana) 58, R. C. Fredericks (Guyana) 54, F. M. Worrell (Barbados and Jamaica) 51, W. W. Hall (Barbados) 48, E. D. Weekes (Barbados) 48, B. F. Butcher (Guyana) 44, C. L. Walcott (Barbados and British Guiana) 44, C. C. Hunte (Barbados) 44.

New Zealand—
J. R. Reid (Wellington) 58, B. E. Congdon (Central Districts, Wellington, Otago) 53, B. Sutcliffe (Otago) 42, G. T. Dowling (Canterbury) 39, R. C. Motz (Canterbury) 32, V. Pollard (Central Districts, Canterbury) 32.

India—
P. R. Umrigar (Bombay) 59, V. L. Manjrekar (Rajasthan) 55, C. G. Borde (Baroda) 55, F. M. Engineer (Bombay) 46, Mansur Ali Khan (Delhi) 46, B. S. Bedi (Delhi) 45, V. Mankad (Rajashan) 44, P. Roy (Bengal) 43.

Pakistan—
Hanif Mohammad (Karachi) 55, Imtiaz Ahmed (Services) 41, Saeed Ahmed (Lahore) 41, Mushtaq Mohammad (Karachi) 38, Asif Iqbal (Karachi) 34, Fazal Mahmood (Punjab) 34, Intikhab Alam (Karachi) 29, Nasim-ul-Ghani (Karachi) 29, Mohamood Hussain (Karachi) 27.

Appeared for two countries

The following players have appeared for two countries in Test matches:—
Amir Elahi for India and Pakistan, J. J. Ferris for England and Australia, S. Guil-

len for West Indies and New Zealand, Gul Mohamed for India and Pakistan, F. Hearne for England and South Africa, A. H. Kardar (previously known as Hafeez) for India and Pakistan, W. E. Midwinter for England and Australia, F. Mitchell for England and South Africa, W. L. Murdoch for England and Australia, Nawab of Pataudi for England and India, A. E. Trott for England and Australia, S. M. J. Woods for England and Australia.

The only man to play for and against both England and Australia is W. E. Midwinter of Gloucestershire and Victoria.

ARMSTRONG, Warwick Windridge (1879–1947)

Born in 1879, this powerful man, who stood six feet two inches and weighed between 18 and 20 stone, became known as "The Big Ship" and was one of Australia's most successful captains. He was also one of the outstanding cricket personalities of his day and never a man to be browbeaten by the authorities.

In the 10 Tests in which he led the Australians against England he was undefeated, winning eight and drawing the other two.

Altogether Armstrong played in 50 Tests and the English cricket followers first saw some measure of his power in 1902 when he scored 172* against Sussex at Hove.

However, he was then only 23 years old and this was nothing to compare with his deeds in subsequent tours.

In that summer of 1902 he had been outshone by the great Vic Trumper, but in his next tour of 1905, the powerful hitter from Victoria topped the Australians' averages with 50.05 (aggregate 1,902 runs) and scored 303* against Somerset at Bath. He made that triple century, the highest ever scored at Bath, in only 315 minutes.

Armstrong visited England again in 1909, missed 1912 and 1919 because of his dispute with the Australian Cricket Board, but then returned for the last time as captain in 1921.

Australia lost only two of their 39 matches on that tour and Armstrong left England with the memory of not only a great all-rounder, but one of the craftiest captains ever to lead a touring side in the mother country.

His highest score in Tests was his 159* v. South Africa at Johannesburg in

1902–03, but for sheer power there was nothing in his career to surpass his 158 against England at Sydney in 1920.

When he retired he had made 16,731 runs in first-class cricket (av. 47.13) including 46 centuries.

Those are outstanding figures but it would be a serious omission if we closed without mentioning his bowling. His slow leg-breaks were renowned for their consistency of length and in England alone he took 443 wickets (av. 16.45). Few visiting bowlers have bettered this. His finest performance with the ball in England was his 8 for 47 v. Nottinghamshire in 1902.

ASHES, The

In August 1882 an Australian side so humiliated England at the Oval that the following mock obituary notice appeared in the *Sporting Times*.

"In affectionate remembrance of English Cricket which died on The Oval, on August 29th, 1882. Deeply lamented by a large circle of sorrowing friends and acquaintances. R.I.P. N.B. The body will be cremated and the Ashes taken to Australia."

In the match to which this referred England had been set 85 to win when they began their second innings at 3.45 p.m. on the second day, but with Spofforth and Boyle bowling so well they lost seven wickets for 70. With only 15 to get and three wickets to fall England still seemed assured of victory, but those last wickets went with only 7 (including three byes) added to the score.

So Australia won this remarkable game by seven runs thanks largely to Spofforth who created an Australian record for these Tests by taking 14 wickets for 90.

In the winter of 1882 an England team, captained by the Hon. Ivo Bligh, went to Australia and it was during this tour that the actual ashes were presented to the England captain.

One of the stumps used in the third Test was burnt and the ashes handed to the England captain in an urn. This urn, and the velvet bag in which it was originally presented, now stands on show in the Imperial Cricket Memorial museum at Lord's, having been bequested to the M.C.C. in the will of Lord Darnley (formerly Hon. Ivo Bligh) on his death in 1927.

ATTENDANCES

The record attendance for a cricket match anywhere in the world was set up at Melbourne on the occasion of the third Test of England's 1936–37 Australian tour.

This game was played on January 1, 2, 4, 5, 6 and 7, 1937 and the aggregate attendance was 350,534. The total receipts were £30,124.

On the third day of that match another world record was created with an attendance of 87,798. This stood until February 11, 1961, when on the same ground a crowd of 90,800 attended the second day of the fifth Test between Australia and West Indies. The total attendance for the five days of this Test was 274,404. Receipts £A65,034 (£52,040 sterling).

The record in England was set up at Leeds on the occasion of the fourth Test between England and Australia in July 1948. The total attendance for the five days was nearly 159,000. Receipts £34,000.

The record attendance for a county game in England was set up at the Oval in July 1906, when Surrey met Yorkshire in W. Lee's benefit match. The final day's play attracted over 30,000 spectators and the aggregate was reckoned to have been over 80,000, although the actual number who paid for admission was 66,923.

It is also interesting to note these 18th and 19th century attendances:

A record was created at the Oval in August 1887, when 24,450 paid for admission to see Surrey and Nottinghamshire. The aggregate for three days was 51,607.

The record crowd for a cricket match in England before 1900 was 63,763. This number attended another meeting between Surrey and Nottinghamshire at the Oval. This was in August 1892. On the first day the attendance was 30,760.

When Three of Kent played Three of England, at the Artillery Ground, Finsbury, July 11, 1743, the crowd was said to number about 10,000.

In the provinces 10,000 crowds were not uncommon in the 18th and 19th centuries. At least that number saw England beat Sussex at Brighton in July 1827, and 16,000 saw Twenty of Sheffield v. All England XI, at Hyde Park, Sheffield, in 1846.

Although the attendances may have been smaller there is no doubt that cricket was followed with as great enthusiasm nearly 200 years ago as it is today. In his

Annals of Cricket W. W. Read reproduced a report of a match played in August 1796 at Walworth for 1,000 guineas between eleven Greenwich Pensioners with one leg and eleven with one arm. Part of the report reads as follows:—

"About three o'clock, whilst those with but one arm were having their innings, a scene of riot and confusion took place, owing to the pressure of the people to gain admittance to the ground. The gates were forced open, and several parts of the fencing were broke down; and a great number of persons have got upon the roof of a stable, the roof broke in, and several persons falling among the horses were bruised. About six o'clock the game was renewed . . ."

AUSTRALIA

See also under SHEFFIELD SHIELD.

The British first settled in Australia towards the end of the 18th century and it is safe to assume that cricket was introduced into that country very soon after this, probably by soldiers who were stationed in the south-eastern regions of the continent around the turn of the century.

The first club to be formed is thought to have been the Hobart Town Club which came into existence in 1832. The name was changed to the Derwent Club in 1837. This was followed by the Melbourne C.C. in November 1838.

Intercolonial matches began in 1851 with a game between Tasmania and Victoria, played at Launceston, and the earliest match to be subsequently recognised as first-class was that between Victoria and New South Wales at Melbourne in 1856. Indeed, this is the earliest first-class match played outside the United Kingdom. New South Wales won by three wickets.

The first touring team to go out to the Australian continent left Liverpool on October 18, 1861, and landed at Melbourne on Christmas Eve.

This team, under the captaincy of H. H. Stephenson of Surrey, was met with great enthusiasm and there was a crowd of over 15,000 to see their opening match at Melbourne against Eighteen of Victoria.

The tour was a remarkable success from every angle, and, of the 12 games played, the visitors won six and lost two, with four

games drawn. The defeats were against Twenty-two of Castlemaine and against a combined Twenty-two of New South Wales and Victoria.

The names of this English team, the majority of whom were Surrey men, are well worth recording here: H. H. Stephenson, G. Bennett, W. Caffyn, G. Griffith, R. Iddison, T. Hearne, W. Mudie, E. Stephenson, C. Lawrence, W. Mortlock, T. Sewell and G. Wells.

The tour was sponsored by two men who were in the catering business in Australia, Messrs. F. Spiers and C. Pond. It was reckoned that they made something like £11,000 from the tour. The players each received £150 and all their expenses.

This was quickly followed by another tour in the winter of 1863–64. George Parr, who had declined an invitation to join the earlier team, captained this side, which included only one amateur, E. M. Grace.

Parr's team was undefeated in their 16 matches of the tour which included four played in New Zealand.

None of these games, nor those played by the third English team in Australia (W. G. Grace's team of 1873–74) were first-class as they were all played against odds. The Australians did not meet an English touring team on level terms until James Lillywhite's tour of 1876–77.

Cricket was thus well established in Australia, and one of the original tourists remained behind to play an important part in the improvement of the standard of the game in that continent. He was C. Lawrence, an all-rounder who played for Middlesex and Surrey. This proficient cricketer stayed in Australia to coach Sydney's top cricket team from the Albert Club.

Lawrence was also the man who introduced Australian cricketers to England when he brought over a team of Aborigines (q.v.) in 1868.

Another Englishman who played a leading part in the early advancement of Australian cricket was W. Caffyn. Also a Surrey player, he stayed behind after the second tour as coach to the Melbourne Club. He subsequently moved to Sydney.

The first Test match between England and Australia was played at Melbourne, March 15, 16 and 17, 1877. The rival captains were J. Lillywhite and D. W. Gregory. This was a triumph for Australia for it was the first time that a representative Australian team defeated an England team on level terms. Australia won by 45 runs, and C. Bannerman made the outstanding contribution to their victory by scoring 165 before he was forced to retire with an injured hand.

Since then England and Australia have brought their total of Test meetings to 224. Of this number England have won 71 and Australia 87.

James Lillywhite must have been impressed with Australian cricket on this tour for he agreed to arrange a visit of a representative Australian team to England in the following summer.

So, in 1878, a team consisting of six men from New South Wales, five from Victoria and one from Tasmania, toured this country under the captaincy of D. W. Gregory. They played 17 eleven-a-side matches (15 of them first-class) and 20 against odds. Of the first-class matches they won seven and were only beaten by Nottinghamshire, Gentlemen of England, Yorkshire and Cambridge University. Their biggest victory was that by 10 wickets against Gloucestershire, all the more remarkable because it was the first defeat by that county at home.

No Test match was included in that first tour and the earliest game in England to be subsequently recognised as a Test was that played against the Australians on their second visit in 1880. In this game, played at the Oval, Australia were beaten by 5 wickets (see under TEST MATCHES).

The Australian Cricket Council was formed in 1892 and they instituted the Sheffield Shield Competition (q.v.) in the season of 1892–93.

The Australian Board of Control was set up in 1905, although the final arrangements of this new board were not completed until the following year. This authority had a stormy passage during its earliest years. Trouble was sparked off between the leading Australian players and the Board when the latter deducted a higher proportion of the profits of the 1909 England tour than had originally been agreed by the players. But the rift between the players and the Board widened into an insatiable disruption when the Board refused to allow the players to appoint their own manager for the 1912 England tour.

The man the players wished to accompany them as manager was F. Laver but as he had already figured in a lengthy argument with the Board when he refused to produce the books of the previous tour he had managed (1909), the Board would not allow him to take charge of the 1912 tour.

Six of Australia's leading players who had been selected to come to England accordingly declined the invitation and the tour was a failure from all points of view.

Fortunately, these differences were largely forgotten by the time that the Board got down to arranging their next overseas tour after the intervention of World War I.

A team was selected from the Australian forces serving in Europe and this played 28 first-class matches in England in 1919, but the first team to set out from Australia after the war clouds had rolled away was that which went to New Zealand in 1920–21. This was quickly followed by a tour of England in 1921 when the Board showed that the quarrel of 1912 was indeed a thing of the past by appointing one of the rebels, W. W. Armstrong, to captain the side.

The most successful Australian team to tour England was that led by D. G. Bradman in 1948. This was the only representative Australian team to complete a tour of the United Kingdom undefeated. In all they played 34 matches (all but three of them first-class), won 25 and drew nine. They won four out of the five Test matches.

The players in this touring team were: D. G. Bradman (South Australia) captain, S. G. Barnes (N.S.W.), A. R. Morris (N.S.W.), A. L. Hassett (Victoria), K. R. Miller (N.S.W.), R. N. Harvey (Victoria), S. J. Loxton (Victoria), R. R. Lindwall (N.S.W.), I. W. Johnson (Victoria), D. Tallon (Queensland), D. Ring (Victoria), W. A. Johnston (Victoria), E. R. H. Toshack (N.S.W.), R. A. Saggers (N.S.W.), W. A. Brown (Queensland), all of whom played in one or more Tests, and also R. A. Hamence (South Australia).

Since their failure to win a single Test in South Africa in 1969–70 or against England at home in 1970–71 Australia have re-established themselves as world champions, losing only five out of 35 Tests up to and including the series with the West Indies in 1975–76. In this period, under the captaincy of either I. M. Chappell or brother G. S. Chappell, they have lost to England only three times in 15 Tests; to West Indies once in 11 Tests, and to New Zealand once in six Tests. Pakistan were beaten 3–0.

Records (Tests)

Highest score for: 758 for 8 declared v. West Indies, at Kingston, June 1955.

C. C. McDonald, b Worrell	127
L. Favell, c Weekes b King	0
A. R. Morris, lbw b Dewdney	7
R. N. Harvey, c Atkinson b Smith	204
K. R. Miller, c Worrell b Atkinson	109
R. G. Archer, c Depeiza b Sobers	128
R. R. Lindwall, c Depeiza b King	10
R. Benaud, c Worrell b Smith	121
I. W. Johnson, not out	27
Extras	25
Total (for 8 wkts. dec.)	758

Highest individual score: 334 by D. G. Bradman v. England, at Leeds, July 1930.

Highest score against: 903 for 7 declared by England, at the Oval, August 1938.

Highest individual score against: 364 by L. Hutton of England, at the Oval, August 1938.

Lowest score for: 36 v. England, at Birmingham, May 1902. (Rhodes 7 for 17, Hirst 3 for 15).

Lowest score against: 36 by South Africa, at Melbourne, February 1932. (Iremonger 5 for 6, Nash 4 for 18, McCabe 1 for 4).

Records (Other matches)

Highest score: 843 v. Oxford and Cambridge Universities Past and Present, at Portsmouth, 1893.

Highest individual score: 345 by C. G. Macartney v. Nottinghamshire, at Nottingham, 1921.

Highest score against: 230* by J. Hardstaff jun. for M.C.C. at Sydney, 1935–36. This was against a side described as an Australian XI. The highest individual score against an Australian touring team is 228 by W. Gunn for Players, at Lord's, 1890.

Lowest score: 18 v. M.C.C., at Lord's, 1896 (J. T. Hearne 4 for 4, A. D. Pougher 5 for 0).

Lowest score against: 17 by Gloucestershire, at Cheltenham, 1896. (H. Trumble 6 for 8, T. R. McKibbin 4 for 7).

Records (Australian States)

New South Wales

Highest score for: 918 v. S. Australia, at Sydney, 1900–01. Highest score against: 1,107 by Victoria, at Melbourne, 1926–27. This is the highest score in Australian first-class cricket. Highest individual score for: 452* by D. G. Bradman v. Queensland, at Sydney, 1929–30 (6 hours 55 minutes—49 fours). Highest individual score against: 365* by C. Hill for S. Australia, at Adelaide, 1900–01. Lowest score for: 37 v. Victoria, at Sydney, 1868–69. Lowest score against: 27 by S. Australia, at Sydney, 1955–56.

Queensland

Highest score for: 687 v. New South Wales, at Brisbane, 1930–31. Highest score against: 821 for 7 declared by S. Australia at Adelaide, 1939–40. Highest individual score for: 283 by P. J. Burge v. New South Wales, at Brisbane, 1963–64. Highest individual score against: 452* by D. G. Bradman for New South Wales, at Sydney, 1929–30. Lowest sccore for: 40 v. Victoria, at Brisbane, 1902–03.

South Australia

Highest score for: 821 for 7 declared v. Queensland, at Adelaide, 1939–40. Highest score against: 918 by New South Wales at Sydney, 1900–01. Highest individual score for: 369 by D. G. Bradman, v. Tasmania, at Adelaide, 1935–36; 365* by C. Hill v. New South Wales, at Adelaide, 1900–01. Highest individual score against: 336 by W. H. Ponsford for Victoria, at Melbourne, 1927–28. Lowest score for: 23 v. Victoria, at Melbourne, 1882–83. Lowest score against: 43 by Victoria, 1896. (In 1876 Victoria scored 29 v. XVIII of S. Australia).

Tasmania

Highest score for: 458 v. Indians, at Launceston, 1947–48. Highest score against: 1,059 by Victoria, at Melbourne, 1922–23. Highest individual score for: 274 by C. L. Badcock v. Victoria, at Launceston, 1933–34. Highest individual score against: 429 by W. H. Ponsford for Victoria, at Melbourne, 1922–23. Lowest score for: 18 v. Victoria, at Melbourne, February 1869. Lowest score against: 57 by Victoria, Launceston, 1851.

Victoria

Highest score for: 1,107 v. New South Wales, at Melbourne, 1926–27. This is the highest score in Australian first-class cricket. Highest score against: 815 by New South Wales, at Sydney, 1908–09. Highest individual score for: 437 by W. H. Ponsford v. Queensland, at Melbourne, 1927–28; (10 hours 20 minutes—42 fours). 429 by W. H. Ponsford v. Tasmania, at Melbourne, 1922–23. Highest individual score against: 357 by D. G. Bradman for S. Australia, at Melbourne, 1935–36. Lowest score for: 15 (one man absent) v. M.C.C. at Melbourne, 1903–04. Lowest score against: 18 by Tasmania, at Melbourne, 1868–69.

Western Australia

Highest score for: 615 for 5 declared v. Queensland, at Brisbane, 1968–69.

Highest score against: 639 by New South Wales, at Sydney, 1925–26. Highest individual score for: 243 by C. Milburn v. Queensland, at Brisbane, 1968–69. Highest individual score against: 356 by B. A. Richards for S. Australia, at Perth, 1970–71. Lowest score for: 38 v. Victoria, at Melbourne, 1892–93. Lowest score against: 54 by S. Australia, 1906.

AVERAGES (BATTING)

Best in a season

Here is a list of the men who have topped the batting averages in England in each season since 1900. The qualification for this list is 25 or more innings.

Season		Inns.	N.O.	Runs	H.S.	Avge.
1900	K. S. Ranjitsinhji (Sussex)	40	5	3065	275	87.57
1901	C. B. Fry (Sussex)	43	3	3147	244	78.67
1902	A. Shrewsbury (Notts.)	32	7	1250	127*	50.00
1903	C. B. Fry (Sussex)	40	7	2683	234	81.30
1904	K. S. Ranjitsinhji (Sussex)	34	6	2077	207*	74.17
1905	C. B. Fry (Sussex)	44	4	2801	233	70.02
1906	T. W. Hayward (Surrey)	61	8	3518	219	66.37
1907	C. B. Fry (Sussex)	34	3	1449	187	46.74
1908	T. W. Hayward (Surrey)	52	1	2337	175	45.82
1909	W. Bardsley (Australians)	49	4	2072	219	46.04
1910	J. T. Tyldesley (Lancs.)	51	2	2265	158	46.22
1911	C. B. Fry (Hants.)	26	2	1728	258*	72.00
1912	C. B. Fry (Hants.)	31	3	1592	203*	56.85
1913	C. P. Mead (Hants.)	60	8	2627	171*	50.51
1914	J. W. Hearne (Middlx.)	43	8	2116	204	60.45
1919	G. Gunn (Notts.)	25	2	1451	185*	63.08
1920	E. Hendren (Middlx.)	47	6	2520	232	61.46
1921	C. P. Mead (Hants.)	52	6	3179	280*	69.10
1922	E. Hendren (Middlx.)	38	7	2072	277	66.83
1923	E. Hendren (Middlx.)	51	12	3010	200*	77.17
1924	A. Sandham (Surrey)	37	2	2082	169	59.48
1925	J. B. Hobbs (Surrey)	48	5	3024	266*	70.32
1926	J. B. Hobbs (Surrey)	41	3	2949	316*	77.60
1927	C. Hallows (Lancs.)	44	13	2343	233*	75.58
1928	J. B. Hobbs (Surrey)	38	7	2542	200*	82.00
1929	J. B. Hobbs (Surrey)	39	5	2263	204	66.55
1930	D. G. Bradman (Australians)	36	6	2960	334	98.66
1931	H. Sutcliffe (Yorks.)	42	11	3006	230	96.96
1932	H. Sutcliffe (Yorks.)	52	7	3336	313	74.13
1933	W. R. Hammond (Glos.)	54	5	3323	264	67.81
1934	D. G. Bradman (Australians)	27	3	2020	304	84.16
1935	W. R. Hammond (Glos.)	58	5	2616	252	49.35
1936	W. R. Hammond (Glos.)	42	5	2107	317	56.94
1937	W. R. Hammond (Glos.)	55	5	3252	217	65.04
1938	D. G. Bradman (Australians)	26	5	2429	278	115.66
1939	G. Headley (West Indians)	30	6	1745	234*	72.70
1946	W. R. Hammond (Glos.)	26	5	1783	214	84.90
1947	D. C. S. Compton (Middlx.)	50	8	3816	246	90.85
1948	D. G. Bradman (Australians)	31	4	2428	187	89.92
1949	J. Hardstaff jun. (Notts.)	40	9	2251	162*	72.61
1950	E. D. Weekes (West Indians)	33	4	2310	304*	79.65

Season		Inns.	N.O.	Runs	H.S.	Avge.
1951	P. B. H. May (Cambridge U. & Surrey)	43	9	2339	178*	68.79
1952	D. S. Sheppard (Cambridge U. & Sussex)	39	4	2262	239*	64.62
1953	R. N. Harvey (Australians)	35	4	2040	202*	65.80
1954	D. C. S. Compton (Middlx.)	28	2	1524	278	58.62
1955	D. J. McGlew (South Africans)	34	2	1871	161	58.46
1956	K. Mackay (Australians)	28	7	1103	163*	52.52
1957	P. B. H. May (Surrey)	41	3	2347	285*	61.76
1958	P. B. H. May (Surrey)	41	6	2231	174	63.74
1959	M. J. K. Smith (Warwicks.)	67	11	3245	200*	57.94
1960	R. Subba Row (Northants)	32	5	1503	147*	55.66
1961	W. M. Lawry (Australians)	39	6	2019	165	61.18
1962	T. W. Graveney (Worcs.)	48	6	2269	164*	54.02
1963	G. S. Sobers (West Indians)	34	6	1333	112	47.60
1964	K. F. Barrington (Surrey)	35	5	1872	256	62.40
1965	M. C. Cowdrey (Kent)	43	10	2093	196*	63.42
1966	G. S. Sobers (West Indies)	25	3	1349	174	61.31
1967	K. F. Barrington (Surrey)	40	10	2059	158*	68.63
1968	G. Boycott (Yorks.)	30	7	1487	180*	64.65
1969	J. H. Edrich (Surrey)	39	7	2238	181	69.93
1970	G. S. Sobers (Notts.)	32	9	1742	183	75.73
1971	G. Boycott (Yorks.)	30	5	2503	233	100.12
1972	R. B. Kanhai (Warwicks.)	30	5	1607	199	64.28
1973	G. M. Turner (Worcs. & New Zealand)	44	8	2416	153*	67.11
1974	C. H. Lloyd (Lancs.)	31	8	1458	178*	63.39
1975	G. Boycott (Yorks.)	34	8	1915	201*	73.65
1976	Zaheer Abbas (Glos.)	39	5	2554	230*	75.11

Notable averages prior to 1900 include the following:

1871	W. G. Grace	35 innings	2739 runs	78.9 average
1873	W. G. Grace	30 innings	2139 runs	71.9 average
1876	W. G. Grace	42 innings	2622 runs	62.18 average

The innings numbered in those last three years above are completed innings only.
In the 1938–39 season in Australia D. G. Bradman recorded an astonishing
average of 153.16 in seven innings with one "not out".

Minor Counties

Here are some of the outstanding averages recorded in Minor Counties cricket:

	Inngs.	Not out	Aver.	Year
T. Copley (Yorkshire II)	8	4	122.00	1959
G. J. Whittaker (Surrey II)	8	2	119.50	1950
T. F. Shepherd (Surrey II)	11	4	101.28	1920
G. J. Whittaker (Surrey II)	11	4	100.42	1939

League Cricket

The following averages are among the best recorded in English League cricket:

	Inngs.	Not out	Aver.	Year
V. L. Manjrekar (Castleton Moor)	21	12	161.77	1956
E. D. Weekes (Bacup)	17	9	158.25	1954
W. Greenhalgh (East Lancs. P.M.)	21	12	116.88	1947
F. M. Worrell (Radcliffe)	25	10	112.93	1951

Best in completed first-class career

Qualification, over 100 innings.

95.14	D. G. Bradman 1927–49	338 innings	43 not out
72.75	V. M. Merchant 1929–51	221 ,,	44 ,, ,,
69.86	G. Headley 1927–54	164 ,,	22 ,, ,,
65.18	W. H. Ponsford 1920–34	235 ,,	26 ,, ,,
65.00	W. M. Woodfull 1921–34	245 ,,	39 ,, ,,
58.24	A. L. Hassett 1932–53	322 ,,	32 ,, ,,
57.69	A. F. Kippax 1918–36	254 ,,	33 ,, ,,
56.37	K. S. Ranjitsinhji 1893–1920	500 ,,	62 ,, ,,
56.10	W. R. Hammond 1920–51	1004 ,,	104 ,, ,,
55.51	L. Hutton 1934–57	815 ,,	91 ,, ,,
55.01	A. R. Morris 1940–54	242 ,,	15 ,, ,,
54.87	G. S. Sobers 1953–74	609 ,,	93 ,, ,,
52.00	H. Sutcliffe 1919–45	1087 ,,	123 ,, ,,

Test Cricket

The leading averages in completed Test careers with at least 50 innings are:

D. G. Bradman (Australia)	80 innings	10 not out	99.94
H. Sutcliffe (England)	84 ,,	9 ,, ,,	60.73
K. F. Barrington (England)	131 ,,	15 ,, ,,	58.67
E. D. Weekes (West Indies)	81 ,,	5 ,, ,,	58.61
W. R. Hammond (England)	140 ,,	16 ,, ,,	58.45
G. S. Sobers (West Indies)	60 ,,	21 ,, ,,	57.78
J. B. Hobbs (England)	102 ,,	7 ,, ,,	56.94
C. L. Walcott (West Indies)	74 ,,	7 ,, ,,	56.68
L. Hutton (England)	138 ,,	15 ,, ,,	56.67
A. D. Nourse jun. (South Africa)	62 ,,	7 ,, ,,	53.81

AVERAGES (BOWLING)

Best in a career

Considering the number of wickets taken and the length of his career the average of 16.71 for 4,187 wickets taken by W. Rhodes (Yorkshire) over a period of 32 years is the most remarkable. He retired at the end of the 1930 season.

The nearest approach to Rhodes' record in more recent times is probably that of W. E. Bowes (Yorkshire) with 16.75, but he took only (comparatively speaking) 1,638 wickets in a career of 19 years from 1928 to 1947.

Tests

Among the men who have taken over 150 Test wickets the bowler with the best average is S. F. Barnes who took 189 wickets at a cost of only 16.43 each.

Best in an innings

The best bowling average for a single innings in a first-class match is 16—6 for 1 by S. Costick for Victoria v. Tasmania, at Melbourne, 1868–69; V. I. Smith for the South Africans v. Derbyshire, at Derby, 1947, and by Israr Ali, for Bahawalpur v. Dacca University, 1957–58.

Tests

Among those players who have taken at least five wickets in a Test innings the best performance as far as the average is concerned is that of E. R. H. Toshack who took 5 for 2 runs for Australia v. India, at Brisbane, in 1947–48.

Best in a match

The most remarkable bowling average ever recorded by a player taking more than 10 wickets in a first-class match is 1.07—13 wickets for 14 runs by F. Morley for M.C.C. v. Oxford University at Oxford, 1877.

Tests

The best bowling average ever recorded by a player taking more than 10 wickets in a Test match is 1.86—15 wickets for 28 runs by J. Briggs, England v. South Africa, at Cape Town, 1888–89.

Best in a season

Here is a list of the men who have topped the bowling averages in England in each season since 1900. The qualification for this list is 100 or more wickets.

Season		Overs	Mdns.	Runs	Wkts.	Av.
1900	W. Rhodes (Yorks.)	1553	455	3606	261	13.81
1901	W. Rhodes (Yorks.)	1565	505	3797	251	15.12
1902	S. Haigh (Yorks.)	799	219	1984	158	12.55
1903	W. Mead (Essex)	971.3	355	1791	131	13.67
1904	J. T. Hearne (Middx.)	1153.3	330	2732	145	18.84
1905	S. Haigh (Yorks.)	831.5	220	1983	120	15.37
1906	S. Haigh (Yorks.)	971.3	209	2540	174	14.59
1907	R. O. Schwarz (South Africans)	711.3	153	1616	137	11.79
1908	S. Haigh (Yorks.)	623.2	176	1380	103	13.39
1909	S. Haigh (Yorks.)	844.2	205	1702	122	13.95
1910	J. T. Hearne (Middx.)	752	253	1523	119	12.79
1911	G. T. Thompson (Northants.)	735.5	199	1889	113	16.71
1912	C. Blythe (Kent)	919.3	241	2183	178	12.26
1913	C. Blythe (Kent)	1120.2	289	2729	167	16.34
1914	C. Blythe (Kent)	1008.4	280	2583	170	15.19
1919	W. Rhodes (Yorks.)	1048.3	305	2365	164	14.42
1920	W. Rhodes (Yorks.)	1028.4	291	2123	161	13.18
1921	W. Rhodes (Yorks.)	963	316	1872	141	13.27
1922	W. Rhodes (Yorks.)	841.1	312	1451	119	12.19
1923	W. Rhodes (Yorks.)	929	345	1547	134	11.54
1924	G. G. Macauley (Yorks.)	1220.4	343	2514	190	13.23
1925	C. W. L. Parker (Glos.)	1512.3	478	3311	222	14.91
1926	W. Rhodes (Yorks.)	892.4	315	1709	115	14.86
1927	H. Larwood (Notts.)	629.2	147	1695	100	16.95
1928	H. Larwood (Notts.)	834.5	204	2003	138	14.51
1929	R. Tyldesley (Lancs.)	1114.3	350	2399	154	15.57
1930	C. W. L. Parker (Glos.)	1016.3	301	2299	179	12.84
1931	H. Larwood (Notts.)	651.3	142	1553	129	12.03
1932	H. Larwood (Notts.)	866.4	203	2084	162	12.86
1933	H. Verity (Yorks.)	1195.4	428	2553	190	13.43
1934	W. J. O'Reilly (Australians)	870	320	1858	109	17.04
1935	H. Verity (Yorks.)	1279.2	453	3032	211	14.36
1936	H. Larwood (Notts.)	679.1	165	1544	119	12.97
1937	H. Verity (Yorks.)	1386.2	487	3168	202	15.68
1938	W. E. Bowes (Yorks.)	932.3	294	1844	121	15.23
1939	H. Verity (Yorks.)	963.3	270	2509	191	13.13
1946	A. Booth (Yorks.)	917.2	423	1289	111	11.61
1947	T. W. Goddard (Glos.)	1451.2	344	4119	238	17.30
1948	W. A. Johnston (Australians)	850.1	279	1675	102	16.42
1949	T. W. Goddard (Glos.)	1187.2	326	3069	160	19.18
1950	R. Tattersall (Lancs.)	1404.4	502	2623	193	13.59
1951	R. Appleyard (Yorks.)	1323.1	391	2829	200	14.14
1952	A. V. Bedser (Surrey)	1184.4	296	2530	154	16.42
1953	L. Jackson (Derby)	741.4	229	1574	103	15.28
1954	R. Appleyard (Yorks.)	1026.3	315	2221	154	14.42
1955	D. Shackleton (Hants.)	1220.2	438	2183	159	13.72
1956	G. A. R. Lock (Surrey)	1058.2	437	1932	155	12.46
1957	G. A. R. Lock (Surrey)	1194.1	449	2550	212	12.02
1958	L. Jackson (Derby)	829	295	1572	143	10.99

Season		Overs	Mdns.	Runs	Wkts.	Av.
1959	J. B. Statham (Lancs.)	977.4	267	2087	139	15.01
1960	J. B. Statham (Lancs.)	844.1	274	1662	135	12.31
1961	J. Flavell (Worcester)	1245.2	300	3043	171	17.79
1962	D. A. D. Sydenham (Surrey)	989.2	295	2030	115	17.65
1963	C. C. Griffith (West Indians)	701.2	192	1527	119	12.83
1964	T. W. Cartwright (Warwicks.)	1146.2	502	2141	134	15.97
1965	H. J. Rhodes (Derby)	646.5	187	1314	119	11.04
1966	D. L. Underwood (Kent)	1104.5	475	2167	157	13.80
1967	D. L. Underwood (Kent)	979.1	459	1686	136	12.39
1968	D. Wilson (Yorks.)	895.5	335	1521	109	13.45
1969	M. J. Proctor (Glos.)	639.3	160	1623	108	15.02
1970	D. J. Shepherd (Glam.)	1123.3	420	2031	106	19.16
1971	P. J. Sainsbury (Hants.)	845.5	332	1874	107	17.51
1972	No player took 100 wickets					
1973	B. S. Bedi (Northants)	864.2	309	1884	105	17.94
1974	A. M. E. Roberts (Hants.)	727.4	198	1621	119	13.62
1975	P. Lee (Lancs.)	799.5	193	2067	112	18.45
1976	No player took 100 wickets					

Notable first-class averages in the years before 1900 include:

1880	A. Shaw (Notts.)	1995	1251	1525	177	8.61
1875	A. Shaw (Notts.)	1741	1022	1499	161	9.50
1878	A. G. Steel					
	(Cambridge Univ. and Lancs.)	1223	447	1542	164	9.66
1879	A. Shaw (Notts.)	1575	924	1259	134	9.53
1882	J. Crossland (Lancs.)	749	332	1015	105	9.70
1888	J. Briggs (Lancs.)	1450	763	1659	160	10.79
1894	T. Richardson (Surrey)	936.3	293	2024	196	10.32

Minor Counties

Some of the most notable season's bowling averages in Minor Counties include the following:

1912	S. F. Barnes (Staffs.)	191	75	376	70	5.37
	C. J. Adamson (Durham)	65	15	193	31	6.22
1895	Eldridge (Wilts.)	107.2	30	274	37	7.15
1946	G. C. Perkins (Suffolk)	304.1	165	332	46	7.21
1932	F. Edwards (Bucks.)	300	97	606	79	7.64

This Minor Counties' list includes only some of those with more than 30 wickets at less than 8 runs each.

League Cricket

Here are a few of the outstanding averages in the Leagues (100 or more wickets at less than 6 runs each):

S. F. Barnes (Porthill)	112 wickets	3.91 average	1907
S. F. Barnes (Saltaire)	150 ,,	4.11 ,,	1922
S. F. Barnes (Porthill)	100 ,,	4.28 ,,	1909
Wallwork (Chalfont St.)	101 ,,	4.59 ,,	1922
S. F. Barnes (Porthill)	114 ,,	4.66 ,,	1913
S. F. Barnes (Saltaire)	107 ,,	4.92 ,,	1917
S. F. Barnes (Porthill)	103 ,,	5.14 ,,	1906
S. F. Barnes (Saltaire)	112 ,,	5.20 ,,	1918
C. C. Griffith (Burnley)	144 ,,	5.20 ,,	1964
S. F. Barnes (Saltaire)	100 ,,	5.36 ,,	1920
S. F. Barnes (Porthill)	122 ,,	5.68 ,,	1908
S. F. Barnes (Saltaire)	112 ,,	5.69 ,,	1921
K. Ramadhin (Radcliffe)	117 ,,	5.72 ,,	1963
F. Taylor (Burslem)	100 ,,	5.91 ,,	1938

Best in a completed first-class career (over 3,000 wickets)

W. Rhodes 1898–1930	4187 wickets	16.71 average
J. T. Hearne 1888–1923	3061 ,,	17.75 ,,
A. P. Freeman 1914–35	3776 ,,	18.42 ,,
C. W. L. Parker 1903–35	3278 ,,	19.46 ,,

Test Cricket

The best average among those with over 200 wickets is 21.57 by F. S. Trueman taking 307 wickets in 67 Tests for 6,625 runs.

B

BAILEY, Trevor Edward
(1923–   )

Born at Westcliff, December 3, 1923, this all-rounder was educated at Dulwich College and made his debut for Essex in 1946. He gained his "Blue" at Cambridge both for soccer and for cricket, and, in 1949, he became the first amateur for 16 years to complete the "double".

He subsequently completed the "double" in 1952, 1954, 1957, 1959, 1960, 1961 and 1962. In 1959 he scored 2,011 runs and captured 100 wickets.

Trevor Bailey joined the Essex administrative staff in 1948 and was the club's secretary, 1954–65. He was Essex captain 1961–66.

He made the first of his 61 Test appearances in 1949 (against New Zealand). His highest score in these matches is 134* v. New Zealand, at Christchurch, in 1950–51.

His record of 2,290 runs and 132 wickets in Test cricket is among the best ever recorded by any Englishman.

A fast-medium right-arm bowler, Bailey took all 10 Lancashire wickets in one innings at Clacton in 1949, while his best Test feat is 7 for 34 against the West Indies, at Kingston in 1953–54. In 1950 he performed the hat-trick against Glamorgan at Newport.

BAILS

See under WICKET, THE.

BALL, The

According to a statement in the diary of Joseph Farrington, the Duke family of Penhurst, Kent, had been making cricket balls for some 250 years before 1811. That would take us back to 1561 and although this fact is recorded by many cricket historians there is some doubt as to the truth of the matter.

The firm of Duke & Son was actually formed in 1760 and before that this family was largely concerned with the making of footwear. However, there is no doubt that they also made cricket balls before 1760, and, according to Haygarth, they were making these balls for over 200 years before 1888.

It is a remarkable fact that the materials used in the making of cricket balls have changed very little during the past 250 years. Originally cricket balls were white but they have nearly always been made with cork and leather.

It is not certain when the idea of dyeing the balls red was first introduced but it is well over 100 years ago as indicated by this quotation from Dickens' "Martin Chuzzlewit", which was published in 1843.

Dickens describes the ledgers of the Anglo-Bengalee Disinterested Loan and Life Assurance Company as having "red backs like strong cricket balls beaten flat".

According to the earliest laws of cricket which were published in 1744 "the ball must weigh between five and six ounces". In 1774 the limits were revised to between 5½ and 5¾ ounces. The size of the ball is not mentioned until 1838 when it is given as between 9 and 9¼ inches in circumference.

The weight of the ball remains the same today, but the size was altered in 1927 to not less than 8 13/16th inches nor more than 9 inches. This alteration was made to allow for expansion which occurs after use.

See also under THROWING THE BALL, LAWS OF CRICKET.

BANNERMAN, Alexander
Chambers (1854–1924)

Born Sydney, March 21, 1854, "Little

Alec" played in 28 Tests for Australia. He actually toured England with the Australian side of 1878 before he had made his first appearance for New South Wales.

A younger brother of Charles Bannerman, Alex was a stubborn "stonewaller" who often annoyed the spectators with his lack of aggression, but he was a wonderful fielder and it was his prowess in the field that secured him a place in his earliest Tests.

Bannerman toured England six times and the best of these seasons was his last visit, in 1893, when he averaged 23.06 in 47 innings and scored 133 in the Australians' record total of 843 against Oxford and Cambridge Universities Past and Present, at Portsmouth.

Bannerman's average in all 28 Tests against England was 23.08, with 1,108 runs in 50 innings. Such figures are not great and they do not give any idea of the value of a man like "Little Alec" who could be relied upon to keep his end up while someone else went for the runs.

He never scored a century in Test cricket, 94 was his highest (Sydney, January 1883), but his stubbornness wore out a lot of bowlers and won his side a lot of games.

The finest example of his stubbornness and resolution was in the second Test of England's 1891–92 Australian tour. Then he had an innings which spread over three days before he was caught by W. G. Grace off J. Briggs for 91.

BARBADOS
See under WEST INDIES

BARDSLEY, Warren
(1883–1954)

Born Warren, New South Wales, Warren Bardsley first came to the fore in 1908–09 and was chosen for the tour of England in 1909.

As things turned out Bardsley always did well in England and during his first tour he set the standard for his future visits.

True, he achieved little of note in the first four Tests of 1909, but in the fifth Test at the Oval he created a record (since equalled) by scoring a century in each innings—136 and 130.

In other matches on that tour he made such scores as 219 v. Essex at Leyton, 211 v. Gloucestershire at Bristol, and 118 v. Warwickshire at Birmingham. He ended the tour topping the Australians' batting averages with 46.38, a total bag of 2,180 runs.

His 219 against Essex was to remain his highest score in England but he exceeded the 2,000-run mark on each of his three tours.

A glutton for cricket Warren Bardsley was undoubtedly Australia's finest left-handed batsman between the two world wars. He never did quite as well in his own country as in England, but in all he scored over 17,000 runs including 53 centuries, with an average of around 50 runs an innings and a highest score of 264.

When considering those figures it should not be forgotten that he was usually an opening batsman.

BARNES, Sydney Francis
(1873–1967)

This great bowler's Test wickets cost an average of only 16.43 apiece, which is easily the best bowling average for any Test cricketer when considered in relation to the number of wickets he took—189.

R. Peel averaged 16.81 but his total of wickets captured was more than 80 less than the bowling marvel from Staffordshire.

Sydney Barnes made an astonishing leap to fame for he was a comparatively unknown bowler when A. C. MacLaren chose him to go to Australia in 1901.

Up to that time Barnes, who was then professional with Burnley, had taken only nine wickets in first-class cricket, but in his first two Tests he took 19 wickets, including 6 for 42 and 7 for 121. In the third Test, however, he broke down with a knee injury and achieved very little for the remainder of the tour. Despite this he still topped England's Test bowling averages with his 19 wickets at 17.00 runs apiece.

Barnes' Test debut in Australia had been exciting enough but he was destined to deal an even bigger blow to the cream of Australian batsmen on their own ground.

He did not go to Australia in 1903–04, but he got 24 Test wickets (av. 26.08) there in 1907–08. Then, in 1911–12, he went out again and it was in the second Test at Melbourne that he took five Australian wickets, Kelleway, Bardsley, Hill, Armstrong, and Minnett, in 11 overs for 6 runs! Nine of those overs were maidens! This, mark you, on a batsman's wicket!

The South Africans also have good reason to remember Sydney Barnes. In the 1912 series in England he took 34 of their wickets, average 8.29, while in South Africa in 1913–14, on matting wickets, in only four Tests, his bag was 49, average 10.93.

One could go on reciting Barnes' figures all day, and every one of them leaves one gasping with amazement. In first-class cricket he took 653 wickets, average 16.93, but it was in League cricket that he spent the greater part of his career and there he was even more astonishing. His total League bag was about 4,000 wickets at a fantastic average of less than 7 runs each.

Sydney Barnes was a fast-medium bowler and his leg-break was a real gem. He played first-class county cricket for Warwickshire and Lancashire as well as minor counties cricket with his native Staffordshire. In the Leagues he played first for Smethwick and subsequently for Rishton, Burnley, Church, Porthill, Saltaire, Castleton Moor and Rawtenstall. He was 57 years of age when he signed for Rawtenstall in 1931, but he went on to take over 115 wickets at a cost of 6.30 runs apiece in his first season with them.

When one considers his record on all types of wickets there is a strong case for naming him the best bowler of all times. He bowled equally well when the ball was either new or old.

BARNES, William (1852–1899)

Among the best bowling averages in Test cricket is that of William Barnes of Nottinghamshire.

In 21 Tests, all against Australia, William Barnes took 51 wickets at an average of 15.54 runs each.

In addition to being an outstanding medium-pace bowler he was also a sound bat for he made 725 runs in those Tests (av. 23.38). His best performance being 134 and 28* at Adelaide in 1884. However, on occasions he was criticised for his stubborn defensive play.

In a first-class career which extended from 1875 to 1894 William Barnes scored 15,429 runs. His highest score was 160. In his best bowling season, 1885, he took 97 wickets at an average cost of 15.53.

BARNETT, Charles John (1910–   )

Born at Cheltenham, son of C. S. Barnett

who played for Gloucestershire, C. J. first played for the county at the age of 16, subsequently turning professional in 1929. He remained with Gloucestershire until 1949 when he joined Rochdale in the Central Lancashire League.

One of the most attractive of batsmen, noted particularly for his off-side play, Barnett, who was also a reliable medium-pace bowler, gave his county outstanding service. He was an opening batsman for many seasons and also opened the bowling on numerous occasions.

At his best during the 1930's he topped 2,000 runs in seasons 1933, 1934, 1936 and 1937.

Barnett first appeared in Test cricket against the West Indies in 1933, being chosen for one match, and then followed this during the winter with a tour of India and three more Tests.

After another Test at home against India, Barnett reached the peak of his international career on the Australian tour of 1936–37. At Adelaide he made his highest Test innings, a score of 129, and at Brisbane, against Queensland, he hit his highest ever score, 259.

Barnett could hit with tremendous power and at Bath in 1934 his innings of 194 included 11 sixes and 18 fours. As many as 11 sixes in a single innings have only been hit by five other players in first-class cricket.

One of Barnett's finest performances as a bowler was taking 6 for 17 in 12 overs against Essex at Clacton in 1936.

BARRINGTON, Kenneth Frank (1930–   )

This dedicated batsman with the square-on stance made his debut for Surrey in 1953 after five years on their ground staff and became one of their most consistent performers topping their averages in 1959, 1960, 1961, 1963, 1964 and 1967.

In 1955 Barrington not only gained his county cap but played in two Tests against South Africa. However, he was not seen in the England side again until the Tests against India four years later. Then he played in all five games and came out with an average of 59.50. His future selection was assured.

In 1959 he scored two centuries in one match for Surrey v. Warwickshire, at Birmingham, 186 and 118*. His highest score was 256 for England v. Australia, at Old Trafford in 1964, and in his very next first-class innings he scored 207 v. Notts.

In Australia in 1962–63 his Test aggregate of 582 was the highest by an Englishman in this series since 1929 when W. R. Hammond scored 905. Indeed, this Surrey batsman was generally at his best on the faster pitches abroad.

He appeared in 82 Tests and is among the elite of batsmen who have scored over 6,000 runs in this class of cricket, and his average for these games (58.67) speaks for itself. One of his most successful series was in South Africa, 1964–65 when his Test average for 7 innings (2 not out) was 101.60.

BAT, The

When cricket first began to grow in popularity the bowling was of the underarm-along-the-ground type. It is, therefore, not surprising to see in old drawings that the bats were suitably shaped to deal with this type of bowling i.e. the weight was in the bottom of the bat which was curved at the end like a hockey stick.

The first straight bat with shoulders is believed to have been made by John Small of Petersfield, Hampshire, in 1773, and the changeover from curved to straight bats was generally completed before 1780.

In those days, and for many years to follow, most bats were made all in one piece. Bats with whalebone handles were made in about 1845 and in about 1853 came the most important innovation in the evolution of the bat—the cane handle.

The oldest bat still in existence is one to be found in the pavilion at the Oval. It is inscribed "J. C." and is said to have belonged to John Chitty, in 1729. Shaped like a hockey stick it weighs 2lb. 4oz.

The old timers used bats of varying shapes and sizes to suit their own requirements, but after a certain Thomas "Shock" White of Reigate went in to bat at Hambledon, in a game between that club and Chertsey, with a bat wider than the wicket, it was decided to introduce legislation limiting the size of bats. The date of that game was September 23, 1771. The new law was made two days later by a committee of the Hambledon club and it limited the width of the bat to 4¼ inches. A metal gauge was kept by the Hambledon club to check the width of all bats, and the size has remained the same ever since.

A limit on the length of the bat was not introduced until 1835. Then, as now, it was a limit of 38 inches, which, of course, includes the handle.

There is no substitute for a good willow in bat making. Many 19th-century players preferred bats made with red willow but for some time now the white willow has been favourite.

Bats vary in weight but the average player today uses one which weighs around 2lb. 3oz. Bigger men use bigger bats and in his autobiography published in 1899, W. G. Grace states "I play with a bat weighing 2lb. 5oz., which, I think, is heavy enough for anybody; but a few ounces make very little difference if the bat is really well balanced".

In *The Jubilee Book of Cricket* (1897) Prince Ranjitsinhji had this to say about bats. "A really good bat is a work of art . . . It is by far the most important instrument an individual cricketer has to select. It must be remembered that no two players are exactly alike, and that consequently nearly every cricketer requires a particular make of bat to suit him".

BATTING

See also under AVERAGES, BIG HITTING, BOUNDARIES, CENTURIES, FAST SCORING, HIGHEST SCORES, LOWEST SCORES, PARTNERSHIPS, SLOW SCORING, STONEWALLER, THOUSAND RUNS.

A keen eye and sharp reflexes are the most important attributes of a good batsman and the art of batsmanship is in the footwork. A good batsman always gets close to the ball before making his stroke.

In his *Hints for Young Cricketers* the Champion once had this to say: "For boys who are learning to bat, an important piece of advice is to play forward as much as possible. On good hard and true wickets nearly every ball can be played forward, and if a boy has once learned to play forward confidently he will soon adapt himself to playing backwards at balls that demand it".

In the old days the majority of batsmen played back to a ball and it was not until the great W. G. Grace made his mark that forward play generally came into vogue. But then the Champion was a genius who combined both styles of play to advantage and there is no doubt that he did more than any man to lay the foundations of the modern style of batting.

Batting (Teams)

In their second innings of the first Test at Leeds in June 1952, India lost their first four wickets without scoring a single run. Roy, Gaekwad, Mantri, and Manjrekar, were dismissed in the course of the first 14 balls sent down by Trueman and Bedser. Nothing like this has ever been known in any other Test match.

Batting through an innings

W. G. Grace and C. J. B. Wood each batted through a completed innings no less than 17 times in their careers. This is a record.

The highest score by an opening batsman who played right through a completed innings is 357* by R. Abel for Surrey v. Somerset, at the Oval, in 1899. The total for that innings was 811 and that is the highest innings through which a batsman has played not out.

Four batsmen have played through both completed innings of a match in England: H. Jupp, Surrey v. Yorkshire, at the Oval, 1874; S. P. Kinneir, Warwickshire v. Leicestershire, at Leicester, 1907; C. J. B. Wood, Leicestershire v. Yorkshire, at Bradford, 1911; V. M. Merchant, Indians v. Lancashire, at Liverpool, 1936.

C. J. B. Wood is the only one to score a century (107* and 117*) in each innings.

Players who have carried bat through a complete innings in Test cricket: W. W. Armstrong, W. Bardsley, J. E. Barrett, W. A. Brown, I. R. Redpath, W. M. Lawry (twice) and W. M. Woodfull (twice) for Australia; R. Abel, L. Hutton (twice), P. F. Warner for England; T. L. Goddard, D. J. McGlew, A. Tancred, J. W. Zulch for South Africa; Nazar Mohammed, Pakistan, G. M. Turner (twice), New Zealand, and C. C. Hunte and F. M. Worrell, West Indies.

BEDFORDSHIRE C.C.C.

Founded: 1847, re-formed 1899. There may have been a county club in existence as early as 1741. Secretary: G. L. B. August, 24 Furzefield, Putnoe, Bedford. Highest score for: 539 for 7 v. Oxfordshire, at Bedford, 1947. Highest score against: 577 for 8 declared by Sir Julian Cahn's XI, 1933; In Minor County game—534 for 8 declared by Hertfordshire, at Stevenage, 1924. Highest individual score for: 234 by A. B. Poole (in 3 hours 14 minutes) v. Oxfordshire, at Banbury, 1936. Highest individual score against: 246 by G. F. Summers of Sir Julien Cahn's XI, 1933; In Minor County game—224 by G. A. Stevens of Norfolk,

1920. Lowest score for: 19 v. Cambridgeshire at Chatteris, 1972. Lowest score against: 23 by Hertfordshire, 1879; In Minor County Championship—37 by Shropshire, 1958. Bowling feats: W. E. King 6 for 7 v. Buckinghamshire, at Bedford, 1922. R. V. Ward all 10 wickets for 72 v. Hertfordshire, 1935. (First player to do this in Minor County Championships). M. Ashenden all 10 for 15 in 8.4 overs v. Shropshire, at Bedford, 1958. Eight were clean bowled and Ashenden did the hat-trick with his last three balls. Colours: Purple, black and white stripes. Badge: Three scallop shells and lion rampant in silver thread and dark blue background. Honours: Minor Counties Champions, 1970, 1972.

BEDSER, Alec Victor (1918–   )

In 51 Tests this dedicated cricketer captured 236 wickets at an average cost of 24.89 runs.

A big man with a big heart, no England bowler ever worked harder than A. V. Bedser of Surrey.

When making his Test debut in 1946—it was against India at Lord's—he took 7 for 49 and 4 for 96. The finest Test debut ever made by an England bowler. Then, as if that wasn't a good enough start, Bedser equalled this in his second Test with 4 for 41 and 7 for 52.

Bowling right-arm medium-fast, Bedser's professional career extended to the end of 1960 season. He took 100 wickets in a season 11 times, his best being 1953 when he captured 162.

The 1953 season was also his finest against Australia for in that series of five Tests he took 39 wickets at an average of 17.48. Only J. C. Laker has taken more Australian wickets in a Test rubber.

In the Nottingham Test during that summer Bedser captured 14 wickets for 99 runs.

Born at Reading, Alec Bedser made his debut for Surrey in 1939 and on return from the war he gained his county cap in 1946.

He performed the hat-trick against Essex in 1953 and his best bowling feats in the County Championship are 8 for 18 against Nottinghamshire in 1952, and 8 for 18 against Warwickshire in 1953, both games being played at the Oval.

Bedser has been a Test Selector since 1962.

BENAUD, Richie (1930–   )

This six foot all-rounder from New South Wales made his debut in first-class cricket in 1948–49 but had the misfortune to suffer a face injury after only one match.

He came back the following season and gradually built up a reputation as a powerful hitter with a first-class driving stroke and one of the finest right-arm leg-break and googly bowlers of all time.

Benaud made his Test debut against the West Indies in 1951–52, and after playing against South Africa in 1952–53 he toured England in 1953.

Following more games against England in Australia he really made his mark as a Test cricketer in the next series against the West Indies. Then, at Kingston he hit a century in 78 minutes and went on to score 121.

It was in South Africa in 1957–58 that he reached his peak as a bowler by bagging 106 wickets for an average of 19.40 and he was made captain for the series against England in 1958–59.

In this rubber he not only maintained his reputation as a leg-break bowler but established himself as one of his country's most forceful captains.

In those 1958–59 Tests he took more wickets than any other bowler on either side, 31 (av. 18.83), and at Melbourne he had the distinction of winning the match even though he had chosen to put England in to bat.

Benaud next led Australia to victory against Pakistan and India in 1959–60, personally accounting for 41 wickets at an average cost of 18.00 apiece.

Another Test rubber victory followed in the exciting series against the West Indies and then Benaud led the Australians to England in 1961. Here he proved himself to be one of the most capable captains ever to lead a Test side, an inspiration to his team and a leader who handled every situation with amazing drive and good sense.

When Benaud retired in 1964 he had captained Australia in 28 of his 63 Tests and never lost a Test rubber while bagging a total of 248 wickets (av. 27.03).

BENEFITS

The record benefit received by a cricketer amounted to nearly £28,000. This was collected by B. L. D'Oliveira (Warwickshire) in 1975.

Whereas a footballer's benefit is subject to Income Tax a cricketer's benefit is not.

The test case was made when the Inland Revenue attempted to tax a benefit which J. Seymour of Kent had received in 1920.

The case was heard by Sir John Simon and he agreed that a cricketer's benefit is a free gift from his employers and admirers and was, therefore, not subject to tax.

A footballer does not enjoy this freedom because payment of benefit is normally laid down in his contract, but no such agreement is made in the case of a cricketer.

J. M. Read's benefit match in 1893 was the Oval Test between England and Australia. The player himself did not take part in this match.

Benefit matches are normally granted by the County Clubs after 10 years' service. The M.C.C. began giving their professionals benefits in the 1850s.

BENSON and HEDGES CUP

A limited over one day match competition inaugurated in 1972 under sponsorship of the tobacco firm. The 17 first-class counties. Oxford and Cambridge Universities (one only each year in turn), or a combined team, and sides representing minor counties North and South are divided into four regions. The top two teams from each region eventually meet on a knock-out basis and the Final takes place at Lord's. Winners: 1972—Leicestershire; 1973—Kent; 1974—Surrey; 1975—Leicestershire; 1976—Kent.

Highest score: 327 for 4 off 55 overs, Leicestershire v. Warwickshire, at Coventry, 1972. Highest individual score: 173* by C. G. Greenidge, Hampshire v. Minor Counties (South), at Amersham, 1973. Lowest completed innings: 62 off 26.5 overs, Gloucestershire v. Hampshire, at Bristol 1975.

BERKSHIRE C.C.C.

Founded: March 12, 1895. However, county cricket was played as early as 1748. A member of the Minor Counties Championship. Secretary: C. F. V. Martin, Leeward, Lee Lane, Maidenhead. Highest score for: 537 v. Devon, at Reading, 1921. Highest score against: 533 by Devon, at Reading, 1926. Highest individual score for: 282 by E. Garnett v. Wiltshire, at Reading, 1908. Highest individual score against: 232 by F. H. Carroll of Devon, at Exeter, 1912. Lowest score for: 39 v. Wiltshire, at Salisbury,

1931. Lowest score against: 54 by Buck-inghamshire, at Slough, 1957. Colours: Green. Badge: County crest (a white hart passing under a polled oak) in white. Minor Counties champions: 1924, 1928, 1953.

BETTING

Cricket in the 18th and early 19th centuries was the object of much wagering and at one period this grew to such proportions that it brought the game into disrepute.

Occasionally this gambling influenced people to give vent to their feelings and it was not uncommon for fighting to break out at cricket matches among the betting fraternity.

In 1748, after a defendant had been found not liable for payment of a betting debt which it was alleged had been incurred over a cricket match, the judge remarked "It is, to be sure, a manly game, and not bad in itself, but it is the ill-use that is made of it by betting above £10 upon it that is bad and against the laws."

Among a number of charges levelled against the game by one critic in 1743 there appeared in *The Gentleman's Magazine*, the following: "It is a notorious and shameless breach of the laws, as it gives the most open encouragement to gambling".

When the Old Etonians met Eleven Gentlemen of England at Newmarket in June, 1751, the game was played for £1,500 and "near £20,000 is depending" in side-stakes.

In September 1786, £4,000 was staked on a match arranged by the Duke of York and a number of gentlemen.

Lord Frederic Beauclerk, a cricketing parson, made no secret of the fact that his wagering on cricket brought him something like 600 guineas a year. He was an all-round cricketer, much respected in the game, and became President of the M.C.C. in 1826. It was Lord Frederic who took the momentous step of banning one of the game's leading professionals, William Lambert, from ever appearing again at Lord's after it had been alleged that the famous Surrey all-rounder had "sold" the match between England and XXII of Nottingham in 1817.

Betting returned to cricket grounds in the 1970's after an absence of over a century. The first to have a betting shop was Trent Bridge in 1971 where Ladbrokes agreed an arrangement whereby the home club took 40% of their profit.

BIG HITTING

See also under BOUNDARIES and FAST SCORING.

Five of the biggest hitters ever seen in first-class cricket have been G. J. Bonnor, G. L. Jessop, C. I. Thornton, A. E. Trott and A. W. Wellard.

G. J. Bonnor of New South Wales and Victoria once hit a ball through the face of the pavilion clock on Melbourne Cricket ground. On another occasion when in practice at Melbourne he hit a ball right out of the ground, a distance of over 160 yards.

Bonnor, who stood six foot six inches tall, did not reserve all his big hitting for Australia. At Bradford, in 1888, when playing for the Australians against Yorkshire, he hit five balls out of the ground. He hit a ball out of the Trent Bridge ground on a previous visit in 1880, and, in the same year, when practising on Mitcham Green, he drove a ball 147 yards.

The year 1880 was a big hitting one for Bonnor. At the Oval he hit a ball so high that he had run two before he was caught by G. F. Grace. The catch was as remarkable as the hit for it was made at a distance of 115 yards from the wicket.

Bonnor drove two balls out of the Lord's ground when playing in a charity match, Smokers v. Non-Smokers, in 1884. Both these hits were made off his fellow-countryman, F. R. Spofforth, the 'demon bowler'.

Many examples of the powerful hitting of G. L. Jessop can be found in this volume under BOUNDARIES and under FAST SCORING.

In two innings at Bradford against Yorkshire, this devastating Gloucestershire batsman hit eight balls clear out of the ground (not merely over the boundary). That was in 1900 when in two innings of the same match he scored 104 in 70 minutes and 132 in 95 minutes.

In the same season Jessop put three balls out of the Scarborough ground and one out of the Lord's ground. This one went over the entrance gate and into St. John's Wood Road.

Another man to hit a ball clear out of the Scarborough ground was C. I. Thornton who also has the distinction of driving clear over the pavilion (not the present pavilion) at Lord's. Thornton performed this last feat during the Eton v. Harrow match of 1868.

One of the biggest hitters of the 19th century, Thornton made his record measured drive at Hove in 1876. The distance is recorded as 168 yards 2 feet. However, this hit though remarkable was made in practice and not in a match, and the distance, though precise, is doubtful. Most evidence points to it being around 160 yards.

In 1866 when playing for the Gentlemen of England v. I. Zingari, at Scarborough, Thornton hit seven sixes, one ball clearing nearby houses and landing in Trafalgar Square. In this particular innings he secored 107* with only 29 strokes!

Another action packed Thornton innings was for Kent v. Sussex, at Tunbridge Wells, in 1869. This included nine sixes. Remember those were the days when a six was recorded for a hit "clear out of the ground".

A. E. Trott must have special mention here because he is the only man who has ever hit a ball over the present pavilion at Lord's. He did this when playing for the M.C.C. against the Australians, July 31, 1899. The ball was sent down by M. A. Noble.

Trott actually made a bigger hit than this over the pavilion at Lord's, only this hit which was made a few weeks before the more historical one did not go clear over the roof, but struck the M.C.C. coat-of-arms, well above the roof, and bounced back among the seats. This hit was off a ball by F. W. Tate in a game between M.C.C. and Sussex.

Somerset batsman A. W. Wellard probably hit more sixes than any other player during the 1930s. In his best season (1935) his total was 72, and during his career he twice hit five consecutive sixes. On the first occasion, at Wells in 1936, he sent seven balls out of the ground and one was lost. On the other occasion, on the same ground in 1937, he drove seven balls out of the ground and only three were recovered.

F. T. Mann of Middlesex once hit two consecutive balls onto the roof of the pavilion at Lord's, and E. Hendren and M. P. Donnelly have also hit a ball onto the same roof.

We have already mentioned Thornton as one of the men who had the satisfaction of hitting a ball over the old Lord's pavillion. Others who achieved this feat included H. E. Meek and W. H. Fowler.

H. E. Meek made his big hit in the Eton v. Harrow game of 1877. The ball actually landed on the roof and bounced over. W. H. Fowler's ball went over the pavilion and clear out of the ground, a distance of over 150 yards. The bowler was A. Shaw.

Fowler was a Somerset player, and on his home ground at Taunton in 1882 he sent a ball from F. R. Spofforth over the pavilion.

Another big hit at Lord's was that made by L. N. Constantine on May 22, 1933. This was remarkable not only for its distance but for its direction. The ball was sent down by M. J. C. Allom and Constantine hit it over the wicket-keeper and over the flag by the players' dressing-room.

In August, 1945, W. R. Hammond hit a six through the open door of the Long Room at Lord's and up against one of the glass showcases. Fortunately no harm was done, but that stroke made history. It was during the England v. Dominions game.

There is another story concerning big hitting on the old Lord's ground in Dorset Fields. Apparently Thomas Lord made an offer of 20 guineas to any player who could hit a ball out of the ground. E. H. Budd achieved this feat but he never received the prize.

Over to the other famous London ground at the Oval where the biggest hit is probably that made by P. G. H. Fender when batting for Surrey v. Kent in 1922. In the course of an innings of 137 he drove one ball from G. J. Bryan over extra-cover and into the street. The distance was well over 140 yards.

One of the biggest hits ever must have been that made by the Hon. Frederick Ponsonby for the M.C.C. against Cambridge University, on Parker's Piece, Cambridge, in 1842. Those were the days before boundaries and Ponsonby ran nine off that hit.

The same number of runs is said to have been made off one hit by Twopenny, a member of the team of Aborigines which toured England in 1868.

The longest drive ever is usually regarded as that made by Rev. W. Fellows of Oxford University in 1856. The distance is said to have been 175 yards, but there is reason to doubt the accuracy of this. The hit was made in practice on the Christ Church Ground at Oxford.

Other big hits include the following:

G. Anderson: Ran 8 off one hit for North of England v. Surrey, at the Oval, in 1862.

L. N. Constantine: Drove a ball from "Eddie" Gilbert out of the ground at Woollongabba, Brisbane. The ball was lost.

G. F. Earle: When playing for Somerset, at Lord's in 1925, hit a ball over the score-board near the printing office.

R. A. Haywood: Hit two consecutive balls from A. Morton out of the Northampton ground. This was in 1919.

H. T. Hewett: In the Somerset v. Sussex game at Taunton in 1892 he sent a ball from W. A. Humphreys over the scorers' box and out of the ground into the churchyard.

V. T. Hill: When playing for Somerset at Taunton he hit a ball from A. E. Trott over the pavilion. On another occasion at Trent Bridge he drove a ball a distance of 124 yards.

E. R. T. Holmes: At the Oval in 1935 when playing for Surrey v. Middlesex he drove a ball over mid-off as far as the wall that surrounds the ground.

C. H. Lloyd: When playing for Lancashire v. Surrey, at the Oval, May 1975, hit a ball over mid-wicket and clear into Harleyford Road—over 120 yards.

P. Marner: Playing for Lancashire v. Hampshire, at Southampton, in May 1960, hit a ball out of the ground and onto the track of the adjoining greyhound stadium. This would be a distance of about 100 yards.

E. H. D. Sewell: At the Crystal Palace when playing for London County v. Surrey in 1904 he made such a tremendous hit that it was measured and found to be 140 yards.

O. G. "Collie" Smith: At Chesterfield, in 1957, when playing for the West Indians against Derbyshire, one of his sixes landed on the roof of the pavilion, another on the edge of the boating lake, and two more went into the crowd.

He also hit two sixes out of the ground when playing at Hastings in 1957, and later in his career in League cricket in May, 1959, at Turf Moor, Burnley, he hit a ball from the Belvedere Road end over the stand and into the middle of the adjoining football ground.

W. J. Stewart: Drove a ball clear out of the Blackpool ground for Warwickshire v. Lancashire, July 1959.

Hon. L. H. Tennyson: Sent a ball from F. E. Woolley over the pavilion at Southampton in the Hampshire v. Kent game of 1920. The distance was measured and recorded as 139 yards, 1 foot 8 inches.

G. Ulyett: When playing at Bramall Lane in 1883 he hit a ball out of the ground and it is said to have landed two streets away.

BLACKHAM, John McCarthy (1853–1932)

There has never been a more competent wicket-keeper than this smallish black-bearded cricket enthusiast from Victoria.

J. M. Blackham made no less than eight tours of England and was one of the very few wicket-keepers who have been chosen to captain a Test team. Between 1885 and 1895 he led Australia in eight Tests against England.

Blackham was also a batsman with an unorthodox style who was good enough to help his side out of trouble on a number of occasions and scored 800 runs in 35 Tests with an average of 15.68. When he made 74 against England at Sydney in 1894–95 he figured in a ninth wicket stand of 154 with S. E. Gregory. This is still an Australian ninth wicket Test record.

However, it was Blackham's lightning speed behind the stumps which won him fame. He could stand up to any bowling, including that of Spofforth, and was referred to in his day as the "prince of wicket-keepers".

An injury received in the first Test of 1894–95 ended his career as a wicket-keeper.

BLYTHE, Colin (1879–1917)

Colin Blythe of Kent was probably one of the half-dozen deadliest slow left-arm bowlers of all time.

He was not a robust man, yet not the least of his qualities was his durability. He bowled unchanged throughout a match on five different occasions.

His name appears on the Roll of Honour of those who met their death in World War I, but in the comparatively short time between making his debut in 1899 (taking a wicket with his first ball) and leaving for the fighting front in 1915, he took 2,506 wickets at an average of 16.81.

In 1907 he captured 17 wickets in one day against Northamptonshire, a record which was not to be equalled for 26 years.

Blythe performed the hat-trick twice; took all ten wickets once (10 for 30), and, in 1912 season, got his average down to 12.26 while taking 178 wickets.

His biggest bag in a single season was 215 wickets (av. 14.54) om 1909.

In Test cricket his finest performance was his 15 for 99 v. South Africa, at Leeds, in 1907, while one of his best innings against Australia was his 6 for 44 at Edgbaston in 1909.

Colin Blythe played in 19 Tests taking 100 wickets at an average of 18.63 runs apiece.

BODY-LINE

See under BOWLING (BODY-LINE).

BORDE, Chandrakant Gulabrao (1934-   )

Only two players, Umrigar and Majrekar, have scored more runs for India in Test cricket than this all-rounder from Poona—a right-handed batsman and leg-break bowler.

His aggregate in 55 Tests is 3,062 (av. 35.60) and it was against the West Indies that he made the greatest impression. In the 5th Test, at Delhi in 1958, he scored 109 and 96, while in the 3-match 1966–67 series in India he averaged 57.66 with two centuries.

Always a determined performer his finest bowling performance was his 4 for 21 v. Pakistan, at Calcutta in 1960–61. It was in that series that he also hit his highest Test score—177* in nine hours at Madras.

Made debut with Mahrashtra in 1952, and was with Baroda 1954–64 before returning to Mahrashtra. Played as a professional in Lancashire League 1957–58 and 1960–62, and toured England in 1959 and 1967.

BOSANQUET, Bernard James Tindal (1877–1936)

Always remembered as the inventor of the googly (still known in Australia as "the Bosie") but he was also a fine batsman.

His googly bowling first attracted widespread attention when he used it as a member of P. F. Warner's team in Australia and New Zealand in 1902–03. His first googly at Sydney clean bowled Victor Trumper.

No Tests were played on that tour and it was in the 1903–04 visit to Australia that his bowling made its mark in the highest class of cricket. Then, in the fourth Test at Sydney it was his googlies which won the Ashes, for in Australia's second innings he took 6 for 51.

Bosanquet's first-class career began

with Oxford University in 1898 and he appeared with Middlesex from 1898 until 1919, twice scoring two centuries in a match for his county.

BOUNDARIES

Boundaries were first mentioned in the Laws of Cricket in 1884 but they had been in use in Australia as early as 1862 and were first introduced at Lord's for the Eton v. Harrow match of 1866.

In his autobiography, W. G. Grace wrote that "there were no fixed boundaries at Lord's when I first played there (this was in 1864). If the ball struck the pavilion a four was allowed—although even that rule was suspended one year—but every other hit had to be run out."

W. G. went on to say that the institution of proper boundaries was thought advisable following an incident involving A. N. Hornby, who chased a ball into the crowd with such determination and energy that spectators were scattered and one old gentlemen "not being sufficiently alert to get out of the way" was rather severely hurt.

Nowadays it is normal practice to allow four runs for a boundary hit, and six runs for a hit that pitches over the boundary, but these scores are subject to alteration on certain grounds in accordance with local custom.

The awarding of six runs for a hit that drops over the boundary line was adopted at some grounds as early as 1906, but until 1910 it was still necessary, in many places, to hit a ball clear out of the ground to get six runs. On these grounds a ball hit clear over the boundary but not out of the ground gained only four runs, or the same as for any ball which reached the boundary.

At one period in Australia about the turn of the century, and until 1906, hits over the boundary were awarded 5 runs.

Prior to the introduction of boundaries, as already mentioned most hits had to be run out. But there was a time when the batsmen were awarded certain scores for boundaries in addition to those actually run off the same hit.

So we have the remarkable score of 10 runs being made for a single hit in a first-class match at Lord's in 1900. This is how it happened.

When batting for Derbyshire against the M.C.C., S. H. Wood sent a ball from C. J. Burnup to the boundary and also ran

4. Two were added for the boundary, but as the result of an overthrow the ball went through to the other boundary and Wood ran another two while two were added for this second boundary, making 10 altogether.

In 1957 it was decided to experiment with a boundary limit of 75 yards from the centre of the pitch, but this compulsory maximum was abandoned for the 1966 season.

Most boundaries

The greatest number of boundary hits in a single innings is 68, all fours, by P. A. Perrin when he made 343* for Essex v. Derbyshire, at Chesterfield, in 1904. At least 14 of these hits landed outside the boundary and would have been sixes under present day rules.

At Bath, in June 1936, H. Gimblett of Somerset hit 18 consecutive boundaries in an innings of 143 against Northamptonshire. They were six sixes and 12 fours.

The record for the most sixes in a single innings of first-class cricket was set up by J. R. Reid at Wellington in a Plunket Shield game for the home side v. Northern Districts in January, 1963. Reid hit 15 sixes in an innings of 296 which lasted for 227 minutes and also included 35 fours.

G. Sobers hit six sixes in one over off M. A. Nash when batting for Nottinghamshire v. Glamorgan, at Swansea, August 31, 1968.

Two of the most remarkable boundary hitting overs on record are the work of A. W. Wellard the six-foot Somerset professional who was born in Kent but was missed by his home county.

In August 1936, at Wells, he hit the last five balls of an over from T. R. Armstrong of Derbyshire for boundary sixes. On that occasion his 86 in 62 minutes included seven sixes and eight fours.

He got another five consecutive sixes on the same ground in August 1938 when facing the bowling of F. E. Woolley of Kent. This time his innings of 57 lasted 37 minutes and included seven sixes.

M. J. Procter hit five consecutive sixes in one over for Western Province v. Australians, at Cape Town, March 1970. The bowler was A. A. Mallett.

The only other player apart from Sobers, Wellard and Procter to hit five consecutive sixes (all in the same over) is D. Lindsay, for South African Fezela XI off W. T. Greensmith of Essex, at Colchester, in June 1961.

V. T. Trumper, the famous New South Wales batsman, hit 22 fives (today these would have been sixes) in an innings of 335 in a club game in Australia in 1902–03.

An Englishman gets the palm for the finest display of boundary hitting in a Test match, for when J. H. Edrich scored 310* against New Zealand, at Leeds, July 1965, his innings included a record total of 238 with boundary hits—52 fours and 5 sixes.

Another of the finest displays of boundary hitting ever seen in Test cricket in England was that of D. G. Bradman at Leeds in July 1930. This was the occasion when Bradman made 334 and this score included 46 fours.

In his next Test appearance on that ground four years later Bradman played an innings of 304 which included 43 fours and two sixes.

When A. C. MacLaren made his record 424 runs (still an English record) for Lancashire v. Somerset, at Taunton, in 1895, his innings included 63 boundary hits—one six and 62 fours.

With regard to the record for the most sixes in a single match this is held by W. J. Stewart of Warwickshire. At Blackpool in 1959 when batting against Lancashire his first innings of 155 included 10 sixes (and 12 fours) and in his second innings of 125 he added another seven sixes (and 12 fours).

In 1935 A. W. Wellard (Somerset) hit a record number of 72 sixes. His most notable innings that season were 68 v. Nottinghamshire, at Nottingham (four sixes and seven fours); 57 (five sixes) and 83 (57 of these in 12 strokes, four sixes, a five and seven fours) v. Essex, at Clacton; 74 (four sixes and eight fours) and 70 (six sixes and five fours) v. Kent, at Maidstone. In this season of 1935 Wellard hit 68 of his sixes in matches for his county.

There is little doubt that Wellard was the most prolific six-hitter in the history of the game. A precise figure is difficult to obtain but it ss claimed that in a career which lasted from 1927 to 1950 he hit over 500 sixes. This is an astonishing figure but when you consider that he hit 129 sixes in only two seasons, 1935 and 1936, then he had plenty of time to hit the others.

See also under BIG HITTING.

BOWLING

See also under AVERAGES (BOWLING), HAT-TRICKS, OVERS, WICKET (BAILS), WIDES, THROWING THE BALL.

All three stumps

In bowling Felix, Charles Lawrence knocked all three stumps out of the ground. Scottish Twenty-Two v. All England XI, at Edinburgh, 1849[1].

In bowling C. R. Filgate (M.C.C.) at Lord's, May 30, 1870, G. Freeman (Yorkshire) knocked all three stumps out of the ground.

"Bosie" (or "Wrong 'un")

See in this section under Googly.

Body-line (or direct attack)

The big dispute over body-line bowling, a dispute which was almost an international incident, took place during the England tour of Australia in 1932–33.

On January 18, 1933, the following cable was sent to the M.C.C. by the Australian Board of Control.

"Body-line bowling has assumed such proportions as to menace the best interests of the game, making protection of the body by the batsmen the main consideration.

"This is causing intensely bitter feeling between the players as well as injury. In our opinion it is unsportsmanlike.

"Unless stopped at once it is likely to upset the friendly relations existing between Australia and England."

The M.C.C. rejected the Australian Board's charge of bad sportsmanship and agreed to a cancellation of the remainder of the tour if the Australians thought this necessary.

Relations between the two countries were, to say the least, strained, and it is difficult for people in England to appreciate the feeling of resentment which existed in Australia towards the visiting cricketers at that time.

The Australian Board of Control had coined the phrase "body-line bowling" to describe what the M.C.C. preferred to call "fast leg-theory bowling".

The Editor of Wisden's in his comments on the situation refused to use the Australian term because he considered it "an objectionable term, utterly foreign to cricket, and calculated to stir up strife".

Fortunately, diplomacy on both sides won out and one of the heroes of the day who deserved nothing but praise for his part in a difficult situation was the England captain, D. R. Jardine.

Leg-theory bowling had been used before this series of Tests but the adoption of this style of bowling was more significant on this occasion because it was used by such a fast bowler as Larwood bowling short of a length.

In November 1934, the M.C.C. issued a communication deploring the use of the type of bowling which in effect constituted a direct attack by the bowler upon the batsman. In order to put a stop to this it was necessary to ensure that all concerned knew what is meant by "direct attack bowling", and so the following ruling was made:

"That the type of bowling regarded as a direct attack by the bowler upon the batsman, and therefore unfair, consists in persistent and systematic bowling of fast, short-pitched balls at the batsman standing clear of his wicket."

Development of bowling

In the earliest days of cricket all bowling was underarm but eventually men like David Harris, William Clarke, and John Nyren developed this type of bowling so well that it was of a class far removed from that one may normally associate with underarm bowling.

David Harris bowled with such accuracy of length and with the ball getting up off the ground so fast that batsmen were forced to move out to the pitch of the ball.

Gradually the bowling arm was raised higher and higher. Indeed, Harris bowled with his hand about the level of his armpit, and towards the end of the 17th century round-arm bowling was introduced, although this type of bowling, or "throwing" as some people called it, met with much opposition.

Round-arm bowling was first used consistently by John Willes of Sutton Valence, Kent, and James Broadbridge of Sussex, but it is said to have been invented by a woman, Christina, a sister (or was it his daughter?) of Willes. She adopted this form of bowling to avoid her billowing skirts when sending down practice balls to her brother.

Even so the arm was not allowed to be raised above the shoulder, and for many years bowlers were constantly being "no-balled" as they raised their arm in an effort to get the ball to rise and also break to the off. In 1828 the hand was allowed to

[1] *Compiler's note:* This incident has often been mentioned but is not substantiated by contemporary reports.

be raised to elbow level, and in 1835 to shoulder level.

William Lillywhite and James Broadbridge were among the most persistent breakers of the law against raising the arm, but it was Edgar Willsher of Kent who brought this matter of overarm bowling to the point where the authorities were forced to take some action.

In the England v. Surrey match at the Oval in 1862 Willsher left the field after being "no-balled" seven successive times by John Lillywhite for raising his hand higher than his shoulder. Thereupon the game was suspended for the day and the following morning Lillywhite was replaced when he stubbornly refused to change his mind about the legality of Willsher's bowling.

This incident, more than any other, led to approval of over-arm bowling with a change in the wording of the laws in 1864.

Incidentally, underarm bowling was still used in first-class cricket for many years after this. The last man to use this type of bowling in a first-class county match was T. J. Molony of Surrey as recently as 1921.

The first man to make the ball break from the off was probably Lambert (Lamborn) "The Little Farmer" of Hambledon. That was in about 1780. He really started something for by the time we reach the turn of the century off-break bowling had become such a fad (it really developed quickly after overarm bowling was legalised) that cricket was in danger of becoming a bore.

Googly bowling changed this and the introduction of the swerve with the new ball did much to enliven the situation.

The first "googly" is usually credited to B. J. T. Bosanquet a medium to fast bowler who took the wicket of S. Coe with the first delivery of this type sent down in 1900.

The next bowler to use the "googly" successfully was R. O. Schwartz in 1903–04. He was one of a quartet of "googly" experts from South Africa, the other three being A. E. Vogler, G. A. Faulkner and G. C. White.

The difficulty with this type of bowling is keeping a good length, and that in addition to the physical strain on the bowler. Schwartz gave up this type of bowling to concentrate on keeping a length.

An accurate length is, of course, the true essence of good bowling, and it is, after all, the bowling rather than the batting which wins most matches.

Fast bowling

Who was the fastest bowler ever? This question is one which causes no end of discussion but it is quite impossible to give a definite answer. Here it will suffice to list a few of the fastest bowlers ever known.

N. A. Knox of Surrey. This bowler took a 25-yard run up before sending the ball down at an astonishing speed. He took 11 for 64 v. Hampshire, at the Oval, in 1906, and 10 for 181 in the famous Surrey v. Yorkshire game which was watched by a crowd of 80,000 in July 1906, also at the Oval.

C. J. Kortright has been described as the fastest of all fast bowlers, but Dr. W. G. Grace, who had played the Essex man's bowling, considered that the bowling of H. W. Fellows and W. Marcon, both of Eton, was even faster.

It is worth noting that these Eton bowlers used an underhand delivery. This is what the Doctor wrote about them:

"Few people nowadays realise how fast they bowled. Kortright, Mold, Richardson, and Lockwood were not nearly as fast. It required two or three long-stops to stop them, and many considered their bowling dangerous to play."

Another fast bowler of the 19th century was George Brown of Brighton. It was this player who once killed a dog instantaneously when it was struck by one of his fast deliveries as it stood among the spectators on the boundary.

In more recent times H. Larwood, "The Nottingham Express" is another candidate for the title of world's fastest bowler. He was one of the very few really fast bowlers ever to top the first-class averages for more than a single season. Larwood was the country's leading bowler in 1927, 1928, 1931, 1932, and 1936.

This Nottinghamshire player was at the centre of the body-line controversy of the 1932–33 tour of Australia. His figures in that fateful third Test when two Australian batsmen were accidentally hurt, were 7 for 126. His Test analysis on the tour showed an average of 19.51 in taking 33 wickets.

Soon after World War II there was F. H. Tyson who played a leading role in England's Test rubber victory in Australia in 1954–55 and was described by John Arlott as the fastest bowler he had ever seen.

Today we have J. R. Thomson and D. K. Lillee, the Australian pair who destroyed England with a bag of 58 wickets between them in the 1974–75 series down under, and the West Indians, A. M. E. Roberts, who captured 35 Australian wickets in the 1975–76 Tests, and M. A. Holding who took 28 England wickets in 1976, including 14 in one Test.

General

In the third Test of the Australian tour of England in 1884 all 11 England players bowled. This is a record for a Test match. The players were W. G. Grace, W. H. Scotton, W. Barnes, A. Shrewsbury, A. G. Steel, G. Ulyett, R. G. Barlow, Lord Harris, Hon. A. Lyttelton, W. W. Read, and E. Peate.

It is also worth noting that it was the wicket-keeper, the Hon. A. Lyttelton, who returned the side's best bowling figures with his underhand lobs—4 for 19.

The match was drawn, Australia scoring 551 in their first innings, and England scoring 346 and 85 for two wickets.

There have been very few other instances of all 11 members of a team bowling in a single innings. One notable occasion was when all the Essendon team bowled against Melbourne University when the latter made their historic 1,094 total at Melbourne in 1898.

One of the most recent occasions when this happened in a first-class match was when all 11 of the Somerset team bowled in the second innings against Leicestershire, at Taunton in July 1957. They could only capture three wickets before time ran out with Leicestershire scoring 295 runs.

At Worcester on August 30, 1949, Worcestershire dismissed the last six Surrey batsmen without any addition to the score which remained at 107. The bowlers were R. O. Jenkins and R. Howorth, and the time taken to dismiss the six batsmen was 15 minutes.

"Googly"

This is the name for a ball which is an off-break sent down with a leg-break action. The earliest successful exponent of this type of bowling was B. J. T. Bosanquet of Eton, Oxford University, Middlesex and England. He claimed that the first wicket he ever took with a "googly" was that of S. Coe of Leicestershire, at Lord's in 1900.

It was in Australia in the 1903–04 tour that he really established googly bowling,

for in the Tests his average of 25.18 for 16 wickets was second only to W. Rhodes. In the fourth Test of that series Bosanquet took 6 for 51 in the Australians' second innings. At one stage he was 5 for 12.

Some authorities name earlier exponents of the googly. J. Phillips, an Australian who assisted Middlesex about the turn of the century is one of them, but he did not use it regularly.

Hat-trick

See separate entry.

Maidens

See separate entry, OVERS.

Most balls in an innings

The world record for the number of balls sent down by one bowler in a single innings was set up by S. Ramadhin when playing for the West Indies against England, at Birmingham, May–June 1957.

In the second innings of this Test he bowled 98 overs (588 balls). His analysis was 98–35–179–2.

Most balls in a match

The record in England was created by S. Ramadhin in the same match as mentioned above. He bowled 31 overs in the first innings and 98 in the second, a total of 774 balls. With these he took 7 for 49 and 2 for 179.

The world record for a match is held by C. S. Nayudu who sent down a total of 917 balls for Holkar v. Bombay, at Bombay, 1944–45.

Most wickets in an over

Several players have taken four wickets in an over. Probably the most remarkable performance was by P. I. Pocock (Surrey) for in the course of his final over against Sussex, at Eastbourne, August 1975, five wickets were taken, four of them bowled with consecutive deliveries and the other man run out. Pocock actually took seven wickets for four runs in his last two overs.

Most wickets in an innings

Several men have taken all 10 wickets in an innings but only four of these have achieved this more than once:

A. P. Freeman, Kent v. Lancashire, at Maidstone, 1929; Kent v. Essex, at Southend, 1930; Kent v. Lancashire, at Manchester, 1931.

J. C. Laker, Surrey v. Australians, at the Oval, 1956; England v. Australia, at Manchester, 1956.

Laker is the only man ever to take all 10 wickets in a single innings of a Test match.

H. Verity, Yorkshire v. Warwickshire, at Leeds, 1931; Yorkshire v. Nottinghamshire, at Leeds, 1932.

V. E. Walker, England v. Surrey, at Oval, 1859; Gentlemen of Middlesex v. Lancashire, at Manchester, 1865.

When E. Barratt took all 10 Australian wickets in their first innings against the Players, at the Oval in 1878, he did not bowl down a single wicket.

The only man to actually bowl down all 10 wickets in a single innings is J. Wisden. This was when bowling for the North v. South, at Lord's, in 1850.

Although it is not a first-class match another remarkable performance is worth noting here. In 1867 A. Dartnell of Broad Green took all 10 Thornton Heath wickets for no runs.

Most wickets in a match

J. C. Laker holds the record with 19 Australian wickets in the fourth Test at Manchester in July 1956.

Laker took nine wickets in the first innings and all 10 in the second. His analysis for the match was 68–27–90–19. An average of 4.7.

A. P. Freeman of Kent took 10 or more wickets in a match on no less than 140 occasions, an outstanding record unapproached by any other bowler. His best was 17 wickets for Kent v. Sussex, at Hove, 1922, and v. Warwickshire, at Folkestone, 1932.

Most wickets in a day

When C. Blythe of Kent achieved the distinction of taking 17 wickets in a match he did so in a single day's play. This was against Northamptonshire, at Northampton, in 1907. Blythe's figures were 10 for 30 and 7 for 18.

Two other bowlers to take 17 wickets in a day: H. Verity, 17 for 91, Yorkshire v. Essex, Leyton, July 1933, and T. W. Goddard, 17 for 106, Gloucestershire v. Kent, Bristol, July 1939.

G. H. Pope took 6 for 34 and 7 for 16 for Derbyshire when they beat Somerset in a single day, at Chesterfield, June 11, 1947.

S. Haigh took 8 for 21 and 6 for 22 for Yorkshire when they beat Hampshire in a single day, at Southampton, May 27, 1898.

Most wickets in a season

This record is held by A. P. Freeman of Kent who took 304 wickets in season 1928. During that season he bowled 1,976.1 overs. His average was 18.05.

In 1933 A. P. Freeman bowled over 2,000 overs and only failed to equal his record by six wickets. This total of 298 wickets is still the second best ever recorded.

A. P. Freeman's complete figures for these two remarkable seasons are as follows:

1928: 1,976.1 overs, 423 maidens, 5,489 runs, 304 wkts., 18.05 av.
1933: 2,039 overs, 651 maidens, 4,549 runs, 298 wkts., 15.26 av.

In 1951 R. Appleyard (Yorkshire) created a record by taking 200 wickets in his first full season in first-class cricket. His average was 14.14.

Records of some of the old-timers show that William Clarke (Nottingham) took 476 wickets in his best season—1854; John Wisden (Sussex) 455 wickets in 1851, and W. Hillyer (Kent) 358 wickets in 1849. Of course, not all these matches were first-class and many were against odds.

Most wickets in a career

The record is held by W. Rhodes, Yorkshire's slow left-arm genius. From 1898 to 1930 he took 4,187 wickets (av. 16.71). In his last season when in his 53rd year he took 42 wickets for Yorkshire at an average of 20.42.

In Tests only the record is held by L. R. Gibbs (West Indies), 309 wickets (av. 29.09).

Most wickets in a Test rubber

The record is held by S. F. Barnes who took 49 wickets in four Tests for England in South Africa in 1913–14.

In the first Test, at Durban, which England won by an innings and 157 runs, Barnes took 10 for 105. In the second Test at Johannesburg he created a new Test record by capturing 17 wickets (8 for 56 and 9 for 103) and England won by an innings and 12 runs.

The third Test was also at Johannesburg and England secured the rubber for the first time in South Africa with a victory by 91 runs. Barnes took 3 for 36 and 5 for 102.

At this stage Barnes needed two more wickets to equal the record of 37 in a Test rubber which had been set up three years earlier in South Africa by W. J. Whitty of Australia. Barnes swept that record aside in the fourth Test which was left drawn at Durban. This time he captured 7 for 56 and 7 for 88.

Barnes did not play in the final Test of that series as he was suffering from a strain. Even so his aggregate for four Tests has never been equalled. His average for those 49 wickets was 10.93.

In some respects an even more astonishingly successful Test rubber for one bowler was the series of only three matched in South Africa in 1895–96. In his rubber England's G. A. Lohmann took 35 wickets at an average cost of only 5.80.

No-ball

The first match in which "no-balls" were recorded was that between the M.C.C. and Middlesex, at Lord's, May 17, 1830.

The highest number of "no-balls" recorded against a bowler in an England v. Australia Test is 12. F. R. Foster (England) was no-balled 12 times at Melbourne, 1912, and E. L. McCormick (Australia) the same number, at Lord's, 1938.

E. L. McCormick sent down 35 no-balls in his first match in England in 1938.

There were 99 no-balls (79 unscored from) in the West Indies v. England Test, Bridgetown, March 1974.

Other outstanding bowling feats

Here are listed just a few of the most outstanding bowling feats which have not already been mentioned in this section.

Before lunch

W. Copson (Derbyshire) took 8 Warwickshire wickets for 11 runs before lunch, June 17, 1937.

C. W. Grove (Warwickshire) 8 Sussex wickets before lunch, June 18, 1952. In that innings he took 9 for 39.

S. Santall (Warwickshire) took 8 for 25 against Essex before lunch, 1898. In 1900 he took 8 for 23 before lunch against Leicestershire. Both games were at Edgbaston.

In 1928 at Cheltenham, W. R. Hammond (Gloucestershire) took 9 Worcestershire wickets, 9 for 23, before lunch.

Wickets with consecutive balls

The feat of taking four wickets with consecutive balls has been performed by several bowlers but never in a Test match.

The outstanding achievement in this respect is that of R. J. Crisp of South Africa. He is the only man to perform the feat of four wickets in four balls on two separate occasions—Western Province v. Griqualand West, at Johannesburg, 1931–32, and v. Natal, at Durban, 1933–34.

At Lord's, in June 1907, on the occasion of his benefit match, A. E. Trott of Middlesex, came very close to taking four wickets with four balls twice in the same innings against Somerset. Unfortunately, he ran out of opposition with his seventh wicket.

John Jackson bowled six men with seven balls for the All England XI against 22 of Uppingham.

H. F. Boyle took seven wickets with eight balls when playing for the Australians against 18 of Elland at Leeds in 1878.

W. H. Copson (Derbyshire) took five Warwickshire wickets with six balls for no runs. The last four of one innings and the first of the next innings. The date was June 17, 1937.

P. I. Pocock (Surrey) took seven wickets with eleven balls, including four wickets with four balls, in a devastating spell v. Sussex, at Eastbourne, Aug. 15, 1972.

Remarkable figures

G. Elliott, 9 for 2. Victoria v. Tasmania, 1857–58.

J. C. Laker, 8 for 2. England v. The Rest, at Park Avenue, Bradford, May 31, 1950.

C. H. Palmer, 8 for 5. Leicestershire v. Surrey, at Leicestershire, May 1955. Finished up with 8 for 7.

D. Shackleton, 8 for 4. Hampshire v. Somerset, at Weston, Aug. 1955.

In 1907 C. Blythe of Kent bowling

against Northamptonshire, at Northampton, took 17 wickets for only 48 runs.

F. R. Spofforth, 7 for 3. Australians v. England XI, at Birmingham, in 1884.

F. E. Field (Warwickshire), 6 for 2. v. Worcestershire, at Dudley, 1914.

The remarkable analysis of two Australian bowlers in England in 1888 are worth studying:

C. T. B. Turner 2,589.3 ov., 1,222 m., 3,492 r., 313 w., 11.38 av.

J. J. Ferris 2,222.2 ov., 998 m., 3,103 r., 220 w., 14.23 av.

Test cricket

In Test cricket the following performances are among the best ever recorded:

J. C. Laker, 19 for 90, England v. Australia, at Manchester, 1956.

S. F. Barnes, 17 for 159, England v. South Africa, at Johannesburg in 1913–14.

J. Briggs, 15 for 28, England v. South Africa, at Cape Town, 1888–89.

G. A. Lohmann, 15 for 45 (8 for 7 in one innings) England v. South Africa, at Port Elizabeth, 1895–96.

C. Blyth, 15 for 99, England v. South Africa, at Leeds, 1907.

W. Rhodes, 15 for 124, England v. Australia, at Melbourne, 1903–04.

H. Verity, 15 for 104, England v. Australia, at Lord's, 1934.

E. R. H. Toshack took 5 for 2 in one innings for Australia v. India, at Brisbane, in 1947–48.

Stumps

See also "All three stumps" in this section:

H. Fellows, the Eton fast bowler of the 19th century, once knocked a stump out of the ground and into the hands of the wicket-keeper standing some 11 yards back.

Unchanged

In season 1907, A. W. Hallam and T. Wass bowled unchanged through 11 innings in Nottinghamshire's County Championship programme.

In two games (against Northamptonshire, at Northampton, and Derbyshire, at Chesterfield) they were unchanged throughout.

Nottinghamshire created a record that season by winning the Championship with only these two regular bowlers. Both Hallam and Wass played in all 19 Championship games. Next to them came J.

Gunn who played in 17 games but bowled far less than half as many overs as Wass.

The analysis of the two principal bowlers was:

A. Hallam 804 ov., 259 m., 1,803 r., 153 w., 11,78 av.

T. Wass 761.1 ov., 188 m., 1,969 r., 145 w., 13.07 av.

In 1911 Warwickshire also won the Championship with virtually only two bowlers, F. R. Foster and F. E. Field. Between them they took 238 wickets, but their figures were not as remarkable as those of Hallam and Wass.

It is a very rare occurrence in modern times for two bowlers to be unchanged throughout a match. Since the war, in England it has only happened three times.

In 1952 D. Shackleton and V. H. D. Cannings were unchanged for Hampshire v. Kent, at Southampton.

In 1958 D. Shackleton and M. Heath bowled unchanged throughout the Hampshire v. Derbyshire match at Burton-on-Trent.

In 1967 B. S. Crump and R. R. Bailey bowled unchanged for Northamptonshire v. Glamorgan at Cardiff.

G. Geary and H. A. Smith bowled unchanged in four consecutive innings for Leicestershire in June 1935.

This run began at Stourbridge where they bowled Worcestershire out for 77 in their second innings. Moving on to Gloucester they bowled that county side out for 72 in only 90 minutes. Gloucestershire, however, batted 10 men with one man ill and the match was not completed due to rain.

The next game was at Northampton, and here Geary and Smith bowled unchanged throughout the match which Leicestershire won in two days. Northamptonshire scored 85 and 79.

The most remarkable bowling by an unchanged pair in a single innings of Test cricket is that of A. E. R. Gilligan and M. W. Tate who bowled South Africa out for 30 at Birmingham in 1924; 11 of those runs were extras and the bowlers' figures were Gilligan 6 for 7, Tate 4 for 12.

BOWLING MACHINE

The first bowling machine, the "Catapulta", was invented in 1837 by Nicholas Felix (or Wanostrocht) the Blackheath schoolmaster who played cricket for Kent, Surrey, and the All-England XI. He gave it to the M.C.C.

BOYCOTT, Geoffrey (1940–   )

One of England's finest opening batsmen this perfectionist, who is capable of scoring heavily on any wicket, made his Test debut against Australia in 1964, less than a year after getting his Yorkshire county cap.

By the summer of 1974 he had played in 63 Tests, scoring 4,579 runs (av. 47.69), including 12 centuries, and his highest score in these matches was his 246* v. India at Leeds in 1967. But then he shocked the cricketing fraternity by asking not to be considered for the 1974–75 tour of Australia and New Zealand. That marked the end of his Test career.

He was appointed Yorkshire captain in 1971 and since his first full season for them in 1963 he has never once failed to top their batting averages. In 1971 he became the first English batsman to head the batting averages at home with a figure in excess of 100—actually 100.12. His highest innings is 261* for the M.C.C. v. President's XI, at Bridgetown, 1973–74.

BRADMAN, Sir Donald George (1908–   )

One of cricket's all-time greats. Don Bradman may not have been the finest batsman ever, that is from an aesthetic point of view, but as a scorer of runs he had no equal. Bradman was a veritable scoring machine, a cold and calculating record maker whose powers of endurance and sheer genius were almost inhuman.

Like most people at the top, Bradman had his critics, but he had no real weakness. He was a batsman who always played to win, a remorseless hitter who often "murdered" the bowling even after his side had gained an easy winning margin.

Bradman played for New South Wales from 1927 to 1934, and South Australia from 1935 until his retirement in 1949.

What W. G. Grace is to England, Sir Donald Bradman is to Australia. At the age of 19 he made a century on his debut in first-class cricket. In his second season he set up a new record for New South Wales with an innings of 340* v. Victoria. When he retired in 1949 he had made 117 centuries, and his aggregate of runs, 28,067, produced an astonishing average of 95.14.

Bradman made 200 runs in 37 separate innings, and six times he passed the 300 mark. His highest score was 452* for New South Wales v. Queensland, at Sydney in 1929–30. His highest in England was 334 for Australia in the Leeds Test of 1930. He was particularly successful in England and his average for four tours is 96.44.

He tops the list of Australians in England with 2,960 runs in 1930, and his 1,690 at home in 1928–29 is the highest in Australia. His career average in Sheffield Shield matches is an astonishing 108.85 with a total of 8,926 runs.

This cricketing genius played in 52 Tests, 24 of them as captain, and he never lost a rubber in the five series of Tests in which he led his side.

In all Tests he scored 6,996 runs, and the remarkable fact is that if he could have scored only four runs when making his final Test appearance at the Oval in 1948 (Hollies bowled him for a 'duck') then his Test average would have been exactly 100. As it was it works out at 99.94, easily the best figure ever recorded by any player with a substantial number of innings.

BRAUND, Leonard Charles (1875–1955)

This versatile all-rounder was missed by Surrey, where he had a trial, and subsequently performed his greatest feats with Somerset.

He was a slow-to-medium pace leg-break bowler who developed a high degree of accuracy. In addition he was a reliable batsman and one of the most competent slip-fielders of all time. He held over 500 catches in his career and his catching of Clem Hill off a leg-glance at Edgbaston in the 1902 Test has been marked down to posterity. To make that particular catch Braund actually moved across from first-slip to leg with almost unbelievable speed and anticipation. Hill was certainly astonished.

Braund appeared in 23 Tests. In Australia's first innings at Melbourne in 1904 he took 8 for 81. In all Tests he took 47 wickets at an average cost of 38.51; 21 of those wickets were taken in one series against Australia, that of 1901–02.

As regards his Test batting, he scored three centuries and completed an aggregate of 987 runs (av. 25.97); 104 in one innings at Lord's against South Africa was his highest in this class of cricket. His all-time best was his 257* v. Worcestershire in 1913.

Braund retired from cricket in 1920 and became an umpire. He was on the list of

first-class umpires until his final retirement in 1938.

BRIGGS, John (1862–1902)

This Lancashire professional began his
career as a batsman and change bowler
but quickly developed into one of his county's finest bowlers.

He was left-hand slow, breaking both
ways. With the bat he was right-handed,
and he was also an agile fielder at cover-
point.

When he made his first appearance for
Lancashire at the age of 16 in 1879 he
gained a place largely because of his
prowess as a fielder, but by 1885 he had
become the county's leading bowler and in
that year he really made his mark by
taking 9 for 29 against Derbyshire, at
Derby.

From then until his retirement in 1900
cheerful John Briggs exceeded 150 wickets
in a season five times. His best season was
1893 when he captured 166 wickets at an
average of 15.89. His best season's
average was 10.49 when taking 160
wickets in 1888.

At Manchester in 1890 Briggs took five
Sussex wickets in seven balls. He took all
10 wickets in an innings against
Worcestershire on the same ground in
1900.

John Briggs made 33 Test appearances.
His best performance in these matches
was his 15 for 28 against South Africa, at
Cape Town in 1888–89, clean balling 14
and getting the other wicket lbw. He took
10 or more wickets in a Test match four
times and in all Tests he captured 118
wickets (av. 17.74).

BROADCASTING

See also under TELEVISION.

The first running commentary of a
cricket match to be broadcast was of the
Essex v. New Zealanders game at Leyton,
in 1927. This commentary was made by
the Rev. F. H. Gillingham.

The first Test match to be broadcast
was England v. Australia, at Nottingham,
in 1930.

BROTHERS

See under FAMILIES.

BUCKINGHAMSHIRE C.C.C.

Founded: January 15, 1891. A county side
was in existence as early as 1741. Member
of the Minor County Championship since
1896. Secretary: P. M. M. Slatter, The
White Cottage, Framewood Road, Stoke
Poges, Bucks. Highest score for: 505 v.
Bedfordshire, 1912. Highest individual
score for: 192* by Wright, 1901. Highest
score against: 505 for 6 declared by
Staffordshire, 1948. Highest individual
score against: 209 by R. Smith of
Staffordshire, 1948. Lowest score for: 15
v. Dorset, at Poole, 1909. Lowest score
against: 15 by Kent II, at Bletchley Park,
1925. Colours: Light green, dark green
and silver. Badge: The Bucks Swan.
Honours: Minor County Champions,
1922, 1923, 1925, 1932, 1938, 1952, 1969.

BURGE, Peter John Parnell (1932–   )

Those who were at Headingley for the
England v. Australia Test in 1964 will not
forget this player's fine innings of 160
which turned the tide and set the
Australians on the road to victory. In that
innings he displayed all his talents as an
attacking batsman of the highest class,
cutting and hooking with an ease seldom
matched in recent years.

Burge made his debut for Queensland in
1952–53 and before retiring in 1968 he
had captained the state side and created a
Queensland record with an innings of 283
v. New South Wales, at Brisbane, in
October 1963.

He had in and out spells in Test cricket
but appeared in 42 of these matches,
scoring 2,290 runs (av. 38.16). His highest
score in Tests was 181 against England, at
the Oval in 1961, and that against
Statham and Trueman at their best.

C

CAMBRIDGE UNIVERSITY C.C.

The idea of an inter-university cricket match originated at Cambridge as early as 1821, the year they first sent a challenge to Oxford, but there is no record of the two sides having met before 1827. It is most surprising to learn that this match has never been played at Cambridge, despite the fact that their famous Fenner's ground was opened as early as 1846.

The University match is, of course, normally played at Lord's, but on each of the five occasions it was played elsewhere it was at Oxford—three times at the Magdalen Ground, and once each at Bullingdon Green and Cowley Marsh.

It was not until 1875 that the Cambridge Cricket and Athletic Clubs secured a lease of Fenner's ground, and the freehold was bought from Caius College in 1892.

Cambridge University C.C. owes much for its early progress to the Rev. A. R. Ward, who was son of William Ward, the man who saved Lord's from the builders in 1825.

It was thanks to this gentleman's untiring efforts that Cambridge University Cricket Club was able to secure the lease of Fenner's and find enough money to build a pavilion. Unfortunately, he did not live long enough to see his club achieve its ambition and secure the ground for its very own in 1892.

Among the more famous Cambridge "Blues" of the 19th century are the Hon. Ivo Bligh (later Earl of Darnley) who was captain in 1881, subsequently played in 19 Tests for England, and was President of the M.C.C. in 1900; Hon. Sir F. S. Jackson, captain 1892–93, 20 England Tests, and President of the M.C.C. 1921; G. L. Jessop, captain 1899, 18 England Tests; Hon. Alfred Lyttelton, captain 1879, 4 England Tests, President M.C.C. 1898; Hon. M. B. Hawke (later Lord Hawke), captain 1885, 5 England Tests, President M.C.C. 1914–18; A. G. Steel, captain

1880, 13 England Tests, President M.C.C. 1902; and K. S. Ranjitsinhji, 15 England Tests. All of these except Lord Hawke and K. S. Ranjitsinhji played in four University matches.

Outstanding Cambridge "Blues" of the 20th century include the following players who have all captained England—G. O. Allen, 25 England Tests; F. R. Brown, 22 England Tests; A. P. F. Chapman, 26 England Tests; E. R. Dexter, 62 England Tests; A. E. R. Gilligan, 11 England Tests; A. R. Lewis, 8 England Tests; F. G. Mann, 7 England Tests; F. T. Mann, 5 England Tests; P. B. H. May, 66 England Tests; R. W. V. Robins, 19 England Tests; D. S. Sheppard, 22 England Tests; and N. W. D. Yardley, 20 England Tests. Oddly enough only Yardley in 1938, Sheppard in 1952, Dexter in 1958, and A. R. Lewis in 1962, captained their University side.

Records

Founded: 1820. Highest score for: 703 for 9 v. Sussex, at Brighton, June 19, 1890. In Varsity match: 432 for 9, 1936. Highest score against: 730 for 3 declared by West Indies, Cambridge, 1950. In the Varsity match: 503 in 1900. Highest individual score for: 254* by K. S. Duleepsinhji v. Middlesex, at Cambridge, 1927. In the Varsity match: 211 by G. Goonesena, 1957. Highest individual score against: 304* by E. D. Weekes for West Indies, 1950. In the Varsity match: 238* by the Nawab of Pataudi, 1931. Lowest score for: 30 v. Yorkshire at Cambridge, 1928. In Varsity match: 47 in 1838. Lowest score against: 32 in the Varsity match, 1878. Colours: Light Blue.

CAMBRIDGESHIRE C.C.C.

Founded: 1891 although a Cambridge Town and County Club was in existence before 1849. Earliest mention is 1813. First appeared in the Minor Counties Championship in 1898. Secretary: R. A.

Taylor, Field View, Linton, Cambridgeshire. Highest score for: 488 v. Suffolk, 1904. Highest score against: 521 for 5 declared by Hertfordshire, 1908. Highest individual score for: 221 by L. T. Reid v. Herts 1909. Highest individual score against: 232 by R. E. Frearson of Lincolnshire, at Grantham, 1925; 247 by Thompson of M.C.C., 1901. Lowest score for: 37 v. Suffolk, 1904; 20 v. Yorkshire, 1861. Lowest score against: 37 by Hertfordshire, 1909. Colours: Maroon, light blue and straw. Badge: The County Crest. Honours: Minor Counties champions: 1963.

CAMERON, Horace Brakenridge (1905–1935)

One of the finest wicket-keepers South Africa has ever produced, H. B. Cameron's life was cut short just when his career had reached its peak.

It was in November 1935, shortly after he had returned home from the victorious South African tour of England, that he died of enteric fever.

During that last tour (his second in England) he had enhanced his reputation as a superb stumper as well as a fearless, hard-hitting batsman. He had stopped the rot at Lord's for when he came in South Africa had lost four for 98, but after an hour and three-quarters of powerful stroke play, Cameron had made 90 out of 126 and South Africa were on the road to victory.

At Scarborough, in his last appearance in first-class cricket, less than two months before his death, he gave further evidence of his power by putting together a score of 160 with a fine display of hard driving, cutting and hooking.

H. B. Cameron made his debut in 1924 and played in his first Test match against England only three years later. He came to England in 1929 and scored 102 against Worcestershire in the opening match of the tour.

He captained South Africa in the last two Tests against England in 1931 and continued to lead his country in their next seven Tests, five against Australia and two against New Zealand.

The worries of captaincy obviously spoilt his form however, especially his batting, but when death ended his career so abruptly he had appeared in 26 Tests, making 1,239 runs (av. 30.22), and dismissed 51 batsmen (39 caught and 12 stumped).

CANADA

Cricket was introduced to Canada by British Army officers at the end of the 18th century and although it has never achieved the popularity of a national game it has always had a keen following around Montreal and Toronto.

In 1840 Toronto met New York at cricket, and a series of matches between Canada and the United States was begun in 1844, thus making this the oldest cricket competition between two countries.

The first overseas tour of a cricket team from England was that sponsored by the Montreal Club in 1859. This was by the All England XI captained by George Parr and John Wisden which went to Canada and the United States and played five games, winning all of them.

Another tour was made in 1868 under Edgar Willsher and this side played six games, winning five and drawing the other one.

The first amateur eleven ever to go overseas from England on a cricket tour also went to North America. This was in 1872 when the side was under the captaincy and management of R. A. Fitzgerald who was then secretary of the M.C.C.

The Canadians first sent a side to England in 1880 but this tour was soon abandoned when they ran into financial trouble. Other representative sides have been over in 1887, 1922, 1936, 1954 and 1974 while a Canadian Colts team has been over on thirteen occasions.

One of the outstanding figures in Canadian cricket for nearly 20 years was W. G. Wookey of Toronto. In one match against the United States this clever bowler took 8 for 4 and 6 for 24! In season 1920 his bag was 115 wickets for 4.22 each!

Matches played in Canada are not generally recognised as first-class. Since the last war only one first-class match has been played there, that between Canada and the M.C.C., at Toronto, in September 1951. Like all matches on this tour it was played on matting, the M.C.C. winning by 141 runs.

Canadian cricket enthusiasts have staged a revival in recent years and more now is being heard of this country in the cricket world. Since 1955 they have been engaged in a drive to improve the standard of the game among youngsters in their Independent (Public) Schools.

In May 1975 Eastern Canada beat the

Australians (en route for England) by 5 wickets in a one-day match at Toronto.

A Junior Inter-Provincial Tournament was established in 1958 when teams from four provinces took part. This tournament is reserved for players under 21 years of age.

The 1961 season saw the first Inter-Provincial Tournament in which all six provinces took part. This was held at Calgary and won by British Columbia.

The Canadian Cricket Association was admitted to Associate Membership of the International Cricket Conference in 1968. The secretary is S. Wells, 581 Avenue Road, Apartment 302, Toronto, Ontario M4V 2K4.

CANTERBURY WEEK

This famous cricket festival first took place at Canterbury in 1842. It was inaugurated by a group of amateur actors and the old Beverley Cricket Club, and the first game, between Kent and All England, was played on their ground. In 1847 the festival moved to the St. Lawrence ground.

Lord Bessborough and his brother, Sir Spencer Ponsonby-Fane, founded the Old Stagers to give theatrical performances in the evenings of the Canterbury Cricket Week.

When, in 1845, it had become evident that it would be difficult to find enough amateur actors who could also play cricket, or at least could find enough time between rehearsals to play cricket at Canterbury, then the famous I Zingari club was formed, and continued a close association with the Canterbury Festival for many years.

CAPTAINS

The greatest number of seasons in which any player has ever captained a first-class county is 28. Two men have led their counties for as long as this—W. G. Grace (Gloucestershire) 1871–1898, and Lord Hawke (Yorkshire) 1883–1910.

The greatest number of seasons in which any player has captained his side to the County Cricket Championship is eight by Lord Hawke (Yorkshire) 1893, 1896, 1898, 1900, 1901, 1902, 1905, and 1908.

The following men have also captained their side to the Championship on at least three occasions:

D. B. Close (Yorkshire) 4—1963, 1966, 1967, 1968.

R. Daft (Nottinghamshire) 6—1871, 1872, 1873*, 1875, 1879*, 1880.

E. W. Dillon (Kent) 3—1909, 1910, 1913.

W. G. Grace (Gloucestershire) 4—1873*, 1874, 1876, 1877.

L. Green (Lancashire) 3—1926, 1927, 1928.

A. N. Hornby (Lancashire) 4—1881, 1882*, 1889*, 1897.

R. Iddison (Yorkshire) 3—1867, 1869*, 1870.

K. J. Key (Surrey) 3—1894, 1895, 1899.

G. Parr (Nottinghamshire) 3—1865, 1868, 1869*.

A. B. Sellers (Yorkshire) 6—1933, 1935, 1937, 1938, 1939, 1946.

A. Shaw (Nottinghamshire) 4—1883, 1884, 1885, 1886.

J. Shuter (Surrey) 6—1887, 1888, 1889*, 1890, 1891, 1892.

S. Surridge (Surrey) 5—1952, 1953, 1954, 1955, 1956.

G. Wilson (Yorkshire) 3—1922, 1923, 1924.

* Championship tied.

When E. J. Radcliffe made his debut in County Cricket it was as captain of Yorkshire v. Northamptonshire, at Hull, in 1909.

Test Cricket

The men who have captained their country in most Test matches are:

England:
P. B. H. May 41, R. Illingworth 31, E. R. Dexter 30.

Australia:
I. M. Chappell 30, R. B. Simpson 29, R. Benaud 28.

South Africa:
H. W. Taylor 18, J. E. Cheetham 15, A. D. Nourse, jun. 15.

West Indies:
G. S. Sobers 39, C. H. Lloyd 22, J. D. C. Goddard 22.

New Zealand:
J. R. Reid 34, G. T. Dowling 20.

India:
Mansur Ali Khan (Pataudi) 37, A. L. Wadekar 16, L. Amarnath 15

Pakistan:
A. H. Kardar 23, Intikham Alam 17.

Professional Captains

The first professional to captain an England Test team in the 20th century was J. B. Hobbs in the fourth Test v.

Australia, Manchester, July 1926. A. W. Carr was chosen captain but had to leave the field when taken ill on the first day.

A. Shaw (Nottinghamshire), H. E. Dollery (Warwickshire), and J. V. Wilson (Yorkshire) were the only professionals to captain County Championship winning sides before the abolition of amateur status in 1963.

A. Shaw did so in 1883, 1884, 1885, and 1886. H. E. Dollery in 1951, and J. V. Wilson in 1960 and 1962.

Essex, Glamorgan, and Hampshire, were the only first-class counties which never had a professional captain prior to 1963.

CARRYING BAT

See under BATTING (Batting through an innings).

CASUALTIES (FATAL)

There has been only one fatal casualty on the cricket field in the history of the first-class game in England and that was G. Summers, a Nottinghamshire professional.

When playing against the M.C.C. and Ground at Lord's in June 1870, he was struck on the head by a rising ball from J. Platts, and died four days later.

In this case death might have been avoided if Summers had taken proper rest after the accident, but he aggravated the injury by taking part in the following day's play and fielding in the blazing sun. This in addition to making the train journey back to Nottingham.

In 1958–59 Aziz, Karachi's 18-year-old wicket-keeper, was hit over the heart by a ball from Dildar Awan, of Services, in the final of the Quaid-e-Azam Cup Tournament, and died in hospital.

There have been other instances of death intervening in cricket matches, but these were deaths from natural causes.

In 1942 A. Ducat (Surrey) collapsed and died while batting at Lord's in a Home Guard match.

Away from the cricket field, in 1751 Frederick Louis, Prince of Wales (eldest son of George II) died from an abscess which, it is said, had formed as the result of a blow in the side from a ball when playing during the previous summer. However, it is by no means certain whether the accident occurred when playing cricket or tennis for he enjoyed both games regularly.

CATCHES

See also under FIELDING, WICKET KEEPER.

Most in an innings

The record for a fielder other than a wicket-keeper is shared by M. J. Stewart (Surrey) who held seven catches against Northamptonshire, at Northampton, 1957, and A. Brown (Gloucestershire) with seven against Nottinghamshire, at Trent Bridge, 1966.

In Tests the record is five by V. Y. Richardson, Australia v. South Africa, Durban, 1935–36.

Most in a match

W. R. Hammond (Gloucestershire) holds the record for a fielder other than a wicket-keeper. When playing against Surrey at Cheltenham in 1928, and fielding in the slips, he held 10 catches—four in the first innings and six in the second. It was in this match that Hammond also scored a century in each innings.

In the fifth Test of the Australian tour of 1901–02 which was played at Melbourne in February–March 1902, 16 England players were caught. That is a record for Test cricket.

The individual record in a Test match is seven by G. S. Chappell (Australia) v. England, Perth, 1974–75.

Most in a season

During season 1928 W. R. Hammond made a record total of 78 catches.

In 1957 M. J. Stewart of Surrey was only one short of this record.

Most in a career

F. E. Woolley of Kent held 1,015 catches during his first-class career which extended from 1906 to 1938. No other player has exceeded 900.

C. Cowdrey (England) holds the record for Test cricket with 120 catches in 114 matches.

Remarkable catches

One of the most remarkable catches ever made was that by G. F. Grace when playing for England against Australia, at the Oval, 1880.

G. J. Bonnor skied a ball from Alfred

Shaw almost out of sight and the batsmen had nearly run three before Grace made the catch at a distance of 115 yards from the wicket.

G. J. Bonnor made the hits for two other remarkable catches. There was one made by A. P. Lucas at the Oval in 1880 and that of G. Ulyett, at Lord's, in July 1884.

Ulyett's catch was made in the England v. Australia Test at Lord's. He was bowling to Bonnor and it was a wonder that Ulyett did not suffer injury as the smack of the ball hitting his outstretched hand was heard all around the ground. Bonnor, of course, was one of the most powerful hitters of all time.

Later when Ulyett was writing his impressions of the match he had this to say about that catch. "I was very foolish for attempting the catch, for if the ball had hit my wrist or arm, it would have snapped the limb as if it were a stick."

Another catch long remembered was that made by Clem Hill in the England V. Australia Test at Manchester in 1902. He had to run some distance to hold a ball from Lilley near the rails.

CENTURIES

Century before lunch

The only instances of a century before lunch on the first day of a Test match are all by Australians—V. T. Trumper, Manchester 1902; C. G. Macartney, Leeds 1926; and D. G. Bradman, Leeds 1930.

Century in debut

See separate section DEBUTS.

Century in each innings

Two centuries in a match are too numerous to list here but W. R. Hammond (Gloucestershire) set up a record by achieving this on seven occasions, four times for his county, and once each for England, M.C.C. and for an England XI.

C. B. Fry (Sussex and Hampshire) came very close to creating a world record. He actually scored a century in each innings of five matches, but in addition there were three other games in which he scored a century in one innings but was out for 99 in the other.

In 1896, at Hove, K. S. Ranjitsinhji (Sussex) actually scored two separate centuries in the same day against Yorkshire. He began his first innings late the previous day but did not score before play ended that evening. His scores were 100 and 125*.

In February 1969 K. D. Walters became the first man ever to hit a double century and a century in a Test match, 242 and 103 for Australia v. West Indies, at Sydney.

Double

The first man to score a double-century was W. Ward who made 278 for the M.C.C. against Norfolk at Lord's on July 25, 1820. It is said that Ward's bat weighed four pounds.

The most double-centuries in a career is the 37 by D. G. Bradman between 1928 and 1949. He made 12 of these in England and 25 in Australia.

In 1930 in England Bradman created another record by scoring six double-centuries in a single season: 334 v. England, at Leeds; 254 v. England, at Lord's; 252* v. Surrey, at Oval; 236 v. Worcestershire, at Worcester; 232 v. England, at Oval; 205* v. Kent, at Canterbury.

Bradman's average for all first-class games on this tour was 98.66!

W. R. Hammond was only one short of Bradman's total with 36 double-centuries when he retired in 1947.

A. E. Fagg of Kent is the only man ever to score a double century in each innings of a first-class match. That was in July 1938 when he made 244 and 202* against Essex, at Colchester.

Fastest centuries

The fastest century on record is that made by P. G. H. Fender for Surrey against Northamptonshire, at Northampton, in August 1920. This was his maiden century in first-class cricket, and he reached the hundred in only 35 minutes.

Fender's innings was interrupted by the tea interval. He scored 91 before tea and then took a further 12 minutes to reach his century. The comparatively slow scoring after tea was due to the fact that his partner at the wicket, H. A. Peach, was then nearing the first double-century of his career and was getting most of the bowling. As soon as Peach had made 200* Surrey declared.

The sixth wicket partnership had produced 171 in 42 minutes. Fender's innings of 113* reads as follows: 1 1 4 4 4 4 4 4 1 1 6 4 1 6 4 4 1 4 4 6 4 3 6 4 1 1 4 4 1 1 6 4 1 4 1.

It was in this match that a record aggregate for a County Championship game was created. Northamptonshire scored 306 and 430; Surrey 619 for 5 declared, and 120 for 2. An aggregate of 1,475.

Another powerful hitter, G. L. Jessop, made 101 in 40 minutes when playing for Gloucestershire against Yorkshire at Harrogate in 1897.

This remarkable innings was also interrupted, this time by the lunch interval. Jessop got 43 in 20 minutes before lunch and 58 in the same amount of time after the resumption.

The fastest century in a Test match was probably that made by J. M. Gregory for Australia v. South Africa at Johannesburg, in 1921–22. Just under 1¼ hours.

A century by J. H. Sinclar for South Africa v. Australia, at Cape Town, in 1902–03, has been variously timed as either 60 or 80 minutes. Although the longer time seems to have been correct it has been said that his innings might have produced a world record but for the time wasted in retrieving balls from outside the ground.

Here are the fastest centuries in first-class cricket at home in each of the last ten seasons.

1967 M. Jahangir, Pakistanis v. Glamorgan, Swansea, 61 minutes.

1968 G. S. Sobers, Nottinghamshire v. Kent, Dover, 77 minutes.

1969 R. G. Pollock, International Cavaliers v. Barbados, Scarborough, 52 minutes.

1970 C. P. Wilkins, Rest of World v. T. N. Pearce's XI, Scarborough, 73 minutes.

1971 B. F. Davidson, Leicestershire v. Northamptonshire, Leicester, 63 minutes.

1972 Majid J. Khan, Glamorgan v. Warwickshire, Birmingham, 70 minutes.

1973 Asif Iqbal, Kent v. M.C.C., Canterbury, 72 minutes.

1974 G. S. Sobers, Nottinghamshire v. Derbyshire, Ilkeston, 83 minutes.

1975 R. N. S. Hobbs, Essex v. Australians, Chelmsford, 44 minutes.

1976 C. G. Greenidge, West Indians v. Nottinghamshire, Trent Bridge, 69 minutes.

The record for the fastest double century is shared by G. L. Jessop, Gloucestershire v. Sussex, Hove, 1903, and C. H. Lloyd, West Indians v. Glamorgan, Swansea, 1976—200 and 201 respectively in 120 minutes.

First Century

The first century yet found recorded in the annals of cricket is that made by Minshull for the Duke of Dorset's XI against Sevenoaks, in 1769. His total was 107.

However, it is quite likely that John Small had exceeded a century before this although there were no precise scores given on many occasions. When Hambledon beat Kent in 1768 Small "fetched above seven score notches from his own bat".

The first century in a Test match was 165* (retired hurt) by C. Bannerman for Australia v. England, at Melbourne, in 1877.

The first man to score two separate hundreds in a single game was W. Lambert. He made 107 and 157 for Sussex v. Epsom, at Lord's, in 1817.

The first man to score a century in each innings of a Test match was W. Bardsley. He made 136 and 130 for Australia v. England, at the Oval, in August 1909.

Maiden centuries

The following scores are remarkable as they were maiden centuries:

337* by Pervez Akhtar for Railways v. Dera Ismail Khan, at Lahore, December 1964.

292* by V. T. Trumper for New South Wales v. Tasmania, at Sydney, 1898–99.

290 by W. N. Carson for Auckland v. Otago, at Dunedin, 1936–37.

282 by H. L. Collins for New South Wales v. Tasmania, at Hobart, 1912–13.

275 by W. A. Farmer for Barbados v. Jamaica, at Bridgetown, 1952.

See also under separate section DEBUTS.

Most centuries in an innings

The most centuries ever made in a single innings is six for Holkar State (912 for 8 declared) against Mysore, at Indore, March 1945. The century makers were Bhandarkar 142, Jagdale 164, R. P. Singh 100, B. B. Nimbalkar 172, Sarwate 101, C. K. Nayudu 101.

The most centuries in one innings of a Test match is five—Australia v. West Indies, at Kingston, June 1955. Australia made 758 for 8 declared. The centuries were scored by C. C. McDonald 127, R. N. Harvey 204, K. R. Miller 109, R. G. Archer 128, R. Benaud 121.

Most centuries in a match

The record for most individual centuries in a match is nine—Bombay (5) v. Maharashtra (4) in 1948.

When N.S.W. met Victoria at Sydney, in January 1928, there were eight centuries made—five by N.S.W. and three by Victoria.

The most centuries scored in one Test match is seven. England (4) v. Australia (3), at Nottingham, June 1938; West Indies (2) v. Australia (5), at Kingston, June 1955.

Most centuries in a season

18 by D. C. S. Compton in 1947. 13 for Middlesex, four for England v. South Africa, and one for South of England v. South Africans.

16 by J. B. Hobbs in 1925. 13 for Surrey, two for Players v. Gentlemen, one for Rest of England v. Yorkshire.

In 1913 C. H. Tichmarsh of Hertfordshire made 21 centuries, including two for his county. This is not a first-class record.

The highest number of centuries scored in a single season of first-class cricket in this country since World War II is 357 in 1947.

It is interesting to note that less than half that number were scored in the abnormally wet season of 1958 when the total reached only 141, the lowest post-war aggregate.

Most centuries in succession

The record for most centuries in successive innings is shared by C. B. Fry, D. G. Bradman and M. J. Procter. Each made six.

C. B. Fry scored six successive centuries in 1901—five for Sussex and the last for an England XI v. Yorkshire at Lord's.

D. G. Bradman equalled his record during the 1938–39 season in Australia, beginning the run with a century for Bradman's XI v. Rigg's XI and following with five centuries for South Australia.

M. J. Procter's six centuries in successive innings were made for Rhodesia in 1970–71, ending with a personal best of 254 v. Western Province.

Most centuries in a career

J. B. Hobbs 197 (175 of them in England), E. Hendren 170 (151 of them in England); W. R. Hammond 167 (134 of them in England), C. P. Mead 153 (145 of them in England). In all matches J. B. Hobbs made a total of 244 centuries.

Most Test Centuries

The record for most centuries in Test cricket was created by D. G. Bradman. He made a total of 29, including two innings of over 300 and ten of 200 or more. Nineteen of his centuries were against England, two against the West Indies, four against South Africa and four against India.

Next to Bradman comes G. S. Sobers who has hit twenty-six centuries for the West Indies plus two for the Rest of the World.

Slowest centuries

See under SLOW SCORING.

Triple centuries

The first man to score a triple century was W. G. Grace who made 344 in 6 hours 20 minutes for M.C.C. v. Kent, at Canterbury, August 1876.

It is worth noting that it was earlier in that same season that W. G. Grace made his record score of 400 (in approx. 13½ hours) for United South of England XI v. Twenty-two of Grimsby, at Grimsby. This, of course, was not a first-class match.

The player who has made the most triple centuries in first-class cricket is D. G. Bradman with a total of six:

340* N.S.W. v. Victoria, Sydney, 1928–29.

425* N.S.W. v. Queensland, Sydney, 1929–30.

334 Australia v. England, Leeds, 1930.

304 Australia v. England, Leeds, 1934.

357 S. Australia v. Victoria, Melbourne, 1935–36.

369 S. Australia v. Tasmania, Adelaide, 1935–36.

CHALLENGE CUP

In January, 1873, the M.C.C. decided to offer a silver Challenge Cup to be competed for on a knock-out basis between county clubs at Lord's.

This was introduced in an effort to stimulate interest in county cricket, but the scheme fell through because most of the counties refused to co-operate.

Only one match was played in this competition. In June 1873, Kent beat Sussex by 52 runs, at Lord's.

CHAPMAN, Arthur Percy Frank (1900–1961)

As captain of England he led his side to victory in six out of nine Tests against Australia and must therefore rank among this country's most successful skippers.

Born at Reading he played much of his earliest cricket for his native Berkshire. He was educated at Uppingham and Cambridge where he obtained his "Blue" playing in the University game in 1920, 1921, and 1922.

In 1924 Chapman joined Kent and played more or less regularly until 1936, finally retiring in 1939.

During his career he proved himself to be a powerful left-handed batsman and a brilliant fielder, especially at silly mid-off. The catch he made to finish Bradman's second innings at Lord's in 1930 will never be forgotten by those who were fortunate enough to be present. Neither will his catching of Woodfull in the first Test at Brisbane in 1928–29.

Chapman is the only man to score a century at Lord's for his University, for the Gentlemen, and for England. In all he scored 27 centuries, his highest score being 260 for Kent v. Lancashire, at Maidstone, in 1927.

He was captain of Kent from 1931 to 1936 and his aggregate score in 19 years of first-class cricket was 16,135 (av. 31.82).

CHAPPELL, Gregory Stephen (1948–   )

This player has proved himself to be Australia's leading batsman in the 1970s. He is also a medium-pace bowler and a brilliant fielder whose 14 catches in the 1974–75 Test series against England is only one short of the record for a Test rubber, while his seven catches v. England at Perth in that series is a Test match record for a non wicket-keeper.

A powerful forcing batsman who made a century in his first Test against England (108 at Perth in 1970–71), he began his first-class career with South Australia in 1966–67 and had a couple of seasons with

Somerset, 1968 and 1969, making 1,163 and 1,330 runs. Headed Australia's batting averages against the Rest of the World in 1971–72 and thrilled Lord's spectators with a superb 131 against England in 1972, topping their averages on that tour with 70.00. Moved to Queensland as captain in 1973.

When he first captained Australia (against West Indies 1975–76) he again headed his team's averages with 117.00, passing the 3,000 Test-run mark in only his 38th Test.

CHAPPELL, Ian Michael (1943–   )

Eldest of the three famous Chappell brothers. Made Test debut for Australia v. Pakistan in 1964 and succeeded Lawry as captain in the final Test of the 1970–71 series with England at a time when his country's Test cricket was in the doldrums after failing to win their last nine matches.

Australia lost their first Test under his captaincy but his positive approach brought victory in 15 of the 30 Tests in which he led them before handing over to brother Greg in 1975. During this period he was always concerned for the welfare of his players and had a number of brushes with officialdom.

In 72 Test appearances he has totalled 5,187 runs (av. 42.86), including 14 hundreds, with a highest score of 196 v. Pakistan, at Adelaide in 1972–73.

Noted for his speedy footwork and tremendous concentration he played for South Australia from 1961 until joining North Melbourne in 1976. As a leg-spin and googly bowler he took 5 for 53 against Rhodesia in 1966–67.

CHEETHAM, John Erskine (1920–   )

This South African made 24 Test appearances for the Union in the immediate post-war period, captaining his side in 15 matches, including three of the five Tests of the 1955 tour of England.

Cheetham made his first-class debut with Western Province in 1939–40 and led them to many successes after the war. In 1950–51 he made the record score for this province—271* v. Orange Free State, at Bloemfontein.

A sound right-handed batsman, especially strong on the on-side, Cheetham scored 883 runs in Test cricket (av. 23.86). He is an engineer by profession.

CHESHIRE C.C.C.

Founded: Early 1800's (earliest reference 1819). Joined Minor Counties Championship 1909. Secretary: B. S. Jones, Tattenhall Road, Tattenhall, Nr. Chester. Highest score for: 415 v. Northumberland, at Jesmond, 1956; 548 v. Shropshire, 1868, Highest score against: 457 for 6 declared by Durham, 1909; 498 by Revellers, 1881; 520 by Philadelphia, 1884§. Highest individual score for: 192 by R. M. O. Cooke v. Yorkshire II, 1971, 205 by V. Royle, 1874. Highest individual score against: 206 by F. Lee of Yorkshire, 1887. Lowest score for: 14 v. Staffordshire, at Stoke-on-Trent, 1909. Lowest score against: 32 by Staffordshire, 1924; 31 by Warwickshire, 1891; 24 by Carnarvonshire, 1883; 17 by Congleton (with T. Marsden) 1838. Colours: Purple, black and silver. Badge: Wheatsheaf. Honours: Minor Counties Champions, 1967.

§ Gentlemen of Cheshire.

CLARKE, William (1798–1856)

William Clarke of Nottingham rates a place among the all-time greats of cricket because he did as much as any man to help popularise the game throughout England.

It was he who founded the famous All England XI in 1846 and managed it throughout its most illustrious period.

Those were the days of the professional captain and Clarke was the first man to skipper Nottinghamshire, a distinction he enjoyed for 20 years from 1835 until the year before his death.

Clarke had a remarkably long career. He first appeared in an important match in 1816 and his last appearance was not until June 1856, when he took a wicket with his last ball for the England XI.

For most of those 40 years William Clarke was the life blood of Nottinghamshire cricket and it was he who laid out the ground at Trent Bridge and made it into one of the first-ever cricket enclosures where spectators paid to watch the game.

His fame rests not only with his flair for leadership and his enterprise in the formulative years of county cricket, but in his own prowess on the field. Never let it be forgotten that he was one of the finest of all under-arm bowlers.

Today, people are inclined to scoff at under-arm bowling, but Clarke had the knack of making such a high delivery and so imparting leg-spin that he held his own against any bowler in the land, either under-arm or round-arm.

The former, Nottingham bricklayer came to be known as "Old" Clarke, although he was only 58 when he died. Only three years before his death he took 476 wickets in the season at an average of about eight runs apiece against all classes of opposition and on all types of pitches, most of them rough. Nothing more need be said in praise of William Clarke and his slow under-arm bowling. Just ponder upon those figures.

CLOSE FINISHES

See FINISHES, EXCITING.

CLUB CRICKET CONFERENCE, The

Nowhere will you find the true spirit of the game of cricket more alive than among the members of this organisation which jealously guards the real tradition of the sport.

The Club Cricket Conference is an organisation of clubs set up to control and safeguard amateur cricket on strictly non-competitive lines in the old amateur tradition. That is cricket for the game's sake.

It was founded in 1915 at a meeting called by Mr. E. A. C. Thompson at the request of a number of clubs. The first A.G.M. was held on March 22, 1916, under the Chairmanship of Sir Home Gordon who became their first President.

Amongst the clubs present at this meeting were Alexandra Park, Malden Wanderers, Honor Oak, G. W. R., Ealing Dean, Amherst, The Derelicts, Becton, Parsons Green, North Middlesex, Catford, Catford Wanderers, Boro' Polytechnic, Arlington & West Ham, Paddington, Merton, Brondesbury, Heathfield, Edmonton, Mitcham, Great Northern Railway, London & North Eastern Railway, Ealing Park, Derrick Wanderers, Western and Hampstead Montrose.

At the present time the Club Cricket Conference consists of about 2,400 affiliated clubs in the counties of Middlesex, Kent, Essex, Sussex, Hampshire, Berkshire, Bedfordshire, Hertfordshire, Buckinghamshire, and some in Oxfordshire, Suffolk, Nottinghamshire, Devon and Somerset.

In recent years the Conference has been honoured by H.R.H. the Duke of Edinburgh becoming its Patron.

COBDEN'S MATCH

See under FINISHES, EXCITING.

COMPTON, Denis Charles Scott
(1918–   )

One of England's most prolific run-getters Denis Compton holds the record for the highest number of runs in a single season (3,816 in 1947) and only four Englishmen have scored more runs in Test cricket. Compton's total in 78 Tests is 5,807 (av. 50.06).

This carefree batsman who gave so much pleasure to thousands of cricket enthusiasts made his debut in 1936 and although only 18 years of age, scored 1,004 runs in his first season. It was only a fortnight after his debut that he made 100* in 105 minutes against Northamptonshire.

Compton made his Test debut against New Zealand in the next season, scoring 65, and then, at the age of 20, became the youngest England player in Tests against Australia. What is more, in his first game against Australia, at Nottingham in June 1938, he made 102.

At that time Denis Compton was also a soccer forward of some distinction with the Arsenal, having signed for them in 1935 and made his First Division debut in September 1936. During the war he made 11 appearances for England which, unfortunately, do not count in the soccer records as full internationals, and he also played in one Victory International against Scotland.

Compton was able to play a good deal of cricket in India during those dark days of 1939–45. He made a notable 249* for Holkar v. Bombay in the Ranji Trophy Final of 1944–45.

Compton's remarkable batting figures have overshadowed all else in his career but it should not be forgotten that he was also a left-arm bowler of no mean ability. As an all-rounder one of his best performances was to score 97 against Auckland and then take 11 wickets for 49 runs.

This popular player's highest score was his 300 for the M.C.C. v. N.E. Transvaal, at Benoni, in 1948–49, and his highest in Test cricket was his 278 in 290 minutes v. Pakistan, at Nottingham, in 1954.

Knee trouble hindered his career around 1956. He made his final Test appearance in the South African tour of 1956–57 and played only a small number of innings in first-class cricket after 1959.

CONGDON, Bevan Ernest
(1938–   )

Succeeded G. T. Dowling as New Zealand's captain in the 3rd Test in the West Indies in 1971–72 and led his country in 17 Tests before handing over to G. M. Turner in 1976.

Since making his debut for Central Districts in 1960–61 this player has proved himself to be one of his country's finest all-rounders. As a batsman able to adapt to almost any conditions he has scored well over 11,000 runs, and as a right-arm medium pace bowler he has captured around 160 wickets at an average of just under 31 runs apiece. He transferred to Wellington in 1971 and Otago in 1972.

His most successful tour was in the West Indies and Bermuda in 1971–72 when he averaged 82.66 in 16 first-class innings including four not-out. But English fans will always remember his 176 in 6 hrs. 50 min. when New Zealand seemed like fighting back to victory at Trent Bridge in 1973. Unfortunately, after such a determined display, victory escaped them. That remains his highest score in Test cricket.

CONSECUTIVE VICTORIES

See under WINNING RUNS.

CONSTANTINE, LORD
(1902–1971)

This West Indian all-rounder was one of the fastest run-getters of all time and a fielder second to none, especially at cover point. In the field he was known as "Electric Heels".

At Leyton in 1928 he scored 130 in 90 minutes against Essex, and in the 1930–31 West Indian tour of Australia he scored a century against Tasmania, at Launceston, in 52 minutes.

Learie Constantine made his debut in first-class cricket in 1921–22 and came over to England for the first time with the West Indian side of 1923. No Tests were played that year, but he was in England again in 1928 and played in all three Tests. In these, however, he did not show his real form except as a fielder.

Constantine gave a better indication of his power in the matches with the Counties on that tour, and established himself as one of the finest all-rounders of the day with an astonishing display against Middlesex at Lord's.

In the first innings of this match he scored 86, then took seven wickets for 57 in 14.3 overs. Following this, when his side required 259 to win and were 121 for 5, he scored 103, including two sixes and 12 fours. He hit one ball from G. O. Allen over extra-cover and well up into the Grandstand.

Such an attractive run-getter was just the man for League cricket, and in 1929 he was snapped up by Nelson. His contract with them restricted his appearances in first-class games, but he was able to tour Australia with the West Indians in 1930–31.

In 1938 he moved to Rochdale and made his final first-class appearance when captaining the Dominions XI which defeated Hammond's England XI, at Lord's, in 1945.

CORNWALL C.C.C.

Founded: 1894 though there were county games as early as 1813. A member of the Minor Counties Championship. Secretary: A. Lugg, "Wendron", 1 Northfield Drive, Truro. Highest score for: 522 for 9 declared v. Devon, at Devonport, 1947. Highest score against: 483 by Devon, 1901. Highest individual score for: 194 by G. Rogers, 1938. Highest individual score against: 233 by E. Burdett of Devon, at Tavistock, 1911. Lowest score for: 31 v. Monmouthshire, 1913. Lowest score against: 46 by Berkshire, 1914. Colours: Black, gold and maroon. Badge: Shield of the Duchy of Cornwall. Honours: None.

COUNTY CHAMPIONSHIP (FIRST-CLASS)

The County Championship was first acknowledged officially by the county secretaries for season 1890 when the scoring of points was determined by deducting losses from wins and ignoring drawn games. For 20 or more years before this, a county championship had been fostered by the sporting press, and during much of this period, the "least matches lost" method was used (although not without qualification) to determine the champion county. From 1887–89 the sporting press had adopted a method, also occasionally to be found in earlier years, of awarding one point for a win and half a point for a draw.

The list of county champions now generally accepted was first published by the Rev. R. S. Holmes in 1893 and this list commenced with the year 1873, in which season the abortive Championship Cup competition was instituted.

In recent years some of the names contained in this list have been disputed and evidence has been produced to show that the list could quite easily be commenced before 1873. Most exhaustive research into this matter has been carried out by Rowland Bowen and readers who are interested in this aspect of early cricket history can do no better than refer to his articles on the subject which appeared in both the 1959 and 1960 editions of *Wisden*. The list which will be found at the end of this section takes into account most of the findings of these articles.

Before referring to this list the following points should be borne in mind (1) Doubts still exist as to the rightful champion county in several seasons up to the adoption of a points system in 1887. (2) The generally accepted commencing year is 1873 although there is no valid reason for this. (3) The official County Championship did not begin until 1890, and it was not until 1894 that the M.CC. took a hand in the control of this championship.

This Champion County for each season since 1865 has been:

1865	Nottinghamshire		1872	Nottinghamshire
1866	Middlesex		1873	Nottinghamshire and Gloucestershire[1]
1867	Yorkshire		1874	Gloucestershire
1868	Nottinghamshire		1875	Nottinghamshire
1869	Nottinghamshire and Yorkshire		1876	Gloucestershire
1870	Yorkshire		1877	Gloucestershire
1871	Nottinghamshire		1878	Undecided[2]

[1]Nottinghamshire are generally bracketed with Gloucestershire but while they played an equal number of games, the former actually won one more than Gloucestershire.

[2]Middlesex appear in most lists despite the fact that Nottinghamshire had a better playing record. Contemporary opinion, however, was undecided.

1879	Nottinghamshire and Lancashire		1928	Lancashire
1880	Nottinghamshire		1929	Nottinghamshire
1881	Lancashire		1930	Lancashire
1882	Nottinghamshire and Lancashire		1931	Yorkshire
1883	Nottinghamshire		1932	Yorkshire
1884	Nottinghamshire		1933	Yorkshire
1885	Nottinghamshire		1934	Lancashire
1886	Nottinghamshire		1935	Yorkshire
1887	Surrey		1936	Derbyshire
1888	Surrey		1937	Yorkshire
1889	Nottinghamshire Lancashire and Surrey		1938	Yorkshire
1890	Surrey		1939	Yorkshire
1891	Surrey		1940–45	No competition owing to the war
1892	Surrey		1946	Yorkshire
1893	Yorkshire		1947	Middlesex
1894	Surrey		1948	Glamorgan
1895	Surrey		1949	Middlesex and Yorkshire
1896	Yorkshire		1950	Lancashire and Surrey
1897	Lancashire		1951	Warwickshire
1898	Yorkshire		1952	Surrey
1899	Surrey		1953	Surrey
1900	Yorkshire		1954	Surrey
1901	Yorkshire		1955	Surrey
1902	Yorkshire		1956	Surrey
1903	Middlesex		1957	Surrey
1904	Lancashire		1958	Surrey
1905	Yorkshire		1959	Yorkshire
1906	Kent		1960	Yorkshire
1907	Nottinghamshire		1961	Hampshire
1908	Yorkshire		1962	Yorkshire
1909	Kent		1963	Yorkshire
1910	Kent		1964	Worcestershire
1911	Warwickshire		1965	Worcestershire
1912	Yorkshire		1966	Yorkshire
1913	Kent		1967	Yorkshire
1914	Surrey		1968	Yorkshire
1915–18	No competition owing to the war		1969	Glamorgan
1919	Yorkshire		1970	Kent
1920	Middlesex		1971	Surrey
1921	Middlesex		1972	Warwickshire
1922	Yorkshire		1973	Hampshire
1923	Yorkshire		1974	Worcestershire
1924	Yorkshire		1975	Leicestershire
1925	Yorkshire		1976	Middlesex
1926	Lancashire			
1927	Lancashire			

The clubs included in the first official championship season of 1890 in the order of finishing were Surrey, Lancashire, Kent and Yorkshire (tied), Nottinghamshire, Gloucestershire, Middlesex, and Sussex.

Since then Somerset were added in 1891, Essex, Derbyshire, Leicestershire, Warwickshire and Hampshire in 1895, Worcestershire in 1899, Northamptonshire in 1905, and Glamorgan in 1921.

All the above clubs have appeared regularly in the County Championship since they were first admitted, with the single exception of Worcestershire who did not appear in season 1919.

With regard to the clubs generally considered as competitors before 1890 it should be noted that Derbyshire was included from 1871 to 1887, and Hampshire was also included by the sporting press in many years between 1865 and 1885.

COUNTY CRICKET COUNCIL

This was a self-constituted body formed in 1887, largely through the efforts of Lord Harris who had strong views about altering the qualification rules.

The council was formed mainly with the idea of drawing up some new rules on qualification and also to divide the counties into three classes.

However, this organisation was doomed from the start because its authority was not recognised in quite the way it should have been while on the question of qualification they themselves agreed to make any alteration without the agreement of the M.C.C.

This acknowledgement of the power of the M.C.C. over County cricket meant that the County Cricket Council was in itself little more than a debating society without mandate.

The end of the Council came in December 1890 when it collapsed through a failure to gain agreement over their much discussed idea of breaking the counties into three classifications with promotion and relegation between each. The system of qualifying matches suggested was not speedy enough to suit the second-class counties and when their amendments to the scheme were proposed the conflict of opinion became so great that a resolution suspending the Council *sine die* was carried by the casting vote of the chairman.

COWDREY, Michael Colin (1932–   )

As a batsman Colin Cowdrey matured quickly. He was one of the youngest players ever to appear at Lord's in an important match when, at the age of 13, he scored 75 and 44 for Tonbridge School. That was in 1946. In 1951 when he had his first full season of County cricket and was awarded his cap with Kent he scored 1,189 runs (av. 33.02).

Cowdrey got his "Blue" at Oxford and captained his University side. In 1954 he made his Test debut in Australia when still not quite 22 and made 40 in his first innings. He got his maiden Test century in his third match (102) and finished that tour with a Test average of 35.44.

A stylish batsman without being flashy and a master of the straight drive, Cowdrey played in a world record total of 114 Tests, captaining England in 27 of these games. He scored two centuries in a match on three occasions, and got his highest score of 307 (in a temperature of 100 degrees) v. South Australia, at Adelaide in 1962–3. The highest score by an Englishman in Australia. A brilliant fielder close to the wicket he also holds the Test record for most catches with a total of 120.

In 1961 he became the first player to score a century in each innings of a match against the Australians in England—149 and 121 for Kent at Canterbury, and he has the distinction of having scored a century against all countries playing Test cricket.

England never had a braver batsman than this player who scored more Test runs than anybody with the single exception of Sobers. Cowdrey's total—7,624 (av. 44.06), including 22 centuries.

CREASE, The

The term "Popping Crease" originated from the days of the late 17th and early 18th century when, instead of a line drawn on the ground across the front of the wicket there was a small hole big enough to take the ball or the bottom of the bat.[1] To score a run it was then necessary for the batsman to put the butt of his bat into this hole before a fielder could pop the ball into it.

This was eventually abandoned (Pycroft says 1702) in favour of a mark on the ground, probably because of the number of injuries sustained by fielders who often had their hands broken by determined batsmen trying to jam their bat in before the ball.

In the earliest Laws handed down, those presumed to date at least from 1744, the popping crease was 3 feet 10 inches from the wicket. The distance was increased to 4 feet in about 1819, or at the same time as the height of the wicket was increased by two inches to 26 inches.

Originally, there was no stipulation as to the length of the bowling crease. The first limit was made in 1774—3 feet long on either side of the wicket.

This was increased to 6 feet 7 inches in about 1821, and to 6 feet 8 inches about five years later.

The increase to its present length of 8 feet 8 inches was not made until 1902.

---

[1] This may be too fanciful for some who prefer to regard the word 'pop' as meaning 'to strike', and therefore the popping crease would simply be the striking crease.

CRICKETERS' ASSOCIATION, The

The players' Union was not formed until October 1967 but it was due to the efforts of their first secretary and founder member, Fred Rumsey, that the Association developed so rapidly, gaining 100% membership among County cricketers and recognition by the cricketing authorities.

CUMBERLAND C.C.C.

Founded: 1884. However, County games were played as early as 1873. Joined Minor Counties Championship 1955. Secretary: N. Wise, 18 Banklands, Workington. Highest score for: 326 for 9 declared v. Northumberland, at Newcastle, 1955. In other matches, 359 v. North Lancashire, 1910. Highest score against: 403 for 9 declared v. Northumberland, at Newcastle, in 1955; 420 for 9 declared by Westmorland, 1910. Highest individual score for: 136 by R. Entwistle v. Lancashire II, at Millom, 1975. Highest individual score against: 172* by R. Collins of Lancashire II, at Old Trafford, August 1959; 216 by P. D. Harrison of Westmorland, 1910. Lowest score for: 36 v. Yorkshire II, at Workington, 1956; 18 v. Westmorland, 1880. Lowest score against: 84 by Durham, Keswick, 1956. Colours: Blue, red and gold. Badge: Cumberland County Coat of Arms. Honours: None.

CURRIE CUP, The

The trophy for the principal tournament of South African cricket was presented by Sir Donald Currie in 1889 at the time of the first tour of South Africa by an English team, and the first tournament was only one match played between Kimberley and Transvaal, at Kimberley, in April 1890.

Normally, this competition between the South African provinces is divided into two sections and the teams play each other at home and away.

Transvaal has won the trophy more often than any other side.

Currently sponsored by South African Breweries, this competition is now officially known as the S.A.B. Currie Cup.

The highest innings total in this competition is 664 for 6 by Natal v. Western Province, Durban, 1936–37. The highest individual score: 279* by R. A. Gripper, Rhodesia v. Orange Free State, Bloemfontein, 1967–68.

D

DAFT, Richard (1835–1900)

Richard Daft of Nottinghamshire began his career as an amateur, subsequently turned professional, and later reverted to amateur.

According to all accounts he was a delightful batsman to watch. In *The Cricket Field* he is described as a batsman who "combined style with effect."

Daft represented the Gentlemen at Lord's in 1858 and in 1860 he was on the side of the Players. He later captained the Players on several occasions.

Daft had a long career and it is worth noting that 17 of his centuries were made after he had passed his 50th birthday.

He succeeded Parr as captain of the All England XI and in 1879 he led a team to America.

Richard Daft virtually retired from first-class cricket in 1880 although he did appear as late as 1891. He actually made his last century, a score of 140, when he was 59, but this was not in a first-class game.

DARLING, Joseph (1870–1946)

A determined forcing batsman who opened for Australia in the majority of his 34 Test appearances between 1894 and 1905, Joseph Darling was captain of the side 21 times.

A left-hander, he was still only 14 years of age when he made 252 out of 470 for St. Peter's College on the Adelaide Oval, but because of his occupation he did not make his debut with South Australia until 10 years later.

He made his Test debut against England in the following season in Australia, and subsequently made four trips to England, three of them as captain. He also played in three Tests against South Africa.

Darling's highest score in England was his 194 at Leicester in 1896, and alto- gether, over here, he scored 6,377 runs (av. 33.56).

DAVIDSON, Alan Keith (1929–   )

Left-handed bat, left arm fast-medium bowler, and a brilliant fielder, Alan Davidson proved himself a splendid all-rounder on his first tour with an Australian side. Many commentators believe him to have been Australia's most penetrative opening bowler. That was to New Zealand in 1949–50 when in a minor match v. Wairapa, at Masterton, he took all 10 wickets for 29 runs in the first innings and then scored 157* in 109 minutes.

He made his Test debut in England in 1953 and his totals for 44 Tests are 1,328 runs (24.59), and 186 wickets (20.58).

Always injury prone, this marred his record on his second visit to England in 1956 but he came again in 1961 and in his three visits he scored 1,821 runs (av. 35.01) and took 144 wickets (av. 21.85).

In the Brisbane Test v. West Indies, in December 1960, Davidson gave one of the finest all-round performances of all time, scoring 44 and 80 as well as taking 5 for 135 and 6 for 87.

DEBUTS

Batting

Several men have scored a century when making their debut in first-class cricket, but only two have distinguished themselves by scoring a century in each innings.

They are A. R. Morris, who made 148 and 111 for New South Wales against Queensland, at Sydney, in 1940–41, and N. J. Contractor, 152 and 102* for Guijerat against Baroda, at Baroda, in 1952–53.

The highest score ever recorded by a player making his debut in first-class cricket is 240 by W. F. E. Marx for

Transvaal against West Griqualand, at Johannesburg, in 1920–21.

In England the record was set up by G. H. G. Doggart who scored 215* for Cambridge University against Lancashire, at Cambridge, in 1948.

Players who have scored centuries on their debut in Test cricket are:

England

R. E. Foster, 287 v. Australia, at Sydney, December 1903.

P. A. Gibb, 106 v. South Africa, Johannesburg, December 1938.

W. G. Grace, 152 v. Australia, The Oval, September 1880.

S. C. Griffith, 140 v. West Indies, Port of Spain, February 1948.

G. Gunn, 119 v. Australia, at Sydney, December 1907.

J. H. Hampshire, 107 v. West Indies, Lord's June 1969.

F. C. Hayes, 106* v. West Indies, The Oval, July 1973.

P. B. H. May, 138 v. South Africa, Leeds, July 1951.

C. A. Milton, 104* v. New Zealand, Leeds, July 1958.

Nawab of Pataudi, 102 v. Australia, Sydney, December 1932.

K. S. Ranjitsinhji, 154* v. Australia, Manchester, July 1896.

B. H. Valentine, 136 v. India, Bombay, December 1933.

P. F. Warner, 132* v. South Africa, Johannesburg, 1898.

Australia

C. Bannerman, 165* (retired hurt) v. England, Melbourne, March 1877.

J. Burke, 101* v. England, Adelaide, February 1951.

G. S. Chappell, 108 v. England, Perth, December 1970.

H. L. Collins, 104 v. England, Sydney, December 1920.

G. J. Cozier, 109 v. West Indies, Melbourne, December 1975.

R. A. Duff, 104 v. England, Melbourne, January 1902.

H. Graham, 107 v. England, Lord's, July 1893.

R. J. Hartigan, 116 v. England, Adelaide, January 1908.

A. A. Jackson, 164 v. England, Adelaide, February 1929.

W. H. Ponsford, 110 v. England, Sydney, December 1924.

K. D. Walters, 155 v. England, Brisbane, December 1965.

South Africa

None.

West Indies

L. Baichan, 105* v. Pakistan, Lahore, 1975.

A. Ganteaume, 112 v. England, Port of Spain, February 1948.

C. G. Greenidge, 107 v. India, Bangalore, 1974.

G. A. Headley, 176 v. England, Bridgetown, 1930.

C. Hunte, 142 v. Pakistan, Barbados, 1957.

A. I. Kallicharan, 100* v. New Zealand, Georgetown, April 1972.

L. G. Rowe, 214 and 100* v. New Zealand, Kingston, February 1972. The only player to score a century in each innings of his Test debut.

B. Pairadeau, 115 v. India, Port of Spain, 1952.

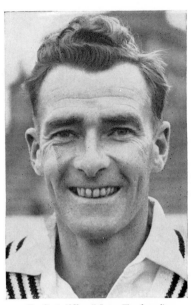
B. Sutcliffe (New Zealand)

P. R. Umrigar (India)

B. Mitchell (South Africa)

E. D. Weekes (West Indies)

LEADING TEST BATSMEN

W. R. Hammond (England)

Sir Donald Bradman (Australia)

LEADING TEST BATSMEN

Hanif Mohammad (Pakistan)

S. F. Barnes—most wickets in a Test rubber

Molly Hide—one of the finest of women cricketers

F. E. Woolley—record number of catches

M. C. Cowdrey (England)

R. N. Harvey (Australia)

G. S. Sobers (West Indies)

J. R. Reid (New Zealand)

LEADING TEST BATSMEN

(*Above*) The West Indians leap jubilantly in the air as the last Australian wicket is broken at Brisbane in December, 1960—the first Test to be tied

TWO HISTORIC EVENTS

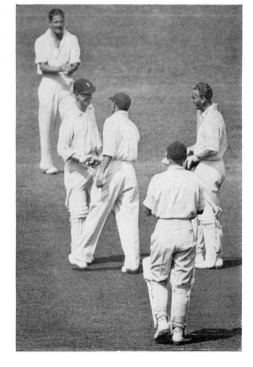

(*Right*) Len Hutton seen receiving the congratulations of Bradman at the Oval in 1938 when he created a world record Test score of 364, still an England record

H. J. Tayfield (South Africa)

R. Benaud (Australia)

L. R. Gibbs (West Indies)

F. S. Trueman (England)

LEADING TEST BOWLERS

(Above) P. B. H. May
captained England in more
Tests than any other player

CAPTAINS
COURAGEOUS

(Left) W. M. Woodfull,
one of Australia's foremost
skippers

Dr W. G. Grace

Sir John Hobbs

THREE MASTERS

K. S. Ranjitsinhji

O. G. Smith, 104 v. Australia, Kingston, 1954.

New Zealand

J. E. Mills, 117 v. England, Wellington, 1930.

R. E. Redmond, 107 v. Pakistan, Auckland, 1973.

B. R. Taylor, 105 v. India, Calcutta, 1965.

India

L. Amarnath, 118 v. England, Bombay, December 1933.

A. A. Baig, 112 v. England, Manchester, July 1959.

Hanumant Singh, 105 v. England, Delhi, 1964.

A. G. Kripal Singh, 100* v. New Zealand, Hyderabad, 1955–56.

D. H. Shodhan, 110 v. Pakistan, Calcutta, 1952–53.

G. R. Viswanath, 137 v. Australia, Kanpur, November 1969.

Pakistan

K. Ibadulla, 166 v. Australia, Karachi, 1964.

Only game

The following men have scored a century in their one and only game in first-class cricket:

N. F. Callaway, 207 New South Wales v. Queensland, Sydney, 1914–15. He was killed during World War I.

H. Grangel, 108 Victoria v. Tasmania, Melbourne, 1935–36.

M. N. Harbottle, 156 Army v. Oxford University, Oxford, 1938.

S. C. Wootton, 105 Victoria v. Tasmania, Hobart, 1923–24.

General

L. C. S. Jerman scored a six off his first ball in first-class cricket when making his debut for Essex v. Surrey, August 10, 1951.

G. Pearce also achieved this distinction when making his debut for Sussex v. Essex, in 1928.

A. C. MacLaren scored a century in his first and last appearances in first-class cricket; 108 Lancashire v. Sussex, at Hove in 1890, and 200* M.C.C. v. New Zealand, at Wellington, in 1923.

Bowling

Several men have succeeded in taking a wicket with their first ball in first-class cricket, but a more remarkable performance is probably that of C. G. Fynn. He did not actually get a wicket with his first ball but he did take two wickets in his first over. This was for Hampshire v. Lancashire, at Bournemouth, July 1930.

F. G. Roberts took 14 wickets in his first County game for Gloucestershire v. Yorkshire, at Dewsbury, 1887.

A. E. Moss took all 10 wickets (for 28 runs) when making his first-class debut for Canterbury v. Wellington, Christchurch, 1889–90.

M. W. Tate took a wicket with his first ball in a Test match. This was in the England v. South Africa Test at Birmingham, in June 1924. He bowled a half-volley on the leg stump to M. J. Susskind who was caught at short-leg by R. Kilner.

Five other bowlers have also taken a wicket with their first ball in Test cricket. They are:

A. Coningham for Australia, 1894–95. R. Howorth for England, 1947. T. Johnson for West Indies, 1939. Intikhab Alam for Pakistan, 1959–60, and G. G. Macaulay for England, 1922–23.

Test appearances

The following players appeared for England in Test cricket during their first season in first-class cricket: D. W. Carr (Kent), K. Cranston (Lancashire), D. B. Close (Yorkshire).

DECLARATION

The law allowing a captain to declare his innings closed was first introduced in May 1889. At that time a captain could declare whenever he pleased in a one day match but only on the last day of a match arranged for more than a single day.

This law helped to cut down the number of drawn games and the farcical throwing away of wickets by batsmen in a hurry to end their innings.

When it was only two years old the law was amended so that a declaration could be made after the start of the lunch interval on the second day.

In the first season after World War II experiments were carried out in County cricket to allow captains to declare on the first day providing that a score of 300 had been made, and in 1951 it was decided to allow declarations in these matches on the first day irrespective of the score. This last alteration was not extended to Test matches until 1957, when the amendment was accepted by the Imperial Cricket Conference and incorporated in the Laws of Cricket.

The following instance of declaration by both sides in a game is sufficiently unusual to warrant inclusion here.

When no play was possible until the third day of the Yorkshire v. Gloucestershire match, at Sheffield, June 1931, the captains decided to go all out for a result on the third day and the chance of 15 points for the winner.

Each, therefore, declared their first innings closed after only one ball had been bowled for four byes. Gloucestershire made 171 in their second innings and then got Yorkshire out for 124.

DEFEATS

Fewest defeats

Several county and touring sides have gone through a season without defeat. Details of these are given under the heading UNDEFEATED in a separate section.

The club with the fewest defeats in the County Cricket Championship since the first official season of that competition in 1890 is Yorkshire; 280 defeats in 2,038 games.

In seven seasons 1922 to 1928 Yorkshire played a total of 208 County Championship games with only nine defeats.

Most defeats in a season

This may not be a reasonable record to include here for so many well beaten teams have often struggled through to hang on for an undeserved draw, and such matches cannot be accounted for. However, the club which has suffered the most defeats in a single County Championship season is Glamorgan with 20 in 1925. They played 26 games and only won one.

Most defeats suffered by an M.C.C. team on an overseas tour which included Test matches is six by J. W. H. T. Douglas' team in Australia in 1920–21. In all matches they played 22, won 9, drew 7, and lost 6.

The Australian side which toured England in 1890 lost 16 first-class matches. The side was captained by W. L. Murdoch. They played 34 first-class games, winning 10, drawing 8, and losing 16.

DENMARK

Cricket was first played in Denmark in about 1866 and today it is one of the two principal cricketing countries (the other is Holland) on the continent of Europe.

The first English team to tour Denmark was the Cleveland C.C. in 1909.

A team from Denmark visited England for the first time in 1926—The Gentlemen of Denmark.

The Danish Cricket Association was formed in 1953, but the game had been under the control of the Ball Game Union (formed 1890) which also covered football and lawn tennis.

DERBYSHIRE C.C.C.

Formed: 1870. Became first-class in 1894, although they had been generally included in the County Championship from 1873 to 1887. Re-admitted to the Championship in 1895. Secretary: D. Harrison, County Cricket Ground, Nottingham Road, Derby. Highest score for: 645 v. Hampshire at Derby, August 1–3, 1898. Highest score against: 662 by Yorkshire, at Chesterfield, August 18–20, 1898. Highest individual score for: 274 by G. Davidson v. Lancashire, Manchester, 1896. Highest individual score against: 343* by P. Perrin of Essex, at Chesterfield, July 18–19, 1904. Lowest score for: 16 v. Nottinghamshire, at Nottingham, July 10–11, 1879, 17 v. Lancashire, at Manchester, 1888. Lowest score against: 23 by Hampshire in 1958. Colours: Chocolate, amber and pale blue. Badge: Rose and crown. Principal venues: Burton-on-Trent, Buxton, Chesterfield, Derby and

Ilkeston. Honours: County Champions, 1936. Gillette Cup: Finalists, 1969.

DEVONSHIRE C.C.C.

Founded: 1824. Joined Minor Counties Championship in 1901. Secretary: M. Whitburn, 2 Osney Gardens, Paignton. Highest score for: 533 for 7 declared v. Dorset, 1902. Highest score against: 621 by Surrey II, at Oval, 1928. Highest individual score for: 235* by D. H. Cole, 1955; 269 by J. F. Scobell, 1866. Highest individual score against: 240 by E. F. Wilson of Surrey II, at Oval, 1928. Lowest score for: 29 v. Berkshire, 1930. Lowest score against: 26 by Monmouthshire, 1922; 25 by Somerset, 1879. Colours: Yellow, blue and black. Badge: Blue lion. Honours: None.

DEXTER, Edward Ralph
(1935–   )

Among the most exciting discoveries of the post-war era Ted Dexter quickly became one of the game's outstanding personalities.

At Cambridge he got his "Blue" for cricket and for golf and captained his University cricket team in his third season (1958). He also made his Test debut that same summer scoring 52 against New Zealand at Manchester.

Although not originally selected for the Australian tour of 1958–59 he was flown out in December to help bolster up a side upset by injuries. He made two Test appearances in Australia without doing himself justice, and it was not until the first of his two Tests in New Zealand that Dexter made his mark in international cricket. In this game at Christchurch he enjoyed an innings of 141 which included 24 boundaries.

Despite this display he was only called upon to make two Test appearances against India at home in 1959, and it was on the tour of the West Indies the following winter that he established himself as a cricketer of the highest class showing the selectors that they had been slow in acknowledging his greatness.

His county, Sussex, also recognised his ability by appointing him captain in 1960 and he rewarded their confidence by hitting the highest aggregate of his career and lifting the county from 15th to 4th place in the Championship.

Entrusted with the captaincy of the England side in India and Pakistan during the winter of 1961–62 Dexter acquitted himself well with a side that was below strength. He followed this with some remarkable all-round performances in the summer of 1962 to be rewarded with the greatest honour of all—the captaincy of England in Australia.

Dexter led England in 30 of his 62 Tests. His captaincy met with some criticism on occasions, whose hasn't? But his reputation as a batsman was enhanced several times over in these games.

His highest score was obtained in a Test match—205 v. Pakistan, at Dacca, in 1961–62, and those who saw his masterly innings of 70 in 80 minutes in a crisis at Lords against West Indies in 1963 will never forget it.

D'OLIVIERA, Basil Lewis
(1931–   )

The first coloured South African cricketer to overcome the primitive conditions in which he was compelled to play at home and rise to County Cricket in England as well as becoming a Test player.

First came to England in 1960 to join Middleton in the Central Lancashire League and topped the League's averages in his first season.

In 1965 this modest man made his Championship debut with Worcestershire and it was only a year later that he was first chosen to play for England.

Since then this right-handed batsman, who is also a reliable off-break bowler, has taken his total of Tests to 44, scoring 2,484 runs (av. 40.06) and capturing 47 wickets (av. 39.55).

The dignified manner in which he bore the stress of being at the centre of the row over the cancellation of the M.C.C. tour of South Africa in 1968, after the South African Government had refused to accept him as a member of the touring team, earned him much praise and undoubtedly led to his being awarded the M.B.E.

DORSET C.C.C.

Founded: About 1845, re-formed 1896. Joined Minor Counties Championship 1902. Secretary: S. Hey, "Greenoaks", Bradford Road, Sherborne. Highest score for: 491 for 6 v. Wiltshire at Sherborne, 1937. Highest score against: 533 for 7 by Devon, at Sherborne, 1902; 603 for 9 declared by Somerset Gentlemen, 1900. Highest individual score for: 203 by G. W. L. Courtenay v. Oxfordshire, at Oxford,

1953. Highest individual score against: 247* by L. Pitchford of Monmouthshire, at Abercarn, 1933. Lowest score for: 28 v. Devon, 1961. Lowest score against: 15 by Buckinghamshire, at Poole, 1909. Colours: Green and white. Flag: Three leopards on a green background. Honours: None.

DOUBLE, The

To achieve the "double" in cricket is to score 1,000 runs and take 100 wickets in a single season.

The record number of "doubles" is 16 by W. Rhodes of Yorkshire. In the 20 playing seasons from 1903 to 1926 he missed the "double" only four times.

The two most outstanding "doubles" are those of G. H. Hirst (Yorkshire) and J. H. Parks (Sussex). In 1906 Hirst scored 2,385 runs and took 208 wickets. In 1937 Parks scored 3,003 runs and took 101 wickets.

In 1949 D. B. Close of Yorkshire achieved the "double" (1,098 runs and 113 wickets) in what was his opening season in first-class cricket. No wonder that he was chosen to play for England that summer.

DOUGLAS, John William Henry Tyler (1882–1930)

This gifted all-round sportsman was not only an outstanding cricketer but an A.B.A. and Olympic boxing champion and a soccer player for England, the Corinthians, and the Casuals.

A powerful man "Johnny Won't Hit Today" Douglas made his debut for Essex in 1901 and captained them from 1911 to 1928. He also captained England in 18 of his 23 Tests, 12 against Australia and six against South Africa, and it was in Australia that the barrackers used his initials in words suitably phrased to express their feelings when annoyed by his stubborn defensive play.

That sort of thing never bothered this batsman, however. Indeed, he seemed to enjoy it, and there was no cooler batsman than J. W. H. T. Douglas when things were difficult.

Douglas, who was educated at Felsted School, reached his peak in 1921 when he scored 1,547 runs and took 130 wickets.

He could not be described as a natural cricketer but he was a fine player who got to the top by sheer hard work and determination.

In 1914 he took 9 for 105 in one innings

at Lord's for the Gentlemen v. Players, and Sir Pelham Warner has since described his efforts as "some of the finest bowling seen in the history of these games".

Douglas performed another fine feat of bowling at Leyton in 1921 when he took 9 Derbyshire wickets for 47. He also bowled a "hat-trick" three times in his career.

An example of his dogged determined batting was his 119 in four hours and a quarter for England v. South Africa in the first Test of the 1913–14 series. He returned from that South African tour second only to Jack Hobbs in the batting averages with 50.00 over 23 innings.

His highest score was 210* v. Derbyshire at Leyton in 1921.

Douglas was drowned in a collision between two ships in a North Sea fog in December 1930.

DRESS

Eighteenth century cricketers wore three-cornered hats, white vests, knee-breeches with silk stockings and buckled shoes. In the case of the Hambledon club and the Earl of Winchelsea's XI, the players had gold or silver lacing around their hats, while Hambledon also wore sky-blue coats with black velvet collars. Their buttons were engraved with the letters "C.C."

About the same time, in the middle of the 18th century, there were many cricketers who preferred to wear a cap which resembled a jockey cap, but at the beginning of the 19th century there was a liking for the high hat or sometimes a straw hat.

Breeches gradually lost favour and trousers were worn with either wide cloth braces or belts with large metal buckles.

It was probably the Universities which first preferred coloured cloth caps, and, in the second half of the 19th century these were often worn with coloured shirts.

However, white shirts were generally adopted well before the end of the 19th century.

About 1860 brown or white shoes were the fashion and it was not until around 1880 that white buckskin shoes came into vogue, since when cricket dress has changed very little.

"DUCK"

A. R. Morris of New South Wales played 100 consecutive first-class innings without failing to score. He nade his first "duck" in his 101st innings which was for Australia against South Africa in the first Test of the 1949–50 series.

Eight M.C.C. batsmen were out for a "duck" (including the first seven in a row) when the side made only 16 runs (in 44 minutes) against Surrey at Lord's in May 1872.

There were seven "ducks" in one innings by the Australians against the Players of England, at the Oval, in 1878. It was in this innings that Surrey's slow left-arm bowler, E. Barratt, took all 10 wickets for 43 runs.

It should also be mentioned here that during that same tour when the Australians beat the M.C.C. at Lord's in a game which provided only four and a half hours actual play, there were seven "ducks" in the M.C.C.'s second innings which totalled only 19 runs.

In the three completed innings of the England v. Australia Test, at Manchester, August 1888, 13 players failed to score, although two of them were "not out".

The record for "ducks" in successive innings is six by A. Wright for South Australia in 1905–06.

DUCKWORTH, George
(1901–1966)

Although born at Warrington, Lancashire, and best remembered as one of that county's finest wicket-keepers, George Duckworth actually made his debut with Warwickshire.

There appeared to be little hope of him superseding the renowned E. J. Smith as regular wicket-keeper with Warwickshire however, and fortunately for Lancashire that county snapped up Duckworth in 1923 on the retirement of B. Blomley.

Duckworth was one of the elite of wicket-keepers who have captured 100 wickets in a season. In 1928 his total was 107, 77 caught and 30 stumped.

In his best matches Duckworth's bag was eight wickets. That was for Lancashire against Kent, in 1928, and against Warwickshire, in 1936.

An outstanding personality who always displayed a wonderful enthusiasm for the game, Duckworth's appeals could usually be heard well outside the ground.

He played in 24 Tests between 1924 and 1936 before losing his place to L. E. G. Ames largely because of the latter's better form as a batsman.

DULEEPSINHJI, Kumar Shri
(1905–1959)

Greatly respected both on and off the field, there have been few, if any, more accomplished batsmen than this Indian Prince who, like his uncle, K. S. Ranjitsinhji, possessed natural gifts which immediately put him streets ahead of the average young man who takes up cricket.

Affectionately known as "Mr. Smith," his first-class career with Cambridge University and Sussex was restricted by ill-health to only eight seasons.

In that so brief career, however, he scored 15.537 runs (av. 50.11) including 49 centuries, with a highest score of 333 for Sussex v. Northamptonshire—a county record. In 1931 he scored four successive hundreds.

Prince Duleepsinhji played in 12 Tests for England and had an average of 58.52 in these games—highest score 173 v. Australia, at Lord's in 1930.

DURHAM C.C.C.

Founded: May 1882. There was an earlier club in the 1870s. Among the original members of the Minor Counties Championship in 1895. Dropped out 1898. Re-entered 1901. Secretary: J. Iley, "Roselea", Springwell Avenue, Durham City. Highest score for: 503 for 2 declared v. Northumberland, 1959. Highest score against: 543 by South Africans, at Sunderland, 1955. In a County match—517 for 8 by Northamptonshire, 1900. Highest individual score for: 217* by E. W. Elliott, 1906. Highest individual score against: 225* by D. M. Green of Lancashire II, August 1961. Lowest score for: 20 v. Staffordshire, 1907. Lowest score gainst: 24 by Yorkshire United, 1874. In Minor Counties Championship—36 by Staffordshire, 1907. Colours: Maroon, blue and gold. Badge: Shield with gold cross between four lions rampant argent. Honours: Minor Counties Champions, 1895 (tie with Norfolk), 1900 (tie with Glamorgan and Northamptonshire), 1901, 1926, 1930, 1976.

E

EDGBASTON

One of the best equipped cricket grounds in England and the headquarters of Warwickshire C.C.C. since 1884, when it was "a meadow of rough grazing land", the Edgbaston ground at Birmingham was first used as the venue for a Test match in May 1902 when torrential rain prevented the England v. Australia match from being completed after the visitors had been all out for 36 in their first innings. The game was a financial disaster.

The finest Test innings played on this ground was P. B. H. May's 285* for England v. West Indies in 1957. This was the occasion when May and Cowdrey created a record 4th wicket Test partnership of 411, and Ramadhin sent down a Test record total of 774 balls.

EDRICH, John Hugh
(1937–   )

A cousin of W. J. Edrich this determined batsman with a solid defence, which always makes him a difficult man to get out, can usually be relied upon to get runs quickly when the need arises. Seldom spectacular but a real class player who has scored 12 centuries in Test cricket, nine of them against Australia.

His highest score in Test cricket was his 310* v. New Zealand, at Leeds in 1965, when his score included five 6's and fifty-two 4's in 8 hours 52 minutes, a sure indication of the power and endurance of this stockily built left-hander. That particular score took him to 1,311 runs in nine consecutive innings, one of the finest spells of run getting in cricket history.

Made debut for Combined Services in 1956 and for Surrey in 1958. Appointed county captain in 1973. Test debut v. West Indies in 1963. Has scored 1,000 runs 18 times, his best being 2,482 (av. 51.70) in 1962. Has scored two centuries in a match three times.

EDRICH, William John
(1916–   )

After making his mark in Minor Counties cricket with his native Norfolk, Edrich joined the ground staff at Lord's in 1934 and when he qualified for Middlesex in 1937 he had one of the most successful first seasons ever enjoyed by any batsman.

During that summer of 1937 he scored 2,154 runs (av. 44.87) with a highest score of 175 v. Lancashire at Lord's.

It was not surprising then that he joined the England side against Australia the following season, but it was a great disappointment when he could only score 67 runs in six innings.

This disappointing run in international cricket continued in the 1938–39 tour of South Africa with only 21 in five innings, but then, at last, Edrich rewarded the faith of the selectors and shocked a lot of critics with a score of 219 in the second innings of the final Test.

Returning to Test cricket after the war Edrich played some of his finest innings in Australia in 1946–47 and against South Africa in 1947. Indeed, 1947 was his finest season. Never missing a chance to hit hard Edrich scored 12 centuries including three double centuries during the summer of 1947, and he and Denis Compton each broke a 31-year-old record for the highest number of runs in a single season. Edrich's aggregate was 3,539 with an average of 80.43. This included his highest ever score, 267* v. Northamptonshire, at Northampton.

When Edrich retired from first-class cricket in 1958 he had made 36,965 runs including 86 hundreds, while as a fast-medium bowler he had taken nearly 400 wickets. He appeared in 39 Tests, shared the captaincy of Middlesex with Denis Compton in 1951 and 1952 and then continued as skipper until the end of 1957. He rejoined Norfolk in 1959.

A war-time R.A.F. pilot and D.F.C., W. J. Edrich also figured in League football with Tottenham Hotspur.

ENDEAN, William Russell
(1924–)

Born at Johannesburg Endean made his debut in 1945–46 but did not become a regular player with Transvaal until 1950.

Then when he was chosen to tour England with the South African side of 1951 he appeared in only one Test.

At that time he was a wicket-keeper as well as a batsman but he was rather overshadowed by John Waite and subsequently gave up wicket-keeping to concentrate on his batting. This move had the desired effect.

In the 1955 tour of England Endean scored over 1,000 runs including an innings of 138* v. T. N. Pearce's XI at Scarborough, and 116* v. England, at Leeds.

In the second Test against England, at Cape Town, in 1956–57, Endean had the unusual experience (unique in Test matches) of being given out "handled the ball".

A brilliant fielder, only two South Africans have held more catches in Test cricket. Endean's total for 28 Tests is 41.

ENGINEER, Farrokh Manekji
(1938–)

Born in Bombay this wicket-keeper batsman made his debut for Combined Services v. West Indies in 1958 and has since played for Bombay, West Zone and (since 1968) for Lancashire.

His Test debut was against England at home in 1961. He proved his ability as a fast-scoring batsman when he made 94* before lunch for India v. West Indies, at Madras in 1966–67, and a century before lunch for West Zone v. Central Zone, at Bombay in 1964–65. His highest score is 192 for Rest of the World v. Combined XI, at Hobart in 1971–72, and his best season behind the stumps was 1970 when he dismissed 91 batsmen, 86 caught and 5 stumped. All but four of these were for Lancashire.

Besides scoring over 13,000 runs he has dismissed over 800 batsmen. His 2,611 Test runs places him in the top five of Indian batsmen.

ENGLAND

Here will be found records of Test matches only.

Highest score for: 903 for 7 declared v. Australia, the Oval, 1938.

L. Hutton, c Hassett, b O'Reilly	364
W. J. Edrich, c Hassett, b O'Reilly	12
M. Leyland, run out	187
W. R. Hammond (capt.) lbw, b Fleetwood-Smith	59
E. Paynter, lbw, b O'Reilly	0
D. Compton, b Waite	1
J. Hardstaff, not out	169
A. Wood, c and b Barnes	53
H. Verity, not out	8
Byes 22, 1–b 19, w 1, n–b 8	50
Total (7 wkts dec.)	903

K. Farnes and W. E. Bowes did not bat.

Highest score against: 729 for 6 declared, by Australia, at Lord's, 1930. Highest individual score for: 364 by L. Hutton v. Australia, at the Oval, 1938. Highest individual score against: 334 by D. G. Bradman of Australia, at Leeds, 1930. Lowest score for: 45 v. Australia at Sydney, January 1887. Lowest score against: 26 by New Zealand, at Auckland, 1954–55 (Appleyard 4 for 7, Statham 3 for 9).

ESSEX C.C.C.

Founded: circ. 1790. Re-formed 1876. Became first-class county in 1894 and were admitted to the Championship in 1895. Secretary: S. R. Cox, The County Ground, New Writtle Street, Chelmsford CM2 0RW. Highest score for: 692 v. Somerset, Taunton, July 11–13, 1895. Highest score against: 803 for 4 declared, by Kent, at Brentwood, 1934. Highest individual score for: 343* by P. A. Perrin v. Derbyshire, Chesterfield, July 19, 1904. Highest individual score against: 332 by W. H. Ashdown, of Kent, Brentwood, 1934. Lowest score for: 30 v. Yorkshire, at Leyton, August 15–16, 1901. Lowest score against: 31 by Derbyshire, 1914, and by Yorkshire, at Huddersfield, July, 1935; (in all matches—22 by Surrey, 1866). Colours: Blue, gold and red. Badge: three scimitars. Honours: None.

ETON COLLEGE

See under PUBLIC SCHOOL CRICKET.

EVANS, Thomas Godfrey
(1920–)

This live-wire wicket-keeper and stubborn batsman succeeded his team-mate, L. E. G. Ames, as England's keeper towards the end of his first full season with Kent.

That was 1946 and Evans was selected for the final Test of that summer against India.

So began a remarkable Test career during which he amassed a remarkable total of 91 appearances for his country.

An unusually spectacular wicket-keeper, Evans made many astonishing catches behind the wicket and among wicket-keepers only A. P. E. Knott has exceeded this player's all-round Test figures—2,439 runs and 219 dismissals.

In all his career he made 811 catches and 249 stumpings. With the bat he registered his highest score at Taunton in 1952 when he notched 144 against Somerset.

EXTRAS

See also under LAWS OF CRICKET, TERMS, LEG-BYE, BOWLING (No-ball).

On July 14, 1842, in a match at Lord's between the M.C.C. and Royal Artillery Club, the Marylebone club's first innings score included no less than 106 extras—Byes 58, wides 48.

The record number of extras in a single innings of a Test match is 57 (Byes 31, leg-byes 16, no-balls 10) New Zealand v. England, at Auckland, February 1930.

The first-class record is generally considered to be 74—Byes 54, leg-byes 16, wides 1, no-balls 3—British Guiana v. W. Shepherd's XI, Georgetown, 1909–10.

F

FAMILIES

Brothers

Many brothers have played together in first-class cricket and they are far too numerous to mention here. Cricket runs in the blood and many families have carried on the cricketing tradition from one generation to another.

In this section we shall reserve space for brothers who have represented their countries in Test matches, and it is really quite surprising how many of these there have been. Indeed, there have probably been more brothers in cricket than in any other international sport.

Three brothers of the Grace family, Dr. W. G., Dr. E. M., and G. F. Grace, appeared together in the England team v. Australia, at the Oval, in September 1880.

The three Hearne brothers all appeared in the South Africa v. England Test, at Cape Town, in 1891–92. A. and G. G. were in the England team, Frank in the South African team.

Before Test matches began the three Newland brothers of Slindon, Sussex, all played for England against Kent at the Artillery Ground, June 18, 1744.

There have been a number of instances of two brothers playing in the same Test team. They are:

Ali, S. Wazir and S. Nazir, for India v. England, at Lord's, 1932, and Madras, 1934.

Amarnath, M. and S., played first together in same Indian Test side v. New Zealand, at Auckland, 1976.

Atkinson, D. and E. for West Indies v. Pakistan, at Bridgetown, 1958.

Bannerman, A. C. and C., of New South Wales, for Australia v. England, at Melbourne, January 1879.

Chappell, G. S. and I. M., first appeared together in the Australian Test team v. England, at Perth, 1970. They provided the first instance of brothers each scoring a century in a single Test innings—v. New Zealand, at Wellington, 1973–74.

Giffen, G. and W. F. of South Australia, for Australia v. England, at Sydney and at Adelaide, in 1892.

Grant, G. C. and R. S. of Trinidad, for West Indies v. England, in all four Tests in the West Indies in 1934–35.

Gregory, D. W. and E. J. of New South Wales, for Australia v. England, at Melbourne, March 1877.

Hadlee, D. R. and R. J. made the first of their Test appearances together for New Zealand v. England, at Nottingham, 1973.

Hands, P. A. M. and R. H. M. played in one Test together for South Africa v. England, 1913–14.

Hearne, A. and G. G. of Kent, for England v. South Africa, at Cape Town, in 1891.

Howarth, G. P. and H. J. of Auckland, appeared together for New Zealand v. England in two Tests in 1974–75.

Mohammad, Hanif, Mushtaq, Wazir and Sadiq. Various combinations of any two have appeared in several Tests for Pakistan, but in only one have three appeared together—Hanif, Mushtaq and Sadiq v. New Zealand, at Karachi, October 1969.

Nayudu, C. S. and C. K., India v. England, at Calcutta and Madras, 1934, Lord's and Manchester, 1936.

Pollock, P. M. and R. G., South Africa in all five Tests in Australia and one in New Zealand 1963–64; all five v. England 1964–65, and all three in England 1965.

Richardson, D. W. and P. E. of Worcestershire, for England v. West Indies, at Nottingham, in 1957.

Rowan, A. M. B. and E. A. B. of Transvaal, for South Africa v. England in four out of five Tests in South Africa in 1948–49, and also in all five Tests in England in 1951.

Singh, A. G. Kripal and A. G. Milkha, for India v. England, at Bombay, November 1961.

Singh, L. Amar and L. Ramji, for India v. England, at Bombay, December 1933.

Stollmeyer, J. B. and V. H. of British Guiana, for the West Indies v. England, at the Oval, August 1939.

Studd, C. T. and G. B. of Middlesex, for England in all four Tests in Australia, 1882–83.

Trott, A. E. and G. H. of Victoria, for Australia v. England, in three Tests in Australia, 1894–95.

The Indian Test team v. England, at Madras in February 1934, included two pairs of brothers—C. K. and C. S. Nayudu, S. Wazir Ali and S. Nazir Ali. The Nayudu brothers appeared together in three other Tests. The Ali brothers in one other Test (see above).

Apart from those just listed, the following brothers have represented their countries in Tests, although not appearing together in the same matches:

Apte, A. L. and M. L. for India.

Archer, K. A. and R. G. for Australia.

Christiani, R. J. and C. M. for the West Indies.

Gilligan, A. E. R. and A. H. H. for England.

Gunn, J. and W. for England.

Gupte, S. P. and B. for India.

Harvey, M. and R. N. for Australia.

McLeod, C. E. and R. W. for Australia.

Marshall, R. E. and N. for West Indies.

Snooke, S. D. and S. J. for South Africa.

Tancred, A. B., L. J. and V. M. for South Africa.

Trumble, H. and J. W. for Australia.

Tyldesley, J. T. and E. for England.

In 1865 on the Sydenham Fields, Bath, the three brothers, E. M., H. M., and W. G. Grace, playing for 18 of the Lansdowne Club against the United All England XI took all the wickets in each innings.

The largest number of brothers to play for a first-class county club is seven of the Foster family who played for Worcestershire. They are B. S., H. K., G. N., M. K., N. J. A., W. L., and R. E.

The brothers W. L. and R. E. Foster both scored a century in each innings for Worcestershire against Hampshire, at Worcester in 1899. R. E.—134 and 101*, W. L.—140 and 172*.

The Hill brothers each scored a century for South Australia v. N.S.W., at Sydney, in 1910–11. C. Hill made 156, and L. R. Hill, 123.

No less than six brothers of the Walker

family of Southgate, Middlesex, played for the Gentlemen against the Players during the 19th century. The most to appear together in one of these games was four, at the Oval, in 1857.

Brothers (Twins)

The following twin brothers have appeared in first-class cricket:

A. V. and E. A. Bedser (Surrey), J. S. and W. H. Denton (Northamptonshire), C. and L. R. Hill (South Australia), A. D. E. and A. E. S. Rippon (Somerset), F. G. and G. W. Stephens (Warwickshire).

The following twins have appeared in minor counties cricket:

E. L. and G. M. Ede (Hampshire), J. H. and D. W. Taylor (Lincolnshire), D. C. and M. E. Thorne (Norfolk).

Father and son

Here are the only instances of father and son having appeared for their country in Test cricket:

England

Hardstaff, J. and J. (Jnr.); Hutton, L. and R. A.; Mann, F. G. and F. T.[1]; Parks, J. H. and J. M.; Tate, F. W. and M. W.; Townsend, C. L. and D. C. H.

Australia

Gregory, E. J. and S. E.

South Africa

Hearne, F. and G. A. (F. also played for England); Lindsay, J. D. and D.; Nourse, A. D. and A. D. (Jnr.); Tuckett, L. and L. R.

New Zealand

Hadlee, W. A. and sons D. R. and R. J.; Vivian, H. G. and G. E.

West Indies

Headley, G. A. and R. G. R.; Scott, O. C. and A. P. H.

India and Pakistan

S. Wazir Ali played for India and his son Khalid Wazir has since played for Pakistan.

Jehangir Khan played for India while his son, Majid Jehangir has since played for Pakistan.

[1] Both father and son captained England.

The Nawab of Pataudi (Mansur Ali Khan) and his father have both captained India since World War II.

D. K. Gaekwad and son A. D. both played for India.

L. Amarnath and sons S. and M. have all played for India.

Several instances have occurred of father and son playing together in the same county side. They include:

W. Bestwick and his son R. Bestwick appeared in the same Derbyshire side in 1922.

In August 1891, H. B. Daft appeared in the Nottinghamshire team together with his father R. Daft in a game against Surrey.

In 1931 G. Gunn scored 183 for Nottinghamshire against Warwickshire, at Edgbaston, and his son, G. V. Gunn, scored 100* in the same match. They played together on several occasions.

A. N. Hornby and his son, A. H. Hornby, played in the same Lancashire side in 1899.

W. G. Quaife appeared with his son B. W. Quaife in several Warwickshire games in the early 1920s.

At Derby, in June 1922, the Quaifes (father and son) and the Bestwicks (father and son) appeared on opposing sides in the Derbyshire v. Warwickshire game.

FAST BOWLING

See under BOWLING (Fast Bowling).

FAST SCORING (INDIVIDUALS)

See also under CENTURIES (Fastest Centuries).

The fastest century ever scored in first-class cricket is that by P. G. H. Fender, of Surrey, at Northampton in 1920. On that occasion this remarkably free hitter not only scored his first century in first-class cricket, but scored it in 35 minutes.

Another great hitter, G. L. Jessop of Gloucestershire was only five minutes outside this record with his fastest century which was scored against Yorkshire, at Harrogate, in 1897.

Jessop, however, created the record for the fastest double-century. This was made at Hove in 1903 when the Gloucestershire batsman reached the 200 mark in 120 minutes against Sussex. This was equalled by C. H. Lloyd with 201 in 120 minutes for the West Indians v. Glamorgan in

1976. In his innings Jessop went on to make 286 in 175 minutes.

When playing for Gentlemen of South v. Players of South, at Hastings, in 1907, Jessop scored 150* in 63 minutes, 191 in 90 minutes.

In 1907 A. H. du Boulay made 402* in 225 minutes. However, this was not in a first-class match, but was for the School of Military Engineering v. R. N. and R.M., at Chatham.

While we are venturing outside the realms of first-class cricket we should recall the innings of A. G. Moyes when playing for Gordon v. Central Cumberland, at Sydney, March 25, 1922.

Well known since for his writing on the game, A. G. Moyes was, of course, the former South Australia and Victoria batsman. In this First Grade club match he played an innings of 218 in 83 minutes! He reached his first 50 in 20 minutes, 100 in 40 minutes, 150 in 62 minutes, and 200 in 72 minutes. His total included seven sixes and 36 fours.

Of the innings which have topped the 300 mark one of the fastest must be that of C. G. Macartney when playing for the Australians against Nottinghamshire, at Nottingham, in 1921. He made 345 in 235 minutes. The 300 was reached in 205 minutes.

F. E. Woolley also reached 300 in 205 minutes when he scored 305* for M.C.C. v. Tasmania, at Hobart in 1911–12.

The time was beaten by D. C. S. Compton when playing for the M.C.C. against N.E. Transvaal, at Benoni, during the 1948–49 tour. He reached 300 in 181 minutes.

For Nottinghamshire against Sussex, at Hove, in May 1911, E. Alletson scored 189 in 90 minutes. At lunch he had scored 47 in 50 minutes but when play resumed Alletson opened up to produce one of the finest spells of big hitting ever known. It included 34 in one over (with two no-balls) off E. H. Killick, and when he was caught by C. L. A. Smith (many considered that Smith was standing outside the boundary), Alletson had scored 142 in 40 minutes!

Concerning the smaller scores the following are well worth noting:

C. C. Inman, 51* in eight minutes, for Leicestershire v. Nottinghamshire, at Nottingham, August 20, 1965. Five sixes and five fours.

C. I. J. Smith, 66 in 18 minutes (50 in 11 minutes) with eight sixes and two fours, for Middlesex v. Gloucestershire, at Bristol, in June 1938.

O. G. Smith of Jamaica scored 46* in 12 minutes for the West Indians against Nottinghamshire, at Trent Bridge, in 1957.

B. Sutcliffe, 46 in 13 minutes for the New Zealanders v. Hampshire, at Southampton, in 1949.

The fastest Test century is probably that of J. M. Gregory who took about 70 minutes to reach treble figures for Australia v. South Africa, at Johannesburg, in 1921–22.

When D. G. Bradman scored 334 at Leeds in 1930 he reached 200 in 214 minutes—a record for a double century in Test cricket.

There are several recorded instances of remarkably fast innings outside of first-class cricket by comparatively unknown batsmen, but one of the fastest made by a first-class player in such a match must surely be that of E. M. Grace for the Thornbury Club in 1873. The time he took to score 295 has been given as 100 minutes!

Partnerships

The fastest scoring partnerships have included the following:

R. R. Relf and C. B. Fry, 150 for the third wicket in 65 minutes, in second innings of Sussex v. Kent, at Canterbury, 1907.

J. B. Hobbs and J. N. Crawford scored 95 in 29 minutes (some say 32 minutes) for Surrey v. Kent, at the Oval, in August 1919. Surrey had been left with 42 minutes in which to get 95 runs to win. The remarkable innings above was carried through in a slight drizzle with poor light, and the winning hit was made at 7.15 p.m.

S. M. J. Woods and G. L. Jessop, two of the fastest scorers on record, combined to put on 50 in eight minutes, and 100 in 16 minutes, in a match at Bristol in 1901. This was not a first-class game.

The record for a first-wicket partnership was set up at Edgbaston in 1904 when E. H. D. Sewell and H. Carpenter scored 142 in 65 minutes for Essex against Warwickshire.

At Old Trafford, in 1905, A. H. Hornby and W. Findlay put on 113 for the ninth wicket in only half an hour for Lancashire v. Somerset.

FAST SCORING (SIDES)

See also under HIGHEST SCORES (THE SIDES)—One day.

In 1907, at Hastings, the Gentlemen of the South scored 313 in 140 minutes against the Gentlemen of the North. This was the innings in which G. L. Jessop scored 191 out of 234 in 90 minutes.

In July 1951, Worcestershire scored 131 for one wicket in 35 minutes against Nottinghamshire, at Nottingham. The batsmen were D. Kenyon 38, G. Dews 43*, and R. O. Jenkins 47*.

Kent scored 219 for 2 in 71 minutes against Gloucestershire at Dover in 1937. This is probably the fastest rate of scoring ever known in England.

At Tonbridge in 1922 Kent scored 621 for 6 declared in only six hours' play. Three players scored centuries during this innings.

FAULKNER, George Aubrey (1881–1930)

This South African all-rounder was a sound batsman, a slow to medium pace googly bowler, and a good fielder.

He was born at Port Elizabeth but became domiciled in England when he was 30 and died in London at the age of 48 after making a name for himself as a cricket coach.

At one time in his career he was recognised as South Africa's leading batsman and when he scored 204 v. Australia, at Melbourne, in 1910–11 he was the first South African to score a double century in a Test match. In England, however, he did rather better as a bowler.

He toured England with the South Africans in 1907 and played a sensational Test at Leeds where he took 6 for 17 in 11 overs, four of them maidens. His average for the three Tests of that series was 12 wickets at a cost of 18.16 apiece.

In the Triangular Tournament of 1912 he was the only South African to make a century—122* v. Australia at Manchester, but apart from that his batting in this series was a disappointment.

His best bowling feat that summer was in the Oval Test against England. In the first innings he took 7 for 84.

After 1912 the South Africans did not visit England again until 1924 but although, between times, Faulkner had played very little first-class cricket, they called upon him to make one more Test appearance during their tour. In this he made 25 and 12, and this brought his final figures in 25 Test appearances to 1,754 runs (av. 40.79) and 82 wickets (av. 26.58).

FAZAL MAHMOOD (1927–   )

Fazal Mahmood, Pakistan's outstanding bowler, has taken more Test wickets than any other Pakistani. When he toured England in 1954 he came as a vice-captain but he later captained Pakistan in 10 Tests.

Mahmood was a bowler with plenty of stamina and one who used the in-swinger as his stock ball. He bore the brunt of the Pakistani attack on their first-ever visit to England in 1954. On that tour he took 77 wickets at an average of only 17.35 runs apiece.

At the Oval he twice broke the back of the England team by taking 6 for 53 and 6 for 46. His average for those four Tests was 20 wickets at 20.40 each.

Fàzal Mahmood enhanced his reputation with many fine displays in League Cricket and with the Pakistan tourists of 1962.

FELIX (WANOSTROCHT, Nicolas) (1804–1876)

A schoolmaster of Camberwell Green, this famous player with the unpronounceable name of Wanostrocht (said to be Flemish) preferred, fortunately enough, to use the name Felix in connection with cricket.

He has earned immortality in this game not so much as a player but as the man who invented batting gloves and also an ingenious bowling machine, the "catapulta". In addition to this his book *On the Bat,* is now a collector's item.

Felix played for Surrey, Kent, and the All England XI, but mostly for Kent, for he moved his school to Blackheath in 1832.

Probably the best left-handed batsman of his day, he was noted for his off-side drive and cut which he executed with some nimble footwork. He was also a good fielder at point, and a lob bowler.

FENNER'S GROUND

Fenner's succeeded Parker's piece as the home of Cambridge University C.C. It was first opened by F. P. Fenner in 1846 but was not leased by the University C.C.

until 1873. The combined University Cricket and Athletic clubs eventually purchased the freehold of the ground from Caius College in 1892.

The first pavilion was erected in 1875, thanks to the efforts of the Rev. A. R. Ward the man who did so much to establish the game of cricket at Cambridge University (q.v.).

FIELDING

See also under CATCHES, WICKET-KEEPER.

Fielding is an important part of the game of cricket although it is often neglected. As many games are lost by bad fielding as are won by good fielding, but it is still a part of the game which so many players tolerate without enthusiasm. Good bowling is often wasted by bad fielding.

There are no figures upon which to base one's judgment of all fielders as they are only credited in the records with stumping or catching a batsman and there are no points for quick and accurate returns or for the prevention of boundaries or quick singles, but these are all part of the fielder's art.

However, on the figures that are available there is no disputing the fact that one of the most accomplished fielders of all time was W. R. Hammond of Gloucestershire. During his first-class career of nearly 30 years he has been credited with 819 catches. Hammond was happy at any place in the field but he was outstanding at cover-point or at first slip, and, during season 1928, he broke all records by making a total of 78 catches which included no less than 10 made in one game against Surrey, at Cheltenham. On that occasion he held four catches in the first innings and six in the second as well as making over 100 runs in each innings.

Only three players have exceeded Hammond's total of catches—F. E. Woolley (Kent) 1,015, W. G. Grace (Gloucestershire) 877, and G. A. R. Lock (Surrey, W. Australia, Leicestershire) 830.

Another brilliant fielder was J. B. Hobbs. His favourite position was cover-point and in 1911–12 tour of Australia he was sharp enough to run out 15 batsmen as well as holding seven catches.

One man who always emphasised the importance of good fielding was Dr. W. G. Grace. In his personal reminiscences published in 1899 he wrote the following:

"I go so far as to say that a really good

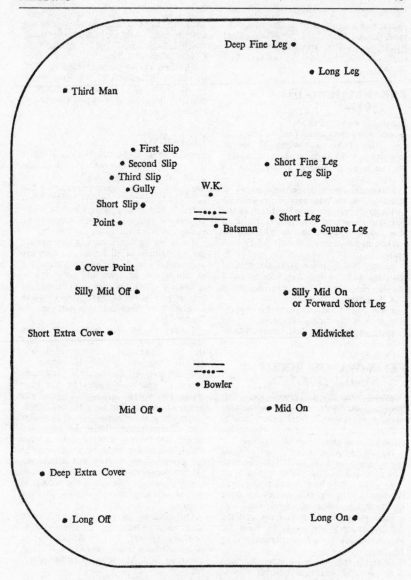

FIELDING POSITIONS FOR A RIGHT-HANDED BATSMAN

Showing the positions in which the fieldsmen can be disposed if so desired. The nine fieldsmen are, of course, placed in certain of these positions according to the type of bowler being used and certain other conditions of the game at any particular time.

fielder often saves as many runs as the best batsman on his side scores, and I firmly believe that a thoroughly efficient fieldsman is worth his place in any team, even if he gets no runs at all."

It would be impossible to list all the outstanding fielders as most of the really great cricketers were good fielders, but here are just a few of the best men in some positions:

Slips—L. C. Braund (Surrey and Somerset), K. R. Miller (Victoria), W. J. Edrich (Middlesex), K. Grieves (Lancashire), W. R. Hammond (Gloucestershire), R. E. Foster (Worcestershire), J. Tunnicliffe (Yorkshire), F. E. Woolley (Kent), H. Trumble (Victoria), G. S. Sobers (West Indies), R. B. Simpson (Western Australia and N.S.W.), J. M. Gregory (N.S.W.).

Gully—A. P. F. Chapman (Kent), D. R. Jardine (Surrey), R. Benaud (N.S.W.).

Silly mid-off or mid-on—G. Brown (Hampshire), J. T. Ikin (Lancashire), A. Iremonger (Nottinghamshire).

Cover-point—L. N. Constantine (West Indies), S. E. Gregory (N.S.W.), J. B. Hobbs (Surrey), G. L. Jessop (Gloucestershire), R. N. Harvey (N.S.W.), C. H. Lloyd (West Indies and Lancashire).

Short-leg—H. F. Boyle (Victoria), G. A. R. Lock (Surrey), M. J. Stewart (Surrey), A. Watkins (Glamorgan).

Third-man—A. O. Jones (Nottinghamshire).

In August 1932 when fielding for Gloucestershire v. Sussex, at Cheltenham, T. W. Goddard stopped the ball with his cap and A. Melville was awarded five runs.

At the Oval in 1938 L. Hutton kicked the ball over the boundary when fielding for England against Australia. His idea was to prevent W. A. Brown from having the strike off the last ball of an over. However, Brown did retain the strike, and Australia were awarded four runs for the boundary and one for the hit.

When fielding at Durban in 1935–36 V. Y. Richardson (Australia) caught five of the last six South African batsmen to be dismissed in the second innings. This is a Test innings record for a fieldsman other than a wicket-keeper.

When fielding at Perth in 1974–75 G. S. Chappell (Australia) caught seven England batsmen. A Test match record for a non-wicket-keeper.

The record for most catches in Test cricket (excluding wicket-keepers) is 120 in 114 games by M. C. Cowdrey.

FINANCES of CRICKET

The Test and County Cricket Board announced a profit of £625,000 from the England-Australia matches of 1975.

Match fees

In the 1840s William Clarke's All England XI received only about £5 or £6 per match and had to pay their own expenses while travelling.

Clarke had a reputation for not being over-generous and this was one of the reasons for the break-up of the team and for the formation of the United All England XI.

1859: The English team which toured Canada and the United States in 1859 under the captaincy of G. Parr each received £50 and their expenses.

1861–62: The English team in Australia under the captaincy of H. H. Stephenson each received £150 and their expenses.

1876: Members of the English team captained by James Lillywhite which toured Australia and New Zealand in 1876–77 each received £150 and expenses.

In 1898 it was decided to pay the England Test players £20 per Test. Thereafter the fee varied from £20 to £40 in each season according to the opposition, until 1938 when it was increased to £50. It became £60 in 1947, £100 in 1957, £120 in 1965, £150 in 1971, £160 in 1974, £180 in 1975, and £200 in 1976.

The fee for umpires in Test matches was increased from £10 to £15 in 1920 and then varied between £18 and £25 until 1947 when they received £40 per Test. In 1956 it was increased to £65, £75 in 1965, £100 in 1971, £125 in 1973, £135 in 1974, £150 in 1975 and £165 in 1976.

Before the formation of the Australian Board of Control the members of touring teams from that continent came over to England on a division of the profits. Players usually had their fares advanced to them by leading clubs and refunded these loans at the end of the tour.

FINISH, EXCITING

It would, of course, be possible to fill several volumes with accounts of games which have provided close and exciting finishes, and the Editor apologises for not being able to include more than a handful here.

The most exciting finish in a Test match in England was probably that in the game with Australia at the Oval in 1882.

England were set to get 85 to win on a sticky wicket. They lost five wickets for 66 and the tension was so great that one spectator collapsed and died.

More wickets went cheaply and England were still 10 short of victory when the last man came in. He got two runs off his first ball but was out to the second ball.

England lost their last five wickets for only 11 runs and the Australians won this game by seven runs.

This was the Test in which Spofforth took 14 wickets for 90 runs—7 for 46 and 7 for 44.

Obviously the most exciting Test match finish was that in the only one of these games which resulted in a Tie—Australia v. West Indies, at Brisbane, in December 1960.

Australia needed six runs to win when the last over was commenced with five minutes left to time. Four extra minutes were allowed for Hall to send down seven balls and end the game. A single was scored off his first ball. Benaud was caught off the second ball and Australia needed only five runs to win with two wickets to fall. There was no score off Hall's third ball, but a bye was run off the next. Another single was added from the fifth ball when Grout was dropped and Australia then needed three runs to win with three balls to come.

Hall's sixth ball was hit by Meckiff and two runs were made before Grout was run-out as they attempted a third.

Last man in was Kline, and with two balls to come Australia still needed one run to win. Kline played the seventh ball away to square-leg but as they attempted to run Meckiff's wicket was hit by an astonishingly fast return from Solomon.

In the first Test of the 1894–95 tour at Sydney, Australia made 586 and England 325 and following on with 437. So Australia needed 177 to win.

They got 113 for two but then rain turned the pitch into a glue-pot overnight and the next day they were all out for 166, Peel taking 6 for 67 and Briggs 3 for 25.

In the fourth Test between England and Australia, at Manchester in July 1902, England were set 124 to win after Australia had made 299 and 86.

England were 4 for 92, 6 for 107, 8 for 109 and 9 for 116. Tate came in needing eight runs but he was bowled by the fourth ball after making only four.

Leaving Test matches another game which provided an exciting finish was that which has come to be known as "Fowler's match". This was Eton v. Harrow match at Lord's in 1910.

Harrow were set 55 to win and victory seemed easy for them, but R. St. L. Fowler took the first six Harrow wickets for only 21 and Harrow were struggling. The atmosphere was terrific as the score went to 29 for 8, 32 for 9, and then came the last man, Hon. H. Alexander (later Field Marshal Alexander). He batted heroically with H. Graham, but when Harrow needed only 10 runs for victory, Alexander touched a ball from A. G. Steel and was caught in the slips.

R. St. L. Fowler had bowled unchanged for more than an hour to see the innings through with a remarkable analysis of 8 for 23.

In 1873 when the M.C.C. and Ground played Surrey Club and Ground, the former had only to make 55 to win. They had scored 204 in their first innings while Surrey had made 105 and 153.

The M.C.C. seemed well on the way to victory when they had scored 26 before the first wicket fell, but then seven more wickets were lost and they still needed 14 to win. They eventually reached 46 for 9, and W. G. Grace and Clayton then went on to make the necessary runs, although not until Clayton had been missed by G. F. Grace.

At Brighton in 1881 the Gentlemen and the Players provided one of the keenest matches ever. In their first innings both sides recorded the same total of 204. The Players then made 112 and when the last man came in for the Gentlemen they needed only five runs to exceed this score.

That last gentleman was A. Appleby, but after he had made three he hit out at a ball from A. Shaw and was caught by the bowler.

So the Players won by one run although, after the match, it was stated that there had been an error in the score and the result should have been a tie.

Although, because of lack of space, we are omitting to mention so many matches which have provided exciting finishes we could not close this section without including the University match of 1870.

As every cricket enthusiast knows this was Cobden's match. No greater scenes of excitement have been witnessed at Lord's than when F. C. Cobden won this match for Cambridge with his historic last over.

Oxford had been set 179 to win and had lost seven wickets when their score was only four short of victory. Who could blame the Cambridge supporters who may have left the ground at this stage but how they must have kicked themselves for missing this.

F. H. Hill took a single off the first ball of Cobden's over —only three runs needed for victory; off the second ball S. E. Butler was caught by A. A. Bourne and the third ball bowled T. H. Belcher off his legs.

Two wickets with two consecutive balls but Oxford needed only three runs to win. One can imagine the feelings of Oxford's last man in, W. A. Stewart.

Down came Cobden's fourth ball, Stewart lifted his bat and was clean bowled. Cambridge had won by two runs.

FIRST, The

The first mention of cricket yet discovered is considered to be that contained in the Royal Household Accounts of King Edward I in 1300. However, it cannot be definitely established that the game named in this account as "creag" bears any positive relationship to cricket.

A more definite reference has been made to "cricket" being played at the Free School of Guildford around about 1550 and this may be the earliest positive mention of the game.

The precise date of this cannot be established as it was contained in a land document dated 1598 in which a certain John Derrick, Q.C., stated that he had known the particular plot of land for fifty years past and "did runne and play there at crickett and other plaies" when he was a scholar at the Free School of Guildford. Derrick was 59 years old at the time this declaration was made.

In 1598 an Italian, Giovanni Florio, produced his dictionary *A Worlde of Wordes,* and in this he defines the word "agrilláre" as "to make a noise as a cricket; to play cricket-a-wicket and be merry". However, this does not give a positive indication that cricket was played in Italy in the 14th century for the words used have been dismissed by an eminent scholar, Andrew Lang, as having no association with the game but being merely rhyming repetition.

The problem with these early references is to establish whether the game mentioned is really the forerunner of the modern game of cricket or whether they refer to one or other of the many similar ball games which were played during the Middle Ages. Because of this, arguments never cease as to the true origin of the game of cricket and early references which are quoted by some cricket historians are deliberately ignored by others.

Strangely enough, although it is generally acknowledged that cricket dates back at least to the 14th century, references to the game in subsequent books of sports are very few until after the end of the 17th century.

In *The Cricket Field* Pycroft draws attention to this absence of cricket from early literature and quotes the following as the only mention of the game in a half dozen 15th and 16th century sporting catalogues examined.

The reference is from Stow's *Survey of London,* dated 1598: "The lower classes divert themselves at foot-ball, wrestling, cudgels, ninepins, shovel-board, cricket, stow-ball, ringing of bells, quoits, pitching the bar, bull and bear-baitings, throwing at cocks, and lying at ale-houses" (!).

R. Cotgrave's *Dictionarie of the French and English Tongues,* 1611, contains another of the earliest references to the game. Here the word "Crosse" is defined as "a Cricket-staffe; or, the crooked staffe wherewith boyes play at Cricket".

The first positive reference to cricket being played outside the United Kingdom was that made by a naval chaplain who informs us that "krickett" was played by men from three of His Majesty Charles II's ships at Aleppo (Syria) May 6, 1676.

The first inter-county match played in England was that between Kent and London, at Lamb's Conduit Fields in 1719.

The first important match of which the full scores are known was that between Kent and All England, on the Artillery Ground, Finsbury, June 18, 1744. A charge of 2/6d. was made to this game which was attended by the Prince of Wales (son of George II), the Duke of Cumberland, and Admiral Edward Vernon. Kent won by one wicket.

FOLLOW-ON, The

The follow-on was first mentioned in the Laws of Cricket in 1835. It was then made compulsory for a side to bat again if they were 100 runs in arrears at the end of the first innings.

In 1854 the margin was reduced to 60 for one-day matches or 80 for longer matches, but 40 years later the limit was increased to 120 runs in three-day matches.

It was not until 1900 that the law was altered to make the follow-on optional. At the same time the margin was increased to 150 runs in a three-day match, 100 for two-day matches, and 75 runs for one-day matches.

The follow-on rule was abolished as an experiment in the County Cricket Championship for two years 1961–62, but when it was reintroduced in 1963 it was also decided to experiment with a follow-on of 200 runs for a match of five days or more. This became Law in 1971.

FOOTBALLER-CRICKETERS

The following men have been capped for England both at cricket and at Association Football:

J. Arnold, former Hampshire county cricket and Oxford City, Southampton, and Fulham, outside-left. Capped at cricket for England v. New Zealand (at Lord's) 1931. Capped at football for England v. Scotland, 1933.

D. C. S. Compton, Middlesex batsman and Arsenal outside-left. Represented England in 78 Tests. Played in 11 war-time soccer internationals for England as well as one "Victory" international v. Scotland. These soccer internationals, however, are not ranked as official.

A. Ducat, Surrey batsman, and Arsenal, Aston Villa and Fulham, wing-half. Cricket v. Australia (at Leeds) 1921. Football for England v. Scotland, Wales, and Ireland, 1919, v. Scotland and Wales, 1920, and v. Ireland, 1921.

R. E. Foster, Worcestershire batsman and Oxford University inside-left. Cricket v. South Africa (3) 1907, Australia (5) 1903–04. Capped at football for England v. Wales, 1900; v. Scotland, Wales, Ireland and Germany, 1901, and v. Wales, 1902. He is the only man to have captained England at both games.

C. B. Fry, Sussex and Hampshire batsman and Corinthians right-back. Twenty-six Tests for England, 1885–1912, and capped at football v. Ireland, 1901.

L. B. Fishlock, Surrey batsman and Dulwich Hamlet, Crystal Palace, Aldershot, Millwall, Southampton, outside-left. Four Tests for England, three v. India and one v. Australia, and capped in England Amateur international v. Wales in 1929.

L. H. Gay, Cambridge University wicket-keeper and Old Brightonians goalkeeper. Capped for England v. Scotland 1893, and v. Scotland and Wales, 1894. Played in one Test against Australia, at Sydney in 1894–95.

W. Gunn, Nottinghamshire batsman and Notts County outside-left. Played in 11 Test matches, all of them against Australia, 1886–99. Capped for England v. Scotland and Wales, 1884.

H. T. W. Hardinge, Kent batsman and Sheffield United inside-forward. One Test v. Australia (at Leeds), 1921, and soccer international for England v. Scotland, 1910.

E. Hendren, Middlesex batsman and outside-right with Manchester City, Coventry City and Brentford. Played for England at cricket in 51 Tests, and at football in "Victory" international v. Wales, 1920—not ranked as a full international.

Hon. A. Lyttelton, Middlesex batsman and Old Etonians forward. Played in four Tests against Australia, 1880–84. Capped for England v. Scotland in 1877.

H. Makepeace, Lancashire batsman and Everton wing-half. Played in four Tests in Australia, 1920–21. Capped for England at soccer v. Scotland, in 1906, 1910 and 1912, v. Wales, 1912.

C. A. Milton, Gloucestershire all-rounder and Arsenal outside-left. Six Test appearances in 1958 and 1959. Capped at soccer v. Austria, 1951.

J. Sharp, Lancashire batsman and Everton outside-right. Played in three Tests against Australia, 1909, and for England at soccer v. Ireland, 1903, v. Scotland, 1905.

W. Watson, Yorkshire and Leicestershire left-handed batsman and former Halifax Town and Bradford City manager, Huddersfield Town and Sunderland wing-forward or wing-half. Twenty-three Tests for England during the 1950s and capped at soccer v. Ireland and Italy, 1950, v. Wales and Yugoslavia, 1951, as well as a "Victory" international v. Wales, 1946.

Apart from those already mentioned an attempt has been made to list below some of the men who have made their mark in both first-class cricket and first-class football. The years given are intended only as an approximate guide to the period during which the player appeared.

Player	Cricket Club	Football Club	Period
Ashton, C. T.	Essex	Corinthians	1920–40
Bailey, P. R.	Northamptonshire	Gillingham	1960s
Balderstone, J. C.	Yorkshire Leicestershire	Huddersfield Town, Carlisle United, Doncaster Rovers	1960–70s
Barnard, H. M.	Hampshire	Portsmouth	1950–60
Bates, D.	Sussex	Brighton	1950–60
Barron, W.	Northamptonshire	Northampton Town	1940–50
Bell, R. V.	Middlesex, Sussex	Chelsea	1950–60
Bennett, D.	Middlesex	Arsenal, Coventry City	1960s
Birley, F. H.	Lancs., Surrey	Oxford Univ.	1870s
Buxton, I. R.	Derbyshire	Derby County, Luton Town, Notts County, Port Vale	1960–70s
Close, D. B.	Yorkshire	Leeds Utd., Arsenal, Bradford City	1950–60
Carter, H. S.	Derbyshire	Sunderland, Derby County, Hull City	1940s
Cook, T. E.	Sussex	Brighton	1920s
Compton, L. H.	Middlesex	Arsenal	1950s
Cox, G.	Sussex	Arsenal, Fulham	1930s
Cross, G.	Leicestershire	Leicester City	1960–70s
Cumbes, J.	Lancashire, Surrey, Worcestershire	Tranmere Rovers, W.B.A., Aston Villa	1960–70s
Daft, H. B.	Nottinghamshire	Notts County	1890s
Devey, J.	Warwickshire	Aston Villa	1890s
Dews, G.	Worcestershire	Plymouth Argyle, Middlesbrough, Walsall	1950–60
Drake, E. J.	Hampshire	Southampton, Arsenal	1930s
Ducat, A. M.	Surrey	Aston Villa	1920s
Dyson, J.	Lancashire	Manchester City, Tranmere Rovers	1950–60s
Etheridge, R. J.	Gloucestershire	Bristol City	1950–60
Foreman, D. J.	Sussex	Brighton	1950–60
Fox, W. V.	Worcestershire	Wolverhampton Wand.	1920s
Gardner, F. C.	Warwickshire	Coventry City, Newport County	1950s
George, W.	Warwickshire	Aston Villa	1900s
Grieves, K.	Lancashire	Bolton Wanderers, Bury	1950–60
Hall, I. W.	Derbyshire	Derby County, Mansfield Town	1960–70s
Harrison, B. R. S.	Hampshire	Crystal Palace	1950–60
Hemsley, E. J. O.	Worcestershire	Shrewsbury Town, Sheffield Utd.	1960–70s
Hill, L. W.	Glamorgan	Newport County, Swansea Town	1960–70s
Hodgson, G.	Lancashire	Liverpool, Aston Villa, Leeds Utd.	1920s
Horton, H.	Hampshire	Blackburn Rovers, Southampton	1950s
Hulme, J. H. A.	Middlesex	Arsenal, Huddersfield Town, Newcastle Utd., England	1930s
Jepson, A.	Nottinghamshire	Port Vale, Stoke City, Lincoln City	1950s
Leary, S. E.	Kent	Charlton Athletic, Queen's Park Rangers	1950–60
Lubbock, E.	Kent	Wanderers, Old Etonians	1870s

Player	Cricket Club	Football Club	Period
Meyer, B. J.	Gloucestershire	Bristol Rovers, Plymouth Argyle, Newport County, Bristol City	1950–60
Mitchell, F. R.	Warwickshire	Birmingham City	1940s
Needham, E.	Derbyshire	Sheffield United	1890–1900
Nepean, C. E. B.	Middlesex	Oxford University	1870s
Nicholls, R. B.	Gloucestershire	Bristol Rovers, Cardiff City, Bristol City	1950–60
O'Linn, S.	Kent and S. Africa	Charlton Athletic	1950–60
Ottoway, C. J.	Kent, Middlesex	Oxford University	1870s
Paravincini P. J. de	Middlesex	Old Etonians	1880s
Poole, C. J.	Nottinghamshire	Gillingham, Mansfield Town	1950–60
Pressdee, J.	Glamorgan	Swansea Town	1950–60
Renny-Tailyour, W. H.	Kent	Royal Engineers	1870s
Rist, F.	Essex	Charlton Athletic, Colchester United	1950s
Russell, S.	Middlesex	Brentford	1950–60
Scott, M. E.	Northamptonshire	Newcastle United, Darlington	1950–60
Smith, D. R.	Gloucestershire	Bristol City, Milwall	1950–60
Standen, J. A.	Worcestershire	Arsenal, Luton, West Ham United, Millwall	1950–60
Stephenson, G. R.	Derbyshire, Hampshire	Derby County, Shrewsbury Town, Rochdale	1960s
Stewart, M. J.	Surrey	Charlton Athletic	1950–60
Storer, H.	Derbyshire	Derby County, Burnley	1920–30
Sugg, F.	Yorkshire, Derbyshire, Lancs.	Sheffield Wed., Derby County, Burnley, etc.	1880s
Suttle, K. G.	Sussex	Chelsea, Brighton	1950–60
Swallow, R.	Derbyshire	Arsenal, Derby County	1960s
Taylor, K.	Yorkshire	Huddersfield Town, Bradford P.A.	1950–60
Tindall, R. A. E.	Surrey	Chelsea, West Ham United, Reading, Portsmouth	1950–60
Titmus, F. J.	Middlesex	Watford	1950–60
Ufton, D. G.	Kent	Charlton Athletic	1950–60
Walden, F.	Northamptonshire	Tottenham Hotspur, Northampton Town	1920s
Walker, W.	Nottinghamshire	South Shields	1920s
Watkins, W.	Glamorgan	Plymouth Argyle, Cardiff City	1950–60
Whitfield, H.	Sussex	Old Etonians	1870–80
Wynard, E. G.	Hampshire	Old Carthusians	1880s

A number of the old-time amateurs are included in the above list who played soccer for such clubs as Old Carthusians, Wanderers and Old Etonians. Some of these were before the days of the Football League. But those mentioned all appeared in an F.A. Cup final and would therefore be rated as first-class footballers. Apart from these Cup Finalists no attempt has been made to include any *amateur* footballers who have not appeared regularly in the Football League or in a full international.

FOURTH INNINGS

The record fourth innings total is 654 for 5 wickets by England against South Africa at Durban in the "timeless" Test of the 1938–39 tour.

When that score had been reached on the tenth day the game had to be abandoned because the England team had to catch a boat home. They then needed only 42 more runs to win.

The record fourth innings total in England is 507 for 7 by Cambridge University v. M.C.C. at Lords, 1896.

FREEMAN, Alfred Percy (1888-1965)

Only one man (W. Rhodes) has taken more wickets in first-class cricket than A. P. ("Tich") Freeman, who played for Kent from 1914 until 1936. During that lengthy career he captured 3,776 wickets at an astonishing average of 18.42 runs apiece.

Without doubt A. P. Freeman was one of the three best slow bowlers in the history of the County Championships, but, oddly enough, with the possible exception of the 1928 series against the West Indies, he seldom showed the same form in Test cricket.

Nevertheless, A. P. Freeman has many distinguished records outside of the Tests. He is the only bowler to capture all ten wickets in an innings on three separate occasions; he bagged over 100 wickets in a season no less than 17 times; holds the record for a single season with 304 wickets (av. 18.05) in 1928, and also takes second place with his 298 wickets (av. 15.26) in 1933. He performed the "hat-trick" on three occasions.

One of Freeman's finest innings was his 9 for 11 against Sussex at Hove in 1922. He followed this in the second innings with 8 for 56.

That wasn't the only time this little man with the big heart took 17 wickets in a match; 10 years later, at Folkestone, he took 8 for 31 and 9 for 61 against Warwickshire.

Most of Freeman's balls were leg-breaks, and it is safe to say that very few batsmen mastered him on English wickets.

FRY, Charles Burgess (1872-1956)

Educated at Repton and Oxford University, C. B. Fry was one of the finest all-round sportsmen this country has ever known.

Not only was he a great cricketer, but he got his soccer "Blue", played that game for England and won an F.A. Cup finalist's medal with Southampton. He was also a fine Rugby player for Blackheath and the Barbarians and only an injury prevented him from gaining his "Blue" at this sport. He did, however, get a third "Blue" and this was for athletics in which he created a record for the long-jump which was not beaten for 21 years.

After playing for Surrey from 1891 to 1893 he went on to earn cricketing fame with Sussex, playing for them from 1894 to 1908, captaining them during the last four seasons. In 1908 he took up his life's work on the training ship *Mercury* in Hampshire but from 1909 to 1921 he made first-class appearances for that county in about five seasons only.

Apart from his prowess as a sportsman he was a brilliant scholar, a journalist, and a politician who took a great interest in the League of Nations, but failed to gain election to the House of Commons. He was even suggested as the new King of Albania but this was one position he declined to accept.

The greater part of his life was devoted to the training of seamen and he did not retire from this occupation until the age of 78, just six years before he died.

C. B. Fry originally came out as a bowler, but subsequently became one of England's finest batsmen. He had an upstanding orthodox style, sometimes described as rather stiff, but he was renowned for his driving and his strong back play.

He played in 26 Tests (captain in 9) and would have played in many more if he had not refused invitations to tour Australia. His only Test tour abroad was to South Africa in 1895–96.

He scored a double-century 16 times during his first-class career and got two separate hundreds in a match on five occasions. In his first season, 1901, he scored six centuries in succession and ended the season with an aggregate of 3,147 runs (av. 78.67).

His highest score was 258* for Hampshire v. Gloucestershire at Southampton in 1911.

G

GAMBLING

See under BETTING.

GATE RECEIPTS

World record gate receipts for a cricket match were taken at Melbourne in December 1974 for the Australia v. England Test—£140,000.

The record for a match in England is £119,692 for England v. Australia, at Lord's, 1975.

GENTLEMEN v. PLAYERS

The first match between the Gentlemen and the Players took place on the original Lord's ground, July 7, 1806. The Gentlemen (with W. Beldham and W. Lambert) won by an innings and 14 runs.

They also won the second of these matches (by 82 runs) which was played only a fortnight later on the same ground, but then, for some reason or another, there was no further Gentlemen v. Players match until 1819 when the Players won by six wickets.

It was soon found that the Gentlemen were no match for the Players except when they were given odds and usually they played with more men on their side than the Players. In 1832 and again in 1837 it was even decided to handicap the Players by having them defend larger wickets, but the Players still won on both of these occasions.

A shortage of bowlers was the Gentlemen's chief weakness and as the Players won game after game and the Gentlemen often found it difficult to muster a full side interest sank to its lowest ebb in the 1840s. J. H. Dark, the proprietor of Lord's was one enthusiast who did most to keep this series going.

Following a surprise victory by the Gentlemen in 1853 they did not win a single game until 1865. Then, in the second of these games to be played in that year and the second in which W. G. Grace appeared, the Gentlemen won by eight wickets. There is no doubt that the advent of the great W. G. did much to increase enthusiasm for the match both among the participants and the public.

The Gentlemen v. Players match later lost some of its appeal to the general public, owing to the ever increasing number of other games, while of course, the greatest honour a 20th century cricketer may receive is to appear in a Test match. But, in the days before Tests the greatest honour was to be called upon to play for either the Gentlemen or the Players in these annual games.

W. G. Grace was not the first man to score a century in this match (T. Beagley of Hampshire did that for the Players in the Coronation Match of 1821) but the Doctor reached a century in 15 innings and his highest score was 217, at Brighton in 1871. He also figured in the Gentlemen's record first wicket stand of 203 with A. J. Webbe, at Lord's, in 1875, as well as a record second wicket stand of 240 with G. F. Grace, at Brighton in 1871.

W.G.'s achievements may have been surpassed in other fields but he still reigns supreme in the history of the game between Gentlemen and Players.

It is worth noting that W.G. celebrated his 58th birthday on July 18, 1906, by scoring 74 in his last appearance for the Gentlemen. Altogether he scored 6,008 runs and took 271 wickets in these games, both totals being unbeaten.

At the passing of W. G. the Players re-asserted their superiority and coming more up to date we find that after World War II the Gentlemen were only able to win one of the matches.

A Gentlemen v. Players match was first played at the Oval in July 1857, and every year, with the exception of the years of World War I and 1930 and 1933, until 1934. Then, when it had become increasingly difficult to find representative sides both for this and for the games at Lord's, the Oval game was abandoned.

Gentlemen v. Players games also took place at Prince's, Hastings, Scarborough, Folkestone and Brighton.

The highest score ever made by each side in this match was 578 by the Gentlemen in 1904, at the Oval, and 651 for 7 declared by the Players, also at the Oval, in 1934.

The highest individual innings: Gentlemen—232* by C. B. Fry, at Lord's, 1903; Players—266* by J. B. Hobbs, at Scarborough, 1925.

The following men appeared for both sides:

R. Daft, E. J. Driver, W. J. Edrich, J. H. Parsons and W. R. Hammond.

This fixture was abandoned in 1963 following the abolition of amateur status in cricket.

GIBBS, Lancelot Richard (1934–)

During the 1960s there was no finer off-spinner in the world than this West Indian who made his Test debut against Pakistan in place of Ramadhin in 1957 but did not really establish himself until the Australian tour of 1960–61. There he performed the hat-trick in the Adelaide Test, and completed the series with 19 wickets (av. 20.78).

By 1970 he had captured more Test wickets than any other West Indian and it was thought that he was on the decline, but when he returned to the side for the visit of the Australians in 1972–73 he again showed himself to be the most effective off-spinner around, taking 26 wickets (av. 26.8).

One of his most devastating spells was against India at Bridgetown in 1961–62, when, in 15.3 overs after the interval on the last day, he took 8 for 6 against a team determined to hold out for a draw. At Old Trafford in 1963 he captured 11 England wickets for 157 to help his side gain their first Test win on this ground.

It was in the 6th Test at Melbourne in 1976 that this player surpassed Fred Trueman's record bag of Test wickets and took his total to 309 (av. 29.09) in 79 matches. He also took another three wickets for the Rest of the World side.

GILLETTE CUP

For many years the idea of a Knock-out Competition as a crowd puller for county cricket was frowned upon, but with attendances on the decline the suggestion was finally accepted by the Advisory County Cricket Committee in December 1961.

Subsequently the Committee accepted a grant from Gillette as sponsors of the new competition and it was inaugurated in 1963 with one innings matches limited to 65 overs (since reduced to 60). No bowler is allowed more than 12 overs in an innings. In the Cup Final there is a reduction to 50 overs per innings with bowlers limited to 10 overs each.

Entries are restricted to the 17 first-class counties and the top five Minor counties (excluding 2nd XI teams).

Winners: 1963 and 1964—Sussex; 1965—Yorkshire; 1966—Warwickshire; 1967—Kent; 1968—Warwickshire; 1969—Yorkshire; 1970 and 1971 and 1972—Lancashire; 1973—Gloucestershire; 1974—Kent; 1975—Lancashire; 1976—Northamptonshire.

Highest innings score: 371 for 4 off 60 overs, Hampshire v. Glamorgan, at Southampton, 1975. Highest individual score: 177 by C. G. Greenidge for Hampshire v. Glamorgan at Southampton, 1975.

There are also Gillette Cup competitions in Australia, South Africa and the West Indies.

GIFFEN, George (1859–1927)

This Australian who was born at Adelaide became one of the finest all-rounders of his day. He was a medium pace bowler of remarkable endurance and a stylish batsman.

Giffen completed the "double" in three of his five tours of England and in his finest all-round display for S. Australia (v. Victoria, Adelaide, 1891–92) he scored 271 and also captured 16 wickets for 166.

He took all 10 wickets for 66 runs in one innings for Australian XI v. The Rest, in 1883–84 and in one match against Victoria, at Adelaide, in 1885–86 he took 17 wickets.

His finest all-round performance in his 31 Test appearances (all against England) was probably that in the first Sydney Test of 1894–95. Then he scored 161 and 41 and took 4 for 75 and 4 for 164. In that Test rubber he not only scored 475 runs (av. 52.77) but also captured 34 wickets (av. 24.11).

Giffen, who captained Australia in four

Tests, scored 1,238 Test match runs (av. 23.35) and took 103 wickets (av. 27.09).

GLAMORGAN C.C.C.

Founded: 1888, although an older club had been in existence for more than 10 years from about 1864. Admitted to the County Championship in 1921. Secretary: W. Wooller, 6 High Street, Cardiff CF1 1YU. Highest score for: 587 for 8 declared v. Derbyshire, at Cardiff, 1951. Highest score against: 653 for 6 declared by Gloucestershire, at Bristol, 1928. Highest individual score for: 287* by E. Davies v. Gloucestershire, at Newport, 1939. Highest individual score against: 302* by W. R. Hammond of Gloucestershire, at Bristol, 1934, and 302 by the same player at Newport, 1939. Lowest score for: 22 v. Lancashire, at Liverpool, 1924. (In Minor Counties Championship, 20 v. Wiltshire, at Chippenham, 1905). Lowest score against: 33 by Leicestershire, at Ebbw Vale, 1965. In Minor Counties Championship, 32 by Carmarthenshire, 1910). Colours: Blue and gold. Badge: A daffodil. Honours: Minor Counties Champions 1900 (tied with Durham and Northamptonshire), County Champions 1948, 1969.

GLOUCESTERSHIRE C.C.C.

Founded: Date not established although a county side appeared as early as 1839; 1871 is the year generally given for the formation of the club now in existence. Secretary: A. S. Brown, County Ground, Bristol BS7 9EJ. Highest score for: 653 for 6 declared v. Glamorgan, at Bristol, 1928. It is also worth noting that in 1927, against Essex, at Bristol, Gloucester forced a draw with a score of 405 for 2 before end of play. Highest score against: 774 for 7 declared by the Australians, at Bristol, 1948. In County games: 607 by Nottinghamshire, Bristol, 1899, and 607 for 6 declared by Kent, Cheltenham, 1910. Highest individual score for: 318* by W. G. Grace v. Yorkshire, Cheltenham, August 17, 1876. Highest individual score against: 296 by A. O. Jones of Nottinghamshire, Nottingham, 1903. Lowest score for: 17 v. the Australians, Cheltenham, August 1896; In County match: 22 v. Somerset, Bristol, 1920. Lowest score against: 12 by Northamptonshire, Gloucester, 1907 (slow bowler G. Dennett took 8 for 9 in one innings, and 15 for 21 in the match). Colours: Blue, gold, brown, sky-blue, green and red. Badge: City and County of Bristol's coat of arms. Honours: County Champions: 1873 (generally bracketed with Nottinghamshire), 1874, 1876, 1877. Gillette Cup: Winners 1973.

GLOVES

There is some dispute as to the inventor of protective batting gloves. There may have been earlier instances of these gloves being worn by batsmen but it is now generally accepted that they were first worn by N. Wanostrocht (Felix) in about 1835. These were kid gloves with small pieces of rubber glued on them.

Soon afterwards, in the early 1840s we note that tubular india-rubber batting gloves were introduced at Lord's by Robert Dark.

As regards wicket-keepers' gloves, these were introduced by the famous cricket gear manufacturers, Duke & Son, in 1848, but in those early days they did not afford the same protection and comfort as those worn today.

In his book *A Few Short Runs*, Lord Hawke tells us that in his early days (this would be about 1875–80) they "were of yellow, and subsequently brown leather, which used to get so hard that they had to be wetted to make them really useful".

GODDARD, John Douglas Claude (1919–)

John D. C. Goddard of Barbados was an all-rounder of outstanding ability. He bowled right-arm medium pace and batted left-handed, being renowned for his stubborn defence but also capable of hitting out when the opportunity arose. In addition he was also a brilliant fielder.

A successful captain, he led the West Indies in England in 1950 and 1957 and in all he appeared as the West Indies skipper in 22 Tests.

He made his debut in first-class cricket when he was only 16. His highest score was 218* v. Trinidad at Barbados in 1943–44. This was the game in which he figured in a fourth wicket stand of 502 with F. M. Worrell.

In 1947–48 he took 5 for 31 v. England at Georgetown, and at the Oval, in 1950, he took 4 England wickets for 25 in the first innings.

GODDARD, Trevor Leslie
(1931–   )

This all-rounder was an extremely accurate left-arm medium pace bowler, a fine fielder, and a steady batsman who opened the innings for South Africa in nearly all of his 41 Tests.

He proved his dependability as a batsman at Cape Town in the second Test against Australia in 1957–58. South Africa were skittled out for 99 but Goddard batted through the innings to make 56*.

Goddard made his debut in Test cricket when he toured England in 1955. In the first innings of the final Test of that series he took 5 wickets for 31 and completed the rubber with a bag of 25 wickets (av. 21.12).

Goddard first appeared for Natal 1952–53. His highest score was 222 for N. E. Transvaal v. Western Province 1966–67. In the 1959–60 season v. Border, at East London, he performed the "hat-trick" and took 6 for 3.

He captained South Africa in 13 Tests.

GOMEZ, Gerald Ethridge
(1919–   )

Another remarkable West Indian all-rounder, G. E. Gomez of Trinidad was a high-scoring batsman, a defensive bowler of medium pace, and an excellent field.

His deadly accuracy as a bowler made him one of the most difficult men to play and a high proportion of his overs in Test cricket were maidens.

One of his best feats with the ball was his 9 for 24 in one innings against South Zone at Madras in 1948–49. At Sydney in 1951–52 when bowling unchanged throughout the first innings of the match he took 7 Australian wickets for 55, and it was in this tour that he took 30 wickets (av. 19.76).

GRACE, Dr. William Gilbert
(1848–1915)

Nothing can be written in praise of W. G. which has not already appeared in print. The Grand Old Man of English Cricket did more to popularise this game than any other player and was the outstanding personality of his day or since.

Everyone knows that he was a man of splendid physique with a large beard. He had remarkable stamina.

Born at Downend, Bristol, in 1848, he was the fourth of five brothers and was only nine when he first appeared for West Gloucestershire C.C. His earliest big score was 51 for that club against Clifton in 1860 at the age of 11. He was 15 when he first played against the famous All England XI, and, in the following year, made his debut at the Oval and at Lord's.

Four men have since scored more runs in first-class cricket but when one considers the type of wickets he played on for the greater part of his career then his first-class aggregate of 54.896 (av. 39.55) is still the most remarkable figure of all. Add to this his aggregate of 2,876 wickets taken at an average cost of 17.92 and you have something of the measure of the greatness of Dr. W. G. Grace. It should also be noted that he never bagged a "pair" throughout his entire career.

No man was ever a better fielder to his own bowling. Generally he fielded at point, but when bowling he would follow-up and move over to act as an extra mid-off. He bowled slow-medium leg breaks. In 1877 he took 17 wickets for 89 for Gloucestershire v. Sheffield.

His highest score in a first-class match was 344 for the M.C.C. v. Kent at Canterbury, in 1876. This stood as a record for 19 years. He also scored a triple-century (318*) for Gloucestershire v. Yorkshire at Cheltenham in 1876, and (301) v. Sussex at Bristol in 1896. Apart from these scores he reached a double-century on 10 other occasions, and scored a century in each innings of three matches. In all he scored 126 separate centuries.

Grace's most prolific scoring season was 1871. Then he scored 2,739 runs (av. 78.25). That season he also took 78 wickets (av. 16.64). His best bowling season was 1875—191 wickets (av. 12.92).

This brilliant cricketer was captain of Gloucestershire from 1871 to 1898 and captained England in 13 Tests, all against Australia. In these Tests he was only on the losing side three times.

W. G. Grace was 60 years of age when, in 1908, he played his last innings in first-class cricket.

GRAVENEY, Thomas William
(1927–   )

In a first-class career extending over 23 seasons this graceful batsman delighted purists all over the world with his elegant stroke-play.

His career total of 47,793 runs (av.

44.91) included 122 centuries. His highest score was obtained in Test cricket—258 v. West Indies at Trent Bridge in 1957, a series in which he averaged 118.00 over five innings, are one out. Graveney's best season was 1956 when he hit 2,397 runs (av. 49.93).

Amazingly this great batsman was out of favour with the Test selectors after the 1962–63 tour down under and he was stuck on a total of 55 Test appearances until being recalled against against the West Indies in 1966. Then he showed the selectors the error of their ways by topping England's batting averages yet again and went on to take his total of Tests to 79, his last at the age of 42, against the West Indies at Old Trafford in 1969 when he scored 75.

Graveney, made his debut for Gloucestershire in 1948, was appointed County captain in 1959, but when he was succeeded in the captaincy of C. T. M. Pugh in 1961 he left the county.

After being lost to Championship cricket for a year while qualifying for Worcestershire Graveney came back as good as ever and not only helped his new county to win the Championship for the first time in their history in 1964 but repeating the performance the following season.

Graveney subsequently joined Queensland and was that state's coach for more than two years.

GREGORY, Jack Morrison (1895–1973)

A member of one of Australia's most famous cricketing families, J. M. Gregory was a great all-rounder.

Standing well over six feet tall he was a powerful left-handed batsman, a frightening fast bowler, and a very fine slip fielder. He made six catches in the final Australia—England Test at Sydney in 1920–21.

J. M. Gregory first made his mark in the A.I.F. team of 1919 and was chosen for all five Tests against the England touring team in the following season.

Scoring 1,146 runs (av. 36.96) in 24 Test appearances he also captured 85 wickets at an average of 31.15 apiece.

His most remarkable displays as an all-rounder were those in his first series against England in 1920–21. In the second Test he scored 100 in Australia's only innings and took 7 for 69 and 1 for 32. In the third Test he scored 10 and 78* and

took 2 for 108 and 3 for 50. In the fourth Test he followed with 77 and 76* and 1 for 61 and 0 for 31 (bowling only 14 overs). In the final Test he scored 93 in his one innings and in all took 3 for 79.

GREGORY, Sydney Edward (1870–1929)

Australia never produced a more copybook stylist than Sydney Gregory. Although on the short side he was the master of every stroke and used his feet so well that he could hook with the best.

He made 58 Test appearances, his first against England in 1891–92 and his last against England in the Triangular Tournament of 1912. In the 1912 series he captained his country in all six Tests.

S. E. Gregory probably rates with the best half-dozen cover-points ever seen in cricket.

His best score in Test cricket was 201 v. England at Sydney in 1894–95. In 1909 he helped create a record Australian first-wicket partnership for Tests against England, (not beaten until 1964) when he and W. Bardsley put on 180 in 135 minutes at the Oval.

GRIFFITH, Charles Christopher (1938–   )

This player's performance in England in 1963 marked him down as one of the outstanding fast bowlers in the history of Test cricket, for during that triumphant West Indian tour he took 32 Test wickets at an average of 16.20 and also topped the season's averages with a bag of 119 wickets at a cost of only 12.83 runs apiece.

Height and build helped Griffith establish himself as a batsman's terror for he stands 6ft. 4in. and weighs around 15 stone and this allied to his speed made him a difficult bowler to play. His action was questioned on a number of occasions, but the fact is that he was only twice "no-balled" for throwing.

In 28 Tests he took 94 wickets for an average of 28.54.

GRIMMETT, Clarence Victor (1891–   )

Born in New Zealand, Grimmett eventually played for Victoria and South Australia and was Australia's finest leg-break bowler between the two wars.

Slow with a round-arm action his Test debut at Sydney in the final game of the

1924–25 series was nothing less than sensational. In England's first innings he took 5 for 45 and followed this with 6 for 37. This made him Australia's top bowler for the series with an average of 7.45.

In England his first Test appearance was awaited with some apprehension and his reputation as the terror of England's batsmen was further enhanced when he made his Test match debut at Leeds in July 1926. In this game he dismissed 5 for 88 and 2 for 59. At the end of that series he was again Australia's top bowler with 13 wickets at an average of 31.84.

In all his 37 Test appearances Grimmett, renowned for his accuracy, took 216 wickets (av. 24.21). Only R. R. Lindwall, G. D. McKenzie and R. Benaud, exceeded these figures in Test cricket for Australia.

GUNN, George (1879–1958)

A member of the illustrious Nottinghamshire cricketing family George Gunn Senior was one of the cleverest batsmen that county has ever produced. When he had his eye in there was no shifting him for he was the master of any type of bowling, and but for his liking for non scoring strokes which always looked so easy but failed to please the crowds he would probably have played in many more than 15 Tests during a first-class career which extended from 1902–1932.

There was one stubborn innings at Nottingham in 1929 when he batted for 5 hours 20 minutes to make 58. But he was a man of moods and when it suited him he could score as fast as anyone.

At Trent Bridge, in 1913, he took six hours to score 132 in Nottinghamshire's first innings against Yorkshire, but then in the second he hit 109 in 85 minutes and was still at the wicket when rain stopped play.

His highest score was 200 for Nottinghamshire v. Derbyshire at Nottingham in 1923 and he celebrated his 50th birthday by scoring 164* for Notts v. Worcestershire in 1929.

When making his Test debut at Sydney in 1907, he scored 119, but after appearing in 10 more Test during the next five years, there was a gap of more than 17 years before he was again called upon to represent England in four Tests in the West Indies in 1929–30.

His son continued to play for Nottinghamshire after George senior's retirement in 1932, but in 1931 they had the distinction of playing together in the same match (v. Warwickshire) and both scoring centuries in the same innings—a unique record.

GUPTE, Subhas Pandhrinath (1929–   )

India's finest leg break and googly bowler. Gupte was born in Bombay and made his first-class debut in 1948–49.

The first of his Test appearances was in the 1951–52 season but he missed the England tour the following summer. However, he came over and joined Rishton in the Lancashire League in 1954 and played for them each season until 1958. Then had two seasons with Heywood before joining Lancaster in 1960.

In 1954–55 he became the first Indian to take 10 wickets in an innings—10 for 78 for Bombay v. Pakistan Services and Bahawalpur XI.

His best effort in Test cricket was his 9 for 102 in the first innings of the Kanpur Test against the West Indies in December 1958. In all Tests for India he captured 149 wickets (av. 29.54).

GUYANA

See under WEST INDIES.

H

HALL, Wesley Winfield (1937–)

One of the fastest bowlers of the post-war era. Disappointed on his his first tour of England in 1957 but subsequently improved remarkably and got his 100th Test wicket in only his 20th game.

In the West Indians' tour of India and Pakistan in 1958–59 he took 46 wickets (av. 15.08) in eight Tests and was the first bowler to perform the "hat-trick" for the West Indies in a Test match.

Further enhanced his reputation in the 1959–60 series against England. In the first innings at Kingston he took 7 for 69.

After distinguishing himself on tour in Australia in 1960–61 he returned there to establish himself as a great favourite with Queensland. Also delighted Lancashire League fans with some great bowling for Accrington.

One of his most remarkable feats of fast bowling was at Lord's in 1963 when he bowled unchanged for 40 overs, never slackening his pace, and took 4 for 93.

In 48 Tests he took 192 wickets (av. 26.38).

HAMBLEDON C.C.

Hambledon is generally referred to as the "Cradle of Cricket" and although this may not be strictly accurate there is no doubt that the men of Hambledon were the first to develop the game along lines approaching the art and class of the more modern cricket.

The Hambledon club was founded in about 1750. The date has never been definitely established and it is possible that there was a Hambledon club before then, but 1750 is the year now generally accepted.

Two of the club's leading lights right from the start were the Rev. Charles Powlett and Richard Nyren. The latter kept the Bat and Ball Inn which overlooked their original ground on Broad-halfpenny Down about two miles from Hambledon. He was also secretary of the club during its best years.

The club drew most of its members from the farming community of the area and, in particular, from around Fareham. They were unbeaten until 1769, and in 1772 they scored a resounding victory over Twenty-two of England. Indeed, so skilled did these men of Hambledon become in the art of cricket that they were just about the only club which could take on the Rest of England and beat them.

No cricket lover should fail to read about the heroes of Hambledon as originally set down by John Nyren in his *Young Cricketer's Tutor* and *The Cricketers of my Time.* These delightful accounts of this famous club have since been quoted in many more recent publications. One of them, *The Hambledon Men* by E. V. Lucas is particularly recommended.

The Hambledon Club probably reached its zenith in 1777 for it was in June of that year on The Vine, at Sevenoaks, that they defeated the Rest of England by an innings and 168 runs.

In about 1780 the club moved its home ground to a spot on Windmill Down to the west of the village.

As more and more of the important matches were being played nearer to London so the Hambledon club faded from the scene. Several of their best men were enticed away by offers of good pay, and the founding of the M.C.C. in 1787 really sealed the fate of the old club. One of the men who helped form the M.C.C., the eighth Earl of Winchelsea, was President of the Hambledon Club at that time.

Hambledon played their last game, against Twenty-two of Middlesex at Lord's, in 1791.

The Rev. John Mitford paid this tribute to the men of Hambledon:

"Great and illustrious eleven! fare ye well! in these fleeting pages at least, your

name shall be enrolled. What would life
be, deprived of the recollection of you?
Troy has fallen, and Thebes is a ruin. The
pride of Athens is decayed and Rome is
crumbling to the dust. The philosophy of
Bacon is wearing out, and the Victories of
Marlborough have been overshadowed by
greater laurels. All is vanity but Cricket;
all is sinking into oblivion but you.
Greatest of all elevens, fare ye well!"

In 1908 a stone monument was erected
on Broadhalfpenny Down in memory of
the original Hambledon C.C.

HAMMOND, Walter Reginald (1903–1965)

One of England's greatest cricketers, W.
R. Hammond, who scored more runs in
Test matches than any other batsman
apart from M. C. Cowdrey and G. S.
Sobers, is numbered among the 30 or so
bowlers who have taken most Test wickets
for England; and holds the record for the
highest number of catches in a single
match and in a single season.

Powerfully built, Hammond made his
debut in 1920 and became one of the most
immaculate and attractive batsmen in the
world, renowned for his off-side play. In
addition he was a clever medium-pace
bowler and a slip-fielder second to none.

On his first tour of Australia in
1928–29 he scored 905 runs in five
successive Test innings and finished the
series with an average of 113.12. No other
English batsman has matched this in
Australia. At Sydney he enjoyed an
innings of 251.

Three times in his career Hammond
topped the 3,000 run mark in a single
season—1933, 1937 and 1938. He got his
highest score of 336* against New
Zealand at Auckland in 1932–33. His best
in England was on his home ground at
Gloucester, 317 against Notts. in 1936.

In all, Hammond scored 167 separate
centuries and created a world record by
scoring two separate hundreds in a single
match on seven occasions.

World War II prevented Hammond
from creating an aggregate record, but he
notched up 50,493 runs and retired with
an average of 56.10.

Born at Dover (Kent objected to his
playing for Gloucestershire when he first
appeared), Hammond played as a professional until 1937 when he created quite a
stir by retiring from the paid ranks and
continuing as an amateur. In the following
year he was chosen to captain England, a

position he held in 20 Test matches. He
was also Captain of Gloucestershire from
1939 to 1946.

HAMPSHIRE C.C.

Founded 1863. Became first-class 1895.
Secretary: E. D. R. Eagar, County
Ground, Southampton SO9 2TY. Highest
score for: 672 for 7 declared v. Somerset,
at Taunton, July 20–22, 1899. Highest
score against: 742 by Surrey, at the Oval,
May 6–8, 1909. Highest individual score:
316 by R. H. Moore v. Warwickshire, at
Bournemouth, 1937. Other matches, 323*
by Sir F. E. Lacey, v. Norfolk at
Southampton, May 30, 1887. Highest
individual score against: 302* by P.
Holmes, Yorkshire, at Portsmouth, 1920.
Lowest score for: 15 v. Warwickshire, at
Edgbaston, June 1922 (Hants. won by 155
runs). Lowest score against: 23 by York-
shire, at Middlesbrough, May 20, 1965.
Other matches: 17 by Gentlemen of
Wiltshire, 1835. Colours: Blue, gold and
white. Badge: Tudor rose and crown.
Honours: County Champions: 1961, 1973.
John Player League: Champions, 1975.

HANDLED BALL

When A. Rees (Glamorgan) was given out
"Handled Ball" v. Middlesex, at Lord's,
August 20, 1965, it was the first time this
decision had been given in first-class
cricket in England since July 1907 when
A. D. Nourse, sen. (South Africans)
suffered a similar fate against Sussex, at
Hove.

Before 1899 a batsman was given out if
he handled a ball which had become
lodged in his clothing, but in that year a
new law was introduced declaring any
such ball "dead", and so allowing a
batsman to remove it without being given
out.

HANIF MOHAMMAD (1934–   )

One of five cricketing brothers, Hanif
developed so quickly that he had
established himself as an opening batsman
of the highest class before reaching his
nineteenth birthday.

On his first tour abroad, that to India in
1952 when he was still only 17, he made
121and 109* in the opening match against
North Zone, and a brilliant 203* in the
sixth match v. Bombay.

No player has ever shown better ability to sustain concentration over long spells at the wicket, and one of the best remembered of many innings demonstrating his determination and endurance was his 187* in 9 hours 2 minutes of the Lord's Test of 1967.

Batting for Pakistan against the West Indies at Barbados in 1957–58 he was at the wicket for 16 hours 10 minutes (the longest innings on record) to score 337, and in 1958–59, this player who had been nicknamed "Little Tich" created another world record by scoring 499 for Karachi v. Bahawalpur at Karachi.

Hanif Mohammad captained Pakistan in 11 of his 55 Tests and his total of 3,915 runs (av. 43.98) in these matches places him far ahead of any other Pakistani batsman. He scored two separate hundreds (111 and 104) against England at Dacca in 1961–62, and his total of 12 Test centuries is far higher than any of his countrymen.

HARDSTAFF, Joseph jnr. (1911–   )

This delightful batsman pleased the crowds in many parts of the world with his flashing strokes. He made his debut with Nottinghamshire in 1930 and in time became recognised as their fastest scoring batsman.

Hardstaff, son of a former England and Nottinghamshire player, made his first appearance in Test cricket against South Africa in 1935 and played in 23 of these matches.

1937 was his best season for then he won the Lawrence Trophy for the fastest hundred of the season—scored in 51 minutes for Nottinghamshire against Kent at Canterbury, got the highest score of his career, 266 v. Leicestershire at Leicester, and also scored 243 against Middlesex and 214* against Somerset, finishing the season with an aggregate of 2,540 runs. He retired in 1955 having scored 31,847 runs (av. 44.35).

HARRIS, David (1758–1803)

A potter from Odiham, David Harris became one of Hambledon's greatest bowlers and one who did most to influence the development of the game.

He was described as a model bowler, extremely graceful, very accurate, and a really fine upstanding character who was loved by all.

Nyren informed us that Harris's mode of delivering the ball "was very singular. He would bring it from under his arm by a twist, and nearly as high as his armpit, and with his action push it, as it were from him. How it was that the balls acquired the velocity they did by this mode of delivery, I never could comprehend. His balls were very little beholden to the ground; it was but a touch and up again; and woe be to the man who did not get in to block them, for they had such a peculiar curl they would grind his fingers against the bat".

Harris was a glutton for bowling and no man ever practised harder. In later years he was severely handicapped by the gout, but still he persevered, hobbling to the game on his crutches and then resting in an armchair on the field between spells of bowling.

He was forced to give up the game in 1798 and when he died five years later, he was only about 45.

HARRIS, Lord (1851–1932)

Described as a "true English Gentleman", the 4th Lord Harris was one of the most highly respected personalities of the game. He began his cricket career at Eton and Oxford University, and subsequently played for Kent, captaining them from 1875 to 1889, which was the last season in which he played regularly.

Unfortunately for the game his political career interrupted his cricket. In 1885 he became Under-Secretary for India, and later Governor of Bombay, a post he occupied until the expiration of the office in 1895. While in India, he was able to do a lot to influence the progress of the game in that country.

Kent owed much to Lord Harris for he was not only a gifted player for them, but captain, secretary, chairman and president. He was also president of the M.C.C. in 1895.

Lord Harris appeared in four Tests (they were not as numerous in his day) and he captained England on each occasion.

It was, however, as one of the leaders of the game that Lord Harris made his greatest contribution. Few men have done more for the welfare of cricket and cricketers. He was a leading personality on the Committee at Lord's for many years from 1875 and was chiefly responsible for the establishment of the ill-fated County Cricket Council in 1887.

A stylish batsman and an excellent fielder, Lord Harris made his highest score, 176, against Sussex in 1882.

HARROW SCHOOL
See under PUBLIC SCHOOL CRICKET.

HARVEY, Robert Neil
(1928-   )
Neil Harvey was not yet 20 years of age when he made his mark in top class cricket with an innings of 153 for Australia against India at Melbourne in 1948 and earned himself a place in his country's team which toured England the following summer.

Over here he was not brought in until the fourth Test at Leeds, but he promptly showed himself to be one of the finest left-handed batsmen in the world with a great display while scoring 112.

In the tour Harvey totalled 1,129 runs (av. 53.76) and when he came again in 1953 he scored 2,040 (av. 65.80) including an innings of 202* v. Leicestershire. In 1956 however, his aggregate dropped to 976 (av. 31.48) although he did register one of his highest scores here, 225 v. M.C.C. at Lord's.

Neil Harvey, who comes from a cricketing family and is one of five brothers, made a total of 79 Test appearances. Only Sir Donald Bradman himself has scored more runs for Australia that this batsman with the twinkling footwork whose aggregate was 6,149 (av. 48.41).

Outside of Australia it is the South Africans who have reason to remember this aggressive batsman the best. There, in 1949–50, he averaged 76.30 scoring 1,526 runs. In the 1952–53 tour of the Union he created a record for an Australian in South Africa by scoring 834 runs in the Tests alone with an average of 92.66.

Harvey's highest score was 231* for New South Wales v. South Australia, at Sydney in 1962–63.

HASSET, Arthur Lindsay
(1913-   )
This diminutive Australian from Victoria succeeded Sir Donald Bradman as his country's captain in 1949.

As a batsman he could either annoy the crowd with his stubborn defensive play or provide a display of sheer dynamite. One of his most blistering innings was his 94 on a rain-sodden pitch at Sheffield against Yorkshire during his first English tour in 1938. Generally, however, he was known to be rather cautious.

Hassett made his debut in 1932–33 and played his first Test matches in England in 1938. When he retired in 1953 he had appeared in 43 Tests, scoring 3,073 runs (av. 46.56). His highest Test innings was his 198* v. India, at Adelaide, in 1947–48. In 1950–51 he scored 232 for Victoria against the M.C.C.

HAT-TRICK
The bowlers' feat of taking three wickets with three consecutive balls became known as a "hat-trick" when, in about 1858, it was the practice in some clubs to present the successful bowler with a new hat.

However, the idea may have originated much earlier for it is a fact that David Harris, the famous bowler of the Hambledon era, was once presented with a gold-laced hat for outstanding bowling, although this was not for taking three wickets with three balls.

The record number of hat-tricks by any one bowler in first-class cricket is seven by D. V. P. Weight of Kent.

Six men have performed two hat-tricks in a single match, but the most remarkable of these is the record of A. E. Trott. When playing for Middlesex against Somerset at Lords in his benefit match of 1907 he took four wickets in four balls and subsequently took another three in three balls, both hat-tricks occurring in the same innings.

J. S. Rao is the only other bowler to perform two hat-tricks in the same innings. This was for Services v. Northern Punjab, at Amritsar, 30 November, 1963.

The other four double hat-trick men are:

R. Jenkins, Worcestershire v. Surrey, at Worcester, 1949.

T. J. Matthews, Australia v. South Africa, at Manchester, 1912.

C. W. L. Parker, Gloucestershire v. Middlesex, at Bristol, 1924.

A. Shaw, Nottingham v. Gloucestershire, at Nottingham, 1884.

HAWKE, LORD (1860–1938)
Great friend of all cricketers, both amateur and professional. The 7th Lord Hawke was educated at Eton and Cambridge, where he won his "Blue" and

subsequently became the leading personality of the Yorkshire C.C.C. and one of the most able administrators the game has ever known.

Captain of Yorkshire from 1883 to 1910, a Test selector, and a member of the Committee of the M.C.C. for many years as well as president and treasurer of that august body. He was also president of Yorkshire for 40 years.

English cricket has had no finer ambassador. Lord Hawke led teams to India, America, New Zealand, West Indies, Canada, and the Argentine, and as a captain he proved himself a skilful strategist as well as a fine leader and sportsman.

Lord Hawke played his last first-class innings in 1911 when he reached 16,092 runs (av. 20.71).

HAYWARD, Thomas Walter (1871–1939)

For many years Tom Hayward was a Surrey opening batsman and his many remarkable partnerships with Jack Hobbs, between 1905 and 1914, are still recalled with great enthusiasm by those who were fortunate enough to witness them. During those years these two appeared together in something like 40 stands of a hundred or more runs.

Hayward, who was born at Cambridge, first appeared for Surrey in 1893. He was a member of a famous cricketing family for both his father and grandfather had played for Surrey, and his uncle, Thomas Hayward, was a leading Cambridgeshire player for many years.

Thomas W. Hayward was a batsman noted for his forward play. He was also a medium pace bowler who took nearly 500 wickets in his career for an average of under 23 runs apiece.

He first scored over 1,000 runs in a season in 1895, and, thereafter he topped the 1,000 run mark in each of the next 19 seasons up to his retirement in 1914. By that time he had aggregated 43,518 runs (av. 41.80).

His highest score was his 315* for Surrey v. Lancashire at the Oval in 1898. Three times he hit two separate hundreds in a match, and in all he scored 104 centuries, carrying his bat through an innings on at least eight occasions.

We have already mentioned Hayward's first wicket stands with Hobbs. Two of the best were the 352 v. Warwickshire, at

Oval, 1909, and 313 against Worcester, at Worcester, in 1913.

HAZARE, Vijay S. (1915–   )

This prolific run-getter first made his mark on Indian cricket with an innings of 316* for Maharashta v. Baroda in 1939–40. This was the first triple-century scored in Indian cricket.

During the war Hazare scored a further triple-century, 309 out of 387 for The Rest v. The Hindus and judging by these two scores, one would not think that this player has often been criticised for extreme caution. But then Hazare was remarkable for his unruffled concentration at the wicket as well as being known as a real fighter. He was also a medium-pace defensive bowler, of some merit.

Hazare made his debut in the international field when he toured England in 1946, but at the time he did not quite come up to expectations.

In Australia in 1947–48, however, he scored two separate hundreds in the fourth Test at Adelaide, 116 and 145, and in England in 1952 he headed his side's Test averages with a total of 333 (55.50).

He captained his country in 14 Tests and scored more runs at home than any other Indian batsman.

HEADINGLEY CRICKET GROUND

This ground at Leeds was opened in 1892 and became the headquarters of the Yorkshire County Cricket Club in 1903.

The attendance record for a Test match in England was set up at Headingley in 1948, when, in five days over 158,000 people paid to see England and Australia.

HEADLEY, George Alphonso (1909–   )

Known as the "Bradman of the Caribbeans" George Headley of Jamaica was one of the West Indies' most successful batsmen.

He made his debut in these matches against England in 1929–30 before he was 21, and did not make his last Test appearance until 1953–54. In 22 appearances his aggregate of runs produced one of the best averages among all the leading West Indian players—60.83.

Headley made 176 in his first Test, a century in each innings of his third Test, and 223 in his fourth. On his first tour of

Australia he scored 193 at Brisbane and 105 at Sydney.

At Lord's, in 1939, he created a Test record for the ground by scoring two separate hundreds.

Headley played his highest Test innings against England at Kingston in 1934–35 when he scored 270*.

As one considers this player's remarkable Test average the figures become even more significant when one remembers that his aggregate was amassed during a period when the West Indies were generally fighting a losing battle. Just consider his record between 1930 and 1939. In those years he scored 2,135 runs in Test cricket with an average of 66.71. His aggregate was more than a quarter of all the runs scored by the West Indians in those Tests!

George Headley was particularly well known in League cricket in England and his son, Ronald, was with Worcestershire 1958–74 and has since played in the Birmingham League and one-day cricket with Derbyshire.

HEARNE, John Thomas (1867–1944)

J. T. Hearne of Middlesex was one of the most successful bowlers of all time. Bowling right-handed with a perfect action, and sending down mostly off-breaks, he captured 3,061 wickets at an average cost of less than 18 runs each.

He made his debut for Middlesex in 1888, and did not retire from first-class cricket until 1923, when, at the age of 56, he made his last appearance for the M.C.C. v. Scotland at Edinburgh.

His finest season was 1896. During that campaign he took his hundredth wicket on June 12, a record not equalled for 35 years, and still not beaten, and went on to amass a total of 257 wickets (av. 14.28).

Hearne played in 12 Tests. His first against South Africa in 1891–92, and his last against Australia in 1899. In these matches he took 49 wickets (av. 22.08). Against Australia, at the Oval, in 1896, he took 10 for 60, and during their next visit (1899), at Leeds, he performed the "hat-trick" and was the only Englishman to perform this feat in a Test at home until Loader did so on the same ground v. West Indies in 1957.

It is worth noting that when J. T. last topped the first-class bowling averages he was in his 44th year. This was 1910 when he took 119 wickets (av. 12.79).

HEARNE, John William (1891–1965)

This dapper Middlesex player was one of that county's finest all-rounders. He batted in effortless style and bowled slow leg-breaks.

"Young Jack", as he was called to differentiate between him and J. T. Hearne, was not yet 21 when he made his first century (114) for England v. Australia in 1911–12 at Melbourne.

For the most part, however, J. W. was not particularly successful in Test matches, but he certainly made up for this with his remarkable consistency in county cricket.

He made his debut for Middlesex in 1909. In 1911 he completed the "double", and in 1913, 1914 and 1920 he exceeded 2,000 runs as well as capturing over 100 wickets. The fifth and last season in which he completed the "double" was 1923.

Against Essex, at Leyton, in 1914, he not only enjoyed an innings of 106* but he took 14 wickets for 146. At Lord's in 1923 he scored 140 and 57* and took 12 Sussex wickets for 128.

Never robust, "Young Jack's" career was interrupted by ill health after 1923, and although he continued until 1936 he missed many games and was never quite able to maintain the all-round brilliance of those peak years between 1913 and 1922.

HEIGHT

Shortest

Among the shortest men ever to appear in first-class cricket are:

R. Baggulay (Nottinghamshire), J. Briggs (Lancashire), W. Cornford (Sussex), A. P. Freeman (Kent), S. E. Gregory (New South Wales), T. W. Gunn (Surrey), F. Hearne (Kent and Western Province), R. Humphrey (Surrey), F. Jakeman (Northamptonshire), H. Jupp (Surrey), William Lillywhite (Sussex), H. Phillips (Sussex), H. Pilling (Lancashire), W. G. Quaife (Warwickshire), K. G. Suttle (Sussex), F. Walden (Northamptonshire), D. J. Ward (Glamorgan), D. Whittaker (Lancashire), J. Wisden (Sussex), H. Wood (Surrey).

All of these are or were under 5 foot 6 inches tall. The shortest—A. P. Freeman, T. W. Gunn and F. Jakeman, only 5 foot 2 inches.

Tallest

Among the tallest are:

A. T. C. Allom (Surrey) 6 foot 10½ inches.

P. Dunkels (Warwickshire), 6 foot 10 inches.

N. A. Paul (Warwickshire), J. D. F. Larter (Northamptonshire), A. W. Greig (Sussex), J. N. Graham (Kent), 6 foot 7½ inches.

R. I. Jefferson (Surrey), 6 foot 7 inches.

G. J. Bonnor (New South Wales and Victoria), P. Hodgson (Yorkshire), H. R. Kingscote (Gloucestershire), J. H. Phillips and R. G. D. Willis (Warwickshire), all 6 foot 6 inches.

A. S. M. Oakman (Sussex), G. B. Lawrence (Rhodesia), Brig. Gen. H. W. Studd (Middlesex and Hampshire), W. Barclay Delacombe (Derbyshire), G. W. Ricketts (Surrey), all 6 foot 5 inches.

A. R. MacGibbon (Canterbury), W. E. Bowes (Yorkshire), F. J. Andrew (Gloucestershire), R. O. Collinge (Central Districts, Wellington), C. C. Griffith (Barbados), R. M. Poore (Hampshire), J. H. Sinclair (Transvaal), 6 foot 4 inches.

T. J. Durston (Middlesex), W. H. Fowler (Somerset), H. Trumble (Victoria), all 6 foot 3½ inches.

HENDREN, Elias Henry "Patsy" (1889–1962)

One of the game's most entertaining personalities, Hendren was renowned for his Cockney wit. He was a fast scoring batsman, especially well remembered for his short-arm hook, but possessing every stroke in the book.

Hendren made his debut for Middlesex in 1907, and in all his first-class cricket scored 57,611 runs (av. 50.80) before announcing his retirement in 1938.

His highest score was 301* for Middlesex v. Worcestershire at Dudley, in 1933, and in all, he made 170 centuries, a figure exceeded only by J. B. Hobbs.

Hendren was always a fast scorer at Lord's, and he hit a century in his last appearance there in a county match.

In his younger days this popular Middlesex batsman was also a soccer player of outstanding ability. He played outside-left for Manchester City, Coventry City, and Brentford, and was good enough to represent England in a "Victory" international in 1919.

HERTFORDSHIRE C.C.C.

Founded: March 8, 1876 (The Minor County with the longest continuous existence). County matches were played as early as 1838. Hertfordshire were original members of the Minor Counties Championship in 1895. Secretary: C. Garrison. 147A High Street, Waltham Cross. Highest score for: 534 for 8 declared v. Bedfordshire, 1924. Highest score against: 521 by Bedfordshire, 1928; in all matches, 547 for 4 declared by Surrey II, 1895. Highest individual score for: 223 by Golding, 1903. Highest individual score against: 231 by J. H. Human of Berkshire, at Cokenach, 1932. Lowest score for: 31 v. Northamptonshire, 1902; in all matches, 19 v. M.C.C., 1875. Lowest score against: 20 by Buckinghamshire, at Aykesbury, 1903. Hertfordshire have the distinction of taking part in the first match ever to be played on the present Lord's Cricket Ground, meeting the M.C.C. there in 1814. Colours- Dark blue, dark green and yellow. Badge: Hertfordshire Hart. Honours: Minor Counties Champions 1936, 1975.

HIGHEST SCORES (INDIVIDUALS)

See under names of the various competitions for one-day records.

Before lunch

The highest score before lunch is 197 by W. R. Endean on the first day for Transvaal v. Orange Free State,, Johannesburg, December 1954. There was 3 hours play before lunch.

Career aggregate

The highest aggregate of runs in first-class cricket is 61,237 by J. B. Hobbs from 1905 to 1934. His total included 197 centuries, another record.

Hobbs' aggregate is the more remarkable when one recalls that he did not make his debut until he was 22 years of age. He also missed four seasons during the first World War, and, in 1921, injury and illness prevented him from playing in all but one county match. In fact, 1921 was one of only two seasons in which he failed to exceed 2,000 runs in a spell of 12 years after World War I.

Runners-up to Hobbs are F. E. Woolley with 58,969 runs from 1906 to 1938, and

E. Hendren with 57,611 from 1907 to 1938. Woolley hit 145 separate centuries and Hendren 170.

Tests

The highest aggregate of runs in Test cricket is 8,032 by G. S. Sobers for West Indies, including 26 centuries, in 93 matches.

M. C. Cowdrey comes second with 7,624 (22 centuries) in 114 matches.

Lord's

The highest individual score ever made at Lord's is 316* by J. B. Hobbs for Surrey v. Middlesex, 1926. This was a personal best for Hobbs and was one better than the previous Lord's record of 315* by P. Holmes for Yorkshire v. Middlesex in 1925 (another personal best).

One ball

The highest score off one ball is 10 by S. H. Wood for Derbyshire v. M.C.C. at Lord's, 1900. The unusual circumstances are recorded in this volume under BOUNDARIES.

One day

The highest individual score ever made in one day's cricket is 345 by C. G. Macartney for the Australians v. Nottinghamshire, at Nottingham in 1921. He reached this total in just under four hours, and the innings included 4 sixes and 47 fours.

The wicket was a batsman's dream and Macartney and C. E. Pellew combined in a devastating fourth wicket partnership which put on 291 in 1¾ hours. Macartney reached 300 in 3 hours 25 minutes.

This was indeed a sorry occasion for Nottinghamshire cricket for despite the state of the wicket they were out for 58 and 100 and were beaten by an innings and 517 runs.

The highest score ever made by an Englishman in one day's cricket is 331* by J. D. Robertson for Middlesex v. Worcestershire, at Worcester, 1949. His innings lasted the full 6½ hours play and when stumps were drawn Middlesex were 623 for 5 and declared their innings closed.

Tests

In Test cricket the record is held by D. G. Bradman with 309 for Australia v. England, at Leeds, 1930.

In this innings Bradman got his century before lunch and after the dismissal of his opening partner, A. Jackson, he shared in a second wicket partnership of 192 with W. M. Woodfull and 229 for the third wicket with A. F. Kippax.

At the end of that first day's play Australia were 458 for 3 wickets. Bradman went on the next day to make 334 before being caught at the wicket by G. Duckworth.

One innings

Seven men have scored over 400 runs in a single innings of first-class cricket. The record is held by Hanif Mohammad with 499 for Karachi v. Bahawalpur, at Karachi, Jan. 1959. He was at the wicket for 10 hours 35 minutes and his innings included 64 fours.

Runners-up are:

D. G. Bradman, 452* for New South Wales v. Queensland, at Sydney, January 1930; 6 hours 55 minutes, and including 49 fours.

B. B. Nimbalkar, 443* for Maharashtra v. Kathiawar, at Poona, Ranji Trophy match, 1948–49. Here it should be noted that Nimbalkar was denied the opportunity of attempting a new record because Kathiawar conceded the match when Maharashtra had scored 826 for 4 against their own first innings score of 238.

W. H. Ponsford, 437 for Victoria v. Queensland, at Melbourne, 1927–28; 10 hours 20 minutes, and including 42 fours.

Ponsford is the only player ever to make over 400 in two separate innings, for, in addition to the above, he also scored 429 for Victoria v. Tasmania, at Melbourne, 1922–23. On this occasion he was at the wicket for nearly eight hours and his innings included 42 fours.

Aftab Baloch, 428 for Sind v. Baluchistan in Quaid-e-Azam trophy, Karachi, February 1974.

A. C. MacLaren, 424 for Lancashire v. Somerset, at Taunton, July 1895; 7 hours 50 minutes, and including 1 six and 62 fours.

All of the above innings were played in either the 19th or 20th centuries. As a matter of interest the highest innings on record in an important 18th century match was 167 by J. Aylward for

Hambledon v. All England, at Sevenoaks, June 1777.

The highest score in Test cricket by a No. 11 batsman is 62* by A. E. E. Vogler, South Africa v. England, Cape Town, 1905–06.

Tests

The record individual innings in Test cricket in 365* by G. S. Sobers for the West Indies v. Pakistan, at Kingston. 1957–58; 10 hours. 8 minutes, and including 38 fours.

This beat the Test record created by L. Hutton in the famous Oval Test against Australia in 1938. Hutton's innings of 364 lasted for 13 hours 20 minutes and included 35 fours.

Minor Counties

The highest individual score in Minor Counties Championship—282 by E. Garnett for Berkshire v. Wiltshire, at Reading, 1908.

In a match involving any county outside of the first-class Championship record is 331 by W. F. Forbes for Mr Fellowes XI v. Huntingdonshire in 1881.

In a match involving two minor county sides the record is 323* by Sir F. E. Lacey for Hampshire v. Norfolk, at Southampton, 1887.

Minor Cricket

Here are a few notable innings made outside of either first-class or minor counties cricket.

628* by A. E. J. Collins for Charles House v. North Town, at Clifton Preparatory School, June 1899. Collins was then aged only 13 and his innings was spread over six or seven days, lasting 6 hours 50 minutes.

566 by C. J. Eady for Break o' Day v. Wellington, at Hobart, Tasmania, March 8, 15, 22, and April 5, 1902. Though spread over four days the innings actually lasted less than eight hours.

515 by D. R. Havewalla for B.B. and C.I. Railway v. St. Xavier's at Bombay, 1933–34.

506* by J. C. Sharp, Melbourne Church of England Grammar School v. Geelong College, at Melbourne, March 1915.

In League cricket the record innings is 306* by "Collie" Smith for Burnley v.

Lowerhouse in the Lancashire League, June 1959.

In this innings Smith hit several balls out of the ground while scoring 56 boundaries, but these only counted as fours on the West End Ground where there are no sixes.

One match

The highest score in a match is the single innings figure of 499 by Hanif Mohammad, Karachi v. Bahawalpur, Karachi, 1958–59.

In England the record was set up by A. E. Fagg who scored a total of 466 (244 and 202*) for Kent v. Sussex, at Colchester, 1938.

Tests

The highest individual score in a Test match is a total of 380 (247* and 133) by G. S. Chappell, Australia v. New Zealand, at Wellington. 1973–74.

One month

In all games during August 1876, W. G. Grace made a total of 1,389, but some of these runs were scored in matches which are not rated as first-class.

The record is held by Sir L. Hutton with 1,294 runs in 16 innings, including seven centuries, in June 1949.

One over

G. S. Sobers became the first batsman to score 36 off a six-ball over when playing for Nottinghamshire v. Glamorgan, at Swansea, August 31, 1968. He hit six sixes off M. A. Nash.

In a six-ball over, but one which included two no-balls, E. Alletson (Nottinghamshire) scored 34 off E. H. Killick (Sussex) at Brighton, in 1911. The scoring strokes were 4–6–6–4–4–4–6.

C. C. Inman (Leicestershire) also scored 32 off a six-ball over at Nottingham, August 20, 1965, but all of N. Hill's balls were slow full tosses. Notts were aiming to give away runs and encourage Leicestershire to declare.

C. C. Smart (Glamorgan) scored 32 (6–6–4–6–6–4) v. Hampshire, Cardiff, July 1935.

I. R. Redpath, 32 off a six-ball over for the Australians v. Orange Free State, Bloemfontein, 1970.

In 1936, at Wells, A. W. Wellard

(Somerset) hit T. R. Armstrong (Derby-shire) for five consecutive sixes to score 30 in a six-ball over.

Two years later, on the same ground, Wellard repeated this performance by hitting F. E. Woolley (Kent) for five successive sixes and a single in a six-ball over.

This record of five sixes off five successive balls was equalled at Chelmsford in 1961 when D. Lindsay for the South African Fezele XI v. Essex hit the last five balls of an over from W. T. Greensmith for sixes. He did not score off the first ball of the over.

M. P. Proctor also hit five sixes off consecutive balls—Western Province v. the Australians, at Cape Town, March 1970.

Seven other players have scored 30 or more off a single over in a first-class match. They are:

J. Mercer (Glamorgan) 31 off R. Howorth (Worcestershire) at Cardiff, 1939; 6–2–4–6–0–6–6–1.

D. G. Bradman (Australians) 30 off A. P. Freeman (England XI) at Folkestone, 1934; 4–6–6–4–6–4.

H. B. Cameron (South Africans) 30 off H. Verity (Yorkshire) at Sheffield, 1935; 4–4–4–6–6–6.

P. L. Winslow (South Africans) 30 off J. T. Ikin (Lancashire) at Old Trafford, 1955; 4–4–6–6–4–6.

D. Wilson (Yorkshire) 30 off R. N. S. Hobbs (M.C.C.) at Scarborough, 1966.

Majid Jahangir Khan (Pakistanis) 30 off R. C. Davis (Glamorgan) at Swansea, 1967, 6–0–6–6–6–6.

R. M. Edwards (Governor-General's XI) 34 of an eight-ball over v. West Indians, Auckland, 1969; 4–0–4–4–6–6–6–4.

In Test cricket the record is 25 off an eight-ball over, B. Sutcliffe (19), R. W. Blair (6), for New Zealand v. South Africa, Johannesburg, 1953–54.

Outside of first-class cricket, A. E. Lawton, playing for Darley Dale against Cromford, at Cromford, August 24, 1907, scored 30–22–34 off three consecutive overs.

See also under BOUNDARIES.

One season

The record aggregate for a single season was created by D. C. S. Compton in 1947. His figures are well worth setting out in detail:

May: 73, 7, 52, 34, 6, 25 22, 18, 97, 88*, 112, 110. Total 644.

June: 154, 34, 88, 65, 163, 50*, 208, 4, 15. Total 781.

July: 115, 6, 151, 33, 11, 129, 48, 110, 13*, 30. Total 646.

August: 100, 106, 4, 137*, 16, 168, 53, 113, 178, 19*, 60, 85. Total 1,039.

September: 17, 139, 101, 30, 87*, 86, 246. Total 706.

This made a grand total of 3,816 runs (2,033 for Middlesex in the County Championship). His average was 90.85.

Another Middlesex batsman also broke the old record in that dry summer of 1947. W. J. Edrich made a total of 3,539 runs, average 80.43.

Prior to 1947 the record had stood for 40 years, having been set up in 1906 by T. Hayward with a total of 3,518 (2,814 for Surrey in the County Championship) average 66.37.

Among the older records, that of W. G. Grace stands out, not only because his aggregate was scored in only 39 innings, but because, in those days, there were no boundaries and every stroke had to be run out. We refer to his aggregate of 2,739 runs (av. 78.25) in 1871 the first time any batsman had passed the 2,000-run mark in a single season.

In Australia, where far fewer matches are played, the aggregate record for a single season was set up by D. G. Bradman with a total of 1,690 runs in 24 innings in 1928–29.

County Championship

The record for a single season of County Championship matches only was created by C. P. Mead of Hampshire with 2,843 runs (av. 81.22) in 1928.

Tests

The record aggregate for a Test rubber is 974 by D. G. Bradman in the five Tests in England in 1930. He scored 8 and 131 at Nottingham, 254 and 1 at Lord's, 334 at Leeds, 14 at Old Trafford, and 232 at the Oval. Average 139.14.

Successive innings

C. B. Fry, D. G. Bradman and M. J. Procter each scored a century in six successive innings. See under CENTURIES.

In only three successive innings in August 1876, W. G. Grace scored a total of 839 runs; 344 for M.C.C. v. Kent, at

Canterbury; 177 for Gloucestershire v. Nottinghamshire, at Clifton; and 318* for Gloucestershire v. Yorkshire, at Cheltenham.

Two overs

Although not a first-class match the performance of J. H. Hunt when playing for Sidmouth v. Quixoties, at Sidmouth, in 1907, is worth recording. He scored 52 in 11 balls in two overs, hitting 4 sixes and 7 fours.

See also under THOUSAND RUNS IN MAY.

HIGHEST SCORES (THE SIDES)

See under names of the various competitions for one-day records.

The highest scores made for and against each county are given under the respective county names. The highest scores in Test matches are given under each country.

Fourth innings

The record score in a fourth innings is 654 for 5 by England against Sough Africa, at Durban, in the "timeless" Test of the 1938–39 tour.

England were set 696 to win but the match had to be abandoned when the time came for the England team to catch their boat home.

The England innings:

L. Hutton, b Mitchell	55
P. A. Gibb, b Dalton	120
E. Paynter, c Grieveson b Gordon	75
W. R. Hammond, st Grieveson b Dalton	140
L. E. G. Ames, not out	17
W. J. Edrich, c Gordon b Langton	219
B. H. Valentine, not out	4
Extras	24
Total (5 wkts.)	654

One day

The record number of runs in a single day's play is 721 by the Australians v. Essex, at Southend, Whit-Saturday, May 15, 1948.

This remarkable score was made in 348 minutes as follows:

S. G. Barnes, hit wkt. b R. Smith	79
W. A. Brown, c Horsfall b Bailey	153
D. G. Bradman, b P. Smith	187
K. R. Miller, b Bailey	0
R. A. Hamence, c P. Smith b R. Smith	46
S. J. E. Loxton, c Rist b Vigar	120
R. A. Saggers, not out	104
I. W. Johnson, st Rist b P. Smith	9
D. T. Ring, c Vigar b P. Smith	1
W. A. Johnston, b Vigar	9
E. R. H. Toshack, c Vigar b P. Smith	4
Extras (b 7, n-b 2)	9
Total	721

Note that the above total, although scored by a single side, represents the record for a day's play and has not been exceeded by the aggregate of two opposing sides.

In Test cricket the record is 503 for 2 by England v. South Africa, at Lord's, June 30, 1924. England had 28 when the day began and the opening pair, Hobbs and Sutcliffe put on 268 for the 1st wicket. A. E. R. Gilligan declared the innings closed shortly before 5.30 pm.

One innings

The record innings total was set up by Victoria in 1926–27, at Melbourne. Playing against New South Wales they made 1,107.

It is interesting to note that when these two sides next met only four weeks later, at Sydney, Victoria were all out for 35.

Victoria also topped the 1,000 mark against Tasmania, at Melbourne, in 1922–23. Then they made 1,059.

Another side which produced a score of over 1,000 runs, although not in a first-class match, was Melbourne University.

Playing against Essendon, at Melbourne, March 5, 12, 19, 23, 1898, they ran up a total of 1,094 runs. Only one batsman on their side made less than 20 and five players made centuries.

In this marathon Essendon sent down 263.3 overs before getting the University out, and even then the last man was caught by one of his own side who was fielding as a substitute. Essendon, with three men absent, replied with a total of 76.

The record Test innings total is 903 for 7 declared by England v. Australia, at the Oval, in August 1938. Details of this innings appear under ENGLAND.

The highest innings recorded in England in any match is 920 by Orlean's Club v. Rickling Green, at Rickling Green, August 1882.

In County games the record is 887 by

Yorkshire v. Warwickshire at Edgbaston, May 7-9, 1896. Yorkshire's total was made in 10 hours 50 minutes.

One match

The record aggregate for a single match is 2,376 for 38 wickets, Bombay v. Maharashtra, in the semi-final of the Ranji Trophy, at Poona, 1948-49.

Next to this comes an aggregate of 2,078 for 40 wickets, Bombay v. Holkar, at Bombay, 1944-45.

Those are the only two aggregates which exeed 2,000 runs.

The records in each of the other principal cricketing countries are:

England: 1,723 for 31 wickets, England v. Australia, Leeds, 1948.

Australia: 1,929 for 39 wickets, N.S.W. v. S. Australia, Sydney, 1925-26.

South Africa: 1,981 for 35 wickets, South Africa v. England, Durban, 1939. A record for all Tests.

West Indies: 1,815 for 34 wickets, West Indies v. England, Kingston 1929-30.

New Zealand: 1,905 for 40 wickets, Otago v. Wellington, Dunedin, 1923-24.

Pakistan: 1,460 for 21 wickets, Pakistan v. Commonwealth XI, Lahore, 1963-64.

One wicket

The record for one wicket is 555 for 1 declared by Yorkshire against Essex, at Leyton, June 1932.

P. Holmes, not out	224
H. Sutcliffe, b Eastman	313
Extras	18
Total (for 1 wkt.)	555

Mitchell, Leyland, Barber, A. B. Sellars, Wood, Rhodes, Macaulay, Verity and Bowes did not bat.

It should also be noted that Sutcliffe threw his wicket away as soon as a new record opening partnership had been created. The previous record being 554.

In 1914, at Leyton, Middlesex scored 464 for 1 declared against Essex:

Hon. R. Anson, c Fane b Douglas	97
F. A. Tarrant, not out	250
J. W. Hearne, not out	106
Extras	11
Total (for 1 wkt.)	464

Clarke, Hendren, Mann, Doll, Little-john, Murrell, Hearne, and Peat did not bat.

HILL, Clement (1877-1945)

Many authorities consider Clement Hill to have been Australia's best-ever left-handed batsman. In his earliest years he was also a wicket-keeper, but he soon gave up that and developed into an aggressive batsman.

Clem Hill first appeared for South Australia at the age of 16, and at the age of 19 he was a last-minute choice for the Australian side to tour England in 1896. An innings of 206 for South Australia helped the selectors decide in his favour.

Unfortunately, Hill did not shine on that tour and indeed he was never to be quite the same batsman in England as he was on the faster wickets of his homeland.

At Melbourne in the fourth Test of England's 1897-98 tour, he scored a brilliant 188. At Lord's in 1899 he hit 135, and back in Australia in 1901-02 series of Tests he had three successive innings against England of 99, 98 and 97.

In his 49 Test appearances this powerful batsman scored 3,402 runs (av. 39.55) including seven centuries. His highest Test innings was 191 against South Africa, at Sydney, 1910-11.

In all first-class matches his highest score was 365* for South Australia v. N.S.W., at Adelaide in 1900-01.

HIRST, George Herbert (1871-1945)

One of England's most successful professional all-rounders, G. H. Hirst made his debut for Yorkshire at the age of 17 and enjoyed a career in first-class cricket which extended over a period of 40 years. During this time he not only scored 36,203 runs (av. 34.05) but captured 2,727 wickets at an average cost of only 18.77.

A fast left-hand bowler and a big hitter Hirst completed the "double" in 17 seasons. His best was 1906 when he scored 2,385 runs and took 208 wickets.

Hirst deceived many batsmen by making the ball swerve in the air, and one of his finest spells of bowling was in the Yorkshire v. Lancashire match of 1910, at Leeds, when in one innings he took 9 for 23.

He played in 24 Tests between 1897 and 1909 but was never quite as good in these games as he was for his county. However, he took 59 Test wickets at an average of 30.00 and scored 792 runs (av. 22.62).

Hirst made his highest score, 341, v. Leicestershire, at Leicester, in 1905.

HISTORY

An article under this heading would be only so much repetition of what appears under other various headings in this volume. Each section is, of course, a piece of cricket history.

However, no doubt many readers will be looking to this section to find something about the early development of the game. They are asked to refer to the following headings:

Ball: Bat: Boundaries; Crease; Dress; First; Gloves; Laws of Cricket; Pads; Wicket.

HITTING

See under BIG HITTING.

HOBBS, Sir John Berry (1882–1963)

Hobbs was the finest batsman on all types of wickets that the world has ever seen. In a brilliant career which extended from 1905 to 1934 he scored 61,237 runs (av. 50.65), a record aggregate which also included a record number of 197 separate hundreds.

Born at Cambridge, the eldest of 12 children, Hobbs played for his home county and then tried to join Essex. However, astonishing as it may seem now, that county turned him down and he made his first-class debut with Surrey in 1905.

Essex could not have been long in regretting their decision for his second game for Surrey was against them and Hobbs made 155.

Hobbs made the first of the 61 Test appearances on the 1907–08 Australian tour, scoring 83 in his first innings. His last appearance for England was in 1930 against Australia, at the Oval.

In his first Test Hobbs opened with F. L. Fane and in his last he opened with H. Sutcliffe. During his career he figured in 166 first-wicket stands of a hundred or more runs. The highest of these was the score of 428 with A. Sandham against Oxford University, at the Oval, in 1926. There were many other notable partnerships with Hayward, Rhodes and Sutcliffe, the best in Test cricket being 323 with W. Rhodes against Australia, at Melbourne, in 1911–12. This is still a first-wicket record in the England—Australia series.

Hobbs made his highest score and a record for the Lord's ground when playing for Surrey v. Middlesex in 1926. On that occasion he scored 316*.

In addition to being the world's outstanding batsman. Hobbs was a great fielder at cover-point. In the earlier part of his career he was also a more than useful slow-medium pace bowler who actually topped the averages in 1920 with 17 wickets at a cost of 11.82 runs apiece.

It may not be generally appreciated that Hobbs was aged 51 when he made his last century in first-class cricket, and this was against the leading side of the season, Lancashire. On that occasion, at Manchester in 1934 (it was Duckworth's Benefit match) Hobbs scored 116 and 51*.

HOLLAND

A cricket club was formed at Utrecht as long ago as 1855, and the oldest club still in existence in Holland, UD (Deventer), traces its history back to 1875.

There is more organised cricket in Holland today than in any other continental country, most of it on matting wickets, and the KNCB, the national body which governs the game, was formed in September 1883 and now has a membership of around 60 associations and clubs.

The first match between English and Dutch teams took place when Uxbridge C.C. visited Holland in 1881, while the first Dutch team to visit England came over in 1892.

A notable day in Dutch cricket history is August 29, 1964, when they beat the Australians by three wickets in a one-day match.

HUISH, Frederick Henry (1872–1957)

This Kent player never appeared in a Test match but he is one of the elite of wicket-keepers who have captured 100 wickets in a single season. Huish actually did this in two seasons, 1911 and 1913.

When he dismissed 100 batsmen in 1911 (62 caught and 38 stumped) Huish was the first wicket-keeper ever to reach a century. He improved on this record with 70 caught and 32 stumped in 1913.

It was during the former season that he gave his most remarkable performance in a single match. For Kent against Surrey, at the Oval, he dismissed 10 batsmen, creating a record (which still stands) by stumping nine of them.

In all matches for Kent between 1895 and 1914 he dismissed 1,262 batsmen, catching 906 and stumping 356.

HUNTE, Conrad Cleophas (1932–   )

After proving his ability as a batsman and brilliant out-fielder with Barbados this delightful stroke player scored 142 when making his first Test appearance for the West Indies.

That was against Pakistan at Bridgetown in 1957–58 and he subsequently proved his tremendous powers of concentration in many fine innings.

He figured in the West Indians' record 2nd wicket partnership of 446 with G. Sobers against Pakistan at Kingston in that same 1957–58 series, and got his highest score, 263, v. Jamaica at Georgetown in 1961–62.

Well known in Lancashire League cricket, Hunte was the West Indies vice-captain in England in 1963 when he topped their Test averages with 58.87 including a dogged 8½-hour innings of 186 at Old Trafford, and again in 1966 when he delighted with a skilfully executed 135 in the First Test at Old Trafford, and thrilled the crowd at Taunton with 206* (2 sixes and 31 fours) against Somerset.

This reliable opener's last Test series was in India in 1966–67. In 44 Tests his aggregate was 3,245 (av. 45.06).

HUTTON, Sir Leonard (1916–   )

A determined batsman of classical elegance, Hutton would have shone at any period in the history of Test cricket, but in the immediate post-war seasons he stood out like a beacon when England's batting often looked shaky.

Hutton made his debut for Yorkshire in 1934 and during that season, at Worcester, he made 196.

The Times then had this to say about the 18-year-old Pudsey lad. "He is a young batsman who applies himself to batting with the passionate concentration of a scientist dissecting a beetle." So it remained throughout his illustrious career.

Hutton disappointed with nought and one in his Test debut v. New Zealand, at Lord's, in 1937, but he scored a century in his first appearance against Australia, at Nottingham, the following summer, and, of course, it was this series of Tests which ended with his record knock of 364 in 13 hours 20 minutes at the Oval. (This Test record was beaten by one run by G. Sobers of the West Indies in 1957–58). In four Test innings during the summer of 1938 Hutton averaged 118.25.

Hutton's Test figures of 6,971 runs (av. 56.67) have only been exceeded among the England batsmen by M. C. Cowdrey and W. R. Hammond. The total includes 19 centuries.

In all first-class cricket Hutton scored 40,140 runs with an astonishing average of 55.51. He retired from first-class cricket in 1957, and only had two more innings—in 1960.

ILLINGWORTH, Raymond (1932–)

Another Yorkshire cricketer born in Pudsey, this all-rounder helped his county to win the Championship seven times before moving to Leicestershire in 1968 and becoming that county's captain. But it was as England's captain that he has earned undying fame, winning the Ashes in Australia in 1970–71 and retaining them in England in 1972.

His most successful season with the bat was 1959 when he scored 1,726 runs (av. 46.64), while he reached his peak as an off-break bowler in 1968 with 131 wickets (av. 14.36). He captained England in 31 Tests 1969–73, losing only five. Also captained England v. Rest of the World in 1970.

Illingworth got his highest score for Yorkshire v. Indians, at Sheffield in 1959 when he made 162. Took 9 for 42 for Yorkshire v. Worcester, at Worcester in 1957.

IMTIAZ AHMED (1928–)

This Pakistani was a batsman/wicket-keeper of the highest class. During his first tour of England, in 1954, he scored over 1,000 runs and dismissed 86 batsmen (including three catches made when not keeping wicket).

Imtiaz Ahmed had made himself known to our cricketers before this. At Bombay, in March 1951, he played an innings of 300* against the second Commonwealth XI.

His highest Test innings was that against New Zealand, at Lahore, in October, 1955, when he scored 209.

In 1961–62 he captained Pakistan in the Tests against England, and by the end of 1962, when he topped 1,000 runs in England, and had missed only one of the 42 Tests played by his country, he had scored 2,079 Test runs and dismissed 93 batsmen from behind the wicket.

When England scored 544 for 5 declared in the first Test of 1962 he kept wicket without conceding a single bye.

INDIA

See also under RANJI TROPHY.

With a spin attack the like of which we had not seen for several years India proved themselves to be the new "world champions" by beating the West Indies in 1970–71 and then emerging victorious over England (holders of the Ashes) both at home and away.

August 24, 1971 has gone down in history as Indian cricket's finest day, for it was then that they clinched their first-ever Test victory in England, winning by 4 wickets at The Oval.

This standard has not quite been maintained more recently, but there is no doubt that India are more of a power in Test cricket today than they have ever been, and one of their most remarkable victories was in the 3rd Test of their West Indies tour in 1976. In this match, at Port of Spain, they were set 403 to win and achieved victory with six wickets to spare.

The earliest cricket to be played in India was probably that at Cambay by sailors of the East India Company in 1721.

The Old Etonians met the Parsees in 1784 and the Calcutta Cricket Club is believed to have been in existence as early as 1792.

In 1804 the Old Etonians met the Rest (all civil servants of the East India Company) on part of the famous Eden Gardens at Calcutta and it was in this game that R. Vansittart scored 102 for the Old Etonians—the first century on record in India.

A cricket club was established by the Parsees in Bombay in 1841 and it is this religious sect which has done most to establish the game on the Indian continent. The Hindus formed their first cricket club in 1866 and the Mohammedans in 1883.

The first cricket team to visit England from India was the Parsees team of 1886 but they met with little success winning only one of their 28 matches and losing 19.

The first representative India side visited England in 1911 under the captaincy of H.H. the Maharajah of Patiala, and in a programme of 23 matches they included 14 first-class games. Altogether they won only six (including two first-class).

The first team to go out to India from England was that under the captaincy of G. F. Vernon in 1889–90. The team was composed entirely of amateurs and in a tour of 13 matches (including two in Ceylon) they suffered one defeat—by the Parsees.

There is no doubt that the prowess of K. S. Ranjitsinhji did much to encourage more Indians to take up cricket but following the falling off in enthusiasm for the game on that continent after World War I two Englishmen contributed much towards a revival. They were J. B. Hobbs and H. Sutcliffe, who toured India at the special invitation of Maharajkumar Sir Vijayu of Vizianagarum, in 1930–31.

Indian records

Test matches

Highest score for: 539 for 9 declared v. Pakistan, January 1961:

M. L. Jaisimha c Intikhab b Hussain	32
N. J. Contractor c Intikhab b Haseeb	81
D. K. Gaekwad c and b Haseeb	9
V. L. Manjrekar b Haseeb	30
P. R. Umrigar b Haseeb	117
C. G. Borde not out	177
A. G. Milkha Singh c Fazal b Haseeb	18
B. K. Kunderam b Haseeb	12
R. B. Desai st Imtiaz b Nasimul	18
R. Surendranath st Imtiaz b Nasimul	6
B. Gupte not out	17
Extras	22
Total (9 wkts. dec.)	539

Highest individual score for: V. Mankad 231 v. New Zealand, Madras, January 1956. Highest score against: 674 by Australia, at Adelaide, 1947–48. Highest individual score against: 256 by R. Kanhai of West Indies, at Calcutta, 1958–59. Lowest score for: 42 for 9 (one man absent hurt) v. England, at Lord's, 1974. Lowest

score against: 101 by England, at the Oval, 1971 (Chandraekhar 6 for 38).

Other matches

Highest score: 612 for 6 declared by India in England, 1946 v. Rest of India, at Calcutta, 1946–47. Highest score against: 608 for 8 declared by Commonwealth Xi v. India XI, at New Delhi, 1949–50. Highest score in India; 912 for 8 declared by Holkar v. Mysore, at Indore, 1944–45. Lowest score in India: 21 by Muslims v. Europeans, at Poona, 1915–16. Highest individual score in India: 443* by B. B. Nimbalkar for Maharashtra v. Kathiawar, at Poona, 1948–49. Highest individual score on tour: 252* by P. R. Umrigar v. Cambridge Univ. 1959.

INNINGS

See also under CENTURIES, FOURTH INNINGS, HIGHEST SCORES, LOWEST SCORES.

Longest (Individual)

The longest individual innings in first-class cricket lasted 16 hours 39 minutes. This was the time Hanif Mohammad of Pakistan was at the wicket in the first Test against West Indies, at Bridgetown, Barbados, January, 1958. He made 337 before being dismissed.

L. Hutton was at the wicket for 13 hours 20 minutes when making 364 for England v. Australia, fifth Test, at the Oval, August 1938. This is the second longest innings in Test cricket.

Some of the old-timers may have exceeded the above times but unfortunately in the majority of cases there is no precise record of their actual time at the wicket. However, it is known that John Small once batted for three days for Hambledon against England, and when William Ward made 278 at Lord's for the M.C.C. v. Norfolk, his innings was spread over three days. Other old-timers' innings spread over three days include one by Tom Sueter when playing for Lord Tankerville's side at Chertsey in 1767 when only 17 years of age.

Longest (Sides)

This is difficult to establish as no precise times are given in most reports of matches. However, there seems little doubt that the longest innings for any first-class side is the same as that mentioned above for an individual. Pakistan's innings continued for a short time after Hanif Mohammad was caught by Alexander off Atkinson soon after tea.

Most

The record number of innings in a single season is 70 by the Sussex player, A. H. H. Gilligan, in 1923.

Shortest (Sides)

Among the shortest innings in first-class cricket are the following:

M.C.C. and Ground were all out for 16 runs in 44 minutes v. Surrey, at Lord's, in May 1872.

M.C.C. were out for 19 runs in 57 minutes in their second innings against the Australians, at Lord's in 1878.

Oxford University were all out for 12 in 75 minutes v. M.C.C., at Oxford, 1877.

South Africa were all out for 30 in 50 minutes v. England at Edgbaston, June 1924.

Worcestershire were all out for 25 in 75 minutes v. Kent, at Tunbridge Wells, June 15, 1960.

England all out for 45 in 80 minutes v. Australia, at Sydney, January 1887.

Australia dismissed by England for 36 runs in less than 1½ hours at Edgbaston, May 1902.

At Old Trafford, in July 1952, India were bowled out twice on the same day in 3¾ hours play for 58 and 82.

The above innings were all played out, but the shortest on record is that of Lancashire v. Nottinghamshire, at Liverpool, in July 1956. Lancashire declared after only one ball, and that took a wicket.

Lancashire were leading by 121 runs on the first innings after the second day had been lost through rain. In an effort to force a win Edrich declared after Hilton had been caught by Poole with the first ball off Walker, leaving 95 minutes for play. At the end of that time Nottinghamshire were 93 for 7.

INTERNATIONAL CRICKET CONFERENCE

The International Cricket Conference was originally constituted under the title of The Imperial Cricket Conference in 1909 when rules were drawn up to control Test matches.

The original members were the M.C.C.

and the Australia and South African Cricket Control Boards.

India, New Zealand and the West Indies were admitted to the conference in 1926, and Pakistan in 1952.

South Africa dropped out in 1961 when they left the Commonwealth.

The present title was adopted in 1965 when it was decided that countries outside the Commonwealth could become members.

INTIKHAB, ALAM (1941–)

Pakistani all-rounder, right-hand batsman and leg-break googly bowler, who made debut for Karachi in 1958 when aged 16 years 9 months. He made Test debut v. Australia, at Karachi in December 1959 when still a couple of weeks short of his 18th birthday.

After a total of 43 Tests his bag of 108 wickets (av. 37.63) places him second only to Fazal Mahmood among Pakistani bowlers, and he has also played five matches for the Rest of the World v. England in 1970, and five v. Australia in 1971–72.

Captained Pakistan in 17 Tests from 1969 to 1975 and has been with Surrey since 1969. Performed the hat-trick for Surrey v. Yorkshire at The Oval in 1972 and his highest score in England for the county—139 v. Gloucestershire on the same ground in 1973. At Hobart in 1972–73 he took eight Victoria wickets for 54, while his career best innings is 182 for Karachi Blues v. Pakistan International Airways B, at Karachi in 1970–71.

IRELAND

The first cricket match on record in Ireland was that played for 1,000 guineas a side at Phoenix Park, Dublin, in 1792. This was between a garrison eleven led by Colonel Charles Lennox and a team styled as All Ireland.

Many readers may be surprised to learn that the first representative national side to cross the sea to play cricket was not George Parr's XI of 1859 but an Irish XI which met the M.C.C. at Lord's in May 1858.

A county club existed in Carlow as long ago as 1829 and there is little doubt that Kilkenny also boasted a cricket club at that time. Neither of these clubs nor, for that matter, any other of the county clubs, with the possible exception of Cork, have enjoyed a continuous existence. Most of them faded out at the time of Parnell's Land League agitations in the eighties or were finally abandoned during the hectic days of World War I.

Today nearly all cricket in Ireland is played on a competitive basis in Leagues, but there is also a regular programme of Internationals.

I ZINGARI C.C.

This is the most famous of all wandering cricket clubs. They were founded in 1845 by the Ponsonby brothers—Lord Bessborough and Sir Spencer Ponsonby-Fane, together with J. L. Baldwin and R. P. Long.

Their first match was played against Newport Pagnell, August 25, 1845.

It was the I Zingari who first established the Canterbury Cricket Week and were also connected with the establishment of the Scarborough Festival.

One of the club's finest victories was at Lord's in 1904, when they defeated the Gentlemen of England (including J. E. Raphael, C. J. Kortright, K. J. Key, and H. T. Hesketh Prichard).

The name of the club is Italian for "the gypsies" and the colours are black, red and gold, signifying "out of darkness, through fire, into light".

Membership can only be obtained by invitation, and according to the rules of the club "the entrance be nothing, and the annual subscription do not exceed the entrance".

J

JACKSON, Sir Frederick Stanley (1870–1947)

An elegant, orthodox batsman, right-hand fast-medium bowler, and cover-point fielder, this Cambridge "Blue" became one of England's finest all-rounders.

Selected to play for England, while still at Cambridge in 1893, he scored 91 at Lord's in his first Test innings against Australia.

One of his outstanding performances in the following season was to bowl unchanged with S. M. Woods in both innings for the Gentlemen v. Players, getting them out for 108 and 107.

The gentleman's first-class career extended from 1890 to 1907 but his services to cricket continued for a long period after that. In 1921 he was president of the M.C.C. and in 1934 he was chairman of the England Test Selectors.

Over 18 seasons the average cost of the 506 wickets he captured for Yorkshire was only 19.18. In all matches he dismissed 770 batsmen (av. 20.28) and scored 15,782 runs (av. 34.76)

Unfortunately he was never able to go out to Australia, but he captained England in the Test rubber at home in 1905, a series in which England were undefeated, while Jackson won the toss five times, and headed both the bowling and batting averages.

JAMAICA

See under WEST INDIES.

JARDINE, Douglas Robert (1900–1958)

After getting his "Blue" as a Freshman at Oxford, and playing in the University matches of 1920, 1921 and 1923, Jardine made his debut for Surrey and became one of England's outstanding amateur batsmen in a career which lasted until 1937.

Jardine's name will forever be linked with the "Bodyline" controversy of the 1932–33 Australian tour. This is unfortunate as he was the captain who had to carry out a plan conceived by others, but it is to his credit that he did his unpopular duty without a murmur.

A determined man was D. R. Jardine. An unemotional captain, strict disciplinarian, and a batsman, who displayed a perfect style. He was also a slow bowler of some quality and an excellent field, usually in the gully. He skippered England in 15 Tests.

As a batsman he could be very stubborn. At one stage of the Australian Test at Brisbane in 1933 he did not score in 83 minutes.

His highest score was 214* for the M.C.C. v. Tasmania in 1928–29.

JESSOP, Gilbert Laird (1874–1955)

This fearless hitter was criticised by the purists because his batting style was so unorthodox, but maybe that is why he was one of the outstanding personalities of the game in the early 1900s.

Today, there is a continued plea for brighter cricket: another G. L. Jessop would certainly satisfy that plea for when this famous Gloucestershire batsman was around there was always plenty of excitement. He could hit balls of all lengths.

Jessop captained Cambridge University in 1899, his fourth season in the side. He played for Gloucestershire for 20 years from 1894 to 1914 and was their captain from 1900 to 1913 and county secretary from 1909 to 1911.

Ruthless in his treatment of bowling, Jessop could cut a ball better than most of his contemporaries, and he scored a high proportion of his runs behind the wicket.

Jessop's batting so overshadowed anything else he did, that it is not generally remembered that he was also a fast bowler of class who took 851 wickets at an average of 22.91 each. In addition he was an outstanding fielder at cover-point.

Reference to Jessop's powerful batting can be found elsewhere in this volume under BIG HITTING, BOUNDARIES and FAST SCORING, but one innings which stands out in his remarkable career was at the Oval in the Test with Australia of 1902. Set 263 to win, England had lost 5 for 48 when "Croucher" Jessop went to the wicket. In 75 minutes he scored 104 and England went on to win by one wicket.

He scored 28 runs off an over on two occasions.

Unfortunately, poor health affected his performances later in his career but when he retired this great all-rounder had scored over 200 runs on five occasions and his aggregate of 26,764 (av. 32.67) included 53 centuries. Highest score was 286 (in 175 minutes) Gloucestershire v. Sussex at Hove in 1903.

JOHN PLAYER LEAGUE, The

Sunday League cricket among the first-class counties was inaugurated in 1969 with this competition sponsored by the tobacco firm, John Player and Sons.

The matches are decided on a single innings basis with a limit of 40 overs and no-one bowling more than eight overs. Winners get 4 points and there are 2 points for a tie.

Winners: 1969 and 1970—Lancashire, 1971—Worcestershire, 1972 and 1973—Kent, 1974—Leicestershire, 1975—Hampshire, 1976—Kent.

Highest innings score: 307 for 4 off 38 overs, Worcestershire v. Derbyshire, at Worcester, 1975. Highest individual score: 155* by B. A. Richards for Hampshire v. Yorkshire, at Hull, 1970.

JOHNSON, Ian William (1918–)

One of Australia's finest all-rounders in the immediate post-war period Ian Johnson made his debut with Victoria in 1935–36 but did not appear in Test cricket until 1946.

A right-handed bat, right-arm off-break bowler, and brilliant slip fielder, Johnson made 45 Test appearances including 17 as captain. In these matches he topped the 1,000 runs and got among the dozen best Australian Test Bowlers of all time by taking 109 wickets at an average cost of 29.19.

One of his best performances in England was to take 7 for 42 against Leicestershire in 1948. In all matches of that, his most successful England tour, he took 85 wickets (av. 18.37).

Highest score 132* v. Queensland, at Melbourne in 1948–49.

JOHNSTON, William Arras (1922–)

This fast-medium left-arm bowler made his debut with Victoria in 1945–46 and first hit the headlines during the Indian tour of Australia in 1947–48. In four Tests he took 16 Indian wickets for an average of 11.37 and when playing for his State against the visitors he took their first three wickets without a run being scored.

Coming to England in 1948 he played in all five Tests taking 27 wickets (av. 23.33). He was here again in 1953 but only took 7 wickets in his three Tests (av. 49.00).

Johnston made the last of his 40 Test appearances during the England tour of 1956. In all these matches he took 160 wickets (av. 23.90), a Test aggregate which has only been beaten by six Australians.

In England Johnston is particularly well remembered by Yorkshiremen, for at Bradford in 1948, on a sticky-dog, he took 6 for 18 and 4 for 22.

A peculiarity of Johnstons's career is that although he was no batsman he topped the 1953 tour of England batting averages with 102.00. He batted 17 times and was not out 16 times!

K

KANHAI, Rohan Babulal (1935–   )

Only Sobers has made more runs for the West Indies than this enterprising batsman whose total in 79 Tests is 6,227 (av. 47.53) with a highest innings of 256 v. India, at Calcutta in 1958–59.

Since making his debut for British Guiana in 1954–55 he has played for Western Australia, Tasmania, and (since 1968) for Warwickshire, as well as in English and Scottish League cricket.

Helped Warwickshire to win the Championship in 1972, the year in which he succeeded Sobers as captain of the West Indies, and he led his country to victory in series in England in 1973, and at home to England in 1973–74. In all he captained the West Indies in 13 Tests.

One of the finest innings of his career was his 157 for the West Indies, at Lord's in 1973 when his side scored 652 for 8 declared.

KELLY, James Joseph (1867–1938)

One of Australia's best ever wicketkeepers, James J. Kelly of New South Wales made his debut in 1894–95 and retired in 1905.

The first of his 36 Test appearances came in 1896 when he visited England. He was here again in 1899, 1902 and 1905, tours in which he also showed himself to be a more than useful batsman.

Against Warwickshire at Edgbaston in 1899 he scored 103, and at Bristol, in 1905, he and F. Laver put on 112 for the last wicket. On that occasion Kelly's contribution was 74.

In his 36 Tests (33 against England and 3 against South Africa) he dismissed 63 batsmen, catching 43 and stumping 20.

His best performance was to catch 8 England batsmen in the 4th Test of the 1901–02 series.

KENNEDY, Alexander Stuart (1891–1959)

For a few years after World War I this Scot was one of the finest all-rounders in England, but although he played in all five Tests in South Africa in 1922–23 he never appeared in a Test match at home.

His absence is surprising when one examines his record, for Kennedy captured 31 wickets (av. 19.32) in those five Tests while in all matches on that South African tour his bag was 82 wickets (14.12). In England where he qualified for Hampshire, and took more wickets for them than any other player, he achieved the "double" on five occasions from 1921 to 1930. His best season was 1922 when he bagged 205 wickets for only 16.80 apiece and also scored 1,129 runs (av. 22.13).

At the Oval, in 1927, in one of his 16 appearances for the Players, he took all 10 of the Gentlemen's wickets in the first innings of 37 runs.

A. S. Kennedy took 2,874 wickets in first-class matches at an average cost of 21.24, as well as scoring over 16,000 runs before he finally retired in 1936.

KENT C.C.C.

Founded: 1859. Reformed 1870. Secretary: M. Fenner, St. Lawrence Ground, Canterbury. Highest score for: 803 for 4 declared v. Essex, Brentwood, 1934. Highest individual score for: 332 by W. H. Ashdown v. Essex, Brentwood, 1934. Highest score against: 676 by the Australians, Canterbury, 1921; 627 for 9 declared by Worcestershire, Worcester, July 31—August 2, 1905. Highest individual score against: 334 by Dr. W. G. Grace for M.C.C., Canterbury, August 1876. Lowest score for: 18 v. Sussex, Gravesend, 1867 (one man absent). In all matches—6 v. Bexley (with Lord Frederick Beauclerk and Hammond) 1805. Lowest score against: 16 by

Warwickshire, Tonbridge, 1913. Colours: Red and white. Badge: White horse on a red background. County Champions 1906, 1909, 1910, 1913, 1970. Kent II have won the Minor Counties Championship 1951, 1956. Benson & Hedges Cup: Winners, 1973, 1976. Gillette Cup: Winners, 1967, 1974. Finalists, 1971. John Player League Champions, 1972, 1973, 1976.

KIPPAX, Alan F. (1897–1972)

This fast scoring batsman made his debut for New South Wales in 1919 and, after scoring 82* for an Australian XI v. M.C.C., at Brisbane, in 1924–25, he was selected for the final Test of that season.

After that he made 21 more Test appearances including six in England five in 1930, and the other (his final Test) in 1934.

Kippax made his highest score of 315* for his home state v. Queensland, at Sydney, in 1927–28. He was at the wicket for 6 hours 28 minutes, and his innings included 41 fours.

With J. E. Hooker, he holds world record for 10th wicket stand—307 for N.S.W. v. Victoria, at Melbourne, 1928–29. Kippax scored 240 out of the 307.

A delightful batsman with an attractive style, in all he scored 43 separate centuries and retired in 1936 with an average of 75.69. He scored more runs for N.S.W. in Sheffield Shield matches than any other player—6,096 (av. 70.88).

KNIGHTS OF CRICKET

The following men have been knighted for their services to cricket.

Sir Donald G. Bradman. Knighted January 1, 1949, following his retirement from first-class cricket.

Sir Neville Cardus. Knighted 1967 for services to cricket and music.

Sir John B. Hobbs. Knighted in the 1953 Coronation year.

Sir Leonard Hutton. Knighted in the Birthday Honours list of 1956.

Sir Francis E. Lacey. Knighted in 1926

following his retirement after 28 years as secretary of the M.C.C.

Sir Henry D. G. Leveson-Gower. Knighted 1953 for his services to cricket as a legislator and Test Selector.

Sir Garfield S. Sobers. Knighted 1975 near the end of a career which established him as the world's greatest all-round cricketer.

Sir Frederick C. Toone. Knighted 1929 after three tours in Australia as manager of the M.C.C. and 26 years as secretary of Yorkshire C.C.C.

Sir Pelham F. Warner. Knighted Coronation Honours 1937 after many years as one of cricket's finest ambassadors.

Sir Frank Worrell. Knighted 1964 after more than 20 years in first-class cricket including 51 Tests.

KNOCK-OUT COMPETITION

See under GILLETTE CUP.

KNOTT, Alan Philip Eric
(1946–   )

This wicket-keeper's six dismissals in the 1976 Test rubber with the West Indies took his total to 221 (204 caught and 17 stumped) a new Test career record among the world's wicket-keepers. He also dismissed another 14 in the five matches against the Rest of the World in 1970.

It is obvious that this player, who made his debut for Kent in 1965, can, with normal luck, take his Test wicket-keeping figures to a new high which may never be exceeded, for he has still only completed nine years in the England team. T. G. Evans, who previously held the wicket-keeping record, enjoyed a Test career spread over 13 years and was five years older than Knott when making his England debut.

Knott's ability as a batsman must not be overlooked. He has made two centuries in a match—127* and 118* for Kent v. Surrey, at Maidstone in 1972, and got his highest score of 156 for the M.C.C. v. South Zone, at Bangalore in 1972–73. In 78 Tests he has scored 3,595 (av. 33.28).

L

LAKER, James Charles (1922–   )

Born in Yorkshire, this talented slow off-break bowler made his debut with Surrey in 1946 and in 60 overs took 8 wickets at a cost of 21.12. Not bad for a beginner, but it gave no inkling of great deeds to come.

In his second season this former Bradford League player .topped Surrey's bowling averages with 66 wickets (av. 16.65). He took over 100 wickets in his third season and never dropped below the century in any of the remaining 11 seasons before his premature retirement. His best total was 166 (av. 15.32) in 1950.

That was the summer in which he first hit the headlines as a record-breaker, for, in the Test Trial, at Bradford, he took eight wickets for only two runs!

The season 1956 was the one for which he will always be remembered. Twice in that campaign he took all 10 of the Australian tourists' wickets. The first time was for his county, at the Oval—10 for 88. The second time was for his country, in the Manchester Test—10 for 53.

It was the first time that all 10 wickets had been taken by one bowler in a Test innings. In all, Laker took 19 wickets for 90 runs in that match, another world record for all first-class cricket. That such a remarkable feat should have been performed for the first time in a Test match made it an even greater triumph.

Laker retired from first-class cricket at the end of 1959 but he returned in 1962 to play three seasons with Essex. Career figures 1,944 wickets (av. 18.40).

LANCASHIRE C.C.C.

Founded: 1864. Secretary: A. K. James, Old Trafford, Manchester M16 0PX. Highest score for: 801 v. Somerset, Taunton, July 1895. Highest individual score for: 424 by A. C. Maclaren (7 hours 50 minutes) v. Somerset, Taunton, July, 1895. Highest score against: 634 by Surrey, the Oval, August 1898. Highest individual score against: 315* by T. Hayward of Surrey, the Oval, August 1898. Lowest score for: 25 v. Derbyshire, Manchester, May 1871; 28 v. the Australians, Liverpool, 1896. Lowest score against: 22 by Glamorgan, Liverpool, 1924. At a time when Derbyshire were not considered first-class they scored only 17 against Lancashire, at Manchester, July 1888. Colours: Red, green and blue. Badge: Red rose. County Champions: 1879 (tie with Nottinghamshire), 1881, 1882 (tie with Nottinghamshire), 1889 (tie with Nottinghamshire and Surrey), 1897, 1904, 1926, 1927, 1928, 1930, 1934, 1950 (tie with Surrey). Lancashire II have been Minor Counties Champions 1907, 1934, 1937, 1948, 1949, 1960, 1964. Gillette Cup: Winners, 1970, 1971, 1972, 1975. Finalists 1974. John Player League Champions, 1969, 1970.

LARWOOD, Harold (1904–   )

Nowadays when one mentions Larwood of Nottinghamshire most people think first of the unfortunate bodyline controversy of 1932–33. This is a pity because Larwood was a remarkable fast bowler of such accuracy that he would have carved himself a niche in cricket history without becoming involved in that upheaval.

Larwood made his debut for Nottinghamshire in 1924 and during a career in which he was eventually hampered by ill health he took 1,427 wickets at an average cost of 17.51 before he gave up in 1938.

There is no doubt that the 1932–33 tour of Australia told on him both mentally and physically. During that tour he took 33 Test wickets (16 clean bowled) but. thereafter, he never bowled as fast and never appeared in another Test.

In his 14 seasons Larwood topped the 100 wicket mark eight times. His best being in 1932 when he took 162 (av. 12.86).

LAW, The and CRICKET

When King James produced his *Book of Sports*, a list of sports permitted on Sundays, cricket was not mentioned. This was in 1617.

However, in the accounts kept by the churchwardens of Eltham in 1654 there is reference to seven men having been fined two shillings each for playing cricket on "ye Lord's Day".

Cricket was not lawful on any day of the week until 1845, all games having been banned by an Act of Parliament introduced during the reign of Henry VIII.

One of the most interesting Law cases involving cricket was that which arose out of an injury sustained by Miss Bessie Stone, of Cheetham, Lancashire.

This lady was struck on the head by a ball hit *out of* the Cheetham Cricket Ground and she sued the club.

At the Manchester Assizes in 1948 Mr. Justice Oliver found in favour of the club but Miss Stone appealed against this decision and had the verdict reversed, being awarded damages of £104 19s. 6d. and costs amounting to £449.

By this time the case had attracted the attention of every cricket club in the country. The decision of the Court of Appeal could have a far reaching effect and so it was decided by the M.C.C. and the National Cricket Club Association that the matter should not be allowed to rest. So, in May 1951, a further appeal came before the House of Lords. Fortunately for cricket their Lordships reversed the decision once again and awarded the Cheetham Club costs against Miss Stone amounting to £2,000.

Because it was felt that this case was so important to the welfare of all cricket clubs the M.C.C. and the National Cricket Club Association got together and paid Miss Stone's costs.

LAWRY, William Morris (1937–   )

One of Australia's finest left-handed batsman, W. M. Lawry burst upon the Test cricket scene when he scored 130 out of 238 at Lord's in 1961 against the bowling of Statham and Trueman. That was only his second appearance as his country's opening batsman.

By the time his Test career was brought to an abrupt end (he was dismissed from the captaincy in 1971 as well as being surprisingly dropped from the side) he had scored 5,234 runs (av. 47.15) in 67 Tests.

Often criticised for negative thinking and defensive play, it was this that led to his downfall as captain, but he was still much too good a batsman to be discarded.

He scored more runs for Victoria than any other player ever did, including an innings of 266 v. N.S.W., at Sydney in 1960–61. His highest score in Tests was 210 v. West Indies, at Bridgetown in 1964–65, and this, mark you, against the fast bowling of Hall and Griffith, when, with R. B. Simpson, he was involved in an opening stand of 382, only 31 short of the world record in Test matches. There was never a batsman better equipped to score off fast bowling.

LAWS OF CRICKET

Apart from Articles of Agreement drawn up for certain matches played for high stakes the earliest comprehensive code of Laws which has been discovered is that believed to have been drawn up in 1744. The earliest version of these laws to be printed appeared in *The New Universal Magazine* in November 1752.

These were laws prepared by the London Club and were to govern cricket at the Artillery Ground, Findbury. They may have been drawn up specially for the first grand match which was played on that ground between Kent and All England, June 18, 1744. However, whether or not this is true is of little importance, but there is no doubt that these Laws of 1744 were a revision of much earlier laws. There are in existence today, copies of Articles of Agreement for particular matches arranged by the nobility, agreements which include many rules governing the actual conduct of the game. These agreements were necessary when such games were played for high stakes.

In 1755 a copy of the Laws was printed for the first time in booklet form by M. Read, and sold by W. Reeve in Fleet Street, London. These differed only slightly in the wording from the 1752 version and may therefore, be the same as those drawn up in the 144. Here they are in detail:

The Game at Cricket,
as settled by the several
Cricket-Clubs,
particularly that of the
Star and Garter, In Pall-Mall

The Pitching of the first wicket is to be determined by the toss of a Piece of Money. When the first Wicket is pitch'd, and the Popping-Crease cut, which must be exactly three Feet Ten Inches from the Wicket, the other Wicket is to be pitch'd directly opposite, at Twenty-two Yards Distance, and the other Popping Crease cut Three feet and Ten Inches before it.

The Bowling-Creases must be cut in direct line from each stump.

The stumps must be Twenty-two Inches long, and the Bail Six Inches.

The Ball must weigh between Five and Six Ounces.

When the wickets are both pitch'd, and all the Creases cut, the Party that wins the Toss-up may order which Side shall go in first, at his Option.

Laws for the Bowlers—Four Balls and Over.

The Bowler must deliver the Ball, with one Foot behind the Crease, even with the Wicket; and when he has bowl'd one Ball, or more, shall bowl to the Number of Four before he changes Wickets, and he shall change but once in the same innings.

He may order the Player that is in at his wicket, to stand on which side of it he pleases, at a reasonable distance.

If he delivered the Ball, with his hinder Foot over the Bowling-Crease, the Umpire shall call no Ball, tho' it be struck, or the Player be bowl'd out; which he shall do without being ask'd, and no Person shall have any right to question him.

Laws for the Strikers—or Those that are Inn.

If the Wicket is bowl'd down, it's out. If he strikes, or treads down, or falls himself upon his Wicket in striking (but not in over-running) it's out. A Stoke, or Nip, over or under his Bat, or upon his Hands (But not arms) if the Ball be held before it touches the Ground, though it be hugg'd to the Body, it's out.

If in striking, both his feet are over the Popping-Crease, and his Wicket put down, except his Bat is down within, it's out.

If he runs out of his Ground to hinder a Catch, it's out.

If a Ball is nipp'd up, and he strikes it again wilfully, before it came to the Wicket, it's out.

If the Players have cross'd each other, he that runs for the Wicket that is put down, is out: If they are not cross'd, he that returns is out.

If in running a Notch, the Wicket is struck down by a throw, before his Foot, Hand or Bat is over the popping Crease, or a stump hit by the Ball, though the Bail was down, it's out.

But if the Bail is down before, he that catches the ball must strike a Stump out of the Ground, Ball in Hand, or else it's not out.

If the Striker touches, or takes up the Ball before it has lain quite still, unless ask'd by the Bowler, or Wicket-Keeper. it's out.

Bat, Foot, or Hand over the Crease.

When the Ball has been in Hand by one of the Keepers, or Stoppers, and the player has been at Home, he may go where he pleases till the next Ball is bowl'd.

If either of the Strikers is cross'd, in his running Ground, designedly, the same must be determined by the Umpires.

N.B. The Umpires may order the Notch to be scored.

When the ball is hit up, either of the Strikers may hinder the Catch in his running Ground; of if it is hit directly across the Wickets, the other Player may place his Body anywhere within the Swing of the Bat, so as to hinder the Bowler from catching it; but he must neither strike at it, nor touch it with his Hands.

If a Striker nips a Ball up just before him, he may fall before his Wicket, or pop down his Bat, before it comes to the Wicket, to save it.

The Bail hanging on one Stump, though the Ball hit the Wicket, it not out.

Laws for the Wicket-Keepers.

The Wicket Keepers shall stand at a reasonable Distance behind the Wicket, and shall not move till the Ball is out of the Bowler's Hand, and shall not, by any Noise, incommode the Striker; and if his Hands, Knees, Foot, or Head be over, or before the Wicket, though the Ball hit it, it shall not be out.

Laws for the Umpires.

To allow Two Minutes for each Man to come in when one is out, and Ten Minutes between each Hand.

To mark the ball that it may not be changed.

They are sole Judges of all Outs and Inns; of all fair or unfair Play; of all frivolous delays; of all Hurts, whether real or pretended, and are discretionally to allow what Time they think proper before the Game goes on again.

In Case of a real Hurt to a Striker, they are to allow another to come inn, and the Person hurt to come inn again; but are not to allow a fresh Man to play, on either Side, on any Account.

They are sole Judges of all Hindrances;

crossing the Players in running and standing unfair to strike, and in Case of Hindrance may order a Notch to be scored.

They are not to order any Man out, unless appealed to by one of the Players.

These Laws are to the Umpires jointly.

Each Umpire is the sole Judge of all Nips and Catches; Inns and Outs; good or bad runs, at his own Wicket, and his Determinations shall be absolute; and he shall not be changed for another Umpire, without the Consent of both sides.

When the four Balls are bowl'd he is to call Over.

These laws are separately.

When both Umpires call Play three times, 'tis at the Peril of giving the Game from them that refuse to play.

When one reads through these earliest Laws of the Game one is surprised to find how little the game has changed during the past 200 years or more.

Here in chronological order are the main revisions and details of a few of the more important changes:

1771 Width of bat limited to 4½ inches

1774 The Laws of the Game were revised by a committee formed by Representatives of London, Middlesex, Hampshire, Surrey and Sussex.

Ball to be between 5½ and 5¾ ounces.

Choice of pitch is the privilege of the visiting team, but it must be within 30 yards. of a point selected by the home team.

L.B.W. Mentioned for the first time. The striker is out if he "puts his leg before the wicket with a design to stop the ball, and actually prevents the ball from hitting his wicket by it".

1788 Laws revised by the M.C.C.

Rolling, watering, covering, mowing and beating of the pitch permitted by mutual consent of the opposing teams.

No run if striker is caught.

L.B.W. only if ball pitches in a straight line to the wicket.

1798 New ball may be demanded at start of each innings.

Size of wicket increase to 24 by 7 inches.

New Law introduced which provides a penalty of five runs against a

fielder who stops a ball with his hat.

1810 Selection of the pitch to be made by the Umpires within 30 yards of a point selected by the sides.

Toss for choice of innings.

Striker may score off a "No ball". The striker may be run-out after playing a "No-ball" but not by any other way.

Bowlers not allowed to raise bowling hand above the elbow.

1811 Wides added to the score but called "byes".

1819 Height of wicket increased to 26 inches.

Popping Crease to be 4 feet from the wicket.

Striker can be out "Hit wicket" if any part of his dress breaks the wicket.

1823 Restrictions imposed on the use of substitutes. Not allowed to bowl, keep wicket, or field at point, middle wicket or long stop (to a fast bowler), except by agreement.

Umpires select the pitch.

Six runs allowed for "lost ball."

L.B.W. if ball strikes any part of the batsman's person providing the ball was delivered in a straight line to the wicket.

Size of the wicket increased to 27 by 8 inches.

1828 "Wide" first mentioned in the scoring. Previously the allowance for a "wide" was entered as a "Bye".

1835 Round-arm bowling legalised but the hand must not be raised above the shoulder.

Substitutes not allowed to bowl.

"Follow on" introduced. Side has to bat again if 100 runs behind on the first innings.

1838 Size of ball must be between 9 and 9¼ inches in circumference.

A wicket of three stumps is specified for the first time in the official rules

The practice of allowing a fresh bowler two trial bowls is discontinued.

1839 L.B.W. now requires a ball to be pitched straight irrespective of the line of its delivery.

1840 Ten minutes interval between innings.

1845 Ball no longer "dead" on the call of "Wide".

Umpires must change ends after each side has had one innings.

1849 Pitch may be swept and rolled between the innings.

1854 Limit of runs for a "Follow on" is reduced to 60 runs in a one-day match, or 80 in games of a longer duration.

1864 Over-arm bowling is now permitted as wording of law is revised to read simply that "the ball must be bowled".

1884 New complete revision of the laws. Boundaries officially mentioned for the first time.

1889 Over increased from four to five balls.
Bowler must not bowl two overs in succession.
Batting side may declare at any time on the last day.

1894 "Follow on" limit increased to 120 runs, in a three-day match.

1899 Ball lodging in a batsman's clothing is "Dead".

1900 "Follow on" limit increased to 150 runs for a three-day match, 100 runs for a two-day match, and 75 runs for a one-day match.
The enforcement of this "follow on" becomes optional.
Over increased to six balls.

1902 Bowling crease is lengthened to 8 feet 8 inches.

1927 Ball must be between 8 13/16 and 9 inches in circumference.

1931 Size of the wicket increased to not less than 27 inches nor more than 28 inches. In the latter case the width to be 9 inches instead of 8 inches.
Time allowed for sweeping and rolling the pitch reduced from 10 to 7 minutes.

1937 L.B.W. Law now includes the ball pitching on the off-side of the wicket, provided it hits some part of the striker between wicket and wicket.

1947 Complete revision of the Laws. Last over of match must be completed before "time" is called, if either captain so demands.
Over may be of six or eight balls.
No longer necessary for bowler to have his back foot "grounded".

1957 Declaration allowed at any time.

1969 Limitation of two leg-side fielders behind the popping-crease.

THE LAWS OF CRICKET
(Current in 1977)
Printed by permission of the M.C.C.
(A) THE PLAYERS, UMPIRES AND SCORERS

The Sides

1. A match is played between two sides of eleven players each, unless otherwise agreed. Each side shall play under a Captain who before the toss for innings shall nominate his players who may not thereafter be changed without the consent of the opposing Captain.

Notes

1. If a Captain is not available at any time, a deputy must act for him to deal promptly with points arising from this and other Laws.

2. No match in which more than eleven players a side take part can be regarded as First-class, and in any case no side should field with more than eleven players.

Substitutes

2. A substitute shall be allowed to field or run between the wickets for any player who may during the match be incapacitated from illness or injury, but not for any other reason without the consent of the opposing Captain; no substitute shall be allowed to bat or to bowl. Consent as to the person to act as substitute in the field shall be obtained from the opposing Captain, who may indicate positions in which the substitute shall not field.

Notes

1. A player may bat, bowl or field even though a substitute has acted for him previously.

2. An injured batsman may be "Out" should his runner infringe Laws 36, 40 or 41. As *Striker* he remains himself subject to the Laws; should he be out of his ground for any purpose he may be "Out" under Laws 41 and 42 at the wicket-keeper's end, irrespective of the position of the other batsman or the substitute when the wicket is put down. When *not the Striker* the injured batsman is out of the game and stands where he does not interfere with the play.

The Appointment of Umpires

3. Before the toss for innings two Umpires shall be appointed, one for each end to control the game as required by the Laws with absolute impartiality. No Umpire shall be changed during a match without the consent of both Captains.

Note

1. The Umpires should report themselves to the executive of the ground 30 minutes before the start of each day's play.

The Scorers

4. All runs scored shall be recorded by Scorers appointed for the purpose; the Scorers shall accept and acknowledge all instructions and signals given to them by the Umpires.

Note

1. The umpires should wait until a signal has been answered by a scorer before allowing the game to proceed. Mutual consultation between the scorers and the umpires to clear up doubtful points is at all times permissible.

(B) THE IMPLEMENTS OF THE GAME AND THE GROUND

The Ball

5. The ball shall weigh not less than 5½ ounces, nor more than 5¾ ounces. It shall measure not less than 8 13/16 inches, not more than 9 inches in circumference. Subject to agreement to the contrary either Captain may demand a new ball at the start of each innings. In the event of the ball being lost or becoming unfit for play, the Umpires shall allow another ball to be taken into use. They shall inform the batsman whenever a ball is to be changed.

Notes

1. All cricket balls used in First-class matches should be approved before the start of the match by the umpires and captains.

2. In First-Class matches, the Captain of the fielding side may demand a new ball after the prescribed number of overs has been bowled with the old one. The Governing Body for cricket in the country concerned, shall decide the number of overs applicable in that country, which shall not be less than 75 overs, nor more than 85 overs (55 to 65 eight ball overs). In other grades of cricket regulations will not apply unless agreed before the toss for innings.

3. Any ball substituted for one lost or becoming unfit for play should have had similar wear or use as that of the one discarded.

The Bat

6. The Bat shall not exceed 4¼ inches in the widest part; it shall not be more than 38 inches in length.

The Pitch

7. The Pitch is deemed to be the area of ground between the bowling creases, 5 feet in width on either side of the line joining the centre of the wickets. Before the toss for innings, the executive of the ground shall be responsible for the selection and preparation of the Pitch; thereafter the Umpires shall control its use and maintenance. The Pitch shall not be changed during a match unless it becomes unfit for play, and then only with the consent of both Captains.

The Wickets

8. The Wickets shall be pitched opposite and parallel to each other at a distance of 22 yards from stump to stump. Each wicket shall be 9 inches in width and consist of three stumps with two bails upon the top. The stumps shall be of equal and of sufficient size to prevent the ball passing through, with their top 28 inches above the ground. The bails shall be each 4⅜ inches in length, and, when in position on top of the stumps, shall not project more than ½ inch above them.

Notes

1. Except for the bail grooves the tops of the stumps shall be dome-shaped.

2. In a high wind the captains may agree, with the approval of the umpires, to dispense with the use of bails (see Law 31, Note 3).

The Bowling and Popping Creases

9. The bowling crease shall be marked in line with the stumps: 8 feet 8 inches/2.64 metres in length; with the stumps in the centre. The popping crease shall be marked 4 feet/1.22 metres in front of and parallel with the popping crease and shall extend a minimum of 6 feet/1.83 metres either side of the line of the stumps. The return crease shall be marked at each end of the bowling crease, at right angles to it, and shall extend forward to join the popping crease, and a minimum of 4 feet/1.22 metres behind the wicket. Both the return and popping creases shall be deemed unlimited length.

Note

1. The distance of the popping crease from the wicket is measured from a line running through the centre of the stumps to the inside edge of the crease.

2. Whenever possible, the popping crease and the return crease shall be redrawn during each interval.

(C) THE CARE AND MAINTENANCE OF THE PITCH

Rolling, Mowing and Watering

10. Unless permitted by special regulations, the Pitch shall not be rolled during a match except before the start of each innings and of each day's play, when, if the Captain of the batting side so elect, it may be swept and rolled for not more than 7 minutes. In a match of less than three day's duration, the Pitch shall not be mown during the match unless "special regulations" so provide. In a match of three or more day's duration, the pitch shall be mown under the supervision of the Umpires before play begins on alternate days after the start of a match, but should the pitch not be mown on any day on account of play not taking place, it shall be mown on the first day on which the match is resumed and thereafter on alternate days. (For the purpose of this Law a rest day counts as a day.) Under no circumstances shall the Pitch be watered during a match.

Notes

1. The Umpires are responsible that any rolling permitted by this Law and carried out at the request of the captain of the batting side, is in accordance with the regulations laid down and that it is completed so as to allow play to start at the stipulated time.

The normal rolling before the start of each day's play shall take place not earlier than half an hour before the start of play, but the captain of the batting side may delay such rolling until 10 minutes before the start of play should he so desire.

2. The time allowed for rolling shall be taken out of the normal playing time if a captain declare an innings closed either (a) before play starts on any day so late that the other captain is prevented from exercising his option in regard to rolling under this Law, or (b) during the luncheon interval later than 15 minutes after the start of such interval.

3. Except in the United Kingdom, if at any time a rain affected pitch is damaged by play thereon, it shall be swept and rolled for a period of not more than 10 consecutive minutes at any time between the close of play on the day on which it was damaged and the next resumption of play, provided that:—

(i) The umpire shall instruct the groundsman to sweep and roll the pitch only after they have agreed that damage

caused to it as result of play after rain has fallen warrants such rolling additional to that provided for in Law 10.

(ii) Such rolling shall in all cases be done under the personal supervision of both umpires and shall take place at such time and with such roller as the groundsman shall consider best calculated to repair the damage on the pitch.

(iii) Not more than one such additional rolling shall be permitted as a result of rain on any particular day.

(iv) The rolling provided for in Law 10, to take place before the start of play, shall not be permitted on any day on which the rolling herein provided for takes place within two hours of the time appointed for commencement of play on that day.

Covering the Pitch

11. The pitch shall not be completely covered during a match unless special regulations so provide covers used to protect the bowler's run up shall not extend to a greater distance that 3½ feet in front of the popping creases.

Note

1. It is usual under this Law to protect the bowlers' run up, before and during the match, both at night and, when necessary, during the day. The covers should be removed early each morning, if fine.

Maintenance of the Pitch

12. The Batsman may beat the Pitch with his bat, and Players may secure their footholds by the use of sawdust, provided Law 46 be not thereby contravened. In wet weather the Umpires shall see that the holes made by the Bowlers and Batsmen are cleaned out and dried whenever necessary to facilitate play.

(D) THE CONDUCT OF THE GAME

Innings

13. Each side has two innings, taken alternately, except in the case provided for in Law 14. The choice of innings shall be decided by tossing on the field of play.

Notes

1. The captains should toss for innings not later than 15 minutes before the time agreed upon for play to start. The winner of the toss may not alter his decision to bat or field once it has been notified to the opposing captain.

2. This Law also governs a one-day match in which play continues after the

completion of the first innings of both sides, (*See also* Law 22).

Following Innings

14. The side which bats first and leads by 200 runs in a match of five days or more, by 150 runs in a three-day or four-day match, by 100 runs in a two-day match, or by 75 runs in a one-day match, shall have the option of requiring the other side to follow their innings.

Declarations

15. The Captain of the batting side may declare an innings closed at any time during a match irrespective of its duration.

Note

1. A captain may forfeit his second innings. In this event, the interval between innings shall be 10 minutes and his decision must be notified to the opposing captain and umpires in sufficient time to allow seven minutes rolling of the pitch.

16. When the start of play is delayed by weather Law 14 shall apply in accordance with the number of days' play remaining from the actual start of the match.

Start and Close of Play and Intervals

17. The Umpires shall allow such intervals as have been agreed upon for meals, 10 minutes between each innings and not more than 2 minutes for each fresh batsman to come in. At the start of each innings and of each day's play and at the end of any interval the Umpire at the Bowler's end shall call "Play" when the side refusing to play shall lose the match. After "Play" has been called no trial ball shall be allowed to any player, and when one of the Batsmen is out the use of the bat shall not be allowed to any player until the next Batsman shall come in.

Notes

1. The umpires shall not award a match under this Law unless (i) "Play" has been called in such a manner that both sides can clearly understand that play is to start, (ii) an appeal has been made, and (iii) they are satisfied that a side will not, or cannot, continue play.

A batsman shall be considered to have commenced his innings once he has stepped on to the field of play.

2. It is an essential duty of the captains to ensure that the "in-going" batsman passes the "out-coming" one before the latter leaves the field of play. This is all the more important in view of the responsibility resting on the umpires for deciding whether or not the delay of the individual amounts to a refusal of the batting side to continue play.

3. The luncheon interval shall be limited to the number of minutes in the previous agreed period if an innings ends within 10 minutes of the scheduled commencement.

4. Bowling practice *on the pitch* is forbidden at any time during the game.

5. No bowler shall have a trial "Run-up" after "Play" has been called in any session, except at the fall of a wicket, when an umpire may allow such a trial "Run-up" if he is satisfied that it will not cause any waste of time.

18. The Umpires shall call "Time", and at the same time remove the bails from both wickets, on the cessation of play before any arranged interval, at the end of each day's play, and at the conclusion of a match. An "Over" shall always be started if "Time" has not been reached, and shall be completed unless a batsman is "Out" or "Retires" within 2 minutes of the completion of any period of play, but the "Over" in progress at the close of play on the final day of a match shall be completed at the request of either Captain even if a wicket fall after "Time" has been reached.

Notes

1. If, during the completion of the last over of any period of play, the players have occasion to leave the field the Umpires shall call "time". In the case of the last over of the match, there shall be no resumption of play and the match shall be at an end.

2. The last over before an interval or the close of play shall be started, provided the umpire standing at square leg, after walking at his normal pace, has arrived at his position behind the stumps at the bowler's end before time has been reached. The above provision will apply if the batsman is "out" off, or "Retires" after the last ball of an over when less than two minutes remain for play at the conclusion of the match.

3. In the final stages of a match, the umpires shall indicate when one hour of playing time remains (according to the agreed hours of play). From that moment, and providing a result is not reached earlier, the game shall continue for a minimum of 20 6-ball overs (15 8-ball overs).

In the event of play being interrupted (including intervals or stoppages for rain, bad light, etc.), the number of overs to be bowled shall be reduced in proportion to the time lost, in the ratio of one over for every three minutes (four minutes for 8-ball overs) or part thereof lost.

If a new innings starts within the last hour of a match, the minimum number of overs to be bowled shall be calculated on the basis of one for each three minutes, or part of three minutes (four minutes for 8-ball overs) remaining for play, when the innings is started.

Whenever the minimum number of overs has been bowled before the agreed time for the close of play, the match shall continue (in the absence of a result) until the agreed time for close of play.

If, during the last hour of the match, a bowler is unable to complete the over for any reason, the remaining balls shall be bowled by another bowler.

(Both captains may agree before the match to forgo the conditions of this Note subject to such agreement being permitted by "Special Regulations".)

Scoring

19. The score shall be reckoned by runs. A run is scored:—

1st. So often as the Batsmen after a hit, or at any time while the ball is in play, shall have crossed and made good their ground from end to end; but if either Batsman run a short run, the Umpire shall call and signal "One Short" and that run shall not be scored. The Striker being caught, no run shall be scored; a Batsman being run out, that run which was being attempted shall not be scored.

2nd. For penalties under Laws 21, 27, 29,44 and boundary allowances under Law 20.

Notes

1. If while the ball is in play, the batsmen have crossed in running, neither returns to the wicket he has left except in the case of a boundary hit, or a boundary from extras, or under Laws 30 Note 1 and 46 Note 4 (VII). This rule applies even should a short run have been called, or should no run be reckoned as in the case of a catch.

2. A run is "short" if either, or both, batsmen fail to make good their ground in turning for a further run.

Although such a "short" run shortens the succeeding one, the latter, if completed, counts. Similarly a batsman taking stance in front of his popping crease may run from that point without penalty.

3. (i) One run only is deducted if both

batsmen are short in one and the same run.

(ii) Only if three or more runs are attempted can more than one run be "short" and then, subject to (i) above, all runs so called shall be disallowed.

(iii) If either or both batsmen deliberately run short, the umpire is justified in calling "Dead Ball" and disallowing any runs attempted or scored as soon as he sees that the fielding side have no chance of dismissing either batsman under the Laws.

4. An Umpire signals "short" runs when the ball becomes "dead" by bending his arm upwards to touch the shoulder with the tips of his fingers. If there has been more than one "short" run the Umpires must instruct the scorers as to the number of runs disallowed. (See Note 1 to Law 4).

Boundaries

20. Before the toss for innings the Umpires shall agree with both sides on the Boundaries for play, and on the allowances to be made for them. An Umpire shall call or signal "Boundary" whenever, in his opinion, a ball in play hits, crosses or is carried over the Boundary. The runs completed at the instant the ball reaches the Boundary shall count only should they exceed the allowance, but if the "Boundary" result from an over throw or from the wilful act of a fieldsman, any runs already made and the allowance shall be added to the score.

Notes

1. If flags or posts are used to mark a boundary, the real or imaginary line joining such points shall be regarded as the boundary, which should be marked by a white line if possible.

2. In deciding on the allowances to be made for boundaries the Umpires will be guided by the prevailing custom of the ground.

3. It is a "Boundary" if the ball touches any boundary line or if a fieldsman with ball in hand grounds any part of his person on or over the line. A fieldsman, however, standing within the playing area may lean against or touch a boundary fence in fielding a ball (see also Law 35, Note 5).

4. An obstacle, or person, within the playing area is not regarded as a boundary unless so arranged by the Umpires. The Umpire is not a boundary, but sight screens within the playing area shall be so regarded.

5. The customary allowance for a boun-

dary is 4 runs, but it is usual to allow 6
runs for all hits pitching over and clear of
the boundary line or fence (even though a
ball has been previously touched by a
fieldsman). It is not usual to allow 6 runs
when a ball hits a sight screen full pitch, if
the latter is on or inside the boundary.

6. In the case of a boundary resulting
either from an overthrow or the wilful act
of a fieldsman, the run in progress counts
provided that the batsmen have crossed at
the instant of the throw or act.

7. The Umpire signals "Boundary" by
waving an arm from side to side, or a
boundary "6" by raising both arms above
the head.

Lost Ball

21. If a ball in play cannot be found or
recovered any Fieldsman may call "Lost
Ball" when 6 runs shall be added to the
score; but if more than 6 have been run
before "Lost Ball" be called, as many runs
as have been run shall be scored.

The Result

22. A match is won by the side which
shall have scored a total of runs in excess
of that scored by the opposing side in its
two completed innings; one-day matches,
unless thus played out, shall be decided by
the first innings. A match may also be
determined by being given up as lost by one
of the sides, or in the case governed by Law
17. A match not determined in any of these
ways, shall count as a "Draw".

Notes

1. It is the responsibility of the captains
to satisfy themselves on the correctness of
the scores on the conclusion of play.

2. Neither side can be compelled to
continue after a match is finished; a one-
day match shall not be regarded as
finished on the result of the first innings if
the Umpires consider there is a prospect of
carrying the game to a further issue in the
time remaining.

3. The result of a finished match is
stated as a win by runs, except in the case
of a win by the side batting last, when it is
by the number of wickets still then to fall.
In a one-day match which is not played
out on the second innings, this rule applies
to the position at the time when a result on
the first innings was reached.

4. A "Draw" is regarded as a "Tie"
when the scores are equal at the conclusion
of play but only if the match has been
played out. If the scores of the completed
first innings of a one-day match are equal,

it is a "Tie", but only if the match has not
been played out to a further conclusion.

The Over

23. The ball shall be bowled from each
wicket alternately in Overs of either 8 or
6 balls according to the agreed conditions
of play. When the agreed number have
been bowled and it has become clear to the
Umpire at the Bowler's wicket that both
sides have ceased to regard the ball as in
play, the Umpire shall call "Over", in a
distinct manner before leaving the wicket.
Neither a "No Ball" nor a "Wide Ball"
shall be reckoned as one of the "Over".

Note

1. In the United Kingdom the "over"
shall be 6 balls unless an agreement to the
contrary has been made.

24. A Bowler shall finish an "Over" in
progress unless he be incapacitated or be
suspended for unfair play. He shall be
allowed to change ends as often as desired,
provided only that he shall not bowl two
"Overs" consecutively in one innings. A
Bowler may require the Batsman at the
wicket from which he is bowling to stand
on whichever side of it he may direct.

Bowler breaking down— Completion of the Over

If, during the last hour of the match, a
bowler breaks down and is unable to
complete an over, the remaining balls shall
be bowled by another bowler.

If, during the first 100 overs of the first
innings of either team in a County Championship match, a bowler breaks down and
is unable to complete the over, the
remaining balls shall be bowled by another
bowler.

Dead Ball

25. The ball shall be held to be
"Dead"—on being in the opinion of the
Umpire finally settled in the hands of the
Wicket-keeper or of the Bowler; or on
reaching or pitching over the boundary; or
whether played or not, on lodging in the
dress of either a Batsman or Umpire; or on
the call of "Over" or "Time" by the
Umpire; or on a Batsman being out from
any cause; or on any penalty being awarded
under Laws 21 or 44. The Umpire shall
call "Dead Ball" should he decide to intervene under Law 46 in a case of unfair play
or in the event of a serious injury to a
player; or should he require to suspend play
prior to the Striker receiving a delivery.

The ball shall cease to be "Dead" on the Bowler starting his run or bowling action.

Notes

1. Whether the ball is "Finally settled" is a question of fact for the Umpire alone to decide.

2. An Umpire is justified in suspending play prior to the striker receiving a delivery in any of the following circumstances:—

(i) If satisfied that, for an *adequate* reason, the striker is not ready to receive the ball and makes no attempt to play it.

(ii) If the bowler drops the ball accidentally before delivery, or if the ball does not leave his hand for any reason.

(iii) If one or both bails fall from the striker's wicket before he receives the delivery.

In such cases the ball is regarded as "Dead" from the time it last came into play.

3. A ball does not become "Dead" when it strikes an Umpire (unless it lodges in his dress), when the wicket is broken or struck down (unless a batsman is out thereby), or when an unsuccessful appeal is made.

4. For the purpose of this and other Laws, the term "dress" includes the equipment and clothing of players and Umpires as normally worn.

5. The Umpire signals "Dead Ball" by crossing the arms back and forth at knee level.

No Ball

26. For a delivery to be fair, the ball must be bowled not thrown. If either Umpire be not entirely satisfied of the absolute fairness of a delivery in this respect he shall call and signal "No Ball" instantly upon delivery. The Umpire at the bowler's wicket shall call and signal "No Ball" if, in the delivery stride, no part of the bowler's front foot is behind the popping crease, whether grounded or raised, or if he is not satisfied that the bowler's back foot has landed within and not touching the return crease or its forward extension.

Notes

1. A ball shall be deemed to have been thrown if, in the opinion of either umpire, the process of straightening the bowling arm, whether it be partial or complete, takes place during that part of the delivery swing which directly precedes the ball leaving the hand.

This definition shall not debar a bowler from the use of the wrist in the delivery swing.

2. The striker is entitled to know whether the bowler intends to bowl over or round the wicket, overarm or underarm, right or left handed. An Umpire may regard any failure to notify a change in the mode of delivery as "unfair", if so, he should call "No Ball".

3. It is a "No Ball" if the bowler before delivering a ball throws it at the striker's wicket even in an attempt to run him out (*see* Law 46, Note 4 (vii)).

4. If a bowler break the near wicket with any part of his person during the delivery, such act in itself does not constitute "No Ball".

5. The Umpire signals "No Ball" by extending one arm horizontally.

6. An Umpire should revoke the call "No Ball" if the ball does not leave the bowler's hand for any reason.

27. The ball does not become "Dead" on the call of "No Ball". The Striker may hit a "No Ball" and whatever runs result shall be added to his score, but runs made otherwise from a "No Ball" shall be scored "No Balls", and if no runs be made one run shall be so scored. The Striker shall be out from a "No Ball" if he break Law 37, and either Batsman may be run out, or given out if he break Laws 36 or 40.

Notes

1. The penalty for a "No Ball" is only scored if no runs result otherwise.

2. Law 46 Note 4 (vii) covers attempts to run before the ball is delivered, but should the non-striker unfairly leave his ground too soon, the fielding side may run out the batsman at the bowler's end by any recognised method. If the bowler throws at the near wicket the Umpire does not call "No Ball", though any runs resulting are so scored. The throw does not count in the "Over".

Wide Ball

28. If the Bowler shall bowl the ball so high over or so wide of the wicket that in the opinion of the Umpire it passes out of reach of the Striker, and would not have been within his reach when taking guard in the normal position, the Umpire shall call and signal "Wide Ball" as soon as it shall have passed the Striker.

Notes

1. If a ball which the Umpire considers to have been delivered comes to rest in front of the striker, "Wide" should not be

called, and no runs should be added to the score unless they result from the striker hitting the ball which he has a right to do without interference by the fielding side.

Should the fielding side interfere, the umpire is justified in replacing the ball where it came to rest and ordering the fieldsmen to resume the places they occupied in the field before the ball was delivered.

2. The Umpire signals "Wide" by extending both arms horizontally.

3. An Umpire should revoke the call if the striker hits a ball which has been called "Wide".

29. The ball does not become "Dead" on the call of "Wide Ball". All runs that are run from a "Wide Ball" shall be scored "Wide Balls", or if no runs be made one run shall be so scored. The Striker may be out from a "Wide Ball", if he breaks Laws 38 and 42, and either Batsman may be run out, or given out if he breaks Laws 36 or 40.

Bye and Leg Bye

30. If the ball, not having been called "Wide" or "No Ball", pass the Striker without touching his bat or person, and any runs be obtained, the Umpire shall call or signal "Bye"; but if the ball touch any part of the Striker's dress or person except his hand holding the bat, and any run be obtained, the Umpire shall call or signal "Leg Bye"; such runs to be scored "Byes" and "Leg Byes" respectively.

Notes

1. Leg byes shall be scored only if, in the opinion of the umpire, the striker (a) has attempted to play the ball with his bat, or (b) has tried to avoid being hit by the ball.

In the case of a deflection by the stiker's person, other than in (a) or (b) above, the umpire shall call "dead ball" as soon as one run has been completed, or the ball has reached the boundary and such runs shall be disallowed. The batsmen will return to their original ends.

2. The Umpire signals "Bye" by raising an open hand above the head, and "Leg Bye" by touching a raised knee with the hand.

The Wicket is Down

31. The wicket shall be held to be "Down" if either the ball or the Striker's bat or person completely removes either bail from the top of the stumps, or, if both bails be off, strikes a stump out of the

ground. Any player may use his hand or arm to put the wicket down or, even should the bails be previously off, may pull up a stump, provided always that the ball is held in the hand or hands so used.

Notes

1. A wicket is not "down" merely on account of the disturbance of a bail, but it is "down" if a bail in falling from the wicket lodges between two of the stumps.

2. If one bail is off, it is sufficient for the purpose of this Law to dislodge the remaining one in any of the ways stated, or to strike any of the three stumps out of the ground.

3. If, owing to the strength of the wind, the captains have agreed to dispense with the use of bails (see Law 8, Note 2), the decision as to when the wicket is "down" is one for the Umpires to decide on the facts before them. In such circumstances the wicket would be held to be "down" even though a stump has not been struck out of the ground.

4. If the wicket is broken while the ball is in play, it is not the umpires' duty to remake the wicket until the ball has become "Dead". A fieldsman, however, may remake the wicket in such circumstances.

5. For the purposes of this and other Laws the term "person" includes a player's dress as defined in Law 25, Note 4.

Out of His Ground

32. A Batsman shall be held to be "Out of his Ground" unless some part of his bat in hand or of his person be grounded behind the line of the Popping Crease.

Batsman Retiring

33. A Batsman may retire at any time, but may not resume his innings without the consent of the Opposing Captain, and then only on the fall of a wicket.

Note

1. When a batsman has retired owing to illness, injury, or some other unavoidable cause, his innings is recorded as "Retired, Not Out", but otherwise as a completed innings to be recorded as "Retired, Out".

Bowled

34. The Striker is out "Bowled" if the wicket be bowled down, even if the ball first touch his bat or person.

Notes

1. The striker, after playing the ball, is out "Bowled", if he then kicks or hits it on his wicket before the completion of his stroke.

2. The striker is out "Bowled" under this Law when the ball is deflected on to his wicket off his person, even though a decision against him might be justified under Law 39 L.B.W.

Caught

35. The Striker is out "Caught" if the ball, from a stroke of the bat or of the hand holding the bat, but not the wrist, be held by a Fieldsman before it touch the ground, although it be hugged to the body of the catcher, or be accidentally lodged in his dress. The Fieldsman must have both his feet entirely within the playing area at the instant the catch is completed.

Notes

1. Provided the ball does not touch the ground, the hand holding it may do so in effecting a catch.

2. The act of making the catch starts from the time when the fieldsman first handles the ball. A catch is legitimate if the fieldsman held it while he had both feet inside the boundary edge, but went over the line afterwards.

3. The fact that a ball has touched the striker's person before or after touching his bat does not invalidate a catch.

4. The striker may be "Caught" even if the fieldsman has not touched the ball with his hands, including the case of a ball lodging in the wicket-keeper's pads.

5. A Fieldsman standing within the playing area may lean against the boundary to catch a ball, and this may be done even if the ball has passed over the boundary.

second time he may be out under this Law, but not only if the ball has not touched the ground since being first struck.

7. The striker may be caught off any obstruction within the playing area provided it has not previously been decided on as a boundary.

Handled the Ball

36. Either Batsman is out "Handled the Ball" if he touch it while in play with his hands, unless it be done at the request of the opposing side.

Notes

1. A hand holding the bat is regarded as part of it for the purposes of Laws 36, 37, and 39.

2. The correct entry in the score book when a batsman is given out under this Law is "Handled the Ball", and the bowler does not get credit for the wicket.

Hit the Ball Twice

37. The Striker is out "Hit the ball twice" if the ball be struck or be stopped by any part of his person, and he wilfully strike it again, except for the sole purpose of guarding his wicket, which he may do with his bat or any part of his person, other than his hands. No runs except those which result from an overthrow shall be scored from a ball lawfully struck twice.

Notes

1. It is for the Umpire to decide whether the ball has been so struck a second time legitimately or not. The Umpire may regard the fact that a run is attempted as evidence of the batsman's intention to take advantage of the second stroke, but it is not conclusive.

2. A batsman may not attempt to hit the ball twice, if in so doing he baulks the wicket-keeper or any fieldsman attempting to make a catch.

3. This Law is infringed if the striker, after playing the ball and without any request from the opposite side, uses his bat to return the ball to a fieldsman.

4. The correct entry in the score book when the striker is given out under this Law is "Hit the ball twice", and the bowler does not get credit for the wicket.

Hit Wicket

38. The Striker is out "Hit Wicket" if in playing at the ball he hit down his wicket with his bat or any part of his person, in the following circumstances. *(Experimental additional words to the Law.)*

(1) At any time when playing at the ball.

(2) In setting out for his first run, immediately after playing at the ball.

Notes

1. *"When playing at the ball" shall include a second strike by the batsman to keep the ball out of his wicket.*

2. *Any part of the batsman's dress shall be considered part of his person.*

3. *A batsman in "Not Out" if he breaks*

*his wicket in avoiding being run out or
stumped.*

*4. The term "playing at the ball" in this
Law shall be deemed to mean the action of
a batsman receiving a bowler's delivery
which has not been called "No ball",
regardless of whether such action is, in the
view of the umpire, an attempt by the
batsman to hit the ball or not.*

L.B.W.

**39. The Striker is out "Leg before
wicket"—If with any part of his person,
except his hand, which is in a straight line
between wicket and wicket, even though the
point of impact be above the level of the
bails, he intercept a ball which has not first
touched his bat or hand, and which, in the
opinion of the Umpire, shall have, or would
have, pitched on a straight line from the
Bowler's wicket to the Striker's wicket, or
shall have pitched on the off-side of the
Striker's wicket, provided always that the
ball would have hit the wicket.**

Notes

1. The word "hand" used in this Law
should be interpreted as the hand holding
the bat.

*The following experimental Law came
into force in 1972:—*

*Should the umpire be of the opinion
that the striker has made no genuine
attempt to play the ball with his bat, he
shall, on appeal, give the striker out
L.B.W. if he is satisfied that the ball
would have hit the stumps even though the
ball pitched outside the off stump, and
even though any interception was also
outside the off stump.*

Obstructing the Field

**40. Either Batsman is out "Obstructing
the Field"—If he wilfully obstruct the
opposite side; should such wilful obstruction by either Batsman prevent a ball from
being caught it is the Striker who is out.**

Notes

1. The Umpire must decide whether the
obstruction was "Wilful" or not. The
involuntary interception by a batsman
while running of a throw in is not in itself
an offence.

2. The correct entry in the score book
when a batsman is given out under this
Law is "Obstructing the field", and the
bowler does not get credit for the wicket.

Run Out

**41. Either batsman is out "Run Out"—If
in running or at any time, while the ball is
in play, he be out of his ground, and his
wicket be put down by the opposite side. If
the batsmen have crossed each other, he
that runs for the wicket which is put down
is out; if they have not crossed, he that has
left the wicket which is put down is out.
But unless he attempt to run, the Striker
shall not be given "Run Out" in the
circumstances stated in Law· 42, even
should "No Ball" have been called.**

Note

1. If the ball is played on to the opposite
wicket, neither batsman is liable to be
"Run Out" unless the ball had been
touched by a fieldsman before the wicket
is put down.

Stumped

**42. A Striker is out "Stumped"—If in
receiving a ball, not being a "No Ball"
delivered by the Bowler, he be out of his
ground otherwise than in attempting a run,
and the wicket be put down by the Wicket-
Keeper without the intervention of another
fieldsman. Only when the ball has touched
the bat or person of the Striker may the
Wicket-Keeper take it in front of the
wicket for this purpose.**

Note

1. The Striker may be "Stumped" if the
wicket is broken by a ball rebounding
from the wicket-keeper's person.

The Wicket-Keeper

**43. The Wicket-Keeper shall remain
wholly behind the wicket until a ball
delivered by the Bowler touches the bat or
person of the Striker, or passes the wicket,
or until the Striker attempts a run. Should
the Wicket-Keeper contravene this Law,
the Striker shall not be out except under
Laws 36, 37, 40 and 41 then only subject
to Law 46.**

Notes

1. This Law is provided to secure to the
Striker his right to play the ball and to
guard his wicket without interference
from the wicket-keeper. The striker may
not be penalised if in the legitimate
defence of his wicket he interferes with the

wicket-keeper, except as provided for in Law 37, Note 2.

The Fieldsman

44. The Fieldsman may stop the ball with any part of his person, but if he wilfully stop it otherwise five runs shall be added to the run or runs already made; if no run has been made five shall be scored. The penalty shall be added to the score of the Striker if the ball has been struck, but otherwise to the score of Byes, Leg Byes, No Balls or Wides as the case may be.

Notes

1. A fieldsman must not use his cap, etc., for the purpose of fielding a ball.

2. The 5 runs are a penalty and the batsmen do not change ends.

3. The number of on-side fielders behind the popping crease at the instant of the bowler's delivery shall not exceed two. In the event of an infringement of this rule by the fielding side, the aquare-leg Umpire shall call "No Ball." The Umpire may elect to stand on the off-side, provided he informs the Captain of the fielding side and the Striker of his intention to do so.

(E) Duties of the Umpires

45. Before the toss for innings, the Umpires shall acquaint themselves with any special regulations, and shall agree with both Captains, on any other conditions affecting the conduct of the match; shall satisfy themselves that the wickets are properly pitched; and shall agree, between themselves on the watch or clock to be followed during play.

Notes

1. Apart from "Special Regulations" other conditions of play within the framework of the Laws are frequently necessary, e.g., Hours of play, intervals, etc.

2. The captains are entitled to know which clock or watch will be followed during play.

46. Before and during a match the Umpires shall ensure that the conduct of the game and the implements used are strictly in accordance with the Laws; they are the sole judges of fair and unfair play, and the final judges of the fitness of the ground, the weather and the light for play in the event of the decision being left to them; all disputes shall be determined by them, and if they disagree the actual state

of things shall continue. The Umpires shall change ends after each side has had one innings.

Notes

1. An Umpire should stand where he can best see any act upon which his decision may be required. Subject to this over-riding consideration the Umpire at the bowler's end should stand where he does not interfere with either the bowler's run up or the striker's view. The other Umpire may elect to stand on the off instead of the leg side of the pitch, provided he informs the captain of the fielding side and the striker of his intention to do so.

2. The Umpires must not allow the attitude of the players or spectators to influence their decisions under the Laws.

3. A code of signals for Umpires is laid down in the Notes to the relevant Laws; but an Umpire must call as well as signal, if necessary, to inform the players and scorers.

4. Fair and Unfair Play

(i) The Umpires are entitled to intervene without appeal in the case of unfair play, but should not otherwise interfere with the progress of the game, except as required to do so by the Laws.

(ii) In the event of a player failing to comply with the instructions of an Umpire or criticising his decisions, the Umpires should in the first place request the captains to take action, and if this proves ineffective, report the incident forthwith to the executives of the teams taking part in the match.

(iii) It is illegal for a player to lift the seam of the ball in order to obtain a better hold. In such case the Umpire will if necessary change the ball for one which has had similar wear, and will warn the captain that the practice is unfair. The use of resin, wax, etc., by bowlers is also unfair, but a bowler may dry the ball when wet on a towel or with sawdust.

(iv) Umpires are reminded that any waste of time constitutes unfair play. In the event of the bowler taking unnecessarily long to bowl an over, the umpire at the bowler's end, after consultation with the other umpire, shall take the following immediate action:—

(a) Caution the bowler and inform the captain of the fielding side that he has done so.

(b) Should this caution prove ineffective:—

  (i) Direct the captain of the fielding

side to take off the bowler at the end of the over in progress. The captain shall take the bowler off as directed.

(ii) Report the occurrence to the captain of the batting side as soon as an interval of play takes place.

A bowler who has been "taken off" as above may not bowl again during the same innings.

(v) It is the duty of the Umpires to intervene and prevent players from causing damage to the pitch which may assist the bowlers.

(Purely as a guide, it is suggested that the "danger area" is an area contained by an imaginary line 4ft. from the popping crease and parallel to it, and within two imaginary and parallel lines drawn down the pitch from points 1ft. on either side of the middle stump and 4ft. from the popping crease.)

In the event of a bowler contravening Law 46, Note 4(v), the umpire will:—

(a) In the first instance caution a bowler and notify the other umpire.

(b) If the caution is ineffective, inform the captain of the fielding side, and the other umpire of what has occurred.

(c) Should the above prove ineffective, the umpire at the bowler's end must:—

(i) At the first repetition call "Dead ball" when the over is regarded as completed.

(ii) Direct the captain of the fielding side to take the bowler off forthwith. The captain shall take the bowler off as directed.

(iii) Report the occurrence to the captain of the batting side as soon as an interval of play takes place.

A bowler who has been "taken off" as above may not bowl again in the same innings.

(vi) The persistent bowling of fast short-pitched balls is unfair if, in the opinion of the umpire at the bowler's end, it constitutes a systematic attempt at intimidation. In such event he must adopt the following procedure:

(a) When he decides that such bowling is becoming persistent he forthwith "cautions" the bowler.

(b) If this "caution" is ineffective, he informs the captain of the fielding side and the other Umpire of what has occurred.

(c) Should the above prove ineffective, the Umpire at the bowler's end must:

(i) At the first repetition call "Dead Ball", when the over is regarded as completed.

(ii) Direct the captain of the fielding side to take the bowler off forthwith. The captain shall take the bowler off as directed.

(iii) Report the occurrence to the captain of the batting side as soon as an interval of play takes place.

A bowler who has been "Taken off" as above may not bowl again during the same innings.

(vii) Any attempt by the batsman to *steal a run* during the bowler's run up is unfair. Unless the bowler throws the ball at either wicket (*see* Laws 26, Note 3 and 27 Note 2), the Umpire should call "Dead Ball" as soon as the batsmen cross in any attempt to run, after which they return to their original wickets.

(viii) No player shall leave the field for the purpose of having a rub down or shower while play is actually in progress.

5. GROUND, WEATHER AND LIGHT

(i) Unless agreement to the contrary is made before the start of a match, the captains (during actual play the batsmen at the wickets may deputise for their captain) may elect to decide in regard to the fitness of the ground, weather or light for play; otherwise in the event of disagreement, the Umpires are required to decide.

(ii) Play should only be suspended when the conditions are so bad that it is unreasonable or dangerous for it to continue. The ground is unfit for play when water stands on the surface or when it is so wet or slippery as to deprive the batsman or bowlers of a reasonable foothold, or the fieldsmen of the power of free movement. Play should *not* be suspended merely because the grass is wet and the ball slippery.

(iii) After any suspension of play, the captains, or, if the decision has been left to them, the Umpires, unaccompanied by any of the players, will without further instructions carry out an inspection immediately the conditions improve, and will continue to inspect at intervals. Immediately the responsible parties decide that play is possible, they must call upon the players to resume the game.

Appeals

47. The Umpires shall not order a Batsman out unless appealed to by the other side which shall be done prior to the delivery of the next ball, and before "Time" is called under Law 18. The Umpire at the Bowler's wicket shall answer

appeals before the other Umpire in all cases except those arising out of Laws 38 and 42 and out of Law 41 for run out at the Striker's wicket. In any case in which an Umpire is unable to give a decision, he shall appeal to the other Umpire whose decision shall be final.

Notes

1. An appeal, "How's that!" covers all ways of being out (within the jurisdiction of the Umpire appealed to), unless a specific way of getting out is stated by the person asking. When either Umpire has given a batsman "Not Out" the other Umpire may answer any appeal within his jurisdiction, provided it is made in time.

2. The Umpire signals "Out" by raising the index finger above the head. If the batsman is not out, the Umpire calls "Not Out".

3. An Umpire may alter his decision provided that such alteration is made promptly.

4. Nothing in this Law prevents an Umpire before giving a decision from consulting the other Umpire on a point of fact which the latter may have been in a better position to observe. An Umpire should not appeal to the other Umpire in cases on which he could give a decision merely because he is unwilling to give that decision. If after consultation he is still in any doubt, the principle laid down in Law 46 applies and the decision will be in favour of the batsman.

5. The Umpires should intervene if satisfied that a batsman, not having been given out, has left his wicket under a misapprehension.

6. Under Law 25 the ball is "Dead" on "Over" being called; this does not invalidate an appeal made prior to the first ball of the following "over", provided the bails have not been removed by both Umpires after "Time" has been called.

Notes for Scorers and Umpires

1. (a) Law 4 explains the status of the scorers in relation to the Umpires.

(b) During the progress of the game, if two scorers have been appointed, they should frequently check the total to ensure that the score sheets agree.

(c) The following method of entering "No Balls" and "Wides" (Laws 27 and 29) in the score sheet is recommended.

(i) If no run is scored from the bat off a "No Ball", the latter should be entered as an "Extra", and a dot placed in the Bowling analysis with a circle round it

to show that the ball does not count in the over.

(ii) If runs are scored from the bat off a "No Ball", they should be credited to the striker, and entered in the bowling analysis with a circle round the figure. Such runs count against the bowler in his analysis even though the ball does not count in the over.

(iii) All runs scored from "Wide Balls" are entered as "Extras", and inserted in the bowler's analysis with a cross to indicate that the ball does not count in the over.

2. The following code of signalling between the Umpires and the scorers has been approved:—

Boundaries—by waving the hand from side to side.

A boundary six—by raising both arms above the head.

Byes—by raising the open hand above the head.

Leg Byes—by touching a raised knee with the hand.

Wides—by extending both arms horizontally.

No Balls—by extending one arm horizontally.

The decision "Out"—by raising the index finger above the head.

One Short—by bending the arm upwards and by touching the top of the nearest shoulder with the tips of the fingers of one hand.

3. If the above instructions are properly carried out, cases of disagreement as regards the scores and the results of matches should not occur.

It is, however, important that the captains should satisfy themselves of the correctness of the scores on the conclusion of Play, as errors cannot subsequently be corrected.

It should be noted that, in general, by accepting the result notified by the scorers, the captain of the losing side has thereby acquiesced in the "playing out or giving up" of the match as stated in Law 22.

Regulations for Drying the Pitch and Ground in First-Class Matches

N.B. These regulations are primarily designed for First-Class cricket, and their application in whole or in part in other grades of Cricket is at the discretion of the ground, etc., authorities.

1. Except as provided below, the existing regulations in regard to the rolling of

the pitch and the fitness of the ground for play shall apply. (*See* Laws 10, 12 and 46).

2. (i) To enable play to proceed with the least possible delay after rain, the groundsman shall adopt every practical means to protect or rid the surface of the ground, *other than the pitch*, of water or dampness at any time except while play is in progress.

(ii) Prior to tossing for choice of innings the artificial drying of the pitch and outfield shall be at the discretion of the groundsman. Thereafter and throughout the match the drying of the outfield may be undertaken at any time by the groundsman, but the drying of the pitch shall be carried out only on the instructions and under the supervision of the Umpires. The Umpires shall be empowered to have the pitch dried without a reference to the Captains at any time they are of the opinion that it is unfit for play.

(iii) In wet weather, the Umpires shall see that the foot-holes made by the bowlers and batsmen are cleaned, dried and filled up with sawdust at any time during the match, although the game is not actually in progress.

The groundsman, without instructions from the Umpires, may also clean out in this way foot-holes, provided they are not on any part of the pitch more than 3ft. 6ins. in front of the popping creases.

The drying of the footholds on the pitch itself may be undertaken, as directed by the Umpires, at any time. The Umpires may also direct the groundsman to protect against further rain marks made by the bowlers, even though they be more than 3ft. 6ins. in front of the popping creases, provided that they are not between wicket and wicket, with loose sawdust, which, however, shall be removed prior to the resumption of play.

(iv) The Umpires shall ascertain from the groundsman before the commencement of a match, what equipment is available for drying the pitch artificially.

Any roller may be used, if the Umpires think desirable but only (except as laid down in paragraph [2] [v]) for the purpose of drying the pitch and making it fit for play, and not otherwise. This would allow Umpires to roll the pitch after drying it, say with a light roller, for a minute or two, should they consider it desirable.

(v) When the artificial drying of the pitch, under the supervision of the Umpires, coincides with any interval during the match, after the toss for choice

of innings, the Umpires, and not the captain of the batting side, shall select the roller to be used.

(vi) The fact that the Umpires may have dried the pitch artificially does not take the decision as regards the fitness of the pitch and ground for play out of the hands of the captains, even though the Umpires may have selected the roller to be used for the drying process. Law 46, Note 5 (i) is applicable in such cases.

LEAGUE CRICKET

Under this heading we refer only to the traditional League cricket of the Midlands and North of England, although the attractiveness of this type of cricket has more recently spread further afield with its introduction among the First-class Counties in 1969.

Truly competitive cricket was first played at Batley, Yorkshire, for it was there that they inaugurated a Cricket Cup competition in 1883—the Heavy Woollen District Cup. The first winner was the Heckmondwicke Club.

For some reason or other in the South of England there was until recent years a certain amount of prejudice against league cricket, but there is no doubt that the success of the Northern clubs in County Cricket is derived in some measure from the fact that so many of their players have been "blooded" in the keener competitive atmosphere of League cricket.

Many of the Northern Counties also loan professionals to the League clubs to provide them with valuable experience.

If one were asked to pinpoint the most essential difference between County and League cricket one would have to say that in League cricket it is more important to win that it is in County Cricket where the game's the thing.

County cricket, of course, needs money to keep going but nowhere is the financial aspect of the game given more emphasis than in League cricket where more points mean more spectators and more spectators mean more money.

The spectators who follow English League cricket are as partisan as most football crowds and they are mostly good judges of the game. Slovenly play or slacking in the field is not tolerated, every nerve is strained to gain a victory and so get more points for the climb up the table.

As already mentioned there have been many first-class players who began their cricketing careers in the Leagues. Here are just a few:—G. H. Hirst (Kirkheaton C.C.), Sir L. Hutton (St. Lawrence C.C. Pudsey), P. Holmes (Paddock C.C.), W. Watson (Paddock C.C.), W. Rhodes (Kirkheaton C.C.), M. Leyland (Walsden C.C.), H. Sutcliffe (Allerton Bywater C.C. and Pudsey Britannia C.C.), J. Wardle (Denaby C.C.), S. F. Barnes (Rishton C.C., Burnley C.C., etc.), H. Verity (Rawdon C.C.).

Many people in the South of England imagine that League cricket, like Northern Rugby League, is a professional game, but this is not the case. The fact is that most Leagues allow each club no more than one professional, and many famous county cricketers have rounded off their careers as club professionals in the Leagues, while many Overseas players have also displayed their talents in this class of cricket. Even before the last war there were many League professionals receiving £20 per match.

County cricketers who subsequently became League professionals include: G. Dews (Worcestershire to Dudley), R. E. Foster (Worcestershire to Stourbridge), E. G. Arnold (Worcestershire to Stourbridge), A. O. Jones (Nottinghamshire to Dudley), F. R. Foster (Warwickshire to Moseley), A. Gover (Surrey to West Bromwich Dartmouth), A. Wellard (Somerset to Kidderminster), C. J. Barnett (Gloucestershire to Rochdale and Longton), J. C. Laker (Surrey to Norton).

The principal Leagues and their dates of formation are: Birmingham and District League (the oldest) formed in 1888 and said to have been inspired by the formation of the Football League. Lancashire League (formed 1892) from the N.E. Lancashire League which was formed in 1890, Central Lancashire League (formed 1893 from the S.E. Lancashire League formed in 1892), Huddersfield League (1892), North Staffordshire League (1890), Yorkshire Council (1899), Durham Senior League (1902), Bradford League (1903), and Bassetlaw and District League (1904).

LEG BEFORE WICKET

L.B.W. was first mentioned in the Laws of Cricket in 1774. Prior to this the use of the curved bat, shaped something like a hockey stick and used with a sweeping motion, meant that the batsman stood more to one side of his wicket, but the introduction of the shorter straight bat moved the batsman closer and soon

brought the need for a law to discourage him from stepping in front of his wicket.

In 1774 a player was deemed to be out if he "puts his leg before the wicket with a design to stop the ball, and actually prevents the ball from hitting his wicket by it".

In 1788 it was decided to restrict the application of this law to a ball which "pitched in a straight line to the wicket", and in 1823 a player was out "L.B.W." if the ball which had been delivered in a straight line to the wicket struck any part of his person. The line of the ball's delivery was ignored after 1839 when the law reverted to its 1788 context inasfar as it referred to the pitch of the ball.

The development of the defensive style of batting subsequently caused much concern and several proposals were made to alter this law so as to assist the bowler and discourage "padding" by the batsman.

There was a strong movement towards accepting a proposal that the words "or, should he wilfully cross the wicket to defend it with his person" be added to this law ruling a batsman out, but in 1902 it did not receive the necessary two-thirds majority.

No definite alteration of or addition to the law was made until 1937 when it was extended to include the case of a ball pitching on the off-side of the wicket, and then hitting the striker between wicket and wicket.

When the Laws of Cricket were completely revised in 1947 a slight alteration was made in the wording to show that the striker was not excused if the ball struck his person (except his hand) above the level of the bails; and also to show that he could not be out "L.B.W." if the ball touched his bat or hand *before* striking his person.

In 1972 an experimental Law was introduced which is still in force. See under LAWS OF CRICKET—39 L.B.W.

LEG-BYE

These were recorded for the first time in a game between an England XI and Twenty-two of Edinburgh, May 6, 1850.

However, it is generally assumed that leg-byes were counted for many years before this.

There were 30 leg-byes scored in the West Indies 2nd innings against England, at Old Trafford in 1976—a Test match record.

LEICESTERSHIRE C.C.C.

Founded by 1820. Re-formed 1879.
Admitted to County Championship 1895.
Secretary: F. M. Turner, County Cricket
Ground, Grace Road, Leicester LE2 8AD.
Highest score for 701 for 4 declared v.
Worcestershire, at Worcester, 1906.
Highest individual score for 252* by S.
Coe v. Northamptonshire, Leicester, 1914.
Lowest score for: 25 v. Kent, Leicester,
1912. Before Leicestershire gained first-
class status they made a record low of 23
v. Lancashire, August 1889. Highest score
against: 739 for 7 declared, by
Nottinghamshire, at Nottingham, 1903.
Highest individual score against: 341 by
G. H. Hirst of Yorkshire, Leicester, 1905.
Lowest score against: 24 by Glamorgan, at
Leicester, 1971. Before first-class
status—26 by Surrey, 1886. Colours:
Scarlet and dark green. Badge: A running
fox. coloured gold on a green background.
Honours: County Champions, 1975.
Minor Counties Champions (Leicester-
shire II) 1931. Benson and Hedges Cup
Winners, 1972, 1975. John Player League
Champions, 1974.

LEYLAND, Maurice (1900–1967)

A typically smiling and witty Yorkshireman who made debut for his county in
1920 after some experience in Lancashire
League cricket.

The young Leyland took time to
establish himself but he eventually blos-
somed out into one of the most accomplished left-handed batsmen of his day.
There was certainly none more popular.

Powerfully built, Leyland was a
naturally aggressive hitter, an outstanding
fielder near the boundary, and a slow
left-arm bowler.

In a career which extended to 1948 his
aggregate of 33,660 runs included 80
centuries, the highest being 263 v. Essex,
at Hull, in 1936.

He scored 137 and 53* in his Test
debut, which was against Australia, at
Melbourne, in 1929, and played in a total
of 41 Tests scoring eight further centuries
with a top score of 187 against Australia,
at the Oval, in 1938, when he combined
with L. Hutton to create a record England
second wicket score of 382.

With his "Chinaman" Leyland once
performed the "hat-trick" against Surrey,
at Sheffield, in 1935.

LILLEY, Arthur Frederick Augustus (1867–1929)

A wicket-keeper who had the thrilling
experience of making his debut in first-
class cricket against the Australians.

This was in May 1888 when his county,
Warwickshire, was well beaten, but Lilley
had the satisfaction of stumping Trott and
Bonnor.

Few players can have made such a
memorable start to their careers and
although "Dick" Lilley did not leave any
world records behind him when he retired
in 1911 he was one of the most consistent
wicket-keepers this country has ever
known.

It is not surprising that, after making
such a fine debut, Lilley was never
dropped by Warwickshire until the season
of his retirement. In those 23 years he
dismissed nearly 900 batsmen including
92 in his 35 Test appearances.

Lilley held his place in the England side
for so long because he was not only a safe
wicket-keeper but also a batsman of no
mean ability. He made 16 centuries in his
career with a highest score of 141.

LILLYWHITE, James, Jnr. (1842–1929)

No collection of cricketers' biographies
could possibly be complete without at least
one of the famous Lillywhite family of
Sussex, and James, generally referred to
as Junior was the fourth generation of this
family which achieved so much for this
particular county.

He was an extremely accurate left-
handed medium-paced bowler who made
his debut for Sussex in 1862 and played in
every one of their games until 1881 when
he retired with a bag of 1,140 wickets
taken at an average cost of only 15.38.

One of his finest spells of bowling was
that for the South when he took all 10 of
the North's wickets for 129 at Canterbury
in 1872.

James Lillywhite captained England in
the first two Test matches which were
played in Australia in 1877 and was
largely instrumental in bringing the first
representative Australian team to England
the following year.

LINCOLNSHIRE C.C.C.

Founded 1853. Re-formed 1888, 1900 and
1921. Joined Minor Counties Championship 1896. Dropped out 1914. Re-entered

1924. Secretary: R. J. Charlton, 114 Gloucester Avenue, Grimsby, South Humberside. Highest score for: 458 for 5 declared v. Cambridgeshire, 1925. Highest score against: 458 by Yorkshire II, 1925; 463 for 6 declared by All India, 1911. Highest individual score for: 232 by R. E. Frearson v. Cambridgeshire, at Grantham, 1925. Highest individual score against: 253 by A. Booth of Lancashire II, at Grimsby, 1950. Lowest score for: 34 v. Buckinghamshire, 1937; 18 v. M.C.C., 1889. Lowest score against: 31 by Suffolk, 1910. Most wickets in a season: 81 (av. 11.18) by F. Geeson, 1890. Colours: Green and gold. Badge: The Lincoln Imp in gold. Honours: Minor Counties Champions, 1966.

LINDWALL, Raymond Russell (1921–   )

This fair-haired Australian pace bowler with the smooth action earned himself a big reputation as the opening batsmen's terror with the new ball, and is considered among the greatest of all fast bowlers.

In his first two Tests in England in 1948 he had Washbrook out for 6 and 8, and Hutton out for 13.

Lindwall made 61 Test appearances from 1946 to 1959 and took more wickets than any other Australian bowler in Test history except Benaud and McKenzie—228 (av. 23.05).

A splendid all-round athlete who was also a rugby full-back, Lindwall made three cricket tours of England, 1948, 1953, and 1956. In the first two he topped his side's Test bowling averages with 27 wickets (av. 19.62), and 26 wickets (av. 18.84), but in his third tour his bag was only 7 (av. 34.00).

Also an attractive batsman, he struck his best form against England in the Melbourne Test of 1946–47 and scored 100 in 115 minutes.

It was in that same 1946–47 series that he enjoyed one of his most successful bowling spells taking 7 for 63 and 2 for 46 in the final Test. His best in England was 6 for 20 and 3 for 50, at the Oval, in 1948.

LLOYD, Clive Hubert (1944–   )

Considering this hard-hitting left-handed batsman's performances in the last three or four years it is difficult to believe that his place in the West Indies team was not always certain after making his Test debut against India in 1966–67, more especially as he is almost worth a place for his fielding ability alone.

However, this bespectacled player was somewhat inconsistent as a Test batsman until his trip to Australia in 1973. Since then he has never looked back and was appointed the West Indies captain for the tour of India and Pakistan at a time when his side's Test status was at a low ebb. He has since led them to victory against India at home and away as well as the thrashing of England in 1976.

This dynamic player began his first-class career with Guyana (then British Guiana) in 1963 and has played for Lancashire since 1968, topping this county's batting averages in six of the eight seasons to 1976. One of his most remarkable displays of power was against Glamorgan, at Swansea in 1976, when he equalled Jessop's record for the fastest double-century with 201 in 120 minutes. His 242* for West Indies v. India, at Bombay in 1974–75 is his highest score, while as a right-arm medium pace bowler he took 4 Leicestershire wickets for 48 at Old Trafford in 1970.

LOCK, Graham Anthony Richard (1929–   )

One of the best slow left-arm bowlers of the post-war era, "Tony" Lock was also a confident right-handed batsman and a close fielder who must rank with the finest in the history of the game.

He also made more catches than any other fieldsman in cricket history apart from W. G. Grace and F. E. Woolley. In his best season, 1957, Lock held a total of 64, and this included eight in one match against Warwickshire, at the Oval.

1957 was one of Lock's best seasons in every respect for apart from his magnificent fielding he also dismissed 212 batsmen as a bowler. His average of 12.02 was the best since 1888 by the season's leading bowler, The only season in which Lock exceeded this number of wickets was in 1955 when he captured 216 (14.39).

In a first-class career spread over 26 seasons with Surrey, Western Australia, and Leicestershire, Lock captured 2,844 wickets (av. 19.23) and made 830 catches.

LOHMANN, George Alfred (1865–1901)

One hundred and twelve Test wickets at an average cost of only 10.75 runs each gives this Surrey all-rounder the finest bowling average in the history of international cricket.

W. G. Grace once said that he never met a bowler who used his head more than Lohmann who bowled right-hand and could vary his pace from slow to fast and still maintain his accuracy.

Lohmann's career extended from 1884 to 1897 and during that time he captured over 1,800 wickets at something like 14 runs apiece; played in 18 Tests, in which he took 10 or more wickets on five occasions, and performed the "hat-trick" once.

A bowler of great endurance, he bowled unchanged throughout a match on at least four occasions.

The South Africans suffered the most at his hands, for in the three Tests of the 1895–96 tour of that country he took no less than 35 wickets costing only 5.80 apiece. Nothing quite like this has ever been achieved by any other bowler in a Test rubber, at least not with so few balls. Lohmann delivered only 520 balls in those three Tests.

LONG CAREERS

See also under AGE (OLDEST).

W. G. Grace made his first-class debut in 1865 and his last appearance came 43 years later, in 1908. Several gentlemen have come out of retirement to play one or two games 40 years or so after making their debut but W. G. was playing regularly for at least 35 years. He last topped 1,000 runs in first-class cricket in 1902 when he was 54 years of age.

A. D. Nourse (sen.) began his first-class career in 1896 and continued until the end of the 1934–35 season. So completing 40 years in the game.

G. H. Hirst first appeared for Yorkshire in 1892 and his last appearance was not until 37 years later when he played in a Scarborough Festival match in 1929. He had, however, really retired from active first-class cricket in 1921.

C. E. de Trafford of Leicestershire made his debut in 1884 and his final appearance in 1920.

Players whose careers lasted for 35 years include: W. G. Quaife, who made his first appearance for Warwickshire in 1893 and his last in 1928; E. Smith, Yorkshire, 1888–1923; J. Gunn, Nottinghamshire, 1897–1932; J. T. Hearne, Middlesex, 1888–1923.

33 years—W. H. Ashdown made his debut for Kent in 1914 and did not finally retire until 1947; W. E. Astill, Leicestershire, 1906–1939; G. Cox, Sussex, 1895–1928; C. Hill, South Australia, 1892–1925; A. C. MacLaren, Lancashire, 1890–1923. He virtually retired in 1914 but came back again in 1921.

32 years—W. Rhodes made his debut for Yorkshire in 1898 and his last appearance in 1930; F. E. Woolley, Kent, 1906–1938; A. N. Hornby, Lancashire, 1867–1899.

LONGEST GAME

The final Test of England's South African tour of 1938–39 was spread over 11 days (Nine days actual play). It began on Friday, March 3, as a timeless Test, but had to be abandoned as a draw on March 14, when the England team had to catch their boat home. There was no play on the two intervening Sundays or on Saturday, March 11.

LONGEST HIT

See under BIG HITTING.

LONGEST INNINGS

See under INNINGS (LONGEST).

LORD'S CRICKET GROUND

The present Lord's cricket ground in St. John's Wood Road, London N.W.8 is the third ground of that name.

The first was secured in 1787 by Thomas Lord, a Yorkshireman who was on the staff of the old White Conduit club. Backed by the Earl of Winchelsea and Charles Lennox (later Duke of Richmond), he secured the lease of a piece of land from the Portman Estate. It was situated where Dorset Square now stands, and the first game was played there on May 31–June 1, 1787, between Middlesex and Essex.

The new ground became the headquarters of the Marylebone Cricket Club, but it wasn't very long before Thomas Lord, anticipating the encroachment of the builders upon the site, secured the lease of another piece of ground further west and nearer to St. John's Wood. This was in 1808, but the actual move from Dorset Square to this second ground was not made until May 1811, the turf having been taken up at the old ground and re-laid at the new Lord's.

However, the move was not popular with members of the M.C.C. and apparently there were few regrets when it was decided to cut the new Regent's Canal through the centre of the ground.

So Thomas Lord obtained another site still further west at a rental of £100 a year. This, the present Lord's ground, was opened, complete with tavern and pavilion, in May 1814. The first match was between the M.C.C. and Hertfordshire, the hosts winning by an innings and 27 runs.

Although the ground has always retained the name of its original proprietor Thomas Lord was actually bought out by William Ward for £5,000 in 1825 when the canny Yorkshireman was about to commence building houses on the site.

Ward was succeeded as proprietor by James Henry Dark in 1835, and, in 1860, the freehold of the ground became the property of Isaac Moses, although Dark retained the lease.

The M.C.C. acquired the ground for £18,000 in 1866 and it has been the headquarters of the game ever since. It has also been the headquarters of Middlesex C.C.C. since 1877.

The original pavilion, which was greatly improved through the generosity of William Ward, was destroyed by fire in 1825. With it went most of the old cricket records.

A second pavilion was opened in 1826 and in 1838 an archery ground, a bowling green, and a tennis court, were laid out.

The pavilion was greatly enlarged in about 1866 and at the same time the tavern was replaced with a much improved building. A grandstand was also built.

A third pavilion, the present one, was begun in 1889 and opened in the following year. The Mound Stand followed in 1898, while a further stand was added in 1926 and another in 1934, the Sir Pelham Warner stand in 1958, and the Tavern Stand in 1967.

The area of the ground is approximately five acres, and today Lord's has a capacity of 35,000. The record attendance is 137,915 for the England–Australia Test in June 1953 while the record gate receipts (£119,692) were taken for the England v. Australia Test of 1975.

LOWEST SCORES

See also under Duck.

The lowest totals recorded by each of the county sides, as well as the lowest individual scores are given under the name of each county. Lowest scores in Test cricket are given under the name of each country.

The lowest score ever recorded in an important cricket match is 6 by "The Bs" (one man absent) v. England, at Lord's, 1810.

The record low in a first-class match is 12, by Oxford University (one man absent) v. M.C.C., at Oxford, May 24, 1877, and also by Northamptonshire v. Gloucestershire, at Gloucester, June 11, 1907.

The lowest score in a first-class match outside of England is 13. This score has been recorded in two games in New Zealand—by Wellington v. Nelson, at Nelson, 1862–63, and by Auckland v. Canterbury, at Auckland, 1877–78.

The lowest match aggregate by any one side in England is 42 (15 and 27) by Northamptonshire (one man absent) v. Yorkshire, at Northampton, 1908. Hirst took 12 for 19, and Haigh 6 for 19.

The world record low match aggregate is 34 (16 and 18) by Border v. Natal, at East London, 1959–60. G. Griffin 7 for 11, T. L. Goddard 6 for 4, J. Cole 7 for 17.

The lowest match aggregate is 105 runs for 31 wickets, M.C.C. v. Australians, at Lord's in that astonishing match of 1878. The M.C.C. were all out for 33 in their first innings, but the Australians were then skittled out for 41.

When the M.C.C. went in again they were all out in 57 minutes for only 19 runs. The Australians then took 20 minutes to gain the 12 runs needed for victory with the loss of only one wicket.

Some interesting low scores in other minor matches:

Leeds were out for 12 (including 11 extras) v. Harrogate, in August 1847.

Hereford were out for 4 (including 1 bye) v. The Bar of the Oxford Circuit and The Militia of Hereford, at Hereford, July 1855. Only two players were able to score.

There have been several instances of sides being dismissed for 0 but not in first-class matches.

Kent were all out for 5 in the first innings of a game against Bexley (with three of England), at Bowman's Lodge, Dartford Heath, September 1805. Seven of the Kent side failed to score.

Tests

The lowest score in a Test innings is 26 by New Zealand v. England, at Auckland, March 28, 1955.

J. G. Leggatt, c Hutton b Tyson   1

M. B. Poore, b Tyson	0
B. Sutcliffe, b Wardle	11
J. R. Reid, b Statham	1
G. O. Rabone, lbw b Statham	7
S. N. McGregor, c May b Appleyard	1
H. B. Cave, c Graveney b Appleyard	5
A. R. MacGibbon, lbw b Appleyard	0
I. A. Colquhoun, c Graveney b Appleyard	0
A. M. Moir, not out	0
J. A. Hayes, b Statham	0
Extras	0
Total	26

Tyson 2 for 10, Statham 3 for 9, Appleyard 4 for 7, and Wardle 1 for 0.

England won by an innings and 20 runs.

The lowest match aggregate in a Test is 234 runs for 29 wickets; Australia (153) v. South Africa (36 and 45), at Melbourne, February 1932.

M

MACARTNEY, Charles George (1886–1958)

When this diminutive Australian first took the cricket field his slow left-hand bowling was considered more valuable than his right-hand batting, but subsequently he developed into one of the leading batsmen of his day, and was at his peak in the years immediately after World War I.

The "Governor General", as he was popularly known, toured England four times, 1909, 1912, 1921 and 1926.

As already suggested he did better as a bowler than as a batsman in that first tour (at Leeds he took 11 for 85), but in the Triangular Tournament tour of 1912 we had more than a hint of the high standard he was reaching as a batsman, for he got six separate centuries including a score of 208 against Essex.

As for those two post-war tours it was in these that the spectators were treated to some of the most daring, hard hitting innings ever seen from such a small man.

In 1921 his eight centuries included a score of 345 in a single day against Nottinghamshire, the highest score ever made by an Australian in England. There were seven more centuries on his final tour in 1926, and those who were present have still not forgotten his masterly display in scoring 151 when he and Woodfull added 235 for the second wicket against England at Leeds.

When Macartney retired in 1935 he had amassed a total of 49 separate centuries.

McCABE, Stanley Joseph (1910–1968)

All those who were at Trent Bridge in June 1938 have particular cause to remember this stylish Australian batsman, for it was there, in the first Test of that season, that he put together one of the fastest double-centuries ever seen in International cricket, reaching 232 in 230 minutes before being caught by young Denis Compton off Verity.

McCabe enjoyed batting on English wickets more than many Australians, for it was here that he made his highest score of 240. That was against Surrey at the Oval in 1934.

Making his debut in 1928–29, McCabe was first chosen to represent Australia on the England tour of 1930 when he shone more as a medium-pace bowler.

In all he played in 39 Tests scoring 2,748 runs (av. 48.21).

McDONALD, Colin Campbell (1928–   )

Made his debut in first-class cricket with Victoria in 1947–48 and gradually established himself as one of the finest opening batsmen in Australia.

In 1949–50 he scored 186 in an opening partnership of 337 with K. Meuleman for Victoria v. South Australia at Adelaide, and subsequently an innings of 207 v. New South Wales, at Sydney, in 1951–52, earned him his place in the final Test of that season against the West Indies.

McDonald visited England three times. He did not make a Test appearance on his first tour of 1953, but in 1956 he was one of Australia's opening batsmen in all five Tests, scoring 243 runs (av. 24.30).

In the 1961 England tour he opened for Australia in the first three Tests before a wrist injury cost him his place in the side. His average for five innings, however was only 19.00.

McDonald's highest score was 229 v. South Australia at Adelaide in 1953–54.

McGLEW, Derrick John (1929–   )

South Africa's record breaking opening batsman made his first-class debut in 1947–48 and his first Test appearance in 1951 when he was a surprise choice for the England tour.

McGlew came third in his side's batting averages that season with 38.53, but he moved to top place on his next visit to England in 1955 when he hit five centuries, including scores of 104* and 133 in Tests.

It was during this 1955 tour that McGlew first took over as captain of South Africa and they won both of the Tests in which he led the side; the first time that South Africa had ever won two Tests in a rubber in England.

McGlew proved a stubborn opener with a strong defence and in 1958 against Australia, at Durban, he scored the slowest century ever made (545 minutes) when going on to make 105 in 575 minutes.

At Wellington in 1952–53 he remained on the field for the whole of a Test which lasted for 3½ days and made his highest score of 255*.

McKENZIE, Graham Douglas (1941–   )

The youngest player ever to capture as many as 200 wickets (27 years 6 months) in Test cricket, this powerfully built fast bowler stands second only to Richie Benaud in the list of Australia's most successful Test bowlers. His total—246 (av. 29.78) in 60 Tests.

Made debut for Western Australia in 1959–60 and joined Leicestershire 10 years later.

Glamorgan will always remember McKenzie for he took 7 for 8 when they were all out for 24 v. Leciestershire in August 1971.

MacLAREN, Archibald Campbell (1871–1944)

It is elementary cricket knowledge that this Lancastrian played the highest individual innings ever made by an Englishman—424 for Lancashire v. Somerset, at Taunton, in 1895. On that occasion he batted for 7 hours 50 minutes.

A fine example of correct batting, his execution of driving strokes has never been surpassed.

After distinguishing himself at Harrow he made a sensational debut for Lancashire, in 1890, by scoring 108 against Sussex at Hove.

MacLaren, who captained Lancashire from 1894 to 1896 and from 1899 to 1907, enjoyed one of the longest first-class cricketing careers, for he did not play his last match until 1923.

An outstanding captain, both as a disciplinarian and a tactician, he led the England side in 22 Tests, all against Australia. His total number of appearances in these matches from 1896 to 1909, being 35.

This grand player, who began his first-class career in such remarkable fashion, ended it on the same high note. Leading an M.C.C. team to Australia and New Zealand in 1922–23, when he was in his 52nd year, he scored 200* against New Zealand at Wellington.

MAIDEN CENTURY

The highest innings ever recorded by a player making his maiden century in first-class cricket is 292* by V. T. Trumper for New South Wales v. Tasmania, at Sydney, 1898–99.

MAILEY, Arthur Alfred (1888–1967)

This Australian leg-spin and googly bowler created a record for his country during his first season of Test cricket by taking nine England wickets for 121. This was in England's second innings of the fourth Test, at Melbourne, January 1921.

In England the following summer he was not as successful, and although he did better in his second tour in 1926 he was never quite the same batsman's terror in England as he was on his home wickets. His bag of 36 wickets in that Test series of 1920–21 still remains a record for an Australian bowler against England.

However, while he did not enjoy the same success in Tests in England he did scare a few of the county sides. In 1921 he captured all 10 Gloucestershire wickets for 66, and at Liverpool, in 1926, nine Lancashire wickets fell to him at a cost of 86 runs.

Mailey's first-class career with New South Wales extended from 1913 to 1930 and during this time he captured 779 wickets (av. 24.10).

MANJREKAR, Vijay Laxman (1931–   )

Another Indian cricketer who is well known in England not only because of his tours (1952 and 1959) but also because of his three seasons with Castleton Moor in the Central Lancashire League.

A stylish batsman noted for his strong defence Manjrekar was the youngest member of the Indian touring team in England in 1952 and he got his maiden first-class century, 133, against England in the Leeds Test. It would not be an exaggeration to say that he won that Test with his brave fight against all the odds.

Manjrekar's highest Test score was 189* v. England, at New Delhi in 1961–62, and after completing his 55th Test appearance in 1965 (v. New Zealand) his aggregate of 3,209 runs (av. 39.13) placed him second only to Umrigar among India's most prolific Test scorers.

MANKAD, Mulvantrai "Vinoo" (1917–   )

One of India's most successful all-rounders, this slow left-arm bowler and right-handed batsman bore the brunt of his country's attack in several Tests.

Making his international debut in the second unofficial Test against England, at Lahore, in 1937–38, when only 20 years of age, he was his side's top scorer in both innings with 38 and 88, and he completed that series by heading India's batting and bowling averages.

A powerful man, Mankad, who had 13 years in English League cricket, completed the double with 1,120 runs and 129 wickets, in England in 1946, the first tourist to achieve this distinction in England since L. Constantine did so in 1928.

After 44 Tests (six as captain) Mankad is one of the elite of all-rounders who have scored more than 2,000 runs and captured 100 wickets in the highest company. His total is 2,109 runs (av. 31.47) and 162 wickets (av. 32.31).

Mankad and P. Roy created a world Test record for an opening stand—413 v. New Zealand, at Madras, 1955–56. Mankad's innings of 231 on that occasion is an Indian Test record.

MANSUR ALI KHAN (formerly Nawab of Pataudi) (1941–   )

The youngest man ever to captain a Test team, he was only 21 years 77 days old when he took over the leadership of the Indian side following N. J. Contractor's serious injury in the West Indies in 1962. But, of course, cricket is in his blood, for his father had also played for England

against Australia in the 1930s as well as for India in 1946.

Mansur Ali Khan's career is all the more remarkable when one remembers that he lost the sight of one eye in a motoring accident in 1961 when he was beginning to make a name for himself with Sussex and Oxford University. He had scored a century for the University in his first Varsity match in 1960. After the accident it was feared that he would not play again but 17 months later he made his Test debut for India v. England, at Delhi, and from there he took his total of Test matches to 46, scoring 2,792 (av. 34.90) with his highest score of 203* v. England, at Delhi in 1963–64. He captained India in 33 Tests until succeeded by A. L. Wadekar in 1970–71.

MARYLEBONE CRICKET CLUB

The M.C.C. was formed during the winter of 1787–88 by members of the old White Conduit Club, led by the eighth Earl of Winchelsea, an Old Etonian, and Charles Lennox, who later became fourth Duke of Richmond.

Thomas Lord is also involved in the foundation of the M.C.C. for the new club used his ground at Dorset Square as its headquarters, playing their first game there in June 1788, v. White Conduit Club. The M.C.C. won by 83 runs.

The M.C.C. did not purchase Lord's cricket ground until 1866 when it cost them £18,000. Most of this money was loaned to them by William Nicholson, one of the leading members of their committee.

Since those early days the M.C.C. has grown in stature. It superseded the Hambledon C.C. as the leading club in England and subsequently became recognised as the top authority of the game anywhere in the world. There were no actual laws to sustain this authority, but the sense of purpose and the integrity of the men who have led the club over the years has been respected by cricket lovers everywhere, so much so that they have gladly accepted the guidance and rulings of the M.C.C.

This authority, however, was not established without some opposition. In about 1867 a proposal was made that a Cricket Parliament should be set up. This plan was aired in the *Sporting Life* and it was suggested that the M.C.C. should be superseded as the legislative authority because they were really a South of

England organisation founded when the South was the stronghold of cricket and were not sympathetic towards the expanding Northern cricketing authorities.

The proposal was that a large committee or parliament of cricketing legislators should be elected every year from enthusiasts in every part of the country.

This movement eventually faded out and although a similar proposal was made in more recent years it did not gain the same momentum as the original movement.

However, following the formation of a Sports Council with Government aid for sport it was decided in 1968 to bring cricket into line with other sports by setting up a new central authority—the M.C.C. Council—to include not only members of the M.C.C. itself but also the Test and County Cricket Board (previously the Board of Control for Test matches at Home), the National Cricket Association, and the Minor Counties.

A hundred years ago the membership of the M.C.C. numbered between six and seven hundred. Today it is well over 12,000 plus over 3,000 associate members. In the early days the club colours were sky-blue, but it has since been changed to red and yellow.

CLUB RECORDS

Highest score for: 735 (one man retired hurt) v. Wiltshire, at Lord's, August 1888. In a first-class match—607 v. Cambridge University, at Lord's, 1902. Highest score against: 629 for 8 declared by New South Wales, at Sydney, 1924–25. Highest individual score for: 344 by W. G. Grace v. Kent, at Canterbury, August 11, 1876. Highest individual score against: 281* by W. H. Ponsford for the Australians, at Lord's, 1934. Lowest score for: 15 v. Surrey, at Lords, July 15, 1839. Lowest score against: 12 by Oxford University (one man absent), at Oxford, May 1877. Colours: Red and Yellow. Badge: The letters M.C.C. Ground: Lord's, St. John's Wood, London NW8 8QN. Secretary: J. A. Bailey.

MAY, Peter Barker Howard (1929–   )

A natural gifted batsman, the former Surrey and England captain enjoyed one of the most successful careers in cricket history.

At Cambridge he got his "Blue" playing in 1950, 1951 and 1952. He made his debut for Surrey in 1950 and became the star batsman of that county's remarkable run of seven County Championship seasons 1952–1958, heading their batting averages in six of those summers.

May was first selected to represent England in 1951 and scored 138 in his first innings against South Africa. From 1953 to 1959 he was never out of the England team, making 52 consecutive Test appearances. He captained England a record 41 times.

During his career May headed the batting averages four times, 1951, 1955, 1957 and 1958. His best average was in 1951 when appearing both for Cambridge University and Surrey he scored 2,339 runs (av. 68.79).

He got his top score, 285*, for England v. West Indies, at Birmingham in 1957. On that occasion his fourth wicket stand of 411 with C. Cowdrey created a new Test record.

Following his enforced absence from cricket through ill-health in 1960 May returned in 1961 and made 4 more Test appearances against Australia, so bringing his total to 66 Tests in which he scored 4,537 runs (av. 46.77).

MEAD, Charles Philip (1887–1958)

This Hampshire and Suffolk left-handed batsman was one of the four most prolific scorers in the game's history. Indeed, he scored more runs for Hampshire than any other player ever did for any team.

Making his debut with Hampshire in 1905 after being allowed to slip away from Surrey, where he had been on the ground staff, Mead's career extended over 32 years, during which time he scored 55,061 runs (av. 47.67).

His total of 153 centuries is only exceeded by Hobbs, Hendren, and Hammond.

Twice he topped the averages, in 1913 and 1921, and he exceeded 2,000 runs in a season on 11 occasions, his highest being 3,179 in 1921 when his top score was 280* and his average 69.10. He scored 1,000 runs in a season 27 times, a feat excelled only by two other men, W. G. Grace and F. E. Woolley.

He made seven Test appearances against Australia, and 10 against South Africa, and his highest score in these games was 182* v. Australia, at the Oval in 1921.

MELBOURNE CRICKET GROUND

It is not within the scope of this book to give details of every important cricket ground abroad but that at Melbourne must be included because it is the world's largest cricket stadium.

The first cricket match played on this ground took place in November 1854, and the earliest first-class match ever played outside the United Kingdom was that between Victoria and New South Wales played here in 1856.

The ground is controlled by the Melbourne Cricket Club who played the leading part in establishing big-time cricket in Australia in the nineteenth century.

Ideally situated in the middle of Richmond Park within easy reach of the centre of the city of Melbourne, it has accommodated the largest number of spectators ever seen at cricket matches on any ground.

The record for a single day's play is 90,800 on the second day of the Australia v. West Indies Test in February 1961, and the record for any match is 350,534 for the six days of the Australia v. England Test, January 1937.

Prior to taking over this ground at Richmond Park the Melbourne C.C. (founded 1838) played at Batman's Hill near where Spencer Street Station now stands.

MIDDLESEX C.C.C.

Founded 1863. Secretary: A. W. Flower, Lord's Cricket Ground, St. John's Wood, London, NW8 8QN. Highest score for: 642 for 3 declared v. Hampshire, at Southampton, 1923. Highest score against: 665 by West Indies, at Lords, 1939. In county cricket—596 by Nottinghamshire, at Nottingham, August 15–17, 1887. Highest individual score for: 331* by J. D. Robertson v. Worcestershire, at Worcester, 1949. Highest individual score against: 316* by J. B. Hobbs, for Surrey, at Lord's, 1926. Lowest score for: 20 v. M.C.C., at Lord's, July 25–26, 1864. In county cricket—25 v. Surrey, at the Oval, 1885. Lowest score against: 25 by M.C.C., 1798 (not the present Middlesex C.C.C.). 31 by Gloucestershire, at Bristol, 1924. Colours: Blue. Badge: Three seaxes. County Ground: Lord's. Honours: County Championship winners: 1866, 1903, 1920, 1921, 1947, 1949 (tie with Yorkshire),

1976. Minor Counties Champions (Second XI): 1935. Benson and Hedges Cup Finalists, 1975. Gillette Cup Finalists, 1975.

MILLER, Keith Ross (1919–   )

Personal opinions may differ but if figures count for anything then K. R. Miller is one of the greatest all-rounders in the history of Test cricket. In 55 Tests from 1946 to 1956 the gay cavalier who delighted crowds everywhere scored 2,958 runs (av. 36.97) and bagged 170 wickets (av. 22.97).

On the cricket field Miller was not only a fine player but an outstanding personality. He was essentially an attacking batsman and bowler, and he was also a great slip fielder.

Miller's finest Test rubber was undoubtedly that in the West Indies in 1955. In the five matches he scored 439 runs (av. 73.16) and captured 20 wickets (av. 32.00). In the final Test at Kingston he played an innings of 109 and took 6 for 107 and 2 for 58.

Miller began his first-class career in 1937–38 with an innings of 181 for Victoria v. Tasmania, at Melbourne. After war service with the R.A.A.F., and topping the batting averages in the Victory games of 1945, he moved to N.S.W. in 1946 and began his Test career proper with an innings of 79 against England at Brisbane in December that year.

He made three official post-war tours of England, 1948, 1953, and 1956, and it was during that third tour that he registered his highest ever score, 281* v. Leicestershire.

When Miller rounded off his Test career with innings of 61 and 7* as well as taking 5 for 147 in the match, at the Oval in 1956, he had missed only two Tests in post-war cricket.

One of this great entertainer's finest performances was to take seven South Australia wickets in one innings for 12 runs off 59 balls at Sydney in 1955–56, his last season with N.S.W.

MINOR COUNTIES CHAMPIONSHIP

Records of Minor Counties cricket can be found under the name of each of the Minor Counties.

This competition was inaugurated in 1895 at the institution of P. H. Foley, then Honorary Secretary of Worcestershire

C.C.C. The Minor County Championship, however, was not officially recognised until it was reorganised in 1901.

The move to organise a Minor County Championship had been prompted by the promotion of four more counties to the first-class Championship in 1894. This made it evident that the remaining second-class counties needed some reorganisation if they were to survive, but only seven of them arranged the eight fixtures necessary for inclusion in the first season of the new competition. These counties were Bedfordshire, Durham, Hertfordshire, Norfolk, Oxfordshire, Staffordshire and Worcestershire.

Oddly enough, however, matches with counties outside the competition were allowed to count in the championship and on this basis Norfolk finished joint champions with Durham and Worcestershire.

As already mentioned, the competition was reorganised on a sounder basis in 1901.

Altogether 25 counties have taken part in this competition (not including second XI's) but of these Carmarthenshire, Denbighshire and Monmouthshire, have dropped out, while Worcestershire, Glamorgan and Northamptonshire have been promoted to first-class.

Only one county has played the qualifying number of matches in every season since the inauguration of this competition—Hertfordshire.

Some records

Highest score: 621 by Surrey II v. Devonshire, 1928. Highest individual score: 282 by E. Garnett, Berkshire v. Wiltshire, 1908. Prior to the establishment of this competition Sir F. E. Lacey scored 323* for Hampshire v. Norfolk, at Southampton, in 1887. Lowest score: 14 by Cheshire v. Staffordshire, 1909. The first player to capture all 10 wickets in a Minor Counties Championship game was R. V. Ward, 10 for 72, Bedfordshire v. Hertfordshire, 1935.

Minor Counties Champions:
1895   Norfolk, Durham and Worcestershire
1896   Worcestershire
1897   Worcestershire
1898   Worcestershire
1899   Northamptonshire and Buckinghamshire
1900   Glamorgan, Durham and Northamptonshire

1901   Durham
1902   Wiltshire
1903   Northamptonshire
1904   Northamptonshire
1905   Norfolk
1906   Staffordshire
1907   Lancashire II
1908   Staffordshire
1909   Wiltshire
1910   Norfolk
1911   Staffordshire
1912   Norfolk finished first and Staffordshire second but as they had not met and it was found impossible for them to play a decider so late in the season, the championship was left in abeyance.
1913   Norfolk
1920   Staffordshire
1921   Staffordshire
1922   Buckinghamshire
1923   Buckinghamshire
1924   Berkshire
1925   Buckinghamshire
1926   Durham
1927   Staffordshire
1928   Berkshire
1929   Oxfordshire
1930   Durham
1931   Leicestershire II
1932   Buckinghamshire
1933   Not decided. Norfolk finished top but were beaten by Yorkshire II in the final Challenge match. It was subsequently found that Yorkshire had no right to have played in this match for an error had been made in the points awarded to them and they were in fact third in the table and not second.
1934   Lancashire II
1935   Middlesex II
1936   Hertfordshire
1937   Lancashire II
1938   Buckinghamshire
1939   Surrey II
1946   Suffolk
1947   Yorkshire II
1948   Lancashire II
1949   Lancashire II
1950   Surrey II
1951   Kent II
1952   Buckinghamshire
1953   Berkshire
1954   Surrey II
1955   Surrey II
1956   Kent II
1957   Yorkshire II
1958   Yorkshire II
1959   Warwickshire II
1960   Lancashire II

1961	Somerset II
1962	Warwickshire II
1963	Cambridgeshire
1964	Lancashire II
1965	Somerset II
1966	Lincolnshire
1967	Cheshire
1968	Yorkshire II
1969	Buckinghamshire
1970	Bedfordshire
1971	Yorkshire II
1972	Yorkshire II
1973	Shropshire
1974	Oxfordshire
1975	Hertfordshire
1976	Durham

MITCHELL, Bruce (1909–   )

This South African all-rounder had one of the longest of all Test careers. He made his first appearance for his country in England in 1929 and his last, also against England but at home, in 1949.

At the Oval in 1947 he scored a century in each innings of the fifth Test, 120 and 189*.

Mitchell was, without doubt, one of South Africa's finest opening batsmen. In 1930–31 at Cape Town he figured in an opening partnership with I. J. Siedle which put on 260 against England, a South African Test record for the first wicket.

A slow bowler as well as a stylish batsman, Mitchell took 11 for 95 in his very first match for Transvaal, against Border, at East London, in 1925–26. He was also a brilliant fielder in the slips, and against Australia at Melbourne in 1931–32 he held six catches, four of them in the second innings. This equalled the South African Test record created by A. E. E. Vogler against England in 1909–10.

MONMOUTHSHIRE C.C.C.

Founded 1823. Expired 1934. Competed in the Minor County Championship from 1901 to 1934 inclusive, except season 1920. Highest score for: 479 v. Carmarthenshire, 1909. Highest score against: 538 by Glamorgan, 1901. Highest individual score for: 247 by L. Pitchford, 1933. Highest individual score against: 254 by H. E. Morgan of Glamorgan, 1901. Lowest score for: 22 v. Dorset. Lowest score against: 21 by Herefordshire, 1837. In Championship—31 by Cornwall, 1913. Honours: None.

MORRIS, Arthur Robert (1922–   )

One of Australia's finest openers this brilliant left-handed batsman played in 46 Tests in the first 10 years after World War II.

A fine stroke-maker all round the wicket, he had the distinction of scoring a century in each innings for New South Wales when making his first-class debut. That was against Queensland in 1940–41 at Sydney when his scores were 148 and 111.

Morris did not make quite the same impact in his Test debut for he scored only two and five at Brisbane and Sydney in 1946–47. Fortunately for Australia, however, Bradman chose to persevere with his new batsman, and in his next Test appearance Morris made 155 and followed with scores of 122 and 124*.

Coming to England for the first time in 1948 he topped his side's Test batting averages with 87.00. His average in all matches on that tour was 72.18, and his 290 in 300 minutes will never be forgotten by those who saw it against Gloucestershire, at Bristol.

His Test aggregate of 3,533 (av. 46.48) included 12 centuries, with a highest score of 206 v. England in 7¾ hours at Adelaide in 1951.

MURRAY, John Thomas (1935–   )

When this wicket-keeper batsman retired at the end of the 1975 season he had created a new world record for wicket-keeping dismissals with 1,527 since making debut in 1952. His outstanding season was 1957 when he completed the wicket-keeper's "double" with 1,025 runs and 104 dismissals.

Made Test debut in India in 1961–62, but it is rather surprising that such a remarkably consistent performer behind the stumps should have made no more than 21 Test appearances in such a lengthy career.

He dismissed nine batsmen in a match for Middlesex v. Hampshire, at Lord's in 1965, and in 1967 on the same ground he got six batsmen in one innings of the Test v. India.

MUSHTAQ ALI, Syed (1914–   )

The gay cavalier batsman of Indian cricket. Unorthodox but brilliant when in his best aggressive mood, he was a right-hand batsman and slow left-arm bowler.

On his first visit to England in 1936 he scored 112 in the Test at Old Trafford and helped create what was then an Indian Test record 1st wicket partnership of 203 with V. M. Mankad.

When he made his final Test appearance nearly 16 years later in February, 1952, it was still as an opening batsman and he made 22 against England at Madras.

In a first-class career which extended from 1934 to 1958, his aggregate of 5,013 runs (av. 49.14) in Ranji Trophy games is one of the highest for that competition.

MUSHTAQ MOHAMMAD (1943–   )

One of the world's leading all-rounders and a member of the famous family of five cricketing brothers, four of whom have played Test cricket. When Mushtaq made his first-class debut at the age of 13 years 41 days, playing for Karachi (Whites) v. Hyderabad, he scored 87 and took 5 for 28! Obviously a naturally gifted player.

Made his initial Test century v. India at Delhi in 1959–60 when he was still only 18 years 28 days old—the youngest ever to make a Test century.

Right-hand bat and leg-break googly bowler he joined Northamptonshire in 1964. In 1969 he topped both their batting

and bowling averages. His highest score is 303* for Karachi (Blues) v. Karachi University in 1967–68, while one of his most remarkable feats of bowling was to capture seven Middlesex wickets for 59 runs at Lord's in 1974 when playing for the Pakistan tourists.

MYNN, Alfred (1807–1861)

A powerful man who was over six feet tall and weighed around 18 stone, Alfred Mynn was nicknamed "The Lion of Kent".

In his day he was as great a personality as was W. G. Grace in later years, and Mynn's presence on any ground was sure to increase the attendance by a substantial margin.

With huge hands as strong as could be he was a mighty hitter, a deadly accurate fast round-arm bowler, and a magnificent fielder in the slips.

Alfred Mynn made his debut in 1832. He played for the Gentlemen v. Players in that year and in all but two years until his last appearance in 1852. He captured over 100 wickets in these matches as well as scoring 605 runs.

During his career he was several times single-wicket Champion of England. In these games he beat such renowned men as Felix and James Dearman of Sheffield.

N

NAYUDU, Cottari Kanakayia (1895–1967)

Often described as the "Indian Bradman" this outstanding personality was not only a brilliant batsman but also a clever right-arm slow-medium spin bowler and one of the finest fielders ever.

He first attracted world-wide attention when he had past his 30th birthday and he scored 153 in 100 minutes (11 sixes and 13 fours) against the M.C.C. tourists of 1925–26. He was 37 when he first appeared in England with a representative Indian team but he was the outstanding member of that 1932 tour scoring 1,618 runs (av. 40.45) and taking 65 wickets (av. 25.53).

C. K. Nayudu appeared in seven Tests, captaining the side in four of them, and in his best all-round season at home (1934) he scored 2,567 runs and captured 109 wickets.

In his 1936 visit to England he took 6 Lancashire wickets for 46, while his highest score with the bat was 200 for Holkar v. Baroda when he was 50 years of age.

NETS

Practice nets are believed to have been introduced by Nicolas Felix (Wanostrocht) in about 1845. He recommended the use of these nets in his book *Felix on the Bat.*

NEW ZEALAND

Cricket has been played in New Zealand since the 1830s, and Wellington C.C. is known to have been in existence by 1842.

The first inter-provincial match was played in March 1860 between Wellington and Auckland. This game took place at Mount Cook Barracks. The return was played over two years later at Auckland.

The first English side to visit New Zealand was George Parr's team which went there from Australia in 1864 and played four matches, all against odds, winning three and drawing one.

This was followed by James Lillywhite's team in 1876–77 and they were undefeated in eight matches, all against odds.

In 1877–78 the first representative team to visit England from Australia, D. W. Gregory's team, also played seven games in New Zealand, winning five, drawing one, and losing one.

The first New Zealand team to tour abroad was not until 1898–99 when a side captained by L. T. Cobcroft went to Australia and played four matches, winning one and drawing one.

In view of the proximity of these two countries it is surprising that they have met in only one Test match, that of March 1946 at Wellington when Australia won by an innings and 103 runs.

The first New Zealand team to visit England did not come over until 1927. Then a side captained by T. C. Lowry played 38 matches (including 26 first-class) and surprised the mother country by winning 13 and losing only five. The first-class matches resulted in seven wins, five defeats and 14 draws.

It was only a little over two years after this visit that New Zealand played their first Test matches. This was in 1929–30 when an England team captained by A. H. H. Gilligan was sent out to Australasia with the specific intention of playing four Test matches in New Zealand although their tour actually opened in Australia. England won the first of these Tests, at Christchurch, by eight wickets, but the other three matches were left drawn.

New Zealand has since met all the Test playing countries but with only limited success. They gained their first Test win in 1955–56 when they defeated West Indies, at Auckland, by 190 runs.

Surprisingly enough the first official Test series with Australia did not take place until 1973–74 in Australia and here New Zealand proved that they have become a force to be reckoned with for they might well have won the 2nd Test at Sydney in January but for the interference of rain, and when Australia returned the visit later in the season New Zealand had the satisfaction of winning the Christchurch Test (March 1974) by five wickets.

The principal cricket competition in New Zealand is for the Shell Shield which was first presented in 1975–76 and won by Canterbury.

The New Zealand Cricket Council was formed in 1894 and they were first admitted to the Imperial Cricket Conference in 1926.

Records

Highest score by New Zealand: 551 for 9 declared v. England, at Lord's, 1973. Highest score in New Zealand: 752 for 8 declared by New South Wales v. Otago, at Dunedin, 1923–24. Highest individual score for New Zealand: by G. M. Turner v. West Indies, at Georgetown, 1971–72. Highest individual score in New Zealand: 385 by B. Sutcliffe for Otago v. Canterbury, at Christchurch, 1952–53. Highest score against New Zealand: 663 by Australian XI, at Auckland, 1920–21. Lowest score for New Zealand: 26 v. England, at Auckland, 1954–55. Lowest score in New Zealand: 13 by Wellington v. Nelson, at Nelson, 1862–63; and 13 by Auckland v. Canterbury, at Auckland, 1877–78. Lowest score against New Zealand: 30 by Ireland, Dublin, 1937.

Tests

Highest score for: 551 for 9 declared v. England, at Lord's, 1973. Highest score against: 593 for 6 declared by England, at Auckland, 1974–75. Highest individual score for: 259 by G. M. Turner v. West Indies, Georgetown, 1971–72. Highest individual score against: 336* by W. R. Hammond, at Auckland, 1932–33. Lowest score for: 26 v. England, at Auckland, 1954–55. Lowest score against: 132 by India, at Calcutta, 1955–56.

NICKNAMES

Here are nicknames of a few of the better known players of past and present:
Big Ship—W. W. Armstrong (Victoria).
Bishop—M. C. Kemp (Kent).
Buns—C. I. Thornton (Cambridge U., Kent, Middlesex).
Croucher—G. L. Jessop (Cambridge U., Gloucestershire).

Dinny—J. C. Reedman (S. Australia).
Dodger—W. W. Whysall (Nottinghamshire).
Demon Bowler—F. R. Spofforth (N.S.W., Victoria, Derbyshire).
Gubby—G. O. Allen (Middlesex).
Guvnor—R. Abel (Surrey).
Happy Jack—G. Ulyett (Yorkshire).
Jacker—Sir F. S. Jackson (Cambridge U., Yorkshire).
Jonah—A. O. Jones (Cambridge U., Nottinghamshire).
Little Alec—A. C. Bannerman (N.S.W.).
Lion of the North—G. Parr (Nottinghamshire).
Lion of Kent—A. Mynn (Kent).
Lobster—D. L. A. Jephson (Cambridge U., Surrey).
Lol—H. Larwood (Nottinghamshire).
Little Dasher—H. Graham (Victoria).
Monkey—A. N. Hornby (Lancashire).
Plum—Sir Pelham Warner (Oxford U., Middlesex).
Ponny—W. H. Ponsford (Victoria).
Prophet—J. Daniell (Cambridge U., Somerset).
Surrey Pet—W. Caffyn (Surrey).
Shrimp—Sir H. D. G. Leveson-Gower (Oxford U., Surrey).
Slasher—K. Mackay (Queensland).
Mr. Smith—K. S. Duleepsinhji (Cambridge U., Sussex).
Tich—A. P. Freeman (Kent).
Tiger—E. J. Smith (Warwickshire).

NO-BALL

See under BOWLING (No-ball).

NOBLE, Montague Alfred (1873–1940)

In Test cricket M. A. Noble can be numbered among the half dozen best all-rounders ever to appear for Australia.

As a bowler Noble could always be relied upon to keep a perfect length, and he was once named by no less a judge than Ranjitsinhji as the finest medium-pace bowler he had ever played against.

With the bat he was cool and resouceful, noted for his strong defence, but always ready to rise to the occasion.

A man of unruffled temperament, this was a great advantage to him not only as a batsman but as a captain. He led Australia in 15 of his 42 Tests and proved to be one of his country's most successful skippers. Noble played to win and nothing else mattered as much as victory.

An example of his dour defence was his innings at Manchester in 1899 when he took 5 hours 20 minutes to score 89. On the other hand, against Sussex, in 1905, he hit 267 in 5 hours and also took 6 for 39 in the same match.

The Hove ground was a particular favourite of Noble's for it was there, in 1902, that he made his highest score of 284.

In a first-class career which extended from 1893 to 1919 he made 14,034 runs (av. 40.80).

NORFOLK C.C.C.

Founded: 1760's. Reformed 1876. Among the original members of the Minor County Championship in 1895. Secretary: D. J. M. Armstrong, 4 Roseacre, Bodham, Holt, Norfolk. Highest score for: 695 v. M.C.C. at Lord's, July 1885; in Minor Counties match—526 for 7 declared v. Kent II, 1937. Highest score against: 558 by Hampshire, 1887; in Minor Counties match—550 for 5 declared by Surrey II, 1925. Highest individual score for: 222 by G. A. Stevens, 1920. Highest individual score against: 323* by Sir F. E. Lacey of Hampshire, at Southampton, 1887; in Minor Counties match—249* by B. Constable of Surrey II, 1949. Lowest score for: 11 v. M.C.C., 1831; in Minor Counties Championship—36 v. Buckinghamshire, 1927; in County match—22 v. Cambridgeshire, 1845. Lowest score against: 18 by Staffordshire, 1886; in Minor Counties Championship—39 by Suffolk, 1912; in County match—29 by Hertfordshire, 1882. Honours: Minor County Champions: 1895 (tie with Durham and Worcestershire), 1905, 1910, 1913.

NORTHAMPTONSHIRE C.C.C.

Formed: 1820. Re-formed 1878. Admitted to the County Championship 1905. Secretary: K. C. Turner, County Cricket Ground, Wantage Road, Northampton. Highest score for: 557 for 6 declared v. Sussex, at Hove, 1914. Highest score against: 670 for 9 declared by Sussex, at Hove, 1921. Highest individual score for: 300 by R. Subba Row v. Surrey, at the Oval, 1958. Highest individual score against: 333 by K. S. Duleepsinhji of Sussex, at Hove, 1930. Lowest score for: 12 v. Gloucestershire, at Gloucester, June 1907. Lowest score against: 46 by Derbyshire, at Northampton, 1912. Before becoming first-class there was a score of 29 by Northumberland, 1901. Colours: Maroon. Badge: Tudor Rose. Honours: Gillette Cup winners, 1976. Minor Counties Champions: 1899 (tie with Buckinghamshire), 1900 (tie with Glamorgan and Durham), 1903, 1904. Best in the County Championship: Runners-up 1912, 1976.

NORTHUMBERLAND C.C.C.

Founded: 1834. Competed in Minor County Championship since 1901. No Championship win. Secretary: R. W. Smithson, County Cricket Ground, Osborne Avenue, Jesmond, Newcastle-upon-Tyne. Highest score for: 509 for 7 declared v. Cambridge 1913. Highest score against: 503 for 6 declared by Durham, 1939. Highest individual score for: 221 by L. E. Liddell, 1949. Highest individual score against: 217 by D. F. Walker of Norfolk, 1939. Lowest score: 18 v. M.C.C., 1869; in Minor County match—23 v. Staffordshire, 1946. Lowest score against: 25 by Carlisle, 1939; in Minor County match—43 by Staffordshire in 1896 and again in 1937. Honours: None.

NOTTINGHAMSHIRE C.C.C.

Founded: 1841. Re-organised 1859 and 1866. Secretary: Group Capt. R. G. Wilson, D.F.C., A.F.C., County Ground, Trent Bridge, Nottingham NG2 6AG. Highest score for: 739 for 7 declared v. Leicestershire, at Nottingham, May 25–27, 1903. Highest score against: 706 for 4 declared, by Surrey, at Nottingham, 1947. Highest individual score for: 312* by W. W. Kecton v. Middlesex, at Oval, 1939. Highest individual score against: 345 by C. G. Macartney of the Australians, at Nottingham, 1921; in County match—317 by W. R. Hammond of Gloucestershire, at Gloucester, 1936. Lowest score for: 13 v. Yorkshire, at Nottingham, June 1901. Lowest score against: 16 by Derbyshire, at Nottingham, 1879, and by Surrey, at Oval, 1880. Colours: Green and Gold. Badge: County bage of Nottinghamshire. Honours: County Champions: 1865, 1868, 1869, (tie with Yorkshire), 1871, 1872, 1873 (tie with Gloucestershire), 1875, 1879 (tie with Lancashire), 1880, 1882 (tie with Lancashire), 1883, 1884, 1885, 1886, 1889 (tie with Lancashire and Surrey), 1907, 1929.

NOURSE, Arthur David (1878-1948)

Slow left-arm bowler, left-handed batsman, and a remarkable fielder at short slip, this cheerful personality who was born in Surrey, made 45 Test appearances for South Africa, the first in 1902–03 v. Australia, and the last in 1924 in England.

Nourse made his debut with Natal in 1895 and enjoyed a career which spanned some 40 years. He did not finally retire until 1935 when he was 57 years of age.

During this time he toured England three times, 1907, 1912 and 1924. The second was his most successful visit as an all-rounder, but he actually scored more runs and gained a slightly better average on the last tour when he had reached the age of 46.

His highest score in England was against Hampshire, at Bournemouth, when he went in first wicket down and carried his bat through the remainder of the South Africans' innings to score 213* out of a total of 432. That was in 1912.

Nourse beat this figure only once—at Johannesburg in 1919–20 when he scored 304* for Natal v. Transvaal. But possibly no innings pleased him more than his 93* at Johannesburg in 1905–06 which gave South Africa their first Test victory over England.

NOURSE, Arthur Dudley (1901-   )

This aggressive right-hand batsman was an even more consistent scorer than his father. He scored 2,960 runs in Test cricket which is more than any other South African with the single exception of Bruce Mitchell, although his average of 53.81 is slightly better than Mitchell's.

Nourse Junior's outstanding Test series was that in England in 1947. Then he headed his country's averages for the five matches with 69.00. His highest score was 149 at Nottingham.

This was his second Test tour in England. He was here for the first time in 1935 and while he did nothing special in the Tests that year he scored well in matches with the counties, including a run of three consecutive centuries.

On his third visit in 1951 he finished second in his side's Test averages with 37.62 and played a delightful innings of 208 at Nottingham. It lasted for 550 minutes and it should be noted that Nourse played with a broken thumb, an injury sustained in a previous game only three weeks earlier.

Nourse Junior's highest score in Test cricket was 231 v. Australia, at Johannesburg in 1935–36. For Natal he scored 260* v. Transvaal, at Johannesburg in the following season, his personal best. When he retired in 1953 his career average in Currie Cup matches, 65.85, was the best ever recorded in that competition. In this competition alone he scored 4,478 runs (av. 65.85).

NYREN, John (1764–1837)

We know comparatively very little of John Nyren's competence as a cricketer, but we owe a great deal to this Hampshire man for our knowledge of the illustrious band of enthusiasts who nurtured the game in its earliest days at Hambledon. John Nyren immortalised the Hambledon club in his guides to the game, *The Cricketers of My Time*, and *The Young Cricketer's Tutor*.

John's father, Richard Nyren, was one of the founders of the Hambledon Club, and young John played regularly for them from about 1778 until the club finally disbanded in 1791.

He subsequently appeared for the famous Homerton Club, Hampshire, Montpelier, Middlesex, and for England, and from all accounts it is obvious that he excelled as a fieldsman, usually at point or cover, and in one game at Lord's when playing against Twenty-two of Surrey he caught six.

O

OBSTRUCTING THE FIELD

There have been only six instances in first-class cricket in England of a batsman being given out for obstructing the field. June 1868—C. A. Absolom, Cambridge University v. Surrey, at the Oval. August 1899—T. Straw, Worcestershire v. Warwickshire, at Worcester. June 1901—J. P. Whiteside, Leicestershire v. Lancashire, at Leicester. August 1901—T. Straw Worcestershire v. Warwickshire, at Birmingham. August 1951—L. Hutton, England v. South Africa, at the Oval. May 1963—K. Ibadulla, Warwickshire v. Hampshire, at Coventry.

OLD TRAFFORD, MANCHESTER

The headquarters of the Lancashire County and Manchester Cricket Clubs is one of the finest cricket grounds in the world but, unfortunately, it has a bad reputation for rain.

Only three Test matches have been abandoned without a ball being played and two of them were at Manchester in 1890 and in 1938 against Australia. Many other Tests at Old Trafford have been spoilt by the weather (see under WEATHER, Rain).

The site was first taken over as a cricket ground in 1857 by the old Manchester Cricket Club and they were joined there by the Lancashire County C.C. on its formation in 1864.

The first county match played on the ground was the between Lancashire and Middlesex, in July 1865, and the first Test match was played there in July 1884.

The original pavilion was replaced in 1897. The ground suffered badly through enemy bombing during World War II but a large amount of money was willingly subscribed by sports fans to enable the ground and stands to be completely restored.

In July-August 1926, 78,617 people attended the Lancashire and Yorkshire match at Old Trafford and created a record for a county match on this ground.

OLDFIELD, William Albert Stanley (1897-1976)

One of Australia's finest wicket-keepers. His total of 130 dismissals in Test matches places him among the half dozen best-ever and his 54 stumpings in this class of cricket is still unequalled.

Oldfield first appeared in England with the Australian Imperial Forces team in 1919, and back in Australia during the following season he made his Test debut against England but did not finally suceed H. Carter as Australia's regular wicket-keeper until 1924–25.

In all Oldfield made 54 Test appearances, his last in 1936–37 when he appeared in all five games against England.

Among his many remarkable performances as a wicket-keeper was his five dismissals (1 ct. 4 st.) in one innings against England, at Melbourne, in 1925.

When England scored 521 against Australia, at Brisbane, in 1928–29, Oldfield did not concede a single bye. There were only two byes added to England's score when they made 636 in the next Test of that series, and after England had completed their first four innings of the series and scored 1,923 runs Oldfield had conceded only three byes.

ONE DAY CRICKET

See under BENSON AND HEDGES CUP, GILLETTE CUP, JOHN PLAYER LEAGUE.

OPENING PARTNERSHIPS

See under PARTNERSHIPS.

ORDERED OFF

Players ordered off by their captains in first-class matches: R. Peel (Yorkshire) dismissed by Lord Hawke v. Middlesex, at Sheffield, August 1897; J. H. Newman (Hampshire) dismissed by the Hon. L. H. Tennyson v. Nottinghamshire, at Nottingham, August 1922. He was reinstated in the team the following day to complete the match; A. Ward (Derbyshire) by J. B. Bolus v. Yorkshire, at Chesterfield, June 1973.

O'REILLY, William Joseph (1905–   )

A medium pace leg-break and googly bowler of remarkable endurance this tall Australian, nicknamed "Tiger", was always difficult to master.

He employed a subtle variation of pace which often surprised his opponents and enabled him to record many fine bowling figures.

His best performance in his 27 Test appearances between 1931 and 1946 was his 4 for 75 and 7 for 54 against England, at Nottingham, in June 1943. His average for 28 wickets captured in that particular Test rubber was 24.92.

O'Reilly toured England on two occasions, 1934 and 1938, and it was on that first tour that he got in his best figures for a single innings—9 for 38 against Somerset, at Taunton.

In a first-class career which extended from 1927 to 1945 this whole-hearted player took 774 wickets at a cost of less than 17 runs apiece.

OVAL, The Kennington

In 1845 the Montpelier Cricket Club of Walworth were looking for a new ground and one of their leading members, Mr. William Baker, secured the lease of a market garden from the Duchy of Cornwall. This market garden at Kennington is now the Oval Cricket Ground.

In the same year a meeting was held at "The Horns" public house in Kennington Park Road, and it was decided to form the Surrey County Cricket Club with its headquarters at the new ground.

The first important match to be played there was that between the Gentlemen of Surrey v. the Players of Surrey, August 21–22, 1845.

In 1851 the site was nearly lost for ever as a cricket ground, for plans were then being made by the Duchy of Cornwall to build on it, but fortunately for cricket lovers this scheme was knocked on the head by the Prince Consort who was

acting as regent to the young Duke of Cornwall (later Edward VII).

In 1858 a new pavilion was built and this was replaced some 40 years later by the present structure which was designed by the same architect who had undertaken a similar task at Old Trafford.

Many other sports and pastimes have been staged at the Oval apart from cricket. In the 19th century there were pigeon and poultry shows, as well as athletics, rugby and, of course, association football.

The last-named sport has a particularly strong connection with the Oval, brought about, no doubt, through the interests of one man, Mr. C. W. Alcock.

This remarkable sporting personality was one of the founder members of the Old Wanderers Football Club in 1864 and captained their F.A. Cup winning team in 1872. He also captained England against Scotland in 1875. In 1870 this gentleman, who was a journalist by profession, became honorary secretary (subsequently paid) of the Football Association and in 1872 he became the first full-time paid secretary of the Surrey County Cricket Club. He was secretary of Surrey for 35 years. To continue his journalistic work as well as deal with the affairs of two such important sporting organisations, Mr. Alcock must have been most capable and industrious.

All of the F.A. cup semi-finals and all but one of the finals from 1871–72 to 1881–82 were played at the Oval and the finals continued to be played there until 1892.

It was largely due to the efforts of Mr. Alcock that the Oval had the distinction of staging the first Test Match ever played in this country between England and Australia. As most cricket enthusiasts know only too well this took place on September 6, 7 and 8, 1880, and England won by five wickets.

See also ATTENDANCES.

OVER, The

The earliest code of laws still in existence, those believed to be based on a revision of 1744, show that in those days a bowler changed wickets after delivering four balls. After the fourth ball the umpire was directed to call "Over".

In the early part of the 19th century up to 1838 a fresh bowler was allowed two practice balls providing that even if he took one ball he must carry on to complete the over.

Although there is evidence of five-ball and six-ball overs having been tried at different times before 1889, it was not until that year that the Laws of the game were altered to make five-ball overs compulsory.

In 1900 the law was altered again to increase the over to six balls and so it has remained until this day except that in 1921 certain latitude was made to allow eight-ball overs as preferred in countries overseas.

For instance eight-ball overs were favoured in Australia as far back as 1919 and they were also introduced to England during the Australian tour of 1924–25.

The eight-ball over rule was suspended in Australia for the 1928–29 M.C.C. tour, but reintroduced for the 1936–37 tour and retained in that country ever since except for matches against the M.C.C.

Eight-ball overs were tried as an experiment in this country in 1939 but we returned to the six-ball over immediately peace-time cricket was resumed at Lord's in 1945 and at all first-class matches in 1949.

D. F. Hill bowled a 14-ball over for British Guiana v. Barbados, at Georgetown, October 1946. Umpire A. C. De Barros miscounted and Hill dismissed E. D. Weekes, l.b.w. with the 14th ball.

J. M. A. Marshall bowled an 11-ball over for Warwickshire against Worcestershire at Dudley in 1946. He took a wicket with his sixth ball and due to an error by the umpire he was allowed to bowl a further five balls.

Two overs in succession

A bowler is, of course, prevented by the rules from bowling two overs in succession, but this actually happened in two Test matches.

In the fourth Test of Australia's 1921 tour, played at Manchester in July that year, England declared at 341 for four at 5.40 p.m. and the players left the field. However, a discussion ensued as to whether or not England should have been allowed to declare at that time, for this was actually the first day, there having been no play because of rain on the previous day. The Australians pointed out that at least 100 minutes should have been left for play on what was then to be regarded as the first day of the match.

There was much confusion and England

did not return to the field for 20 minutes, whereupon the Australian captain, W. W. Armstrong, reopened the bowling and completed his second consecutive over.

At Wellington, in March 1951, A. M. Moir (New Zealand) bowled the last over before the tea interval and the first after tea when playing against England.

Maiden over

In 1851 William Clarke bowled 128 consecutive balls for the All England XI against Kent without conceding a run.

During his career Alfred Shaw (Notts) bowled 16,922 maidens in 24,700 overs.

E. Willsher, Kent' fast left-arm bowler, sent down 16 consecutive maiden overs for South v. North at Canterbury in 1871.

H. J. Tayfield, South Africa's off-break bowler, set up a world record in January 1957 at Durban in a Test match against England when he sent down 137 balls without conceding a run. This included 16 consecutive (eight-ball) maiden overs.

At Madras in January 1964, Ragunath G. Nadkarni sent down 21 consecutive six-ball maiden overs (131 balls) for India v. England.

At Taunton in 1949 H. L. Hazell the Somerset slow left-arm bowler delivered 105 consecutive balls against Gloucester without conceding a single run. There were 17 consecutive (six-ball) maiden overs. Hazell's analysis for the innings was 28.3–21–27–8.

In the England–Australia Test at the Oval in August 1882 England bowled 14 consecutive maidens in Australia's first innings when they were all out for 63. 24 of E. Peate's 38 overs were maidens and R. G. Barlow sent down 22 maidens in 31 overs.

OXFORD UNIVERSITY C.C.

In its earliest days the cricket club of the Oxford University was the Magdalen Cricket Club. They played on a part of Cowley Common which was named the Magdalen Ground because it had been used regularly by boys of the Magdalen College Choir School.

This would be in the early 1800's when cricket was not taken very seriously at Oxford and it was often difficult to muster a complete eleven.

The first Oxford and Cambridge match was actually played at Lord's in 1827, but the second was played on the Magdalen Ground two years later. This match continued at Oxford or Lord's until 1850 since when it has made its home at Lord's.

The Oxford eleven also used the ground of the Bullingdon Club and it was not until 1851 that Oxford University Cricket Club acquired the Magdalen Ground as its own home after which it remained their headquarters for 30 years, until they moved northwards to the University Park.

The M.C.C. paid their first visit to Oxford and met the University Club on the Magdalen Ground in May 1832.

It is a peculiarity of the organisation of early Oxford University cricket that there was no appointed captain of the eleven until 1862. Up to that time the affairs of the Club were in the hands of three men who were known either as Managers or Treasurers. Each had equal powers both on and off the field and this must have presented many difficulties.

The outstanding player of 19th-century Oxford University cricket was undoubtedly R. A. H. Mitchell who also played for Leicestershire. Mitchell captained the University XI for three years and his average in the Varsity match was 42.2 in seven innings (one not out). Oxford beat Cambridge in each of the three years he was captain.

Of course there have been many Oxford University men who have distinguished themselves in first-class cricket, but among those who first made their names in the Varsity matches are R. E. Foster (Worcestershire), C. B. Fry (Surrey, Sussex and Hampshire), G. O. Smith (Surrey), Nawab of Pataudi (Worcestershire), Mansur Ali Khan Pataudi (Sussex), M. P. Donnelly (Middlesex, Warwickshire and New Zealand), I. A. R. Peebles (Middlesex and Scotland), Javed Burki (Pakistan).

Those names include two England captains, Foster and Fry, and captains of India, Nawab of Pataudi snr. and jnr., and a captain of Pakistan, Javed Burki. Other Oxford "Blues" who captained England Test teams are D. B. Carr, M. C. Cowdrey, F. L. Fane, Lord Harris, D. R. Jardine, H. D. G. Leveson-Gower, T. C. O'Brien, G. T. S. Stevens, M. J. K. Smith and Sir Pelham Warner, A. H. Kardar, who captained Pakistan in 23 Tests also played for Oxford University in three Varsity matches.

Highest score: 651 v. Sussex at Brighton, June 24, 1895. In Varsity match—503 in 1900. Highest individual scores: 281 by K. J. Key v. Middlesex at Chiswick Park, 1887. In Varsity match—238 by Nawab of Pataudi, 1931. Highest score against: 679 for 7 declared by the Australians, at Oxford, 1938. In Varsity match—432 for 9 declared, in 1936. Highest individual score against: 338 by W. W. Read of Surrey, Oval, June 1888. In Varsity match—211 by G. Goonesena, 1957. Lowest score: 12 (one man absent. Innings completed in 75 minutes) v. M.C.C. and Ground, at Oxford, May 24, 1877. In Varsity match—32 in 1878. Lowest score against: 36 by M.C.C., at Oxford, 1867. In Varsity match—47 by Cambridge University in 1838. Colours: Dark Blue.

OXFORDSHIRE C.C.C.

Founded: 1787. One of the original members of the Minor County Championship in 1895. Dropped out in 1906 but returned in 1922. Secretary: J. E. O. Smith, 4 Queen's Close, Eynsham, Oxford. Highest score for: 460 for 9 declared v. Berkshire, 1947. Highest score against: 539 for 7 declared by Berkshire, 1947; in all matches—547 by M.C.C., 1906. Highest individual score for: 220* by C. Walters, 1924. Highest individual score against: 234 by A. B. Poole of Bedfordshire, at Banbury, 1936. Lowest score for: 33 v. Buckinghamshire, 1925. Lowest score against: 32 by Bedfordshire, 1895. Most wickets taken in a season: 74 by R. V. Divecha, 1949. Colours: Blue and White. Badge: Oxon Ford. Honours: Minor Counties Champions: 1929, 1974.

P

PADS

Robert "Long Bob" Robinson of Farnham, Surrey, is believed to have been the first batsman to wear any form of protection for the legs. This would have been at about the end of the 18th or the beginning of the 19th century. The protection was then in the form of a thin piece of board tied to one leg only.

The use of these was scorned upon and Robinson abandoned the idea. However, a more elaborate form of leg protection was introduced in about 1836 protecting the shins but not the knees.

Thomas Nixon, the Nottinghamshire bowler, is named in *Scores and Biographies* as the inventor of pads, but as the date given is 1841 then it would be wrong to allow him the credit for the idea. Nixon's cork pads were, however, a great improvement on anything which went before.

When one considers the state of the pitches in those days it is obvious that batsmen were pretty tough to withstand the many knocks they must have suffered. Do not forget that at one time it was the fashion to wear tight silk stockings up to the knees and these afforded no protection from the shooters and poppers served up by many of the faster bowlers.

The attitude of many cricketers to the introduction of pads is reflected in a remark made by Lord Frederick Beauclerk when he saw them for the first time. He is said to have expressed the opinion that they would be all right for practice games "but how unfair for a bowler if allowed in a match."

It is no wonder then that pads were not generally adopted until well past the middle of the 19th century.

PAKISTAN

The partition of India in 1947 did not favour Pakistan from a cricketing point of view. They were left with very few first-class players and grounds.

However, the Pakistanis are very keen cricketers and they quickly set about developing the resources left to them in the Sind, N.W. Frontier Province, Baluchistan, about half of the State of the Punjab and Eastern Bengal.

This area included two of the continent's principal grounds, that at Dacca and at Karachi, although following the establishment of Bangladesh in what was formerly East Bengal in 1971, there was a further reduction of Pakistan's resources with the loss of Dacca.

It was at Karachi that Pakistan cricketers first made their mark and put their new country on the cricketing map in 1951–52 by defeating the M.C.C. touring side. Heroes of that victory by four wickets were Khan Mohammad, who took 3 for 45 and 5 for 88, and A. H. Kardar, who played the match-winning innings, scoring 50* in two hours and three-quarters.

That was in December 1951, and it was only 12 months later that Pakistan engaged in their first Test matches, playing five games against India, winning one and losing two.

It was in this series that Pakistan discovered a new star of Test cricket, the 17-year-old Hanif Mohammad. After making a century in each innings of the first match of the tour (against North Zone) he enjoyed innings of 51 in the First Test, 96 in the Third Test, and 56 in the Fifth Test. His average for 18 innings on this tour was 65.50.

Pakistan made their first tour of England in 1954 under the captaincy of A. H. Kardar. Unfortunately this was one of the worst summers for many years but they won one of the four Test matches played (that at the Oval which was won by 24 runs).

A talented Pakistani side twice came close to beating England with some wonderful cricket here in 1971, they have since won only one of their next 14 games, beating New Zealand, at Dunedin, by an innings and 166 runs, thanks largely to some fine spin bowling.

The national championship of Pakistan is played for the Quaid-e-Azam Trophy, a knock-out competition which was established in 1953–54.

The BCCP Patron's Trophy was first played for in 1971, the name being changed simply to Patron's Trophy in 1972.

The Board of Control for Cricket in Pakistan was admitted to the Imperial Cricket Conference for the first time in 1952. It has its headquarters at the National Stadium, Karachi.

Records

Tests

Highest score for: 657 for 8 declared v. West Indies, at Bridgetown, Barbados, 1957–58. Highest score against: 790 for 3 declared, by West Indies, at Kingston, 1957–58. Highest individual score for: 337 by H. Mohammad v. West Indies, at Bridgetown, Barbados, 1957–58. Highest individual score against: 365* by G. Sobers of West Indies, at Kingston, 1957–58. Lowest score for: 87 v. England, at Lord's, 1954. Lowest score against: 70 by New Zealand (Khan Mohammad 6 for 21) at Dacca, 1955–56.

Other matches

Highest score for Pakistan: 580 v. Commonwealth XI, at Lahore, 1963–64. Highest score against Pakistan: 630 for 9 declared by Commonwealth XI, at Lahore, 1963–64. Highest score in Pakistan: 951 for 7 declared, Sind v. Baluchistan, at Karachi, 1973–74. Highest individual score in Pakistan: 499 by Hanif Mohammad, Karachi. v. Bahawalpur, at Karachi, 1958–59. Lowest score against Pakistan: 51 by Scotland, Edinburgh, 1954. Lowest score in Pakistan: 27 by D. I. Khan v. Railways, at Lahore, 1964–65.

PARKER, Charles Warrington Leonard (1884–1959)

When one recalls the many bowling feats of this Gloucestershire player it is astonishing to find that in a first-class career which extended from 1903 to 1935 he only represented England in one Test Match,

against Australia at Old Trafford in July 1921.

The explanation is, of course, that Parker's batting was not nearly as good as other outstanding bowlers available at that time, but even then only one Test appearance for one of the half-dozen best slow left-arm spin bowlers of all times is difficult to understand.

Although he began his career with Gloucestershire in 1903 it wasn't until after World War I that he attracted nation-wide attention.

In 1919 he took 10 for 91 (7 for 60) against the A.I.F. at Clifton, and in the following season he topped the 100-wicket mark for the first time.

After that he never dropped below 100 wickets in any season right up to his retirement in 1935, and in five seasons, 1922, 1924, 1925, 1926, and 1931, he exceeded 200 wickets.

His best average in any of these seasons was in 1930 when his 179 wickets cost only 12.84 each.

Parker performed the "hat-trick" no less than six times, including twice in one game against Middlesex, at Bristol, in 1924.

On another occasion, his benefit match v. Yorkshire, at Bristol in 1922, he actually hit the stumps with five successive balls, but one was a "no-ball".

His many remarkable performances are too numerous to mention, but he took all 10 wickets (10 for 79) against Somerset, at Bristol in 1921, and 17 wickets (9 for 44 and 8 for 12) v. Essex at Gloucester in 1925.

PARR, George (1826–1891)

In the days before the development of "leg theory" bowling George Parr of Nottinghamshire was probably the finest exponent of leg hitting.

Parr used his feet to such purpose that he surprised many a bowler by the manner in which he turned balls to leg which were not delivered on that side.

He soon became one of the leading lights of the famous All England XI, getting off to a remarkable start by scoring a century in his first appearance at Leicester in 1847 and following this with scores of 78* and 64. It should be added that these innings were played against odds when the opposition had 18 or more fielders. No wonder he became known as the "Lion of the North".

In 1856, on the death of William

Clarke, Parr took over as manager of the All England XI, and he was also captain of Nottinghamshire from that year until 1870.

It was George Parr who led the first representative team from this country on an overseas tour. This was combined All England and United England XI which went to Canada and the United States in 1859 and returned undefeated.

In 1863 he also captained the second team to go out to Australia, and whereas the first team, under H. H. Stephenson, had suffered two defeats, Parr's team again returned unbeaten.

Obviously Parr was not only a fine batsman but an outstanding captain who should rank with the best that England has ever produced.

PARTNERSHIP (BATTING,

The record partnership for each wicket in first-class cricket is as follows:

1st wicket: 555 by P. Holmes and H. Sutcliffe, Yorkshire v. Essex, at Leyton, 1932

2nd wicket: 465* by J. A. Jameson and R. B. Kanhai, for Warwickshire v. Gloucestershire, at Birmingham, 1974.

3rd wicket: 456 by Khalid Irtiza and Aslam Ali, for United Bank v. Multan, at Karachi, 1975–76.

4th wicket: 577 by V. S. Hazare and Gul Mohamed, for Baroda v. Holkar, at Baroda, 1946–47.

5th wicket: 405 by D. G. Bradman and S. G. Barnes, for Australia v. England, at Sydney, 1946–47.

6th wicket: 487* by G. Headley and C. C. Passailaigue, for Jamaica, v. Lord Tennyson's XI, at Kingston, 1931–32

7th wicket: 347 by D. Atkinson and C. Depeiza, for West Indies v. Australia, at Bridgetown, 1954–55.

8th wicket: 433 by A. Sims and V. T. Trumper, for an Australian XI v. Canterbury, at Christchurch, 1913–14.

9th wicket: 283 by J. Chapman and A. R. Warren, for Derbyshire v. Warwickshire, at Blackwell, 1910

10th wicket: 307 by A. F. Kippax and J. E. H. Hooker, for New South Wales v. Victoria, at Melbourne, 1928–29.

The 555 put on for the first wicket as mentioned above is a record for any partnership in English first-class cricket. When Sutcliffe was bowled by Eastman for 313, Holmes was 224 not out. There were 18 extras, and Yorkshire declared their first innings closed.

This pair put on a hundred in one hour and forty-five minutes. Their fourth hundred was their fastest, being run up in only 50 minutes.

Once the previous first-wicket record (554 by J. T. Brown and J. Tunnicliffe, Yorkshire v. Derbyshire, at Chesterfield, 1898) had been beaten, Sutcliffe threw away his wicket. But there was a shock immediately after this when the scoreboard was altered to read only 554. Fortunately for Holmes and Sutcliffe it was soon discovered that one no-ball had been missed from the score.

Holmes and Sutcliffe hold the record for the highest number of century partnerships in county cricket. They registered 69 of these for Yorkshire.

A record was created at Taunton in 1960 in a match between Somerset and Cambridge University. The opening pair on each side made a century stand in each innings. G. Atkinson and R. Virgin put on 172 and 112 for Somerset, and R. M. Prideaux and A. R. Lewis 198 and 137 for Cambridge University.

The record partnership for any wicket in a Test match is 451 put on by D. G. Bradman and W. H. Ponsford for the second wicket of Australia's first innings against England, at the Oval, August 1934.

One of the longest partnerships was that of G. Sobers and F. M. Worrell. Playing for West Indies v. England, at Barbados, in 1959–60, they remained together at the wicket throughout the fourth and fifth days. When Sobers was eventually bowled for 226, the partnership had produced 399 for the fourth wicket.

PAY

See under FINANCES OF CRICKET.

PAYNTER, Edward (1901–   )

A resolute left-handed batsman, this Lancashire player will always be remembered for his part in recovering "The Ashes" with D. R. Jardine's team of 1932–33.

Although suffering from tonsilitis he got up from his hospital bed when England were being skittled out at Brisbane and arrived on the ground in time to take his place and play an innings of 83. Two days later he made the hit which won the rubber for England.   Making his debut for Lancashire in 1926 he continued to play for that county until the outbreak of World War II. When the war was over he rounded off his first-class career with the Commonwealth team in India in 1950–51 and subsequently became an umpire for a short time.

Paynter's best season was 1937 when he scored 2,904 runs (av. 53.77), and this was the summer in which he played his highest innings, 322 v. Sussex, at Hove. This is still the highest score by a professional for Lancashire, second only to the 424 by A. C. MacLaren.

Details of Paynter's remarkable innings are well worth mentioning for he compiled this score in a single day's play. He hit 100 in 115 minutes before lunch, 200 in 205 minutes, 300 in 290 minutes, and 322 in 300 minutes.

In his 20 Test appearances Paynter's highest score was 243 v. South Africa, at Durban, in 1938–39.

PEEL, Robert (1857–1941)

Yorkshire has produced many great all-rounders but none better than the diminutive Robert Peel from Churwell, near Leeds.

Peel was a slow left-arm bowler whom C. B. Fry rated as the best of his kind. He was also a talented left-handed batsman and a fine fielder.

He made his debut in 1882 and by the time he retired in 1899 had scored over 12,000 runs as well as capturing 1,754 wickets (av. 16.21).

Peel represented England in 20 Tests from 1884 to 1896 and had his finest success in the 1888 rubber in England when he dismissed 24 Australian batsmen at an average cost of only 7.54. In all Tests he took 102 wickets (av. 16.81).

Unfortunately, Peel never showed his batting ability in Test matches, and indeed, he collected a record number of three "pairs of spectacles".

However, he proved that he could bat well on many other occasions. For example he scored 226* for Yorkshire v. Leicestershire, at Bradford, in 1892, and 210* v. Warwickshire, at Birmingham, in 1896.

His career was cut short in 1897 when he was accused of taking part in a game when unfit to play and was suspended for the remainder of the season. He did not play at all during the following season and after only two or three games in 1899 he was not seen again in first-class cricket.

For Yorkshire Peel took 1,550 wickets

(av. 15.09) and scored 23,398 runs in all classes of matches.

PILCH, Fuller (1803–1870)

After distinguishing himself as a batsman with Norfolk and with Bury he was offered £100 a year to move to Kent and was associated with that county from 1836 right up to the time of his death in 1870, although he actually ceased playing for them in 1854.

As a batsman Fuller Pilch could be rated with the "Champion" himself. He was certainly the finest professional batsman of his day and was recognised as the Champion of England as early as 1833 when, in a single-wicket match, he gave the redoubtable Tom Marsden of Sheffield a thorough beating.

Pilch got his highest score of 160 against the bowling of the great William Lillywhite in 1837 and these two had many a keen tussle with bat and ball.

William Clarke secured Pilch's services for the All England XI in 1847 and he played many innings with that team which helped establish his reputation as the most scientific batsman of his day.

The first player to develop forward play to any marked degree Pilch played with a short-handled bat and his upright stance and superb technique made him an attractive batsman to watch.

Pilch appeared for the Players v. Gentlemen on 24 occasions from 1827 to 1849, and following the end of his playing career he was groundsman and umpire at the St. Lawrence Ground, Canterbury, until two years before his death.

PITCH, The

Although so many other things in cricket have changed it is remarkable to note that the length of the pitch has always been 22 yards, that is from the very first time any length was mentioned. This distance is specified in the earliest code of laws handed down to us which were presumably drawn up in 1744.

However, the rules governing the choice of the pitch for each match have changed from time to time. Originally, the pitch was chosen by the side which won the toss, but in 1774 this became the prerogative of the visiting side with the proviso that they restricted their choice to within 30 yards of a point to be selected by the home side. On neutral grounds it was left to the winner of the toss.

At the beginning of the 19th century it became the practice to leave the choice of pitch to the umpires, although even these gentlemen were restricted to an area within 30 yards of a point selected by the teams. However, by about 1823, the teams lost the right of having some say in the matter. Today the selection of the pitch is left to the home club.

Normally, pitches may only be rolled before the start of each innings and the start of each day's play. Then, at the request of the captain of the batting side seven minutes may be allowed for this purpose.

Rolling, and even watering, was first allowed in the Laws in 1788 and in the early 19th century it was also possible to change the pitch during a game after rain.

In the fourth Test of England's tour of Australia in 1882–83, a fresh pitch was used for each innings on the Sydney ground.

PLUNKET SHIELD

Until 1975 when it was down-graded by the introduction of the Shell Shield this was the principal competition of New Zealand cricket. Originally the shield, which was presented in 1906 by Lord Plunket, Governor-General of New Zealand, was presented to Canterbury and then, competed for on a challenge basis, but from 1921 the trophy was competed for on a League basis. In 1975 the Plunket Shield became the trophy to be competed for in the North v. South Island fixture.

Wellington had been the most successful competitor up to 1975, holding the trophy 16 times.

PONSFORD, William Harold (1900–   )

Here was a batsman who could always be relied upon to get runs, a veritable scoring machine, but at the same time an attractive player.

Ponsford first hit the headlines in 1922–23 by scoring a record breaking 429 for Victoria v. Tasmania, at Melbourne.

On the same ground in 1927–28 he beat that score with an innings of 437 ·v. Queensland, and to this day he remains the only batsman ever to play two innings of over 400 runs.

He made 110 in his Test debut v. England, at Sydney in 1924–25, but when he came to England for the first time in 1926 his tour was interrupted by illness

which prevented him from hitting his best form. On his second visit in 1930 he did a little better but we in England did not see the batsman so renowned as a scorer on Australian wickets until his third and last tour in 1934.

Then, in the fourth Test at Leeds, he scored 181 before being out "hit wicket", and in the final Test, at the Oval, he played a scintillating 266, making a second wicket stand of 451 with D. G. Bradman before he was out, curiously enough, the same as in his previous Test innings—"hit wicket". 451 has only been exceeded on two occasions for a second wicket in a first-class game.

Ponsford's average in that 1934 Test rubber was 94.83.

In 29 Tests for Australia between 1924 and 1934 he scored 2,122 runs (av. 48.22) while in all first-class matches his average rose to over 65.

Ponsford's partnership with E. R. Mayne which produced 456 runs for Victoria v. Queensland, at Melbourne, in 1923–24, is still an Australian first-wicket record.

Another Australian record is his third wicket stand of 389 with S. J. McCabe for the Australians v. M.C.C., at Lord's in 1934. His 281* on that occasion is the highest individual score ever made against the M.C.C., that is, of course, outside of Test cricket.

PRINCE'S GROUND

This was a well known London cricket venue in the 1870s. Situated at Hans Place, Sloane Square, it was the home of Middlesex C.C.C. from 1872 until the end of 1876 when they moved to Lord's.

A few important games were played there after this. W. G. Grace scored 261 for the South v. North, at Prince's in 1877, and the last of the five Gentlemen v. Players matches to be played on this ground took place in July of that year. Soon afterwards, however, the ground was built over and disappeared.

PROCTER, Michael John (1946–   )

Another great all-rounder, when this player from Durban made his Test debut at the age of 20 he captured three Australian wickets for 27 runs in the first innings. and 4 for 71 in the second, his first Test victim being Australian skipper, R. B. Simpson. What a pity that South

Africa's exclusion from Test cricket has curtailed this player's international career for he would surely by now have created record Test bowling figures. In only seven Tests he captured 41 wickets (av. 15.02), the finest average among South African Test bowlers.

At his best John Procter is a brilliant fast bowler with a long run-in and an unusual action, while as a batsman he is reckoned to be one of the world's finest players of spin bowling.

Joined Gloucestershire's staff in 1968 and topped their bowling averages five seasons in succession 1968–1972. His highest score with the bat is 254 for Rhodesia v. Western Province in 1970–71, the season in which he scored six centuries in successive innings, and ended the campaign with an average of 119.50. Only three South Africans have ever captured more wickets than this player.

PROFESSIONAL CAPTAINS
See under CAPTAINS (Professionals).

PRUDENTIAL TROPHY
The Prudential Assurance Company first sponsored international cricket matches in 1972 when three one-day games were played between England and Australia. In the ensuing two years they sponsored the Test matches in England, but the name Prudential Trophy has already gone down in history as the trophy in the first "World Cup" cricket tournament in 1975 when England, Australia, India, New Zealand, East Africa, Pakistan, West Indies and Sri Lanka competed in a series of single innings matches (60 overs) and the West Indies became the first world champions, beating Australia by 17 runs in the Final at Lord's.

The following year the West Indies beat England 3–0 in one-day Prudential trophy matches.

PUBLIC SCHOOL CRICKET
The averages of over 150 Public Schools are listed in *Wisdens* every year but it would be impossible to mention every one of these schools in any detail in this volume. However, no book on English cricket could claim to be comprehensive without some word of Public School cricket for this has often been described as the back-bone of the first-class game in this country. Boys have always been encouraged to take their cricket seriously at Public Schools and many first-class players have emerged from the thorough grounding given in these establishment on the art of cricket.

Westminster School and Eton were probably the first Public Schools to play the game regularly, although Winchester claim the earliest reference to cricket as having been played there by Ken (later Bishop Ken) in about 1650.

There is evidence that Westminster were playing at Tuttle (or Tothill) Fields (now Vincent Square) well before 1720 and they met Eton as early as 1788.

The Sackville family, pillars of Kent cricket, were educated at Westminster, and one of them, Lord Middlesex, was captain of Kent in 1735, seven years after leaving Westminster where he must have played a lot of cricket. His brother, Lord John Sackville, played in the historic Kent and All England game of 1744.

Horace Walpole has mentioned cricket at Eton when he was there, 1728–1734, and it is on record that when Eton and Westminster met on Hounslow Heath in 1796 it was strictly against the orders of their headmaster and the whole eleven was flogged on return to school.

The Eton and Harrow match at Lord's has been for many years one of the more important fixtures in the cricket calendar. It was first played at Lord's in 1822, but there is reason to believe that these two schools met as early as 1800 although the scores of this earlier game have not been found. They certainly played each other at Dorset Square in 1805 when Eton won by an innings and two runs.

If their contribution to the game may be gauged by the number of boys who graduated to the Varsity match then there is no doubt that Eton and Harrow stand supreme in the field of Public School cricket.

Over 300 boys from these two schools have gone on to win their cricket "Blues" and more than a few achieved the distinction of being capped for their country.

Outstanding among these with more than half a dozen Test appearances to their credit are G. O. Allen and B. J. T. Bosanquet of Eton, and F. S. Jackson of Harrow.

To these names we should add that of one of the finest captains in the history of the game, Lord Hawke. Captain of Yorkshire for 28 seasons, this distinguished player first developed his game at Eton.

The pick of the Public School players may be seen each year in their Festival at Lord's. Originally the choice of players was restricted to a small number of schools, but today every effort is made to select a truly representative Public Schools XI for the annual match with the English Schools' C.A.

A full list of the first-class county cricketers who played their earliest games at the Public Schools would fill many pages, but some indication of the class of players developed at these schools may be had from the following:

Charterhouse: G. O. Smith (Surrey), F. L. Fane (Essex), P. B. H. May (Surrey).

Cheltenham: K. S. Duleepsinhji (Sussex), Col. H. W. Renny-Tailyour (Kent), G. E. C. Wood (Kent).

Dulwich: T. E. Bailey (Essex), A. E. R. Gilligan (Surrey and Sussex), H. T. Bartlett (Sussex), S. C. Griffith (Surrey, Sussex), R. D. V. Knight (Surrey, Gloucestershire, Sussex).

Eton: Hon. Ivo Bligh (later 8th Earl Darnley) (Kent), G. O. Allen (Middlesex), B. J. T. Bosanquet (Middlesex), Lord Harris (Kent), Lord Hawke (Yorkshire), Rt. Hon. A. Lyttelton (Middlesex), R. A. H. Mitchell (Leicestershire), The Studd brothers (Middlesex), C. I. Thornton (Kent and Middlesex), F. G. Mann (Middlesex).

Harrow: A. N. Hornby (Lancashire), Hon. Sir F. S. Jackson (Yorkshire), A. C. MacLaren (Lancashire), I. D. Walker (Middlesex).

Highgate: R. W. V. Robins (Middlesex), C. D. Drybrough (Middlesex).

Malvern: H. K., W. I. and R. E. Foster (Worcestershire), E. R. T. Holmes (Surrey), D. J. Knight (Surrey), F. T. Mann (Middlesex), R. W. Tolchard (Leicestershire).

Marlborough: F. M. Lucas (Sussex), A. G. Steel (Lancashire), L. H. Gray (Middlesex), R. H. G. Spooner (Lancashire).

Repton: D. B. Carr (Derbyshire), C. B. Fry (Surrey, Sussex and Hampshire), F. J. G. Ford (Middlesex), L. C. H. and R. C. N. Palairet (Somerset), B. H. Valentine (Kent), J. N. Crawford (Surrey), R. A. Hutton (Yorkshire).

Rugby: D. Buchanan (Warwickshire), Sir Pelham F. Warner (Middlesex), W. Yardley (Kent), E. R. Wilson (Yorkshire).

Sherborne: Rev. D. S. Sheppard (Sussex), A. W. Carr (Nottinghamshire).

Uppingham: A. P. F. Chapman (Kent), A. P. Lucas (Surrey, Middlesex, Essex).

Wellington: G. J. Mordaunt (Kent).

Westminster: Rev. C. G. Lane (Surrey), Lord John Sackville (Kent).

Winchester: D. R. Jardine (Surrey), H. D. G. Leveson-Gower (Surrey), J. R. Mason (Kent), J. Shuter (Surrey), G. H. G. Doggart (Sussex), J. C. Clay (Glamorgan), Mansur Ali Khan Pataudi (Sussex).

In 1921 J. L. Guise of Winchester made 278 against Eton. This is believed to be the highest innings ever recorded in a Public Schools match.

V. Mankad (India)   B. R. Taylor (New Zealand)

Fazal Mahmood (Pakistan)   G. D. McKenzie (Australia)

LEADING TEST BOWLERS

Frank Tyson (Northamptonshire)

W. W. Hall (West Indies)

GREAT FAST BOWLERS

Ray Lindwall (Australia)

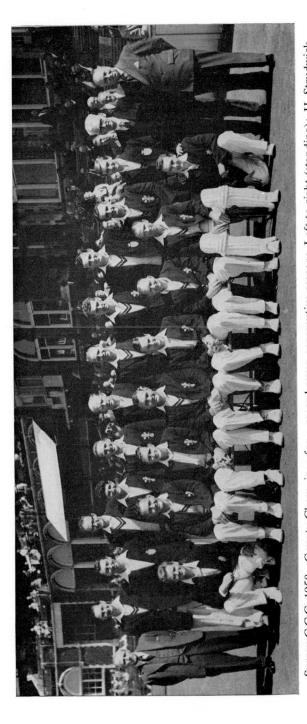

Surrey C.C.C. 1958—County Champions for a record seven consecutive seasons. Left to right (standing): H. Strudwick (scorer), R. C. E. Pratt, M. D. Willett, J. K. Hall, K. Barrington, M. J. Stewart, G. A. R. Lock, T. H. Clark, P. J. Loader, D. Gibson, B. Constable, R. Swetman, J. Tait (masseur), A. Sandham (coach); D. A. D. Sydenham, E. A. Bedser, J. C. Laker, A. V. Bedser, P. B. H. May (captain), A. J. McIntyre, D. G. W. Fletcher, A. B. D. Parsons

L. E. G. Ames (Kent)

J. H. B. Waite (South Africa)

A. T. W. Grout (Australia)

J. T. Murray (Middlesex)

WICKET-KEEPERS SUPREME

The West Indies talented Viv Richards on the way to a score of 291 at The Oval in 1976— the highest Test score by a West Indian in England

(Below) Northampton-shire achieves its first major success by winning the Gillette Cup in 1976. Skipper Mushtaq Mohammad is seen holding the trophy and surrounded by his jubilant team

M. J. Procter (Gloucestershire and South Africa)—scorer of six hundreds in succession in 1970–71

Wilf Rhodes (Yorkshire)—record 4,187 wickets to his credit

J. C. Laker (Surrey and Essex)—record 19 wickets in one match, England v. Australia, 1956

D. C. S. Compton (Middlesex)—record 18 centuries in season 1947

West Indies batsman C. G. Greenidge, who hit the fastest century of the 1976 season— 69 minutes *v*. Nottingham- shire

G. S. Chappell (Australia) has to move quickly to avoid being run out by the West Indies wicket-keeper, D. L. Murray

Undefeated Australian touring team of 1948. Left to right (back row):
R. Lindwall, K. Miller, W. Brown; (middle row): W. Ferguson
(scorer), N. Harvey, D. Ring, E. Toshack, W. Johnston, R. Saggers,
S. Barnes, K. Johnson (manager); (front row): S. Loxton, R. Hamence,
L. Hassett, D. Bradman (captain), C. McCool, A. Morris, I. Johnson.
(D. Tallon does not appear in this group.)

Skipper Ray Illingworth is chaired from the field after England had
regained the Ashes by winning the final Test at Sydney in February
1971

Q

QUALIFICATION

The first rules designed to prevent any player from appearing for more than one county in a single season were drawn up at a meeting in London in December 1872.

These rules which were finally accepted in June 1873 allowed a player to choose at the beginning of each season whether he would play for the county of his birth or the county of his residence. One proviso was that should he choose to play for the latter then he could not play against the county of his birth.

With regard to residential qualification this had to be of a duration of not less than three years for professionals and two years for amateurs. It was a year later that a uniform period of two years was introduced for both classes of players.

The introduction of these qualification rules helped place county championship cricket on a sounder basis. A champion county was recognised for several years before 1873 and although these qualification rules do not appear to have affected the existence or otherwise of a County Championship table at the time, it has since become normal practice to trace the history of the County Championship from that year.

The qualification rules have been altered on a number of occasions and the most recent major revision took place in 1976

The essential difference from the earliest rules and those of the present day is the reduction of the residential qualification period to 12 months. There is also provision for each county to make two "special registrations" of players not qualified under the residential rule. Indeed, in certain special circumstances, such as the player's youth and no qualification for any other county, more than two "special registrations" may be permitted.

Players born or resident in counties which do not play first or second-class cricket, may qualify for the county, the capital of which is nearest to his place of residence or birth.

It is also possible for a player to qualify for a county for which his father has played regularly.

As far as qualification to play for England is concerned, players must either have been born in the British Isles; his father was born in the British Isles and the player has been residing here during the preceding 4 consecutive years and has not played for the country of his birth during that period; resided in the British Isles for the past 10 consecutive years and not played for another country during that time; or begun permanent residence in the British Isles before the age of 14.

R

RAMADHIN, Sonny (1930–   )

When this West Indian came to England for the first time in 1950 he was comparatively unknown, having had very little experience in top class cricket, but by the end of that season he had established himself as one of the best medium-slow right-arm spin bowlers of the post-war era.

Spinning the ball both ways he began quietly enough in the first Test at Manchester with 2 for 90 and 2 for 77, but in the second Test, at Lord's, he completely mastered the England batsmen, bowling 10 consecutive maiden overs in the first innings and 11 in the second innings, and taking 5 for 66 and 6 for 86.

For all matches on this England tour Ramadhin's figures were 135 wickets for 2,009 runs (av. 14.88).

Ramadhin was not the same force in his second Test rubber in England in 1957. He began the first Test just as convincingly (7 for 49 in the first innings) but in the second England innings he was mastered by a fine Cowdrey-May partnership which put on 411 for the fourth wicket and ended the West Indian's reign of terror over English batsmen. This was the innings in which he created a record by bowling 588 balls.

Nevertheless Sonny Ramadhin's Test figures of 158 wickets (av. 28.96) places him among the most successful Test bowlers of all time.

He played for Lancashire 1964–65 and rounded-off his first-class career with a total of 758 wickets (av. 20.24).

RANJI TROPHY

This is the national cricket competition of India. The trophy was presented in 1934 in memory of K. S. Ranjitsinhji.

At the present time over 40 teams compete for the trophy. They are divided into North, South, East, West and Central Zones, and the champion team of each zonal competition which is decided on a points system, then take part in a knock-out competition to decide the winner.

Bombay have won this trophy many more times than any other team, including a run of 15 consecutive victories 1959–73.

RANJITSINHJI, Kumar Shri, afterwards H.H. The Jam Shahib of Nawanagar (1872–1933)

One of the most accomplished batsmen even known "Ranji" executed every stroke to perfection and delighted crowds wherever he played.

He learnt the rudiments of the game when at Rajkumar College, Kathiawar, and perfected his cricket at Cambridge.

Possessing an exceptionally quick eye he could hook even the fastest bowling, and became famous particularly for his leg-glances.

Ranjitsinhji made his debut in English first-class cricket in 1893, and, with the exception of 1898, he played regularly in England until the end of the 1904 season when he returned to India to succeed his father as ruler of Jamnagar.

He came back to England to play cricket in 1908, 1912, and finally in 1920, when, though now blind in one eye, he played three more games for Sussex.

After getting his Cambridge "Blue" and playing for Cambridgeshire Ranjitsinhji made his debut for Sussex against the M.C.C., at Lord's in May 1895, scoring 77* and 150.

Thereafter, with his silk shirt buttoned at the wrists, he became one of the best known and best loved figures in English cricket.

His highest score for Sussex was against Somerset at Taunton in August 1901, 285*, and this was after spending the previous night fishing! When stumps were drawn Sussex had reached 466 for one wicket.

In 1899 he scored 3,159 runs (av.

63.18), but his best season was 1900, for then his average was 87.57 with a total of 3,065 runs in 40 innings. It was during that summer that he scored 222 and 215* in successive innings. In 1901 he followed an innings of 285 with another of 204.

In all, this genial personality played 14 innings of 200 or more runs, and topped 2,000 runs in a season on five occasions.

RANSFORD, Vernon Seymour (1885-1958)

Australia and Victoria left-handed batsman and brilliant cover-point, who played so many delightful innings with such grace and a peculiar gentleness seldom seen in scoring batsmen.

He first appeared for Victoria when only 18 years of age and played in all five Tests against England in Australia four years later.

In 1908-09 season he became the first player to score a century in each innings for Victoria, 182 and 110 v. New South Wales, at Sydney, and was then chosen to tour England.

In the Tests that summer of 1909 he topped the batting average with 58.83, playing a fine not-out innings of 143 at Lord's. Later in the tour he scored 190 on the same ground against the M.C.C.

Ransford was one of the Australian players who took sides against the Board of Control in 1912 and he was never chosen for another Test match.

REDPATH, Ian Ritchie (1941-   )

One of Australia's most prolific run-getters (4,737 runs, av. 43.45) in 66 Tests 1963-76, with a top score of 171 v. England, at Perth in 1970-71, Redpath first established himself as an opening batsman with Lawry in the Victoria team. His highest score is 261 v. Queensland, at Melbourne in 1962-63.

A batsman with a relaxed style, especially sound against fast bowling, he made three centuries in the 1975-76 series against the West Indies, bringing his total of Test centuries to eight.

REGISTRATION RULES

See under QUALIFICATION.

REID, John Richard (1928-   )

This clever all-rounder was the backbone of New Zealand cricket for nearly 20 years and led his country to their earliest Test victories—against West Indies in 1965 and two against South Africa in 1962. In all he captained New Zealand in 34 of his record breaking run of 58 consecutive Tests.

Reid made his debut with Wellington in 1947-48, subsequently transferred to Otago in 1956. His first Test appearances were made in England in the 1949 tour.

In the 1954-55 season he created a record in New Zealand by winning both the Redpath Cup for batting and the Windsor Cup for bowling.

After three seasons in League cricket, 1952-55, he returned to England again in 1958, this time as captain of the New Zealand tourists, and he set his side a fine example, scoring 161 v. Somerset, 118 v. Sussex, and 114 v. Northamptonshire. When he came over as captain in 1965 cartilage trouble in one knee generally prevented him from producing his best form although he hit 165 against Kent.

His most exhilarating innings was his 296 for Wellington v. Northern Districts in 1962-63. This included 15 sixes.

Reid's aggregate of 16,128 (av. 41.35) has only been exceeded by two other New Zealand batsmen—G. M. Turner and B. Sutcliffe.

RHODES, Wilfred (1877-1973)

In selecting only the most successful cricketers for inclusion in this book it is only natural that a large number of superlatives are used in describing their careers. More must now be found to describe this Yorkshireman for as an all-round cricketer he stands second to none having completed the "double" on more occasions than any other player.

Born at Kirkheaton, he made his debut for Yorkshire in 1898 and did not finally retire until 32 years later when he was in his 53rd year.

He first completed the "double" in 1903 and repeated this achievement on another 15 occasions. In these seasons he topped 2,000 runs and 100 wickets twice, 1909 and 1911.

Rhodes was a slow left-arm bowler with no run-up. He had a fine command of spin and break and was probably the best slow bowler ever known on batsmen's wickets.

He took over 100 wickets in a season 23 times, a record, and is also the only bowler ever to collect more than 4,000 wickets in a career.

Rhodes never quite managed to get all ten wickets in a single innings but he did capture as many as nine on three occasions, his best being 9 for 24 for Thornton's XI v. the Australians at Scarborough in 1899. His best match, however, was against Essex at Leyton that same season, when he took 9 for 28 and 6 for 28.

Batting right-handed he got 1,000 runs in a season 21 times and his highest score was 267* for Yorkshire v. Leicestershire, at Leeds, in 1921.

Rhodes made 58 Test appearances and had his finest bowling success against the Australians in 1903–04 when he captured 31 wickets (av. 15.74). However, he probably enjoyed himself the most when he and Hirst bowled the Australians out for only 36 at Birmingham in 1902. In that innings Rhodes took 7 for 17.

RICHARDS, Barry Anderson (1945–   )

Considered by many to be the best since Hammond as a real driver of the ball, this South African's aggregate in his first full season in English cricket with Hampshire in 1968 was 2,395 (av. 47.90) including 130 and 104* v. Northamptonshire, at Northampton. He headed the county's averages that season and has done so in every season since.

In 1976 this batsman hit no less than seven centuries for Hampshire, including two in one match v. Kent, at Southampton.

His 356 for South Australia v. Western Australia, at Perth in 1970–71 is the second highest innings in Australia since the war, only three runs behind R. B. Simpson's total for New South Wales v. Queensland in 1963–64.

RICHARDS, Isaac Vivian Alexander (1952–   )

Superb batsman with an upright, majestic style, Viv Richards from Antigua was seen at his best in 1976 when he scored two double centuries in the Tests in England—232 in the 1st and 291 in the 5th (the second highest score by a West Indian against England) and finished the rubber with 829 runs (av. 118.42). This brought his total in Test cricket during 1976 to 1,710 runs, a calendar-year record which included seven centuries.

This most entertaining of batsmen made his debut for the Leeward Islands in

1971–72. He has since played for Combined Islands and joined Somerset in 1974.

RICHARDSON, Peter Edward (1931–   )

An attacking left-handed batsman who made a great start to his International career when first selected as opener for the Tests against Australia in 1956.

In the first Test at Nottingham he made 81 and 73; got a century (104) in the fourth Test, and finished the rubber with an average of 45.50.

One odd coincidence was that in each of his eight innings of that series Richardson was caught at the wicket; a fact which served to emphasise his weakness in dealing with balls going away on the offside.

Richardson followed this rubber with a tour of South Africa in 1956–57 when he batted for 488 minutes in the first Test to reach treble figures and 525 minutes before he was out lbw for 117.

Richardson's first-class career began with Worcestershire in 1949 and he got his cap in 1952. He captained the county from 1956 to 1958 before moving to Kent in 1959.

He retired in 1965 after making 26,055 runs (av. 34.60). His best season was 1953 when he scored 2,294 runs (av. 39.55), and his highest score was 185 for Worcestershire v. Somerset, at Kidderminster in 1954.

RICHARDSON, Thomas (1870–1912)

One of the greatest fast bowlers of all time, Tom Richardson took 290 wickets at an average cost of only 14.37 each in his best season—1895.

That figure of 290 has only been exceeded by one other player, A. P. Freeman, but the Kent bowler sent down many more balls in each of his two record-breaking seasons.

Among fast bowlers Richardson's record is unparalleled for its consistency and when he was at his peak, in four years 1894–97 (including first-class games played in Australia 1894–95) he took 1,073 wickets (av. 14.69).

At the Oval, in 1894, he took all 10 Essex wickets for 45 runs.

Powerfully built, and noted for his stamina, the lion-hearted Richardson made his debut for Surrey in 1892 and after appearing regularly until 1904 he ended his first-class career the following season by playing one game for Somerset—against the Australians.

ROWAN, Eric Alfred Burchall (1909–   )

Opening batsman from the Transvaal who holds the record for the highest innings in South African first-class cricket, 306* for Transvaal v. Natal, at Johannesburg, in 1939–40. He also set up a record for Transvaal in the Currie Cup competition with an innings of 277* v. Griqualand West, on the same ground, in 1950–51.

Rowan made his debut in 1929–30, and was first chosen to play for South Africa in Test cricket in 1935 when he toured England and played in all five Tests. He did not strike his form in those games but played many graceful innings in other matches doing well enough to head his side's averages with 1,948 runs (av. 44.27).

After appearing against Australia in three Tests in 1935–36 he was not chosen again until England visited South Africa in 1938. Then he scored 156 in the second innings of the second Test.

Rowan made 14 more Test appearances after the war, including all five in the 1951 tour of England when he rounded off his Test career by heading his side's averages once again with 57.22, including a remarkable display at Leeds where he scored 236 and 60*.

ROY, Pankaj (1928–   )

India's former opening right-hand batsman who played in glasses. P. Roy was one of his country's most prolific scorers in post-war cricket.

He made his debut for Bengal v. United Provinces, at Calcutta, in 1946–47, scoring an unbeaten century, and it was five years later that he appeared in his first Test series and scored 140 in his second game against England.

In England, in 1952, however, he collected an unenviable record by being out for nought in five of his seven innings, including a pair in the third Test in Manchester.

Roy appeared in English League cricket and also represented the Indian Football Association at soccer, playing inside-right.

At Madras, in 1955–56, he and V. Mankad created a new Test record for a first wicket partnership by scoring 413 v. New Zealand.

ROYALTY

The first member of the Royal Family to take an active interest in cricket was probably Frederick Louis, Prince of Wales, the eldest son of George II. In 1733 he was so pleased with a game which he saw at Moulsey Hurst between Surrey and Middlesex that he gave a guinea to each player.

He captained both Surrey and London in 1737 and played regularly at East Molesey and Kennington Common. In 1751 he died at Leicester House and it is believed that his death was the result of a blow he had received some time earlier when struck in the side by a cricket ball.

It was Frederick Louis who was chiefly responsible for the first really important cricket match of which the full scores are known today—Kent v. All England, in 1744.

RUGBY AND CRICKET

Men who have represented their country at both rugby and Test cricket:

J. H. Anderson (Western Province), played for South Africa; G. R. D. Dickinson (Otago) for New Zealand; M. P. Donelly (Oxford University, Middlesex and Warwickshire) played cricket for New Zealand, rugby for England; M. K. Elgie (Natal) cricket for South Africa, rugby for Scotland; T. A. Harris (Transvaal) for South Africa; R. H. M. Hands (Western Province) cricket for South Africa, rugby for England; A. N. Hornby (Lancashire) for England; P. S. T. Jones (Western Province) for South Africa; G. MacGregor (Cambridge University and Middlesex) cricket for England, rugby for Scotland; W. H. Milton (Western Province) cricket for South Africa, rugby for England; F. Mitchell (Cambridge University, Yorkshire and Transval) cricket for England and South Africa, rugby for England; O. E. Nothling (New South Wales) for Australia; H. G. Owen-Smith (Oxford University, Western Province and Middlesex) cricket for South Africa, rugby for England; M. L. Page (Canterbury) for New Zealand; A. W. Powell (Griqualand West) for South Africa; A. Richards (Western Province) for South Africa; A. E. Stoddart (Middlesex) for England; J. H. Sinclair (Transvaal) for South Africa; R. O. Schwartz (Transvaal and Middlesex) cricket for South Africa, rugby for England; M. J. K. Smith

(Oxford U., Leicestershire, Warwickshire) for England; R. H. Spooner (Lancashire) for England; M. J. Turnbull (Cambridge University and Glamorgan) cricket for England, rugby for Wales; E. W. Tindill (Wellington) for New Zealand; C. B. Van Ryneveld (Oxford University and Western Province) cricket for South Africa, rugby for England; G. F. Vernon (Oxford University and Middlesex) for England; S. M. J. Woods (Cambridge University and Somerset) cricket for England and Australia, rugby for England.

Other men who have distinguished themselves in both games include:

H. H. Castens (W. Province) capped for South Africa at rugby and captain South African cricketers in England (no Tests) 1894; J. Daniell (Cambridge University and Somerset) capped for England at rugby; H. L. V. Day (Bedfordshire and Hampshire) capped for England at rugby; A. K. Walker (New South Wales and Nottinghamshire) capped for Australia at rugby; W. Wooller (Cambridge University and Glamorgan) capped for Wales at rugby.

RULES

See under LAWS OF CRICKET.

RUN-OUT

In a game between Melbourne and North Melbourne in 1896, R. McLeod was run-out in both innings without having a ball bowled to him. This is believed to be the only case of its kind on record.

At Lord's, August 9–10, 1860, seven of the M.C.C. and Ground team were run-out in their match with Sussex.

RUNS

See under HIGHEST SCORES, LOWEST SCORES.

S

SAEED AHMED (1937–   )

Only Hanif Mohammad has scored more Test runs for Pakistan than this attractive stroke-player who appeared in 41 Tests 1958–1971, including three as captain (v. England 1968–69). His highest Test innings was 172 v. New Zealand, at Karachi in 1964–65. At Lahore in 1961–62 he scored 105 and 102 for PIA v. North Zone, and it was at this time that he scored four centuries in successive innings.

His Test aggregate is 2,991 (av. 40.41).

SANDHAM, Andrew (1890–   )

Despite the fact that he scored one of the highest innings in Test cricket, 325 v. West Indies, at Kingston in 1929–30, and was one of the most prolific scorers in other first-class games, Andrew Sandham never established himself in Test cricket.

He was, however, an unselfish partner for J. B. Hobbs and maybe it was because he allowed the master to take most of the glory that he was not chosen to make more than 14 Test appearances during a first-class career of more than 25 years. Added to this of course is the remarkable opening partnership struck up for England between Hobbs and Sutcliffe.

Nevertheless Sandham was a notable opening batsman in his own right who made 10 double centuries for Surrey and score over 1,000 runs in every season from 1920 to his retirement at the end of 1937.

During this time he figured in no less than 63 first-wicket partnerships with Hobbs which produced a century, their highest being 428 v. Oxford University, at the Oval, in 1926.

Sandham's aggregate of 41,284 (av. 44.82) includes 107 centuries including one in each innings for the M.C.C. v. New South Wales, at Sydney, in 1924–25.

SATURDAY STARTS

Saturday starts for County matches were first introduced in England in 1920 and for the Tests with Australia in 1921.

SCARBOROUGH FESTIVAL

This cricket week is as popular with the Northern cricket followers as the other great cricket festival at Canterbury is with those in the South.

The Scarborough Festival was inaugurated in September 1871 with a game at Castle Yard between Lord Londesborough's XI and The Visitors.

The man who did most to establish this cricket festival was C. I. Thornton of Eton, Cambridge University, Kent and Middlesex. He was associated with the festival for many years and was given the Freedom of the Borough of Scarborough for this work.

Other enthusiasts who have done much to keep the Scarborough flag flying include Lord Hawke, W. W. Leadbeater, H. Leadbeater, and Sir H. D. G. Leveson-Gower, and T. N. Pearce.

SCHWARZ, Reginald Oscar (1875–1918)

Born in Kent and educated at St. Paul's and Cambridge, this all-rounder who became noted particularly for his bowling was one of the men who helped put South African cricket on the map.

Returning to England with the South African team of 1904 he took 65 wickets at an average cost of only 18.26, and when he came over again with the Test team of 1907 he did even better with an aggregate of 137 wickets (av. 11.79).

In England for the Triangular tournament of 1912 he did not do so well, being unable to produce the same pace off the pitch as he had in previous tours. This time he got only 18 wickets which cost 37.33 runs apiece.

Schwarz modelled his style on that of B. J. T. Bosanquet, sending down googlies, and his accuracy made him difficult to play.

His best bowling feats included his 6 for 11 for South Africans v. Northamptonshire, at Northampton in 1907, followed later in the same year by 8 for 55 for M.C.C. v. Gentlemen of Philadelphia, at Mannheim.

The spell of bowling which may have given him the greatest satisfaction was that at Sydney in 1910–11 when, in a Test match, he dismissed Messrs. Trumper, C. Hill, Armstrong Ransford and Cotter, his figures being 5 for 6 at one stage of the Australian innings which eventually totalled 364.

It should be mentioned that R. O. Schwarz made several appearances for Middlesex and also got his "Blue" for Rugby as well as playing that game for England in three internationals. Sad to relate he died of influenza when only 43 years of age.

SCORE-BOARD

Telegraph score-boards were first introduced in the middle of the 19th century. One was seen at Lord's in 1846 and at the Oval in 1848.

When Paget's score-board was brought out in 1884 runs were recorded as soon as they were made alongside the numbers of the two batsmen at the wicket.

It was soon after this that the bowlers were also indicated by means of numbers.

The first detailed score-board was the mammoth mechanical board which was erected at Melbourne in 1884.

Prior to the erection of score-boards the only indication of the state of the game which was given to spectators and players was when the scores were level, for at this point the two scorers always stood up.

SCORE-CARD

The earliest known score-card were printed in 1776 by Pratt who was scorer to the Sevenoaks Vine Club.

However this seems to have been an isolated case and it was not until well into the 19th century that score-cards were made available at most of the principal grounds. The first man to go into the business of printing these at various grounds was Fred Lillywhite. It was in 1848 that he began taking his portable printing press around with him from match to match.

Lillywhite even took his tent and press abroad on the tour of Canada and the United States in 1859.

SCORERS

In the game's earliest days the scorers recorded a run by cutting a notch in a stick.

It should not be forgotten that the word "score" actually means to mark with notches or incisions, and the word "score", meaning twenty, arises out of the practice in some quarters of marking that tally by a larger notch. Because of the lower scores involved in the earliest games it became cricketing practice to make this deeper notch at every tenth run.

In 1706 William Goldwyn wrote this little couplet:
Two trusted friends squat on the rising floor
To notch, with knives on sticks, the mounting score
        (Translated by H.P.–T.)

"Trusted friends" they have been ever since for the position of scorer is an important one, especially with the first-class clubs where they operate under the searching eyes of large numbers of spectators and Pressmen.

SCORES

See also under HIGHEST SCORES, LOWEST SCORES.

The first game of which the scores of each member of the teams is known today was Kent v. All England, at the Artillery Ground, June 18, 1744. These scores were compiled by an anonymous journalist.

The first publication to carry match scores was produced in 1772 by W. Epps. Samuel Britcher began publishing the scores of the more important games in 1791 and continued until 1805. But the most notable work which included the scores of all the more important games from 1744 was Arthur Haygarth's *Scores and Biographies*. Volumes I to IV were produced in 1862 and Volumes V to XIV were subsequently produced by the M.C.C. and published by Longman's between 1876 and 1894. Volume XV appeared in 1925.

Scores and Biographies was followed in 1864 by the first issue of the cricketers' "bible", *Wisden's Cricketers' Almanack* (q.v.).

SCOTLAND

Cricket flourishes in Scotland where counties of the Midland and East have their own championship and Leagues exist for the leading clubs in Edinburgh, Glasgow, Border and North Eastern areas. Most of these clubs employ professionals and the standard is much higher than many Sassenachs are prepared to believe.

The game was introduced to Scotland towards the end of the 18th century by noblemen and gentlemen returning North to their estates, by tradesmen crossing the border to demonstrate their crafts and also by the military stationed in garrison towns such as Edinburgh, Glasgow, Ayr, Stirling and Perth.

The earliest known game was that played in September 1785 on the estate of Earl Cathcart at Alloa between the Hon. Col. Talbot's XI and the Duke of Atholl's XI.

The next game of which record has been found was that played at Aberdeen in 1789 between the 55th Regiment and the Gordon Castle Club.

A well-known English cricket enthusiast among the men who encouraged the growth of the game North of the Border was the fourth Duke of Richmond. In 1790 he was Captain the Hon. Charles Lennox of the 35th Foot stationed at Edinburgh. The castle was illuminated for his arrival!

The first professional was John Sparkes, a Surrey man who had been one of the finest slow break bowlers in England and had coached at Cambridge. He is believed to have been about 57 when he was first engaged by the famous Grange C.C. of Edinburgh in 1834 and he remained with them for nearly 20 years. When he became too old to give much time to bowling he was assisted in his coaching by a younger professional.

Many famous players have gained experience North of the Border and at Galashiels they still claim to have *taught* the great Wilfred Rhodes, for he had a couple of seasons as the local club's professional in 1896 and 1897. Other men whose names spring to mind are Charles Lawrence with Perthshire and Schofield Haigh who was with the same club as well as with Aberdeen.

The Western District Union Championship began in 1893, the Border League in 1895 and the County Championship in 1902.

The club with the oldest minute book, dated 1821, is the Kelso Club, but the Perthshire Club claims to have had the longest continuous existence, having been founded in 1826.

The governing body is the Scottish Cricket Union which was formed in 1908. There was an earlier attempt to establish a Union in 1878 but this lapsed in 1883 and the Grange Club of Edinburgh then acted as the M.C.C. of Scotland until 1908.

SECOND XI CHAMPIONSHIP

This competition was introduced in 1959 primarily to enable players on trial or who had not completed their period of qualification to have more games with the first-class county sides.

Kent Second XI has won this Championship four times (1961, 1969, 1970 and 1976), which is more often than any other county.

SERVICES CRICKET

With more pressing matters needing their attention there was not much time left to develop cricket to any degree in the Army and Navy of the 18th and early 19th centuries.

However, one gentleman who encouraged the Army to take up cricket was the Honourable Charles Lennox (later fourth Duke of Richmond). He had played an important part in the formation of the M.C.C. in 1787, and when he became a Captain and joined the 35th Foot at Edinburgh in 1790 he took his enthusiasm for the game with him across the border.

The first Service side to meet the M.C.C. at Lord's was the Royal Artillery. This was in a 12-a-side match played in June 1818. The R.A., who included one player not in the regiment, won by nine wickets.

The first inter-services match ranked as first-class was that between the Army and the Royal Navy, at Lord's, 1908.

Service commitments obviously prevent a man from playing an active part in first-class cricket but here are just a few who have made their mark in the game while still serving:

Lt. C. H. Abercombie, R.N. (Hampshire), Lt. Cdr. M. L. Y. Ainsworth, R.N. (Worcestershire), Col. (subsequently Canon) J. G. Greig (Hampshire), Col. A. C. Johnston (Hampshire), Brig. Gen. R. M. Poore (Wiltshire, Hampshire and South Africa), Lt. Col. D. C. Robinson (Essex and

Gloucestershire), Brig. Gen. A. J. Turner
(Essex), Brig. Gen. W. N. White
(Hampshire) Major E. G. Wynard
(Hampshire).

SHAW, Alfred (1842–1907)

It was Richard Daft who first called
Alfred Shaw "The Emperor of Bowlers"
and it was a title this Nottinghamshire
man justly deserved when you recall that
in his most successful year (1878), he
captured 201 wickets at an average cost of
only 10.96. That, however, wasn't his best
average, for in 1880 his 177 wickets cost
only 8.54 apiece, a figure that has never
been equalled by anyone taking nearly as
many wickets.

On one occasion for Nottinghamshire v.
Gloucestershire, at Nottingham, Shaw
actually performed the hat-trick" once in
each innings, while at Lord's in 1874,
playing for the M.C.C., he took all 10 of
the North's wickets for 73 runs.

Slow-medium pace with an easy round-
arm action, Shaw captained Nottinghamshire from 1883 to 1886 and played in
seven Tests, captaining the England side
in Australia in 1881–82.

Shaw also played a few games for
Sussex late in his career before retiring
with an aggregate of 2,072 wickets (av.
11.97).

SHELL SHIELD

This is the principal tournament of the
West Indies and similarly of New
Zealand.

The West Indian competition was
inaugurated in 1966 with the re-organ-
isation of their Regional Tournament.
Barbados, Combined Island (Windward
and Leeward), Guyana, Jamaica, and
Trinidad meet each other in 4-day
matches.

The New Zealand competition replaced
the Plunket Shield as the principal
competition in that part of the world in
1975 with Canterbury winning the first
Final.

SHEFFIELD SHIELD

In 1891 Lord Sheffield, a patron of Sussex
cricket and a President of Sussex C.C.C.,
financed a trip to Australia by an England
team captained by W. G. Grace. It was at
the end of this tour that his Lordship
presented a sum of money for the benefit
of cricket in Australia and the Australian

Cricket Council purchased a shield for
competition among the three colonies of
New South Wales, Victoria and South
Australia.

The Sheffield Shield was first competed
for in the following season of 1892–93 and
has continued regularly ever since with the
exception of the years of the two World
Wars.

The three original colonies (now States)
have since been joined by Queensland
(1926) and Western Australia (1947).

Each side in the competition play the
others at home and away and the points-
system is now similar to the County
Championship.

New South Wales have won this trophy
far more often than any of its rivals
including a record run of nine successive
victories 1954–62.

SHORTEST GAMES

Many first-class matches have been
completed in a single day and here are a
few examples of some of the shortest
games:

When the Australians met the M.C.C.
at Lord's in 1878 the game was won by
the visitors in six hours, or only 4½ hours
actual play. The M.C.C. were all out for
33 in 65 minutes, then the Australians
could only reply with 41. In the second
innings the M.C.C. scored 19 and the
Australians made the necessary 12 runs
for the loss of one wicket.

The Australians also defeated an
England XI in 4½ hours at Aston,
Birmingham, in 1884. England 82 and 26,
Australians 76 and 33 for 6.

On Friday, May 27, 1898, Yorkshire
defeated Hampshire, at Southampton, by
an innings and 79 runs in under seven
hours' play. There had been no play
possible on the first day.

When Middlesex met Somerset in
Wilfred Flowers' benefit, at Lord's, in
1899, no play was possible on the first day
because of rain, but on the following day
the match was completed with only three
hours and five minutes play. 30 wickets
fell for 165 runs and Middlesex won by an
innings and seven runs. A. Trott took 11
wickets for 31 runs.

In July 1894 Somerset were beaten in a
single day in two successive games. On
July 17, they were beaten by Lancashire,
and on July 19 they lost to Yorkshire. The
scores were:

Lancashire 231, Somerset 31 and 132,
at Manchester;

Yorkshire 173, Somerset 74 and 94, at Huddersfield.

In August 1954 Surrey beat Worcestershire at the Oval in only five hours play. On the first day Worcestershire were dismissed for only 25 runs, G. A. R. Lock taking 5 for 2, and Surrey declared after scoring 92 for 3 with one hour left for play.

On the second day only one hour was needed to dismiss Worcestershire for 40 and so give Surrey victory by an innings and 27 runs.

The match aggregate of 157 runs for 22 wickets is the lowest ever recorded in a completed County Championship game.

SHORTEST INNINGS

See under INNINGS (Shortest).

SHREWSBURY, Arthur (1856–1903)

The outstanding professional batsman of his day, this Nottinghamshire player scored over 26,000 runs in a career which began in 1875 and continued until he died at the age of 47 in May 1903.

Even at that age the graceful Shrewsbury was still one of the most prolific scorers in the country, and indeed, his last season was his best, for he scored 1,250 runs with an average of 50.00.

Shrewsbury was always a difficult man to get out and there have been few better batsmen than he on a difficult wicket. He was, however, never one to be hustled and generally refused to force the pace. Because of this some of his innings were inclined to be monotonous but he scarcely ever made a bad stroke.

He did, of course, compile many really big scores. His highest was 267, a figure he first recorded for Nottinghamshire v. Middlesex, at Nottingham in 1887, and again v. Sussex on the same ground in 1890. It was, however, some of his lesser scores on difficult wickets that earned him his excellent reputation.

Shrewsbury played in 23 Tests and captained England in seven of them, all in Australia. He won three out of five Tests there in 1884–85 and both of the 1886–87 games.

In the Lord's Test of 1886 he showed his class by scoring 164 against the bowling of Spofforth, Palmer, Garrett and Giffen.

SHROPSHIRE C.C.C.

Founded: Early 1800's. Secretary: H. Botfield, 1 The Crescent, Much Wenlock, Shropshire. Shropshire are the newest members of the Minor Counties Championship having been entered for the first time in 1957. Highest score for: 468 v. Free Foresters, 1880; in Minor County Championship—349 for 7 declared v. Somerset II, 1961. Highest score against: 548 by Gentlemen of Cheshire, 1868; in Minor County Championship—350 for 7 declared by Somerset II, 1961. Highest individual score for: 169 by W. G. Dyas, 1899. Highest individual score against: 201* by W. H. Arundel of Cheshire, 1873; in Minor County Championship—200* by R. A. Diment of Leicestershire II, 1959. Lowest score for: In M.C. Championship—30 v. Warwickshire II, 1962. Minor Counties Champions 1973. Colours: Blue and gold. Badge: County Coat of Arms.

SIMPSON, Reginald Thomas (1920–   )

When this stylish Nottinghamshire opening batsman made his Test debut in England in 1949 against New Zealand, after playing only one previous Test in South Africa, he gave one of the most sensational displays ever seen in Test cricket on the Old Trafford ground.

After passing his 50, he opened up with some fine hitting which brought him another 53 in only 27 minutes before he was caught.

Simpson, who was also a brilliant fielder at cover-point, played in 27 Tests and his highest score in these games was 156* against Australia, at Melbourne, in 1950–51.

He began his first-class career in India during the war, and got his county cap in 1946. He was county captain from 1951 until the end of the 1960 season.

The highest score of his career in which he aggregated 30,546 runs (av. 38.32) was his 259 for the M.C.C. v. New South Wales, at Sydney, in 1950–51. He also scored nine other double centuries for his county.

SIMPSON, Robert Baddeley (1936–   )

Born in Sydney of Scottish parents he first appeared for New South Wales when only 16 years of age in 1953 and developed into one of Australia's finest all-rounders and shrewdest captains, being a sound right-handed batsman, leg-spin bowler and brilliant slip fielder.

He succeeded Benaud as Australia's captain and led them in 29 of his 52 Tests.

Old Trafford fans will always remember this player for he created a record for that ground with his 311 against England in the 4th Test of 1964. That innings lasted for 12 hours 57 minutes. His stubborness sometimes bored the crowd but his innings also produced several spells of really attractive batsmanship.

Simpson, who also had a spell with Western Australia during his career which lasted until 1968, got his highest score of 359 for New South Wales v. Queensland at Brisbane in October 1963.

Only three Australian Test batsmen have scored more than his total of 4,131 runs, while his 99 catches in Tests places him among the elite of fieldsmen.

SINGLE WICKET CRICKET

This type of cricket was very popular in the early part of the 19th century. Unfortunately, however, it was very popular with the betting men too, and because it was easier to bribe the smaller number of players engaged, single-wicket cricket fell into disrepute and by the middle of the 19th century it had almost completely disappeared.

At one time these games were played to decide the Champion Cricketer of England and large crowds were attracted to such contests.

In 1833 Tom Marsden of Sheffield was the recognised single-wicket champion of England, but that year he was decisively beaten at Norwich by Fuller Pilch. The winner making 71 runs in one innings against only 7 runs by Marsden in two innings.

In August 1838 the redoubtable Alfred Mynn defeated another famous single-wicket player, James Dearman of Yorkshire. The match took place at Town Malling for 100 guineas and Mynn won easily after toying with his opponent in order to prolong the game.

Alfred Mynn really clinched his right to be called Champion of England when he beat Felix at Lord's, in 1846, and again at Bromley.

Single wicket cricket was revived in England with a tournament at Scarborough in 1963 and was played in each of the next six years at Lord's.

SLANG
See under TERMS USED IN CRICKET.

SLOW SCORING

In England's second innings at Adelaide in the fourth Test of the 1946–47 tour, T. G. Evans was at the wicket for 97 minutes before making his first run. This is a record. Evans eventually made 10 not out.

H. D. Davies was 0 not out for Glamorgan v. Middlesex, at Lord's, after batting for 61 minutes, May 1960.

One of the most stubborn defensive innings in Test cricket was that of H. L. Collins, at Manchester, in 1921. The Australian opener spent 4 hours 50 minutes making 40 runs before being out lbw.

The slowest century on record was made by D. J. McGlew when he scored 105 in 575 minutes for South Africa v. Australia, at Durban, January 1958.

In 1882 at Nottingham, R. G. Barlow, one of the most consistent stone-wallers of all time, made 5 not out in an innings which lasted for 2½ hours. This was for Lancashire v. Nottinghamshire, and during this innings there was one spell of 1 hour 20 minutes during which Barlow made no score at all.

T. Pierpoint once batted for 7½ hours to make 31 runs for Sussex v. Kent, at Sevenoaks, August 1827.

In 1874 Mr. Easton batted for 2 hours to make 3 runs for Twenty-two of Castlemain against W. G. Grace's England team in Australia.

In 1974 at Chelmsford, B. R. Hardie batted for 142 minutes to score four runs for Essex v. Hampshire.

Another batsman often criticised by the spectators for his refusal to force the pace was the Australian, A. C. Bannerman. At Sydney in January 1887 he was at the wicket for 2 hours to make 15*. Australia's total in that innings was 119 in reply to England's 45.

SMALL, John snr. (1737–1826)

A shoemaker by trade, John Small of Hampshire did more than most to develop the game in its formulative years. Being concerned both as a player and as a manufacturer of the implements used in the game he influenced the style of play to a great degree.

He began playing with the Hambledon Club in 1755 and it was he who conceived the idea of the upright bat, an instrument he himself used to great advantage.

This sign appeared at his home in Petersfield:

Here lives John Small,
Makes bat and ball,
Pitches a wicket,
Plays at cricket
With any man in England.

John Small continued to play in first-class matches until he was 61 years of age and made his last appearance for Hampshire v. M.C.C., at Lord's.

He once batted for three days for Hambledon against England, but there is no record of his score on that occasion. Always a difficult man to get out he had many exciting duels with the famous bowler, Lumpy Stevens. It is said that the introduction of a third stump in either 1775 or 1776 was precipitated by a tense innings in which Lumpy Stevens beat Small's bat three times only for the ball to pass between the two stumps without disturbing the bail.

John Nyren described John Small as "a remarkably well-made and well-knit man, of honest expression, and active as a hare."

SMITH, O'Neill Gordon (1933–1959)

Cheerful "Collie" Smith had a glorious but all too short career in first-class cricket. It was only five years after making his debut that he died from the injuries he received in a motoring accident in Staffordshire.

This West Indian sprang into prominence in the 1954–55 season when, in only his third game for Jamaica he played an innings of 169 against the Australians. Smith followed this by scoring 44 and 104 in his first Test appearance against the same opposition.

A powerful hitter, he once scored six sixes and four fours in an innings of 79, and when he made a century in his first Test appearance against England (161 at Birmingham in 1957) one of his sixes (off Laker) broke roof tiles above the ladies' balcony over long-on.

This exhilarating batting subsequently made him a popular professional in League cricket. He joined Burnley in 1958 and it was on their ground, at Turf Moor, that he made what was probably his biggest hit. He drove the ball from the Belvedere Road end over the stand and into the middle of the adjoining football field. This was the occasion that he hit a century in 78 minutes.

Smith created a record in a Worsley Cup game by scoring 306* for Burnley v. Lowerhouse, in June 1959.

It should be noted that he was an all-rounder for he also bowled off-breaks.

SOBERS, Sir Garfield St. Aubrun (1936–   )

Probably the finest all-rounder in the game's history this West Indian left-hander scored 8,032 (av. 57.78) runs and captured 235 wickets (av. 34.03) in Test matches. No other player has ever been able to achieve such figures in the highest class of cricket.

In addition to his prowess with bat and ball he is also acknowledged to have been a brilliant fielder and one of the game's most astute captains, leading the West Indies to victory against Australia (1964–65), England (1966), and India (1966–67), as well as captaining the victorious Rest of the World team in England in 1970 and in Australia in 1971–72.

The 1966 tour of England saw this great cricketer at his best for he not only topped the Test batting averages with 722 (av. 103.14) but was second in his side's bowling averages with 20 wickets (av. 27.25). Seldom, if ever, has a more versatile left-arm bowler been seen in this country.

Sobers made his Test debut against England in 1953–54 before he had reached the age of 18, being called upon to take the place of the injured Valentine. This was after only two games in first-class cricket.

Apart from his native Barbados he also played for South Australia and League cricket in England before being appointed Nottinghamshire captain in 1968. He retired in 1974, having appeared in 93 Tests plus 10 matches for the Rest of the World. His career aggregate figures are 28,315 runs (av. 54.87) including 86 centuries, and 1,043 wickets (av. 27.74).

His personal best, 365* against Pakistan at Kingston in 1957–58 is a world Test record.

SOMERSET C.C.C.

Founded: 1864. Re-formed 1875. Became a first-class county in 1891. Secretary: Roy Stevens, County Cricket Ground, Taunton. Highest score for: 675 for 9 declared v. Hampshire, at Bath, 1924. Highest score against: 811 by Surrey, at the Oval, May 1899. Highest individual score for: 310 by H. Gimblett v. Sussex, at Eastbourne, 1948. Highest individual score against: 424 by A. C. MacLaren of Lancashire, at Taunton, July 1895. Lowest score for: 25 v. Gloucestershire, at Bristol, 1947. Lowest score against: 22 by Gloucestershire, at Bristol, 1920. Colours: Black, White and Maroon. Badge: The Wessex Dragon. Honours: Minor County Champions: (Second XI) 1961, 1965. Best in County Championship: 3rd in 1892, 1958, 1963, 1966. Gillette Cup Finalists, 1967.

SOUTH AFRICA

Cricket was played in South Africa over 170 years ago. The first match of which any record has been found was one between Officers of Artillery Mess and Officers of the Colony at Cape Town for one thousand dollars a side, January 5, 1808.

However, it is quite likely that cricket had been played at the Cape several years before this by members of the first occupation force who were stationed there between 1795 and 1802.

Visiting Servicemen played the game regularly in the early part of the 19th century but it was really established in that part of the world by pioneers from England who went out to settle there in the 1840's and 1850's. It is known that a club was formed at Port Elizabeth in 1843 and at Bloemfontein in 1855.

By 1876 there were so many cricket teams that the town of Port Elizabeth presented a trophy, "The Championship Bat", for competition in the Cape of Good Hope. This was the first cricket competition in South Africa and it helped create a keener interest in the game for a few years until the inauguration of the "Currie Cup" (q.v.) in 1889 put competitive cricket on a firmer basis.

The season of 1888–89 saw the arrival of the first English touring team in South Africa. This was Major Warton's team of six amateurs and seven professionals, captained by C. A. Smith and M. P. Bowden.

During their stay in the Union they played two Tests matches. The first, at Port Elizabeth, on March 12–13, 1889, which England won by 8 wickets, and the second at Cape Town, a fortnight later,

which England won by an innings and 202 runs.

These matches, and many to follow, were played on matting wickets, and indeed, no first-class match was played on turf in South Africa until 1926–27 season.

England won all of the first eight Tests between the two countries, every one played in the Union, but in 1905–06 South African came into its own when they beat England in four out of five Tests.

South Africa's captain in all five of those momentous games was P. W. Sherwell, a great wicket-keeper and a fine batsman who was also a South African tennis singles champion. One of a family of 11 brothers, Sherwell is among the all-time greats of South African cricket history.

It was Sherwell who captained the first South African side to visit England and engage in Test matches. That was in 1907 when they played three Tests, losing one and drawing two.

The South Africans had actually sent touring teams to England on three previous occasions, but these sides which came over in 1894, 1901 and 1904 did not engage in Test matches, and the first side was not give first-class status.

Sherwell figures in another South African cricket triumph, for he captained the first team from the Union which toured Australia in 1910–11 and succeeded in beating the Australians in one of the five Tests.

The side of 1905–06 and the one which visited England in 1907 played an important part in the development of the game because of their introduction of "googly" bowling in force. Schwarz, Faulkner, Vogler and White were their "googly" experts, and these men played the leading role in England's first defeat by a South African Test team.

In the first Test of England's 1909–10 South African tour, Vogler and Faulkner took all 20 England wickets between them, Vogler taking 12 for 181 and Faulkner 8 for 160.

Those were halcyon days for South African cricket. From the time that they won their first Test against England up to the outbreak of World War I, they won 7 of the 15 Tests played against England in the Union.

South Africa had to wait until 1935 for their first Test win in England but then a well balanced side, captained by H. F. Wade, not only beat England at Lord's, but actually suffered only two defeats in a tour of 39 matches.

After that the South Africans won four more Tests in England, one in 1951, two in 1955, and one in 1965.

In recent years South Africa may have possessed the finest Test team they have ever had, as witness their 4–0 victory over Australia in 1970. How sad, therefore, that the South African Government's policy of apartheid has prevented their talented team from playing Test cricket. Before the break in 1970 they had lost only three of their last 25 Tests.

The South African Cricket Association was formed at a meeting held at Kimberley, April 8, 1890. They were one of the three original members of the Imperial Cricket Conference in 1909 but they dropped out in 1961 after leaving the Commonwealth.

Records

Highest score by South Africa: 692 v. Cambridge University, at Cambridge, 1901. Highest score in South Africa: 676 by M.C.C.. v. Griqualand West, at Kimberley, 1938–39. Highest score against South Africa: 654 for 5 declared by England, at Durban, 1938–39. Highest individual score for South Africa: 274 by R. G. Pollock v. Australia, at Durban, 1969–70. Highest individual score against South Africa: 299* by D. G. Bradman of Australia, at Adelaide, 1931–32. Highest individual score in South Africa: 306* by E. A. B. Rowan, Transvaal v. Natal, Johannesburg, 1939–40. Lowest score for South Africa: 30 v. England, at Port Elizabeth, 1895–96, and v. England, at Edgbaston, 1924†. Lowest score in South Africa by any first-class side: 16 by Border v. Natal, at East London, 1959–60. Lowest score against South Africa: 32 by Derbyshire, Derby, 1947.

†The score included 11 extras and not a single batsman reached double figures. The highest scorer was opening batsman and captain, H. W. Taylor with 7.

Tests

Here are Test records other than those mentioned above:
Highest score for: 622 for 9 declared v. Australia, at Durban, Feb. 1970.

B. A. Richards, b Freeman	140
T. L. Goddard, c Lawry, b Gleeson	17
A. Bacher, b Connolly	9
R. G. Pollock, c and b Stackpole	274
E. J. Barlow, lbw b Freeman	1
B. L. Irvine, b Gleeson	13
H. R. Lance, st Taber, b Gleeson	61
M. J. Procter, c Connolly, b Stackpole	32
D. Gamsy, lbw b Connolly	7
P. M. Pollock, not out	36
A. J. Traicos, not out	5
Extras	27
Total (for 9 wkts. dec.)	622

Lowest score against: 75 by Australia, Durban, 1949–50.

SPECTATORS

See also ATTENDANCES.

Spectators rushed onto the field and assaulted the M.C.C. team at Sydney in 1879 during a match against New South Wales.

W. L. Murdoch was given "run out" by the English umpire, G. Coulthard, and after D. W. Gregory, the N.S.W. captain had come onto the field to protest, and Lord Harris had refused to change the umpire, the irate crowd invaded the pitch.

Eventually Gregory, who had ordered his batsman into the pavilion, relented, and the game was continued.

One of the ugliest scenes in cricket history occurred at Trinidad during the second West Indies—England Test of the 1959–60 tour.

This was the Test rubber in which "bouncers" were so prevalent. In the first Test the England team had defied a veritable barrage of these balls to make 482 but it was obvious that a continuation of this brand of bowling would not make for a congenial atmosphere.

In the second Test at Trinidad the England side came in for a heavier battering and then replied with some bouncers of their own which unsettled the West Indian side so much that they collapsed and had scored 98 for 8 when bottles were hurled onto the pitch.

In no time at all a riot had broken out. The crowd, angry at the dismissal of their side, went mad and over 100 people were hurt in the astonishing scenes which followed with more bottles being broken and then thrown into the throng.

The players escaped from the field and the game was suspended while riot squads cleared the ground. At one time it seemed as though this match would be abandoned, but after the Governor had delivered a lashing speech to the people of Trinidad play was resumed the following day and the Test played out.

Pakistan being in a state of unrest, rioting was widespread during the M.C.C. tour of 1968–69 and the Third Test at Karachi had to be abandoned before England's first innings had been completed.

SPOFFORTH, Frederick Robert (1853–1926)

Probably the greatest bowler Australia ever produced. A number of the records he created in the earliest days of international cricket have since been broken, but considering the number of wickets that he took on visits to this country his average in England is still the best of any bowler from the Antipodes.

Spofforth eventually settled in England and qualified for Derbyshire, but in his five tours with the Australians, 1878, 1880, 1882, 1884 and 1886 he captured 662 wickets at an average cost of only 12.302.

There have been faster bowlers than this six foot three inch Australian, but no one of his speed ever combined such accuracy with such subtle variations of pace; all of which earned him the title of the "Demon Bowler".

His average for the 97 wickets which he captured in first-class games on his first tour in 1878 was only 11.00 and his finest success that season was when, with the aid of H. F. Boyle, the M.C.C. was skittled out twice in one day for scores of 33 and 19: Spofforth took 6 for 4 and 4 for 16.

By the time that Spofforth had returned home from that trip which extended over England, America and New Zealand, his total bag was 764 wickets, taken at an average cost of a little over six runs each!

His astonishing bowling feats are too numerous to mention here for he played in 18 Tests and took 94 wickets (av. 18.41), but another occasion when he demoralised England's best batsmen must be recalled. This was at the Oval in the 1882 Test. England were set only 85 runs to win, but Spofforth took 7 for 44 and England were out for 77. In England's first innings he had taken 7 for 46 and this feat of 14 wickets in a Test match remained the best by an Australian in England until R. A. L. Massie took 16 in 1972.

SRI LANKA

Cricket was first introduced into Ceylon (as Sri Lanka was previously called) by British troops in the 1820s and it was later established by British coffee and tea planters. The first club on record is the Colombo C.C. formed in 1863 and this organisation became the leading authority for the game on the island.

The Hon. Ivo Bligh led the first English team to play in Ceylon in 1882 and almost every international team travelling between England and Australia has played in Ceylon or Sri Lanka in recent years.

The Ceylon C.A. was formed in 1921 thanks to the initiative of Dr. John Rockwood.

Players from the island who have made their mark abroad include Gamini Goonesena (Nottinghamshire and N.S.W.), S. Jayasinghe (Leicestershire), J. D. Piachaud (Hampshire), and Clive Inman (Leicestershire).

STAFFORDSHIRE C.C.C.

Founded: 1871, although County cricket had been played as early as 1852. One of the original members of the Minor County Championship in 1895. Secretary: L. W. Hancock, 4 Kingsland Avenue, Oakhill, Stoke-on-Trent. Highest score for: 505 for 6 declared, v. Buckinghamshire, at Stone, 1948. Highest score against: 569 by Warwickshire, 1888; in Minor County Championship—500 for 7 declared, by Northumberland, at Newcastle-on-Tyne, 1951. Highest individual score for: 217 by A. H. Heath v. Lincolnshire, at Stoke-on-Trent, 1889; in Minor County Championship—216 by E. H. Bourne v. Surrey II, at the Oval, 1922. Highest individual score against: 267 by H. C. Maul of Warwickshire, 1888; in Minor County Championship—200* by B. Lilley of Nottinghamshire II, 1925. Lowest score for: 20 v. Lancashire II, at Stoke-on-Trent, 1936. Lowest score against: 14 by Cheshire, at Stoke-on-Trent, 1909. Minor County Champions: 1906, 1908, 1920, 1927. Colours: Green and Gold. Badge: Staffordshire knot in gold. Principal venues: Longton, Wolverhampton and Stone.

STATHAM, John Brian "George" (1930–   )

Lancashire fast right-arm bowler and left-hand batsman. Quickly came into prominence for after only one season in first-class cricket he was called upon to fly out to Australia to join the M.C.C. touring side. He made his Test debut in New Zealand in March 1951 only nine months after playing his first county game.

Statham represented England on 70 occasions and his bag of 252 Test wickets is only exceeded by the number taken by L. R. Gibbs and F. S. Trueman, while his career total of 2,260 wickets (av. 16.36) places him at the head of all Lancashire bowlers. His bag in County Championship matches alone was 1,683 (av. 15.17).

His best performance was in taking 15 Warwickshire wickets for 89 (including 8 for 34) in 1957, while one of his most successful Test rubbers was that against South Africa in 1960 when he captured 27 wickets (av. 18.18).

STONE-WALLER

See also under SLOW SCORING.

When this term was first used to describe a batsman with stubborn defensive style is not certain although the earliest "stone-waller" so called was probably H. Jupp.

This batsman was born in 1841 and when he began to play for Surrey he soon became known as "Young Stonewall".

Of course, there were stone-wallers long before this term was used. The original stone-waller was probably the late 18th-century batsman, Tom Walker of Hambledon. Nyren described him as a man who had "no nerves at all," and on one occasion he received 170 balls from David Harris and scored only a single. In that particular innings he scored 12 off 320 balls. No wonder he was nicknamed "Old Everlasting".

The term "stone-waller" may have been revived by W. Barnes of Nottinghamshire. For after he had been bowling to R. G. Barlow of Lancashire for 2½ hours at Nottingham in 1882 and Barlow had made only five runs, Barnes remarked "bowling at thee were like bowling at a stone wall!"

The Lancashire professional, R. G. Barlow, who played for his county from 1871 to 1891, was first and foremost a bowler, left-arm slow medium, but he was also one of the most patient defensive batsmen in the history of the game.

Apart from the occasion mentioned above, he also batted for 2½ hours for five runs against Sussex, at Manchester in 1876, and on the same ground against Nottinghamshire in 1890 he was at the wicket for 3 hours to make 19 runs. On another occasion against Nottinghamshire, at Liverpool, he batted for 5¼ hours to make 49!

Other famous stone-wallers are W. Scotton (Nottinghamshire)—opening with W. G. Grace for England against Australia, at the Oval in 1886, he stayed for 3¾ hours to make 34; Louis Hall (Yorkshire)—12* in 2¾ hours against Kent, at Canterbury in 1885; A. C. Bannerman (New South Wales)—91 in 7½ hours for Australia v. England, Sydney, 1892; B. Mitchell (Transvaal) —88 in 7 hours for South Africa v. England, Birmingham, 1929; W. E. Midwinter (Gloucestershire and Victoria) —16* in 3 hours for Australians v. Nottinghamshire, Nottingham, 1878; A. Haygarth—16 in 3 hours for M.C.C., v. Hampshire, 1844, 26 in 4 hours for Gentlemen v. Players, 1846.

STOLLMEYER, Jeffrey Baxter (1921–   )

This tall, stylish West Indian opening batsman was only 18 when he made his Test debut in England in 1939, but he proved himself to be a player of the highest class. When the West Indians were skittled out for 84 at Taunton, the youthful Stollmeyer carried his bat for 45*.

A graceful batsman whose style has been likened to that of Palairet, Stollmeyer scored 2,159 runs in Test cricket and captained the West Indies in 13 of his 32 Test appearances.

He made his highest score, 324, for Trinidad v. British Guiana, at Trinidad, in 1946–47, while in Test cricket his best is 160 v. India, at Madras, in 1948–49. This was the game in which he and A. F. Rae combined to create a West Indies Test record first wicket partnership of 239.

STRUDWICK, Herbert (1880–1970)

This Surrey cricketer will always be remembered as one of the most energetic wicket-keepers in the game's history. He rarely had more than two fielders close in on the leg side and he was often seen racing a colleague for the ball down to long leg.

Strudwick made his debut for Surrey in 1902 and eventually succeeded A. A. Lilley as England's wicket-keeper.

He visited South Africa twice, Australia three times, and also met both of those countries in Tests at home.

When he retired at the end of the 1927 season he had dismissed 1,493 batsmen in his 25 years behind the wicket, an aggregate which was not beaten until 1975 when J. T. Murray retired with a total of 1,527.

Strudwick always reckoned Leyton among his favourite grounds and it was there in 1904 that he performed one of his best feats by catching seven men and stumping one other during the course of a match against Essex.

He was, of course, a great favourite at the Oval, and there, in 1914, he caught six men in one innings against Sussex.

SUFFOLK C.C.C.

Founded: 1864. Joined Minor County Championship 1904. Dropped out in 1914 but rejoined in 1934. Secretary: A. E. D. Garnett, Redgate House, Wherstead, Ipswich. Highest score for: 516 for 6 wickets v. Cambridgeshire at Newmarket, 1908. Highest score against: 515 for 6 wickets by Surrey II, at the Oval, 1912. Highest individual score for: 229 by J. F. Ireland v. Cambridgeshire, at Newmarket, 1911. Highest individual score against: 200* by F. P. Longton of Hertfordshire, at Felixstowe, 1911. Lowest score for: 11 v. I. Zingari, at Thornham Hall, 1883; in Minor County Championship—29 v. Oxfordshire, 1904. Lowest score against: 22 by Bedfordshire, at Woburn Park, 1880; in Minor County Championship—37 by Cambridgeshire, 1904. Colours: Maroon and Old Gold. Badge: Lion. Honours: Minor County Champions 1946.

SUNDAY CRICKET

Cricket was not mentioned in the list of sports permitted on Sundays which was issued by King James in 1617.

At Boxgrove, Sussex, in 1622, five people were summonsed for playing cricket on a Sunday in the churchyard and doing damage to the church.

Sunday cricket was not legal until the Act of 1845 was brought in permitting "games of skill,"

Coming up to date, first class cricket on Sundays was discussed in 1961 but not approved. However, following the lead taken in Australia in 1964–65 it was decided by the first-class counties that a Sunday's play should be included in 12 of their matches during 1966.

The popularity of cricket on these days soon led to the breakthrough in 1968 when it was agreed to inaugurate a new Sunday League competition. See John Player League.

SURREY C.C.C.

Founded: August 1845. Secretary: W. H. Sillitoe, Kennington Oval. London SE11 5SS. Highest score for: 811 v. Somerset, at the Oval, May 29–31, 1899. Highest score against: 705 for 8 declared, by Sussex, at Hastings, July 14–16, 1902. Highest individual score for: 357* (8 hours 30 minutes) by R. Abel, v. Somerset, at the Oval, May 29–30, 1899. Highest individual score against: 300* by F. Watson of Lancashire, at Manchester, 1928, and 300 by R. Subba Row of Northamptonshire, at The Oval, 1958. Lowest score for: 16 v. Nottinghamshire, at the Oval, July 26–28, 1880. Lowest score against: 15 by M.C.C., Lord's, 1839. Colours: Chocolate. Badge: Prince of Wales' Feathers. Honours: County Champions: 1887, 1888, 1889 (tie with Lancashire and Nottinghamshire), 1890, 1891, 1892, 1894, 1895, 1899, 1914, 1950 (tie with Lancashire), 1952, 1953, 1954, 1955, 1956, 1957, 1958, 1971. Benson and Hedges Cup winners, 1974. Gillette Cup Finalists, 1965. Minor County Champions: 1939, 1950, 1954, 1955.

SUSSEX C.C.C.

Founded: 1836. Re-formed 1839, 1857. Secretary: S. Allen, County Ground, Hove, Sussex BN3 3AN. Highest score for: 705 for 8 declared v. Surrey, Hastings, July 14–16, 1902. Highest score against: 726 by Nottinghamshire, at Nottingham, May 16–18, 1895. Highest individual score for: 333 by K. S. Duleepsinhji v. Northamptonshire, at Hove, 1930. Highest individual score against: 322 by E. Paynter of Lancashire, at Hove, 1937. Lowest score for: 19 v. Surrey, at Godalming, July 8, 1830, and v. Nottinghamshire (Sussex had one man absent), Hove, August 14–15, 1873. Lowest score against: 18 by Kent (one man absent), at Gravesend, June 6–7,

1867; 35 by Kent, at Catford, 1894. Colours: Dark Blue, Light Blue and Gold. Badge: Six heraldic martlets. Honours: Gillette Cup: Winners 1963, 1964, Finalists 1968, 1970, 1973. Best in County Championship, 2nd in 1875, 1902, 1903, 1932, 1933, 1934, 1953.

SUTCLIFFE, Bert (1923–   )

One of the best left-handed batsmen of the post-war era, Bert Sutcliffe broke most of the batting records in New Zealand cricket during his career which extended from 1942 to 1966.

In only his second match he scored 146, and, when the M.C.C. visited New Zealand immediately after the war, it was Sutcliffe who made the biggest impression on them with a century in each innings (197 and 128) for Otago.

When visiting England for the 1949 tour he enhanced his reputation still further by scoring 2,627 runs (av. 59.70). Only Sir Donald Bradman has exceeded that figure with a touring side in England.

During that successful tour Sutcliffe scored a century in each innings of a match for the fourth time in his career—243 and 100* against Essex at Southend.

Sutcliffe's highest score is 385 for Otago v. Canterbury, at Christchurch, in 1952–53. He has also topped the 300 mark with 355 v. Auckland, at Dunedin in 1949–50, and his total of 17,283 runs (av. 47.22) has only been exceeded by G. M. Turner among New Zealand batsmen.

SUTCLIFFE, Herbert (1894–   )

As immaculate in his play as in his general appearance, Herbert Sutcliffe of Yorkshire is one of the all-time greats of English cricket.

Making his debut for Yorkshire in 1919 he scored at least 1,000 runs in every season right up to the outbreak of World War II. His best seasons were 1932, when he scored 3,336 (av. 74.13) and 1931 with 3,006 (av. 96.96). That last mentioned average has never been equalled by any English batsman with as many innings in a single season.

As for his Test appearances, Sutcliffe covered himself with glory, and his series of opening partnerships with Sir J. B. Hobbs are legendary.

This remarkable partnership began with Sutcliffe's Test debut against the South Africans in 1924 and produced 15 first-wicket century stands, the highest being 283 against Australia, at Melbourne, 1924–25.

With Yorkshire Sutcliffe formed another great alliance with P. Holmes, and together they made 69 first-wicket century stands, including the world record of 555 v. Essex, at Leyton, in 1932.

Sutcliffe made 149 centuries before he retired in 1945. His highest score being 313 in that record first-wicket partnership with Holmes at Leyton.

In 54 Test appearances between 1924 and 1935 Sutcliffe's highest score was 194 v. Australia, at Sydney, in 1932–33.

His career aggregate was 50,135 runs (av. 52.00).

T

TALLON, Donald (1916–   )

After the Second World War Don Tallon succeeded Barnett as Australia's wicket-keeper and in his very first Test rubber he created a new record (since beaten) for the Australia–England series by dismissing 20 batsmen.

Tallon would have made a name in international cricket much earlier if it had not been for the war, and he was actually considered to be past his best when he made his Test debut in 1946.

He was at the peak of his form in 1938–39, the season in which he equalled a 64-year-old world record by dismissing 12 batsmen in a single match. This was for Queensland v. New South Wales, at Sydney, when he caught nine and stumped three. In the same season he equalled another world record (since beaten) by dismissing seven men (v. Victoria, at Brisbane) in a single innings.

Tallon was also a useful batsman who produced his best when it was most needed. Going in at number eight against England, at Melbourne, in 1946–47, he scored 92, his highest score in 21 Test appearances.

TATE, Maurice William (1895–1956)

Popular, smiling Maurice Tate often distinguished himself as a steady batsman but it was as a bowler that he found fame.

Beginning as a slow off-break bowler with Sussex in 1912 it was not until about 1922 that he made his mark as a fast-medium bowler with real pace off the pitch and a deadly outswinger.

In 1924 he took a wicket with his first ball in Test cricket. This was against South Africa, at Birmingham, when the visitors were dismissed for 30 and Tate took 4 for 12.

Tate played in 39 Tests before he finally retired in 1937. In these games he captured 155 wickets (av. 26.13) and scored 1,198 runs (av. 25.48).

His finest Test series was that in Australia in 1924–25 when he captured 38 wickets in five matches at an average cost of only 23.18. This is still the best performance by any Englishman in Test matches down under.

During his career Tate's bowling overshadowed his batting, but it should not be forgotten that he performed the "double" in eight successive seasons from 1922. His career aggregate of wickets taken is 2,783 (av. 18.16). Twice scored 1,000 runs and took 200 wickets in a season.

TAYFIELD, Hugh Joseph (1928–   )

When this South African off-break bowler captured 37 England wickets in the 1956–57 Test rubber he broke a record which had stood for his country for 46 years.

It was during that series that Tayfield also created another South African Test record by capturing nine wickets in a single innings (9 for 113 at Johannesburg), and the average cost of his wickets at the end of that series was 17.18.

Tayfield made his debut for Natal in 1945–46. Subsequently he played for Rhodesia and later moved to Transvaal.

His first Test appearance was against Australia in December 1949, and after that he played in 15 Tests against England, 14 against Australia and 7 against New Zealand. His total of 170 wickets captured in these games is easily the best of any South African.

Tayfield, who was also a good right-handed bat, had a season in Lancashire League cricket in 1956. His highest score in first-class games was, remarkably enough, made in a Test match—75 against Australia, at Cape Town, in 1949–50.

TAYLOR, Bruce Richard
(1943–   )

New Zealand's most successful bowler, B. R. Taylor captured 111 wickets (av. 26.00) in 30 Tests 1965–73.

He made one of the best Test debuts of any player in 1965, scoring 105 runs in the first innings v. India, at Calcutta (his maiden first-class century) and also taking 5 for 86 in one innings.

A forcing left-handed batsman and fast-medium right-arm bowler who made good use of his height he played his initial first-class game for Canterbury in 1964. Transferred to Wellington in 1970. On the West Indies tour in 1971–72 he captured 46 wickets (av. 21.17) including 27 Test wickets, and scored 216 runs (av. 24.00). In the 3rd Test at Bridgetown he took 9 for 182.

TAYLOR, Herbert Wilfred
(1889–1973)

Some idea of the stature of H. W. Taylor as a batsman may be gauged from the fact that when S. F. Barnes created a Test record by taking 49 South African wickets in the series of 1913–14, Taylor's average for the five matches was 50.80, his highest score being 109 at Durban in the first Test.

However, even that is not considered his best series, for when the M.C.C. next visited South Africa in 1922–23 Taylor topped the Test averages with 64.66, and it was during this rubber that he made his highest Test score, 176 at Johannesburg.

In all his 42 Test matches Taylor scored 2,936 runs (av. 40.77), an aggregate which has only been exceeded by two other South Africans, namely B. Mitchell and A. D. Nourse, junior.

Taylor captained South Africa in 18 consecutive Test matches from 1913 to 1924.

TELEVISION

The first cricket match to be televised was the Test between England and Australia, at Lord's, in June 1938. The commentator was H. B. T. Wakelam.

TERMS USED IN CRICKET

Appended below are a few of the terms peculiar to cricket which may not be self explanatory. Names of fielding positions are given elsewhere under FIELDING.

Barn-door game—another term for a batsman who adopts a dour defensive style which is sometimes referred to as stone-walling.

Bosie—see Googly.

Break—a ball which changes direction after pitching.

Bowled all over the wicket—a term meaning completely or clean bowled.

Bumper or bouncer—a ball which rises sharply off the ground to a height above the level of the waist.

Bye—a run which may be scored other than off the bat.

Chinaman—a left-handed finger spun off-break ball.

Dolly—a ball which seems to float in the air and is easy for catching.

Extras—runs not credited to the batsmen. These are no-balls, byes, leg-byes and wides.

Full toss—a ball which when sent down by the bowler does not pitch between the wickets but travels through the air the full distance to the batsman.

Googly—an off-break ball delivered with a leg-break action.

Leg-break—a ball which turns from the leg side towards the off after pitching.

Off-break—a ball which turns from the off side towards the leg when bowled by a right-handed player.

Pair of spectacles—a batsman who fails to score in both innings of a match is said to have collected a pair.

Played on—a batsman who plays the ball into his own wicket is said to have played on.

Rabbits—the weaker batsmen of a side who are well down in the batting order.

Shooter—a fast ball which skims along the ground instead of rising.

Sticky dog—a sticky wicket.

Stone-waller—a batsman who shows little inclination to score runs and bats defensively.

Swerver—a ball so delivered by the bowler that it curls in the air.

Trimmer—applied particularly to a fast ball that removes the bails without touching the stumps.

Turning wicket—one which is conducive to spin bowling.

Wrong 'un—another term for a type of bowler's delivery known as a googly (q.v.).

Yorker—a full length ball mistimed by the batsman.

TEST APPEARANCES

See under APPEARANCES.

TEST CAPTAINS

See under CAPTAINS.

TEST MATCHES

The first Test match was that played
Between England and Australia, at
Melbourne, March 15–17, 1877.

English teams had visited Australia in
1862, 1864 and 1873, but it was not until
an all-professional team captained by
James Lillywhite went out in 1877 that it
was decided to take the opportunity of
meeting a representative Australian side
on level terms in an eleven-a-side game.

Two of these representative games were
played during this tour and subsequently
they came to be regarded as the first Test
matches.

Both of these games were played at
Melbourne under the auspices of the
Victorian Cricket Association. The first
was won by Australia by 45 runs, thanks
largely to a wonderful innings by C.
Bannerman who scored 165* before he
was forced to retire with a hand injury.

England squared matters with a victory
by four wickets in the second match
played a fortnight later. In Australia's
second innings Lillywhite took 4 for 70,
and Southerton 4 for 46.

Australia's success against England on
this tour encouraged them to take the
plunge and accept an invitation to send a
representative side to England the
following year. However, no Test matches
were played here that summer and what is
regarded as the first Test match ever to be
played in England did not take place until
Australia's next tour in 1880.

It was not known until the last minute
that the Australians were sending a team
to England in that summer of 1880 and
when they arrived it was found difficult to
arrange matches. There was also some bad
feeling still left over from the incident
involving Lord Harris's team in Australia
at Sydney the previous year (see under
SPECTATORS) and the M.C.C. did not
appear too keen about arranging a game
for the visitors against a representative
England XI.

However, good sportsmanship prevailed
and thanks largely to the efforts of Lord
Harris himself, a game was played at the
Oval, on September 6, 7 and 8, which

rung up the curtain on Test cricket in
England. This first game was won by
England by five wickets, Dr. W. G. Grace
scoring 152 and 9* and F. Morley taking
eight Australian wickets for 146.

Incidentally, this was the only occasion
in which as many as three brothers
appeared in the same side in a Test
match—W. G., E. M. and G. F. all playing for England.

The next series of Test matches to be
opened was that between England and
South Africa. This began with two Tests
played at Port Elizabeth and Cape Town
during the M.C.C. tour of 1888–89.

Australia visited South Africa to play
their first Test matches in 1902–03, and
the meetings between these three countries
continued to be the only Test matches
until the West Indies visited England and
played three such games in 1928.

In 1929–30 New Zealand were given
Test status with four games against
England, and in 1930–31 the West Indies
first met Australia.

India played their first Test match at
Lord's in 1932 and Pakistan, of course,
came last with their first Test against
India in 1952.

The biggest victory in Test cricket was
that when England beat Australia by an
innings and 579 runs at the Oval in 1938.

The first Test match in England to last
for more than three days was that between
England and Australia during the
Triangular Tournament of 1912. It was
decided that the final match of the
Tournament, that between England and
Australia which commenced at the Oval
on August 19, should if necessary continue
throughout the week, but England won in
four days.

This game was an exception to the
general rule, for although longer Tests
were played abroad, only three-day Tests
were played in England until 1930 when
they were increased to four days. This was
extended to five days in 1948.

Records

The highest and lowest scores for and
against each country in Test matches is
given under the names of the various
countries.

Summary of results

England v. Australia:
Played 224, England won 71, Australia
won 87, drawn 66.

England v. South Africa:
Played 102, England won 46, South Africa won 18, drawn 38.
England v. West Indies:
Played 71, England won 21, West Indies won 22, drawn 28.
England v. New Zealand:
Played 47, England won 23, New Zealand won 0, drawn 24.
England v. India:
Played 48, England won 22, India won 6, drawn 20.
England v. Pakistan:
Played 27, England won 9, Pakistan won 1, drawn 17.
Australia v. South Africa:
Played 53, Australia won 29, South Africa won 11, drawn 13.
Australia v. West Indies:
Played 41, Australia won 24, West Indies won 7, drawn 9, tie 1.
Australia v. New Zealand:
Played 7, Australia won 4, New Zealand won 1, drawn 2.
Australia v. India:
Played, 25, Australia won 16, India won 3, drawn 6.
Australia v. Pakistan:
Played 9, Australia won 5, Pakistan won 1, drawn 3.
South Africa v. New Zealand:
Played 17, South Africa won 9, New Zealand won 2, drawn 6.
West Indies v. India:
Played 37, West Indies won 17, India won 4, drawn 16.
West Indies v. New Zealand:
Played 14, West Indies won 5, New Zealand won 2, drawn 7.
West Indies v. Pakistan:
Played 10, West Indies won 4, Pakistan won 3, drawn 3.
New Zealand v. India:
Played 19, New Zealand won 3, India won 8, drawn 8.
New Zealand v. Pakistan:
Played 15, New Zealand won 1, Pakistan won 5, drawn 9.
India v. Pakistan:
Played 15, India won 2, Pakistan won 1, drawn 12.

TEST SELECTORS

In the earliest days of Test matches the selection of the England team was in the hands of the representatives of the M.C.C., Surrey and Lancashire. This was changed in 1898 when the Board of Control came into being. Then a committee of three was chosen to select the teams, the captain being co-opted to this committee. In 1938 the committee was increased to four, plus the captain who has a casting vote.

THOUSAND RUNS IN MAY

The record for the shortest period of time to score 1,000 runs in the month of May is held jointly by W. G. Grace and W. R. Hammond.

In May 1895, W. G. Grace, aged 46, scored 1,000 runs in 22 days. He was the first player ever to score 1,000 runs in the month of May. His total, up to and including May 30, was 1,016 and that figure included Grace's hundredth century in first-class cricket. A truly momentous month for the old master.

W. R. Hammond equalled this record in May 1927. Getting his 1,000th run in 22 days he went on to register a total of 1,042 before the first day of June.

Only one other batsman has scored 1,000 runs in the month of May and he is C. Hallows of Lancashire. In 27 days of May 1928, his total reached precisely 1,000.

Four other batsmen, T. Hayward, D. G. Bradman, W. J. Edrich, and G. M. Turner have topped the 1,000 mark by the end of May (Bradman has done this twice), but their four-figure totals include a number of runs scored in the month of April.

G. M. Turner (New Zealanders) is the only player to have scored 1,000 runs by the end of May in the period since World War II. When he achieved this feat in 1973 he got his 1,000th run on the last day of the month.

THROWING THE BALL

Controversy

One of the first bowlers to be accused of throwing or jerking the ball was Richard Francis of Hambledon, Surrey, in the 18th century.

It should be noted that "throwing" at that time and in the early 19th century was the term applied to all balls delivered with round-arm action. The more conservative cricketers refused to acknowledge anything but the under-arm action as real bowling.

When John Willes of Kent bowled round-arm against the M.C.C., at Lord's in 1822, he was repeatedly "no-balled" for throwing. He left the field in disgust and decided never to play again.

So it is seen that the throwing controversy which caused such a stir in 1960 was nothing new in cricket. In 1885 Lord Harris of Kent caused some excitement when he advised his county committee not to play the return match with Lancashire because of a dispute over the legality of the delivery of two of that county's bowlers, J. Crossland and G. Nash. Prior to this Middlesex in 1883 and Nottinghamshire in 1884 had also refused fixtures with Lancashire because of their bowlers.

The throwing controversy flared up again during the 1950's and reached its peak in the 1960 season. In that summer in England, apart from the South African, G. M. Griffin being called for throwing in the Lord's Test, seven English bowlers were also no-balled in first-class matches.

Following instructions from the M.C.C. the umpires began to take a firmer line against the culprits and the Imperial Cricket Conference drew up a new definition of "throwing". But there was a great deal of discussion and a number of alterations to this before it was finally accepted as part of the Laws in 1969. See Law 26.

Record throws

The record distance a cricket ball has ever been thrown is usually claimed to have been 140 yards 2 feet by R. Percival on the Durham Sands Racecourse, Easter Monday, 1884. However, it has been found impossible to verify this achievement in contemporary records. Percival was a left-hander and was the New Brighton professional from 1885 to 1892.

At Clermont, Australia, on December 19, 1872, Billy the Aboriginal is said to have thrown a cricket ball a measured distance of 142½ yards. However, 2½ yards was deducted to "allow for any deviation."

At Toronto in 1872 Ross Mackenzie threw a cricket ball a distance of 140 yards 9 inches.

TIES

There is some dispute as to the first-ever tied match on record, for although it is claimed to have been the game between Hambledon and Kent, at Hambledon, in July 1783, this result was never agreed by the two scorers.

After the game had been declared a tie it was found that one of the scorers had made an error in notching the runs (in those days runs were recorded by cutting notches in a stick). This was Pratt, the Kent scorer, whose error meant that Kent had won. However, the matter was never satisfactorily settled because the Hambledon scorer had "mislaid" his stick.

Tie matches are much rarer nowadays for the law was amended in 1948 so that a "Draw" with scores level can only be regarded as a "Tie" if the match has been played out. Prior to this a "Draw" could also be regarded as a "Tie" if the side to bat last had commenced that innings before "time" had been reached.

The only tie in Test cricket was that between Australia and West Indies, at Brisbane, in December 1960. See under FINISH (Exciting).

TOSS, The

Before 1774 the winner of the toss not only had the right to bat first if he so desired, but also the right to choose the pitch.

After 1774 there was no toss except in matches played on neutral grounds. The choice of innings and the pitch was always the prerogative of the visiting team, and it was not until early in the 19th century that the toss was resumed, although then only for choice of innings.

Captains who have won the toss in every game of a Test rubber of at least four games are:
A. Shaw, for England in Australia, four Tests, 1881–82.
Hon. F. S. Jackson, for England v. Australia, in England, five Tests, 1905.
M. A. Noble, for Australia in England, five Tests, 1909.
H. G. Deane, for South Africa v. England, in South Africa, five Tests, 1927–28.
W. R. Hammond, for England v. Australia, in England, four Tests, 1938.
J. D. C. Goddard, for West Indies in India, five Tests, 1948–49.
A. L. Hassett, for Australia in England, five Tests, 1953.
M. C. Cowdrey, England v. South Africa, five Tests, 1960.*
Nawab of Pataudi, India v. England, five Tests, 1963–64.
G. S. Sobers, West Indies in England, five Tests, 1966, and five Tests v. New Zealand, 1971–72.
A. Bacher, South Africa v. Australia, four Tests, 1969–70.
* M. C. Cowdrey followed this by winning the toss in the first two Tests

against Australia in 1961 and so created a record by winning the toss in 9 consecutive Tests. He had won toss in last two Tests in West Indies 1959–60.

G. S. Sobers (West Indies) created a record by winning the toss 27 times in Test matches.

TOURS

The first overseas tour by a cricket team from England was that made by George Parr's XI in 1859. This team consisted of six professionals from the All England XI and six from the United England XI, and they played five games in Canada and the United States.

The tour was financed by the Montreal Cricket Club and the England team (although not an official representative team, it was one of the strongest sides we could have produced at that time) won all five of their games, returning home with a profit of about £90 per head—a very successful enterprise.

As a matter of interest it is worth noting that their games were played at Montreal, New York, Philadelphia, Rochester and Hamilton, and the names of the players on this historic tour were G. Parr (captain), J. Caesar, W. Caffyn, R. Carpenter, A. Diver, J. Grundy, T. Hayward, J. Jackson, John Lillywhite, T. Lockyer, H. H. Stephenson and J. Wisden. Fred Lillywhite went along as scorer.

The next overseas tour was to Australia. This was a team captained by H. H. Stephenson of Surrey which went out in October 1861 and played 12 matches. More details of this tour may be seen under AUSTRALIA.

The first overseas tour by an amateur team was that to Canada and the United States in 1872 by a side captained by R. A. Fitzgerald and including Dr. W. G. Grace. They played eight games and were undefeated.

Since World War I and with the exception of the years of the Second World War there has been a tour of England by a first-class representative side from abroad in every year except 1920, 1922 and 1925.

Apart from the war years one would have to go back to 1875 to find a year in which no representative side from any of the major cricketing countries was engaged in an overseas tour.

TRENT BRIDGE, NOTTINGHAM

This was one of the first cricket grounds in the country outside of the London area which was enclosed so that an entrance charge could be made to spectators.

The cricket enthusiast who began this enterprise and laid out the new ground was a Nottingham man, William Clarke, and this became the headquarters of his much vaunted All England team.

The ground was opened in May 1838 and the first important match to be played there was one between Nottinghamshire and Twenty-two next best of Nottinghamshire, on September 3, 1838. The first county match proper, Nottinghamshire v. Sussex, was played there in 1840, and the first Test match, England v. Australia, in June 1899.

The pitch at Trent Bridge has always been acknowledged as one of the finest in the country and it was never better than in 1938 when a Test record for this county was created there. In one innings against Australia four of England's batsmen made centuries—L. Hutton 100, C. J. Barnett 126, E. Paynter 216* and D. C. S. Compton 102. This was followed in the first Australian innings with scores of 232 by S. J. McCabe, and in their second innings 144* by D. G. Bradman, and 133 by W. A. Brown. The aggregate number of runs made in this match was 1,496 for 24 wickets, a record for the ground.

The highest individual score ever made at Trent Bridge is 345 in four hours by C. G. Macartney for the Australians v. Nottinghamshire, 1921. This innings included 4 sixes and 47 fours and no other player has ever hit as many boundaries in a single innings on this ground.

TRIANGULAR TOURNAMENT

A reference to the "Triangular Tournament" in cricket means the competition of the summer of 1912 when England, Australia and South Africa met each other in a series of six Test matches in England.

For various reasons the experiment of inviting two representative teams to visit England and meet each other during the same season was not a success and it has never been repeated. The World Cup one-day limited over competition in 1975 was quite a different proposition.

Trouble for the 1912 tournament began with the Australians having a domestic quarrel over the selection of a team manager. The Australian Board of Control rightly refused to entertain the demands of certain individuals and the outcome was that six of their best men were left out of the team.

Another reason for the disappointments of the Triangular Tournament was the weakness of the South African side. They were beaten in five games and drew one.

According to contemporary reports the enthusiasm for this tournament was far below that which had been expected. Having two international touring teams in England at the same time was too much of a good thing. Too many matches were crammed into too short a time.

But the factor which dealt the crowning blow to the tournament was the weather. 1912 was one of the wettest summers for many years.

The tournament was won by England under the captaincy of C. B. Fry. They won four of their six games and drew the other two. They beat South Africa three times, and won once and drew twice with Australia.

One of the games with Australia, that at Lord's, had to be left drawn because there had been less than 3½ hours play on the first two days due to rain. England scored 310 for 7 declared and Australia's total had reached 282 for 7 when stumps were drawn on the final day.

The rain also spoilt the other England–Australia match which had to be left as a draw. This time, at Old Trafford, it was even worse, for play did not commence on the first day until nearly three o'clock, and not until five o'clock on the second day. The third day was a complete wash-out.

In the short time available for play England batted first and scored 203 and the Australian opening pair were still in and had scored 14 when the last ball was sent down.

It was left to the last game of the series for England to prove her right to the top place in the tournament.

In this game at the Oval, played to a finish over four days, England scoring 245 and 175 beat Australia (111 and 65) by 244 runs. England probably owed most for their victory to F. E. Woolley who took 5 for 29 and 5 for 20 in 17.2 overs.

TRINIDAD

See under WEST INDIES.

TRUEMAN, Frederick Sewards (1931–   )

One of the outstanding personalities in post-war cricket, this fiery Yorkshireman was the first man to capture over 300 wickets in Test cricket. His total bag was 307 (av. 21.57).

He made a remarkable start to his Test career in 1952 by sweeping India to defeat. Admittedly, the opposition was not very good, but Trueman carved himself a place among the world's most successful fast bowlers by taking 29 wickets in only 119.4 overs at an average of 13.31 apiece.

In the first innings of the Manchester Test that season the powerful Trueman took 8 for 31 in 8.4 overs, and this is probably the most devastating display of a fast bowler in the history of Tests.

Another of his most successful Tests was that against the West Indies at Edgbaston in 1963 when he took 5 for 75 and 7 for 44. He had one spell in the second innings when he took 5 for 0 in 19 balls.

In that 1963 series Trueman took 34 wickets (av. 17.47).

In addition to being one of England's deadliest fast bowlers, the burly Trueman was also a strong right-handed batsman whose highest score is 104 for his county in 1963.

TRUMBLE, Hugh (1867–1938)

This Australian took more England Test wickets than any other bowler in the history of the game. Playing in 31 Tests against England he bagged 141 wickets at an average cost of 20.88. He also played in one Test against South Africa but failed to take a wicket on that occasion, so his final Test average was 21.78.

Trumble performed the "hat-trick" twice in Tests and once against Gloucester at Cheltenham. He was seen at his best at the Oval in 1902 when against England he bowled unchanged and took 8 for 65 and 4 for 108.

Standing over six feet three inches tall Trumble used his height to advantage when sending down his slow-mediums and in his five tours of England between 1890 and 1902 he captured 606 wickets at an average of 16.68.

It should also be mentioned that Hugh Trumble was no mean batsman. Noted for his powerful defence he figured in an Australian record seventh-wicket stand of 165 with C. Hill, at Melbourne, 1898, his personal contribution being a determined 46.

In addition to this Trumble was a first-rate slip fielder who made 45 catches in Test cricket, a figure which places him among the most successful fieldsmen in international cricket.

TRUMPER, Victor Thomas (1877–1915)

A perfect batsman under all conditions this Australian was one of the most attractive of players and was possibly an even greater batsman than Sir Donald Bradman.

As a boy in Sydney, Trumper was such a good batsman that he was often barred from school games because they found him almost impossible to bowl out.

In *The Complete Cricketer* A. E. Knight wrote that "In Victor Trumper we have seen the very poetry and heard the deep and wonderful music of batsmanship . . . Stylish in the highest sense, orthodox, yet breaking all canons of style, Trumper is just himself."

V. T. Trumper played in 48 Tests, between 1899, when he first toured England, and 1911, when he played in all five Tests against England in Australia. He scored 3,164 runs in these games, averaging 39.06, figures which give no indications of the brilliance of this man.

At Hove in 1899 he scored 300* for the Australians against Sussex. This was his highest innings, but he scored many smaller totals which, under more difficult conditions, were masterpieces of sheer concentration, quick thinking and skilful placing of shots.

On one occasion, at Sydney, he compiled a century in 57 minutes. On another occasion in New Zealand he hit 200* in 2 hours 11 minutes. While at Bristol in 1905 he scored 108 before lunch.

However, it was in 1902 that England saw Trumper at his best, a veritable genius. During that tour he scored 11 centuries including two in one game against Essex. He never failed to score in any of his 53 innings and finished with an aggregate of 2,570 (av. 48.49).

Spectators at the Manchester Test that summer were privileged to witness some of the finest batting ever seen in this country when Trumper and Duff put on 135 for the first wicket and the score at lunch was 173 for one. Soon after lunch Trumper was caught behind the wicket for 104.

Some indication of the impression Trumper made on his contemporaries may be had from the fact that *Cricket Scores and Biographies* devotes over five pages to his biography, while in the same volume players like C. B. Fry, T. Hayward, A. C. MacLaren and K. S. Ranjitsinhji get four, three, one and a half and two and a half respectively.

TYLDESLEY, Ernest (1889–1962)

The Tyldesley family achieved as much for Lancashire as any of the other famous cricketing families did for their respective counties. At least seven Tyldesleys have made their mark with the red rose county and the modest Ernest, the youngest of five brothers, got more runs than any of them.

Making his debut in 1909 he had amassed 38.874 runs (av. 45.46) before he retired in 1936. His best year was 1928 when he had an aggregate of 3,024 (av. 79.57). And that was the season in which he and Frank Watson made 371 for the 2nd wicket v. Surrey at Old Trafford—still a Lancashire record partnership for any wicket.

In all Ernest Tyldesley hit 102 hundreds, including four in succession in 1926, and his highest score was 256* for his county v. Warwickshire, at Old Trafford in 1930.

TYLDESLEY, John Thomas (1873–1930)

Outstanding Lancashire professional batsman noted for his remarkable patience and skill on sticky wickets.

A typical example of this was his display against Australia, at Melbourne, in 1903–04, when he scored 97 and 62, being c Trumble b Howell in both innings.

Tyldesley made his debut for Lancashire in 1895 and, in his second match, against Warwickshire at Edgbaston, he scored 152*.

Very quick on his feet he was a particularly attractive batsman, who could hit out strongly when the opportunity arose.

He topped the 1,000-run mark in 19 consecutive seasons, four times exceeding 2,000 runs, and once (in 1901) his total reached 3,041.

On 13 occasions he scored double centuries, all of them were for his county, and the highest, 295*, was against Kent, at Manchester, in 1906.

Once, at Trent Bridge against Nottinghamshire, when he made 250, he so monopolised the scoring that in a last wicket stand of 141 his partner, W. Worsley, scored only 37.

He hit two separate hundreds in a match on three occasions.

After his retirement from full-time cricket in 1919 he was a coach at Old Trafford for many years.

U

ULYETT, George (1851–1898)

Yorkshire all-rounder, noted especially for his batting. He was a very hard hitter, always ready to punish the bowling.

Making his first appearance for Yorkshire in 1873 he quickly established himself as their leading batsman and was chosen to tour Australia with the first team to play Test cricket in 1876–77.

He toured Australia again in 1878–79, 1881–82, 1884–85, 1887–88. In his third tour he became the first Englishman to score a Test century in Australia, hitting 149 at Melbourne in March 1882.

One of Ulyett's most valuable contributions to Test cricket as a fast bowler was at Lord's in 1884, when, in the Australians' second innings, he took 7 for 36. It was in this game that Ulyett, an outstanding fielder, caught and bowled Bonnor, holding one of the Australian's most powerful drives.

A cheerful, typical Yorkshireman, in his 25 Test appearances Ulyett produced these figures—949 runs (av. 24.33) and 51 wickets (av. 19.82).

UMPIRES

The custom of having two umpires standing at a game dates back many years before the first known rules of cricket were drawn up in 1744. It is believed that there may have been only one umpire at the earliest games of the 15th century, but the year of the first appearance of either one or two umpires has never been established even approximately.

Before the popping crease was introduced in the early days of the 18th century it was necessary to touch the umpire at either end to record a run, and to facilitate this operation the umpire at the striker's end usually stood much closer to the wicket than he does today. The umpires also carried sticks or bats not only to lean upon but to provide a touching base for the batsmen.

Today, umpires may be changed during a match providing the opposing captains agree. This seems to have been the rule ever since 1744 although no provision was made for the changing of umpires when the Laws were revised in 1774.

Up to 1883 each side provided its own umpire in first-class matches but in that year a law was introduced making it compulsory for the umpires to be neutral at County matches. This law was not rescinded until 1948.

Men who have played for England and subsequently umpired Test matches are:

A. E. Fagg (Kent), L. C. Braund (Somerset), H. R. Butt (Sussex), J. F. Crapp (Gloucestershire), A. Dolphin (Yorkshire), J. Hardstaff, senior (Nottinghamshire), N. Oldfield (Lancs and Northants), E. J. Smith (Warwickshire) and H. Young (Essex).

F. Chester officiated in more Test matches than any other umpire. His total had reached 48 when he finally retired in 1955. When Chester began his career with Worcestershire in 1912 he seemed destined to become an England cricketer, but then came the war and when Chester lost part of his right arm during service in the Middle East, his playing career was ended.

Chester, however, was determined to make a name for himself in the cricketing world and he did just that. In 1922 he became a first-class umpire and in more than 30 years he built up a reputation which made him the most famous and respected umpire in the history of cricket. In all he officiated in well over 1,000 first-class matches.

There are normally about 25 umpires appointed each season to stand in first-class county matches.

The Association of Cricket Umpires which was founded in 1953 now has a membership of nearly 2,000.

UMPIRES' SIGNALS

The following signals are normally used by umpires to indicate certain scores, etc., to the scorers.

Boundary—waving an outstretched hand from side to side. .

Boundary six—both arms raised straight above the head.

A wide—both arms extended outwards horizontally.

A bye—open hand raised above the head.

Leg Bye—raising a leg and touching the knee with one hand.

No-ball—extending one arm outwards horizontally.

The decision *"Out"*—raising the index finger of one hand above the head.

"One short"—raising an elbow and touching the nearest shoulder with the fingertips of that hand.

"Dead ball"—crossing the arms back and forth at knee level.

UMRIGAR, Pahlan Ratanji (1926–   )

Another Indian all-rounder who is particularly well known in England for he spent five seasons, 1950–55, in Lancashire League cricket.

One of India's most prolific scorers who batted with great self assurance, Umrigar made his debut as an amateur in 1944–45. In 1948–49 he was chosen for one of the Tests against the West Indies and this was followed with all four Tests against England in 1951–52. Thereafter he was an ever-present in Indian Test teams right up to their Test against Pakistan in February, 1961. A run of 46 consecutive appearances.

Returning to the side in the second Test against England in 1961–62 he took his total of Tests to 59 and scored more runs in this class of cricket than any other Indian—3,631 (av. 42.22).

His highest score is 252* v. Cambridge University in 1959, the highest ever made by an Indian on tour.

On his previous England tour in 1952 he made 229* v. Oxford University, 204 v. Lancashire, and the same score against Kent.

In Test cricket his best is only eight runs short of India's record set up by V. Mankad. Umrigar made 223 v. New Zealand, at Hyderabad, in 1955–56.

As regards his bowling, right-arm medium pace, his best performance is 6

for 36 for Bombay v. Maharashtra in 1956–57.

UNDEFEATED

See also under DEFEATS (Fewest).

County Championship

In the County Championship the following clubs have gone through a season of at least 20 games without a single defeat: Yorkshire 1900, 1908, 1925, 1926, 1928. Lancashire 1904, 1928, 1930. Glamorgan 1969, Warwickshire 1972, Hampshire 1973.

Touring Test teams

Only one representative team from overseas has toured the mother country without suffering a single defeat. This was the Australian team of 1948 captained by D. G. Bradman.

This team engaged in 31 first-class matches, winning 23 and drawing eight. They won four of the five Test matches played.

At the end of the following year the Australians toured South Africa and were undefeated in another 21 first-class matches there. As this was the most successful touring side of all time the names of the men who were engaged in both the tour of England and the tour of South Africa are noted here. They were:

A. L. Hassett, R. N. Harvey, I. W. Johnson, W. A. Johnston, R. R. Lindwall, C. L. McCool, K. R. Miller, A. R. Morris and R. A. Saggers.

It should be added that while the Australians were sweeping all before them in South Africa they had another side in New Zealand. This side was also undefeated (in five games) and it included another three of the members of the victorious 1948 tourists: W. A. Brown (captain), D. T. Ring and D. Tallon.

The last England team to engage in an overseas tour which included Test matches and return undefeated was M. J. K. Smith's side in South Africa in 1964–65. They were undefeated in 17 first-class matches including five Tests.

Four other M.C.C. teams have toured South Africa and returned undefeated in all matches (first-class and otherwise):

W. W. Read's team played 20 matches, including only one first-class match (the Test), in South Africa in 1891–92 and were undefeated.

Lord Hawke's team played 17 matches (five first-class) in 1898–99 and won all but two of these. Those two were left drawn.

W. R. Hammond's team was undefeated on their tour of 1938–39 when they played 18 matches, all but one of which was first-class.

F. G. Mann's team was undefeated in 20 first-class matches there in 1948–49, including five Tests.

UNITED ENGLAND XI

When members of the famous All England XI rebelled against the management of William Clarke, certain players, led by John Wisden and Jem Dean, broke away and formed another professional combination, the United England XI.

This was in 1852 and the United England XI played its first match, against Twenty Gentlemen of Hampshire, at Southampton, August 26 of that year.

For a number of years relations between the All England XI and the United England XI were very strained. Indeed, the members of the new combination refused to take part in any match, except a county match, which was being run by William Clarke. However, a year after Clarke's death in 1856 these two sides were brought together for the first time and persuaded to meet at Lord's for the benefit of the Cricketers' Fund Friendly Society.

Thereafter they continued to meet annually at Lord's until 1867 when, because of a dispute between professionals of the North and South of England this benefit match was transferred to Manchester.

At about that time the United England XI was itself split by this dispute leading eventually to to the formation of another professional combination, the United South of England XI. Soon afterwards the former was entirely disbanded.

The United South of England XI continued for another 21 years but then, in 1880, they too were forced to give up through lack of fixtures and falling gates.

UNITED STATES OF AMERICA

Considering the close ties between the British Isles and the United States of America it is surprising that cricket has not taken an equal hold on both sides of the Atlantic.

However, while the game has not proved as popular in the States it has a much bigger following than many people imagine and is particularly strong in New York, Chicago, California, St. Louis and Philadelphia.

References to the game can be found in America as early as the beginning of the 18th century and the actual scores are known of a game in 1751 when New York beat a London XI. A club had been formed in Boston by 1760.

The United States first met Canada at cricket in New York, September 1844, making it the oldest series of matches between two countries. It was revivied as an annual event in 1963 after a gap of 51 years.

By the time the first touring side went out from England in 1859 interest was such that they were able to attract quite large crowds.

This touring team, captained by George Parr, was the first to leave these islands. They played five games in the United States and in Canada, all against odds, and won all five.

The Civil War which broke out in 1861 certainly marred the development of cricket in the U.S.A. just when it was becoming quite widespread, and it has been suggested that it was this war that established baseball instead of cricket as a leading pastime because of its popularity among the troops.

The first team from the United States to visit England was the Gentlemen of Philadelphia. They came over in 1884 and played 18 games against amateur sides. Of these they won eight, drew five and lost five.

Today, Philadelphia is one of the strongholds of American cricket. A club was formed there way back in 1831 and the actual Philadelphia C.C. came into being in 1854 and the Germantown C.C. a year later.

It was at Philadelphia that the Americans first played a match with an overseas touring team on level terms. The visitors were the Australian XI, which had just toured England for the first time. The Philadelphians earned a draw.

The Gentlemen of Philadelphia came over again in 1889 and played another 12 games against second-class opposition, winning four, drawing five and losing three.

This was a truly amateur combination

and the proceeds of all their matches played in this country were donated to the Cricketers' Fund.

The Philadelphians next tour was a momentous one for North American cricket for this time, in 1897, they were optimistic enough to meet all first-class opposition, including the M.C.C. In all they played 15 matches but only succeeded in winning two—against Sussex and Warwickshire. They drew four games and in two of these victory might have gone their way (against Nottinghamshire and Somerset) had the games been played out.

The outstanding member of this Philadelphian side was J. B. King, a fast bowler. Against Sussex he took 7 for 13 and had the distinction of clean bowling K. S. Ranjitsinhji first ball. His record for the tour was 93 wickets at an average cost of 14.91.

Since then the Philadelphians have played first-class matches on this side of the Atlantic in 1903, when they won six of their 14 matches, and in 1908, when they won only four out of 10. In this their last tour they were captained by J. B. King who returned the following astonishing bowling figures: 338.3 overs, 103 maidens, 958 runs, 87 wickets, 11.01 average.

Before leaving the Philadelphians it is worth noting that they succeeded in defeating the Australian XIs of 1893, 1896 and 1912. The Australian touring teams which visited England played matches in America in 1878–79, 1893–94, 1896–97 and 1912–13. In addition to these visits they also sent teams direct to America in 1913 and in 1932–33.

Apart from J. B. King one of the outstanding personalities of cricket in the United States was the Charterhouse, Cambridge, Sussex and England player, Sir C. Aubrey Smith. When he became a film actor he carried his enthusiasm for the game with him to Hollywood and was President of the South California Cricket Association until his death in 1948.

The first official representative U.S.A. team to visit England came in 1968, gaining valuable experience although winning only two of their 21 games with 11 drawn.

Apart from this team and the Philadelphians already mentioned, cricket tours of England have been made by Haverford College, Winnetka, University of California, and Prior of Philadelphia.

The United States Cricket Association with a membership of about 100 clubs was formed at a meeting in St. Louis,

Missouri, in December in 1961. The secretary is R. A. McLaren, 494 Maymont Drive, Ballwin, Missouiri, 63011.

The United States were elected to associate membership of the International Cricket Conference in 1965.

UNIVERSITIES

See also under CAMBRIDGE UNIVERSITY C.C., OXFORD UNIVERSITY C.C. and FINISH, Exciting (for Cobden's match).

The first University match was played at Lord's about June 4, 1827. It seems that there was only time for one innings each and the match was not finished. Oxford scored 258 and Cambridge 92.

The return match did not take place until two years later when it was played on the Magdalen Ground at Oxford and the home side won by 115 runs.

The third meeting was not until 1836, but since 1838 the two Universities have met every year with the exception of the seasons blotted out by two World Wars.

All of these games have been played at Lord's with the exception of the following: 1829, 1846, 1848—at Magdalen Ground, Oxford; 1843 at Bullington Green, Oxford; 1850 at Cowley Marsh, Oxford. Oddly enough there is no record of any game ever taking place at Cambridge.

The biggest victory in these games was that in 1923 when Oxford won by an innings and 227 runs.

In this historic match, Oxford, captained by R. H. Bettington, scored 422. The only Freshman in the side, C. H. Taylor, played a graceful innings for 109.

Cambridge's chances of matching this score were spoilt by a thunderstorm during the interval between innings which lasted all through the night and well into the morning of the second day. They were out for 59 and following on scored 136. In that second innings they found themselves up against R. H. Bettington in his most devastating form. The Oxford captain took 8 wickets for 66.

Cambridge's biggest win over Oxford was achieved in 1957 when they gained victory by an innings and 186 runs. This was the match in which G. Goonesena made the highest score ever by a Cambridge man in the University match—211. He also figured in a seventh-wicket stand of 289 with G. W. Cook which is a record for any wicket by either side in these matches.

Batting first, Oxford were out for 92, O.

S. Wheatley taking 5 for 15 with his medium-fast deliveries.

By the end of the first day Cambridge had lost five wickets for 108, but then Goonesena took command and batted for most of the second day before declaring the innings closed after being dismissed with an hour left to play.

Oxford made a valiant attempt to save the game and opening batsman I. M. Gibson did particularly well to score 63, but after he was run out there was little resistance and with some fine bowling by the man of the match, Goonesena, who took 4 for 40, Oxford were out for 146 with a couple of hours to spare.

The University match of 1977 will be the 133rd official match of the series. In the games played so far Cambridge hold a slight lead with 51 wins to Oxford's 45. 36 games have been drawn.

V

VALENTINE, Alfred Louis (1930–   )

Accurate slow left-arm spin bowler from Jamaica who made his name in England in 1950 when he created a West Indian record for a Test rubber by capturing 33 wickets (av. 20.42).

That was a glorious summer for the West Indies and particularly for that remarkable pair Ramadhin and Valentine.

Ramadhin actually took more wickets than Valentine over the whole tour but Valentine was the first West Indian to take at least 10 wickets in a Test match more than once. That season he took 11 for 204 at Manchester and 10 for 160 at the Oval. The Manchester game was his Test debut!

Again at Manchester in 1950, when playing against Lancashire, he took 8 for 26 and 5 for 31. At Canterbury he took 5 Kent wickets for only 6 runs.

Valentine played in Birmingham League cricket during 1952, and when he returned to England again in 1957 he was not the same force.

However, on his last tour, in Australia in 1960–61 he proved that he was still one to be reckoned with when bowling with typical effortless ease against Tasmania, he took 5 for 33 and completed the tour with a bag of 39 wickets which was second only to W. Hall.

VERITY, Hedley (1905–1943)

Yorkshire have rarely been short of a good left-arm bowler and Hedley Verity was one of the finest that county ever had.

Born at Leeds, Verity first appeared for Yorkshire Colts in 1926. He subsequently played as a professional for Accrington in the Lancashire League and with Middleton in the Central League, before making his debut in Yorkshire's county side in 1930.

In his first full season with Yorkshire in 1931 he hit the headlines by taking all 10 Warwickshire wickets for 36 runs at Leeds, and he repeated this performance in the following season on the same ground by taking all 10 Nottinghamshire wickets for 10 runs with only 52 balls.

Hedley Verity was well nigh unplayable on sticky wickets, indeed many critics rate him the best-ever spin bowler on a sticky wicket, and although that is purely a matter of opinion this player produced some remarkable figures to back his supporters.

From 1931 to the outbreak of World War II Verity never captured less than 150 wickets in a season. In his best summer, 1936, he bagged 216 (av. 13.18).

He made his debut in Test cricket against New Zealand in 1931 and played in a total of 40 Tests, capturing 144 wickets (av. 24.37). In this class of cricket his finest display was against Australia at Lord's in 1934. On that occasion he took 7 for 61 and 8 for 43.

No mean batsman, he shared in England v. India record Test stands for 8th, 9th and 10th wickets (since beaten), and scored 101 v. Jamaica in 1936.

A very determined man was Hedley Verity, remarkable for his strength of character. He died of wounds in Sicily in July 1943, when serving as a Captain in the Green Howards.

VILJOEN, Kenneth George (1910–1974)

South African whose first-class career extended from 1926 to 1948, playing for Griqualand West, Orange Free State and the Transvaal, and averaging 59.06 runs in Currie Cup matches, a figure which places him among the half dozen soundest batsmen ever to take part in that competition.

Viljoen represented South Africa in 27 Tests. The first against England at Johannesburg in December 1930, and the last more than 18 years later at Port Elizabeth v. England, in March, 1949. In the 1947 England tour he finished second in his side's batting averages with 1,441 runs (av. 49.68). Against Sussex at Hove he played an innings of 201*.

Always a sound orthodox middle-of-the-order batsman, Viljoen got his highest score, 215 for Griqualand West v. Western Province at Kimberley in 1929–30. His best in Test cricket was 124, at Manchester, in 1935, when he batted at number three.

Following his retirement from the field he managed a number of South African touring teams and also became President of the South African C.A.

VOCE, William (1909–   )

Tall Nottinghamshire left-arm fast bowler who made his debut in 1927, and will always be remembered for the part he played in the "body line" tour of 1932–33. That was, however, a part he preferred to forget for on his return from that tour, in which he took 15 Test wickets (av. 27.13), he and Larwood declared that they would rather not take any further part in International cricket.

Voce was not called upon to meet the Australians in the 1934 Test series, but, fortunately for England, he subsequently relented and was recalled to Test cricket in 1936 for the final game against India. After this he accepted an offer to accompany the M.C.C. team on their 1936–37 tour of Australia.

Here again Voce was at his best, even better than in his previous tour. This time he headed the averages, capturing 26 Test wickets at 21.53 runs each. At Sydney he took the wickets of O'Brien, Bradman and McCabe with four consecutive balls, taking 4 for 10 and 3 for 66.

Voce went to Australia again after World War II in 1946–47.

As well as a successful bowler Voce was also a better than average hard-hitting batsman. His highest score was 129 v. Glamorgan in 1931. He never succeeded in performing the "double" but he got 1,020 runs in 1933 when he totalled 73 wickets. He topped 100 wickets in a season on six occasions before retiring in 1947.

In Test cricket he took 98 wickets at a cost of 27.88 runs each.

W

WAITE, John Henry Bickford (1930–)

One of the finest wicket-keeper batsmen of modern times, this South African scored 2,405 runs in Test cricket as well as capturing 141 wickets. That total of wickets has only been exceeded by A. P. E. Knott, T. G. Evans and A. T. W. Grout in this class of cricket. Waite enjoyed an innings of 134 v. Australia at Durban in 1958.

In the 1961–62 tour of New Zealand, Waite, who hails from Johannesburg, created a record by capturing as many as 26 wickets in a Test rubber. He scored over 1,000 runs in England in 1951 and topped the South Africans' batting averages here in 1960.

At Durban in season 1959–60 he scored centuries in each innings—159* and 134* for Transvaal v. Natal in the Currie Cup.

WALCOTT, Clyde Leopold (1926–)

Tall hard-hitting batsman from Barbados who was one of the most consistent scorers in the history of Test cricket.

A schoolboy prodigy, Walcott played for Barbados at the age of 16 and soon became noted for his driving and skilful back-play. He subsequently developed such a muscular frame and long reach that he became one of the most terrific hitters in the game.

Making his Test debut against England in the 1947–48 series he never really got going, but in his next series in India in 1948–49 he made consecutive scores of 152, 68, 54, 108, 43, 11 and 16 (av. 75.33).

Walcott's greatest success was in the 1954–55 Australian tour of the West Indies. Then he scored a century in each innings of a Test, not once but twice. 126 and 110 at Trinidad, and 155 and 110 at Kingston. He actually scored five centuries

in that Test rubber, a world record, and finished with an average of 82.70.

Walcott's highest score was 314* for Barbados v. Trinidad in 1945–46.

WALES

With only one county in the first-class championship many people are apt to believe that cricket in Wales begins and ends with Glamorgan C.C.C., but this is a misconception.

The earliest inter-county match involving at least one (if not two?) Welsh counties was that played in August 1825 between Monmouthshire and Breconshire, and although there is no account of their earlier games it is known that a Monmouthshire club had existed two years before this.

Pembrokeshire played their first match in 1830, Montgomeryshire in 1853.

The Monmouthshire club was among the members of the Minor County Championship from 1901 until (with the exception of 1920) 1934, when it was taken over by Glamorgan C.C.C.

However, not too much about Monmouthshire lest that old argument is raised as to whether it was part of England or part of Wales.

Apart from Glamorgan, county cricket in Wales has been most enthusiastically contested among the northern counties. Clubs like Carnarvonshire, Denbighshire, Flintshire and Montgomeryshire were playing each other in the North Wales Cricket Association for several years before World War I. And with the addition of Anglesey in 1928 these counties have competed against each other more or less regularly ever since.

Carmarthenshire (1908–11), Denbighshire (1930–31, 1933–35), Glamorgan (1897–1920), Monmouthsire (1901–14, 1921–34), have appeared in the Minor County Championship.

The principal League competition in Wales is the South Wales and

Monmouthshire, formed in 1926. Star players from this League who have risen to the first-class game with Glamorgan include Emrys Davies, Haydn Davies, W. G. A. Parkhouse, C. C. Smart and E. C. Jones. Parkhouse, who hails from Swansea, did, of course, play for England, as did M. J. Turnbull, C. F. Walters and J. C. Clay before him.

In its hey-day, between the two World Wars, Welsh League cricket also boasted many famous professionals and none more popular than Percy Holmes of Yorkshire.

WALTERS, Kevin Douglas (1945–   )

An adventurous type of batsman who has produced some of his most brilliant innings when really needed, this Australian is also a medium-pace bowler who has surprised a lot of batsmen, but he has seldom been seen at his best in England where he has toured three times.

A typical example of his value to a side in trouble was at Auckland in 1973–74. Australia were 37 for 4 when he came in, but he stayed to make an unbeaten 104, reaching his half century in 99 minutes and his century in 158 minutes. Only three other Australian batsman reached double figures in that innings, the highest of them only 45.

In one game for New South Wales v. South Australia in 1964–65 he enjoyed an innings of 253 as well as taking 7 wickets for 63, and against the West Indies, at Sydney in 1968–69 he became the first batsman to score a double century and a century (242 and 103) in a Test match.

WARDLE, John Henry (1923–   )

This player's first-class career ended abruptly amidst a considerable amount of publicity towards the end of the 1958 season. Following differences between the player and the Yorkshire C.C.C. the county dispensed with his services at a time when he had already been selected by the M.C.C. for a further tour of Australia. After his dismissal the M.C.C. withdrew their invitation.

So one of the finest slow left-arm bowlers of the post-war era was lost to first-class cricket. Only the previous year Wardle's popularity with the Yorkshire supporters had been confirmed when his benefit realised £8,129.

Making his debut for the county in 1946

he totalled over 100 wickets in 10 of his 12 full seasons before his withdrawal.

He was first called upon to appear in a Test match when touring the West Indies in 1947–48, but he had no success, and it was not until the West Indies visited England in 1950 that he again represented his country.

After that he was an almost automatic choice and brought his total of Tests to 28, ending with the second Test against the West Indies in 1957. In all these matches he took 102 wickets (av. 20.39).

Wardle was also an aggressive left-handed batsman who made several useful contributions to his side's score in Tests and other matches.

After 1958 he played League cricket for Nelson and Minor Counties for Cambridgeshire.

WARNER, Sir Pelham Francis (1873–1963)

Middlesex have particular reason to feel proud of this true cricketing gentleman, for no man has done more to establish that county as a major force in the first-class game. But then all the cricket enthusiasts in England owe much to Sir Pelham Warner for he was one of the greatest ambassadors of the game who ever went on tour from this country.

Educated at Rugby and Oxford, where he got his "Blue", Sir Pelham Warner made his debut for Middlesex in 1894 and continued to play regularly for them until the end of the 1920 season. He was captain from 1908 until his retirement and had the satisfaction of leading them to the championship in that last season of 1920.

In all "Plum", as he was affectionately known on the cricket field, hit 60 centuries in first-class cricket, including 32 at Lord's.

He made his Test debut when he toured South Africa in 1898–99, carrying his bat through the innings for 132*. This is still the only occasion an Englishman has accomplished this in a Test v. South Africa.

Sir Pelham Warner captained England in Australia in 1903–04 and in South Africa in 1905–06. In addition he also led a touring team to America in 1897 and 1898 and to Australia in 1911–12. On this last tour, however, illness prevented him from playing in the Tests.

An attractive batsman with a fine upright stance he made his highest score,

244, for the Rest v. Warwickshire, at the Oval in 1911.

Sir Pelham was a Test selector and was chairman for seven seasons. He was President of the M.C.C. in 1950.

Editor of the authoritative and popular magazine *The Cricketer* for many years, Sir Pelham received his knighthood in 1937 for his services to the game.

WARWICKSHIRE C.C.C.

Founded: 1826. Re-formed 1884. Granted first-class status in 1894 and admitted to the Championship in 1895. Secretary: A. C. Smith, County Ground, Edgbaston, Birmingham B5 7QU. Highest score for: 657 for 6 declared v. Hampshire, Birmingham, July 24–26, 1899. Highest score against: 887 by Yorkshire, at Birmingham, May 7–9, 1896. Highest individual score for: 305* by F. R. Foster v. Worcestershire, at Birmingham, June 1, 1914. Highest individual score against: 316 by R. H. Moore of Hampshire, at Bournemouth, 1937. Lowest score for: 16 v. Kent, at Tonbridge, 1913. Other matches, 15 v. Dublin University, 1893. Lowest score against: 15 by Hampshire, at Birmingham, June 1922. Colours: Blue, Yellow and White. Badge: Bear and Ragged Staff. Honours: County Champions: 1911, 1951, 1972. Second XI were Minor Counties Champions 1959 and 1962. Gillette Cup: Winners, 1966, 1968, Finalists, 1964, 1972.

WASHBROOK, Cyril (1914–   )

When this famous Lancashire opening batsman was recalled to the England side against the Australians in the third Test of 1956 he was 41 years of age and had been absent from Test cricket for more than five years. Nearly everyone said that his selection was a mistake, but this attractive player proved them wrong.

That summer England had drawn the first Test and lost the second, but Washbrook, coming in at a crucial time in the Leeds Test, played a brilliant innings of 98 which virtually won the match.

Making his debut in 1933 Washbrook scored 152 v. Surrey at Manchester in his second match and quickly developed a style which always pleased the spectators.

During his career, which ended in 1959, he topped 1,000 runs in a season 20 times. His best was 2,662 (av. 68.25) in 1947.

He first appeared for England in 1937

and became a regular opening partner with L. Hutton. In South Africa in 1948–49 this partnership produced a record England first-wicket stand of 359.

As well as a consistent batsman Washbrook was a fine fielder at cover. His highest score is 251* for Lancashire v. Surrey, at Manchester, in 1947.

Washbrook captained Lancashire from 1954 to 1959 and is now a Test selector.

WEATHER:

Blizzard

At Rochester, New York, in October 1859, greatcoats and gloves were worn by the players in a match between George Parr's England XI and a Combined XXII which was played in a blizzard.

Heat

In July 1868 at the Oval a game between Surrey and Lancashire was stopped for an hour because of the intense heat.

The temperature in the sun exceeded 150 degrees (111.4 in the shade) during the Australia and England Test at Adelaide in January 1908.

Rain

The worst summers on record in England when cricket was badly hit by rain were those of 1879, 1888, 1901, 1903, 1912, 1927, 1954, 1956, 1968 and 1974.

In 1903 six County Championship matches were abandoned without a ball being played. Five matches were abandoned in 1912 and in 1927, and four matches in 1901, 1954, 1956 and 1967.

Particularly bad days have included the following:

July 23, 1936: No play in any of seven matches in progress.

May 26, 1948: No play in six first-class matches.

May 17, 1955: No play in all six matches due to weather.

June 27, 1958: Only one innings (by Glamorgan v. Hampshire) was possible in seven matches.

May 27, 1967. No play in all 10 first-class matches.

June 28, 1968. No play in all 8 first-class matches.

The only Test matches which have been abandoned because of rain without a ball being played were those between England and Australia at Old Trafford in August

1890 and in July 1938, and at Melbourne December–January 1970–71.

At Old Trafford in August 1931 no play was possible before 3.15 on the third and last day in the Test between England and New Zealand.

On the first day of the 1926 Old Trafford Test between England and Australia only six minutes' play was possible before rain washed out the rest of that day.

WEEKES, Everton de Courcy (1925–   )

Short, thick-set, confident, carefree, that's Everton Weekes from Barbados. But he was also a nimble and powerful stroke player who developed into one of the most prolific run-getters in post-war cricket.

Making his debut in 1944–45 he was brought into the West Indies side during the M.C.C. tour of the islands in 1947–48. In the first three Tests he made only moderate scores but he virtually won the fourth Test for the West Indies with an innings of 141.

This was the first of a run of five successive Test centuries (a world record) for in the tour of India in 1948–49 he scored 128 (at New Delhi), and 194 (at Bombay), 162 and 101 (at Calcutta). In his next Test innings he was run out when his score had reached 90. His average for Test matches on that Indian tour was 111.28, a figure that has seldom been exceeded in a Test rubber.

Weekes did almost as well on his next tour of India, in 1952–53, with an aggregate of 716 runs and an average of 102.28.

English spectators had a first taste of his powerful batting and many unorthodox scoring strokes when he joined Bacup in the Lancashire League in 1949 and set up a League record with an aggregate of 1,470 runs.

His first Test appearance in England followed in 1950 and although he did not score as many as expected in the four Tests he again headed his side's averages for the whole tour with a total of 2,310 (av. 79.65). It was on this tour that he created a record for a West Indian tourist in England with an innings of 304* v. Cambridge University.

During that summer he scored four other double-centuries: 232 v. Surrey, at the Oval, 279 v. Nottinghamshire, at Nottingham, 246* v. Hampshire, at Southampton, and 200* v. Leicestershire, at Leicester. Only Bradman, with six in

1930, has exceeded this score of five double-centuries in a single season.

WEIGHT

Among the heaviest men who have taken part in first-class cricket are the following:
W. Foulke (Derbyshire), about 23 stone.
W. W. Armstrong of Victoria, 22 stone.
D. J. Durston (Middlesex) 19½ stone.
George Brown of Sussex ("Brown of Brighton"), and Dr. W. G. Grace of Gloucestershire, 18 stone.

WEST INDIES

As in so many other parts of the world it was British troops who introduced cricket to the West Indies in the early part of the 19th century.

Records are scarce but it is known that the 59th Foot defeated the Trinidad Club in 1842 and even at that early date the home club had been in existence for some time. Clubs were also formed in the other island capitals at about the same period.

The first inter-colonial match was played in Barbados in February 1865. The home side easily beating British Guiana.

Trinidad entered the inter-colonial cricket field in 1869 but matches were few and far between until the early 1880's when the game really established itself in that part of the world.

Indeed, such rapid strides were made that in 1886 a representative West Indian side toured the United States and Canada under the management of G. N. Wyatt of British Guiana and captained by L. R. Fyffe of Jamaica.

The Americans made a return visit to the West Indies in the following year.

In 1891 a triangular tournament between Barbados, British Guiana and Trinidad proved such a success that it was decided to institute a regular inter-colonial cup competition. This trophy was subscribed for throughout the West Indies and first put up for competition in 1893 and continued until 1939.

Interest was further stimulated in 1895 by the arrival of the first touring team from England. This was a team captained by R. S. Lucas of Middlesex. They played 16 matches, winning 10, losing 4 and drawing 2. Barbados, Jamaica, Trinidad and St. Vincent were the four sides to defeat the Englishmen.

In 1896 two amateur teams from England toured the West Indies. One was captained by Lord Hawke and the other by Mr. A. Priestley. There was some unpleasantness between the two sides but the West Indians were certainly provided with a wealth of good cricket.

The West Indians came to England for the first time in 1900 and although they were disappointed at being refused first-class status their side, captained by Aucker Warner, was an enthusiastic one. Early defeats killed the interest of the home spectators and the tour was a failure from a financial point of view, but the side gained valuable experience and succeeded in defeating the Minor Counties, Leicestershire (Sir Pelham Warner played in this one match, captaining the West Indies), Hampshire, Surrey and Norfolk.

West Indies' most successful batsman on this tour was C. A. Ollivierre who scored 883 runs (av. 32.70). His finest innings was against Leicestershire where he opened with P. Warner (Sir Pelham) and 238 runs were on the board before "Plum" was out for 113. Then Ollivierre went on to make 159.

After this tour Ollivierre remained behind in England to qualify for Derbyshire and play for them until the end of 1907 season.

The first English side including professionals which toured the West Indies went out in 1904–05. They were captained by Lord Brackley and although they were only defeated in three of their 20 games (10 first-class) they found that the West Indians were improving their standard of cricket.

The West Indians were far more optimistic about their chances on their second England tour in 1906 when a side captained by H. G. B. Austin played 19 matches, including 13 first-class matches. But although they generally did show better form than they had done in 1900 they could only win three first-class games. They caused a shock by defeating Yorkshire (admittedly not at full strength) by 262 runs, and also gained victories over South Wales (by 278 runs) and Northamptonshire (by 155 runs).

After that the West Indians did not come to England again until 1923 when they won six first-class matches under the captaincy of H. G. B. Austin. It was in this tour that G. Challenor of Barbados established himself as one of the world's finest batsmen at that time. He came third to Hendren and Mead in the first-class averages of the season with 1,556 runs (av. 51.86). As for the West Indies bowling this was headed by G. Francis (Barbados)

82 wickets (av. 15.58) and G. John (Trinidad) 49 wickets (av. 19.51). It seemed that West Indian cricket had really made its mark.

No wonder then that the M.C.C. decided to send a really strong team to the West Indies in 1926 and include three games against fully representative sides in their itinerary. These games were not given Test status, however.

The M.C.C. team on this tour was captained by the Hon. F. S. G. Calthorpe and included Lionel Tennyson, P. Holmes, R. Kilner, F. Root and E. Astill.

The first of the three unofficial Tests was abandoned as a draw when rain stopped play. The West Indies had been on the verge of defeat. The second was won by the M.C.C., but in the third game the tourists were themselves saved from defeat by rain.

Obviously the West Indies were ready to be granted Test status and so they played their first official Tests on their next visit to England in 1928. Unfortunately, however, they were beaten by an innings in all three of these matches played that summer.

F. R. Martin (Jamaica) topped their Test batting averages with 175 runs (av. 29.16) and H. C. Griffith (British Guiana) took 11 wickets (av. 22.72).

Since then the West Indians have toured England in 1933, 1939, 1950, 1957, 1963, 1966, 1969, 1973 and 1976. Their most successful tours have been in 1950, 1963, 1966 and 1976. In each of those years they won three of their Test matches. In 1950 and 1966 their leading batsmen E. D. Weekes and G. S. Sobers respectively topped the averages in this country, and in 1963 West Indians topped both the batting and bowling averages—G. S. Sobers with 47.60 and C. C. Griffith with 119 wickets taken at a cost of only 12.83 runs apiece. In 1976 M. A. Holding was the most economical bowler in the country taking 55 wickets (av. 14.38), including 14 in the 5th Test at The Oval (8 for 92 and 6 for 57).

The West Indians also took part in the Prudential World Cup tournament in England in 1975 and won all five of their games, beating Australia by 17 runs in the Final.

They made their first Australian tour in 1930–31; their first to India and Pakistan in 1948–49, and their first to New Zealand in 1951–52. The colour bar has prevented a meeting with South Africa.

Records

Tests

Highest score for: 790 for 3 declared v. Pakistan, at Kingston, 1957–58:

C. Hunte, run out	260
R. Kanhai, c Imtiaz, b Fazal	25
G. Sobers, not out	365
E. D. Weekes, c Hanif, b Fazal	39
C. L. Walcott, not out	88
Extras	13
Total (3 wkts dec.)	790

Highest score against: 849 by England, at Kingston, 1929–30. Highest individual score for: 365* by G. Sobers v. Pakistan, at Kingston, 1958 (a world record—Tests). Highest individual score against: 337 by Hanif Mohammad of Pakistan, at Barbados, 1957–58. Lowest score for: 76 v. Pakistan, at Dacca, 1958–59. Lowest score against: 74 by New Zealand, at Dunedin, 1955–56 (Ramadhin 6 for 23).

Other matches

Highest score for: 730 for 3 declared v. Cambridge University, 1950. Highest score against: 676 for 8 declared by Harlequins, at Eastbourne, 1928. Highest individual score for: 304* by E. D. Weekes v. Cambridge University, at Cambridge, 1950. Highest individual score against: 264 by W. R. Hammond of Gloucestershire, at Cheltenham, 1950. Lowest score for: 33 v. R. A. Bennett's XI, at Georgetown, 1901–02. They scored only 19 v. United States, Georgetown, 1887–88, but this was not first-class. Lowest score against: 50 by Yorkshire (R. Ollivierre 7 for 23), Harrogate, 1906.

Barbados

Highest score for: 753 v. Jamaica, at Bridgetown, 1951–52. Highest score against: 692 for 9 declared by British Guiana, at Georgetown, 1951–52. Highest individual score for: 314* by C. L. Walcott v. Trinidad, at Trinidad, 1945–46. Highest individual score against: 281* by W. R. Hammond for M.C.C., Barbados, 1934–35. Lowest score for: 54 v. Trinidad, at Port of Spain, 1905–06. Lowest score against: 16 by Trinidad, at Bridgetown, 1941–42.

Guyana

Highest score for: 692 for 9 declared v. Barbados, at Georgetown, 1951–52.

Highest score against: 750 for 8 declared by Trinidad, at Port of Spain, 1946–47. Highest individual score for: 268 by H. P. Bayley v. Barbados, at Georgetown, 1937–38. Highest individual score against: 324 by J. B. Stollmeyer of Trinidad, at Port of Spain, 1946–47. Lowest score for: 22 v. Barbados, at Bridgetown, 1864–65. Lowest score against: 45 by Trinidad, at Port of Spain, 1868–69.

Jamaica

Highest score for: 702 for 5 declared v. Lord Tennyson's XI, at Kingston, 1931–32. Highest score against: 753 by Barbados, at Bridgetown, 1951–52. HIghest individual score for: 344* by G. A. Headley v. Lord Tennyson's XI, at Kingston, 1931–32. Highest individual score against: 275 by W. A. Farmer of Barbados, at Bridgetown, 1951–52. Lowest score for: 33 v. R. A. Bennett's XI, at Kingston, 1901–02. Lowest score against: 80 by Combined Islands, at St. John's, Antigua, March 1971.

Trinidad

Highest score for: 750 for 8 declared v. British Guiana, at Port of Spain, 1946–47. Highest score against: 726 for 7 by Barbados, at Bridgetown, 1926–27. Highest individual score for: 324 by J. B. Stollmeyer v. British Guiana, at Port of Spain, 1946–47. Highest individual score against: 314* by C. L. Walcott of Barbados, at Port of Spain, 1945–46. Lowest score for: 16 v. Barbados, at Bridgetown, 1941–42. Lowest score against: 33 by A. Priestley's XI, at Port of Spain, 1896–97.

WHITE CONDUIT CLUB

A number of the aristocracy who were keen on cricket and were members of the Star and Garter Club of Pall Mall, London, used to play on the White Conduit Fields at Islington, and in 1752 they formed a cricket club taking the name of their ground.

However, a few of the important gentlemen who took part in these games at Islington soon felt that a pitch on public fields was not up to the standard of such an exclusive club. Two of these gentlemen, the Earl of Winchelsea and Charles Lennox, then persuaded one Thomas Lord, an employee of the White Conduit

Club, to rent a private ground where the club could play their games.

So, the first Lord's ground at Dorset Square was opened in 1787 and the White Conduit Club played their first matches there in the summer of that year. But during the following winter they dropped their original name and became the Marylebone Cricket Club.

WICKET, The

The earliest batsmen probably defended a convenient tree stump but subsequently these countrymen (for cricket was born in the countryside and not in the towns) adopted a target formed by two upright sticks with a third piece resting across the tops. This was similar to the hurdle which formed the entrance to their sheep-pens, a small wicket gate with a horizontal rail known as a "bail". Hence the adoption of these names, stumps, wicket and bail, in the game of cricket.

The earliest wickets before 1702 were generally about a foot high and two foot wide and it was originally the practice to dig a small hole under each wicket into which the batsman had to pop his bat to score a run.

One can imagine that there must have been many scarred and broken knuckles in those days as the fielder attempted to run-out the batsman by popping the ball into this hole before the bat. No wonder, therefore, that it was eventually decided to dispense with the hole although the memory of the old system is retained today in the name "popping crease".

The first regulation wicket in the Laws of 1744 was 22 inches high and 6 inches wide with a popping crease cut in the ground at a distance of 46 inches before the wicket.

There is some doubt as to the precise year in which a third stump was introduced, but it was almost certainly in either 1775 or 1776, despite the fact that Pycroft names the first occasion as a match between Hambledon and England at Sevenoaks in June 1777.

Even then there was only one bail across the top of the three stumps and the use of two bails was not generally adopted until about 1786 although Haygarth makes reference to two bails in a game as early as September 1776.

In 1798 the wicket was increased in size to 24 inches by 7 inches, and it was also about this time that the Earl of Winchel-

sea experimented with the idea of using a fourth stump.

By 1821 the wicket had been increased to measure 26 inches by 7 inches with the popping crease moved a further two inches from the wicket.

In 1872 the M.C.C. experimented at Lord's with a wicket 29 inches by 9 inches but it was not until 1931 that any further alteration was made in the regulation size, it being increased to its present measurements of 28 inches by 9 inches.

Bails (Record distance)

In first-class cricket the record is held by R. D. Burrows of Worcestershire. When bowling W. Huddleston of Lancashire, at Manchester, June 29, 1911, he sent a bail a distance of 67 yards 6 inches.

It is on record that in a match between New Town and North West Hobart, played at Hobart, Tasmania, November 21, 1925, A. O. Burrows clean-bowled a batsman and sent a bail a distance of 83 yards, 1 foot, 9 inches.

The record distance for a bail in England was set up by a Minor County player, Dr. A. F. Morcom. When bowling for Bedfordshire v. Suffolk, at Wardown Park, Luton, in 1908, he sent a bail 70¼ yards.

WICKET-KEEPER

In the earliest days there was no wicket-keeper, at least not as a specific member of the team as we know him today. The bowlers took turn at keeping wicket at either end but they did not stand up close to the wicket and stumping was rare and not recorded as such in the scores.

It is generally acknowledged that the earliest specialist wicket-keeper was Tom Sueter, a builder and carpenter of Hambledon. He was also an outstanding left-handed batsman and played first for Hambledon and subsequently for Surrey until about 1791.

According to K. S. Ranjitsinhji the best wicket-keeper available should always be selected for a side without any regard for his batting ability, and in his *Jubilee Book of Cricket* the Prince went as far as to say that a really good wicket-keeper saves more runs than any single batsman gets.

The wicket-keeper with most dismissals to his credit in an entire career of first-class cricket is J. T. Murray of Middlesex. From when he first appeared for his county in 1953 until his retirement in 1975 his total reached 1,527.

As regards stumping, the record is held by L. E. G. Ames of Kent and England. From 1926 to 1950 his total reached 415.

The record number of dismissals by a wicket-keeper in a single innings is eight by A. W. Grout (all caught) for Queensland v. Western Australia, at Brisbane, February 1960.

Grout also shares the record for Test cricket with six in an innings when making his debut for Australia v. South Africa, at Johannesburg, 1957–58. This record was equalled by D. Lindsay, South Africa v. Australia, at Johannesburg, 1966–67, J. T. Murray, England v. India, at Lord's, 1967, and by S. M. H. Kirmani, India v. New Zealand, at Christchurch, 1976.

The match record of 12 dismissals is shared by three men—E. Pooley, Surrey v. Sussex, at the Oval, 1868; D. Tallon, Queensland v. New South Wales, at Sydney, 1938–39; and H. B. Taber, New South Wales v. South Australia, at Adelaide, 1968.

In Test cricket the match record is nine (eight caught and one stumped) by G. R. Langley for Australia v. England, at Lord's 1956.

The most dismissals by a wicket-keeper in a single season is 127 (79 caught and 48 stumped) by L. E. G. Ames of Kent and England in 1929. He also registered the second highest total with 121 (69 caught and 52 stumped) in 1928.

From another aspect the performance of T. G. Evans of Kent when playing for England v. Australia, at Sydney, in 1946–47, should never be overlooked. In their single innings Australia scored 659 for 8 declared, but Evans did not concede a single bye. This is the highest ever Test innings recorded without byes.

At Cheltenham in 1893 W. H. Brain of Gloucestershire stumped three Somerset batsmen off three consecutive balls from C. L. Townsend. He is the only wicket-keeper ever to achieve this stumping hat-trick.

WIDES

"Wides" were not entered in the scores as such until 1827. Prior to this they had been treated simply as "Byes".

The first match in which "wides" were actually recorded is believed to have been that between Sussex and Kent, at Brighton, September 17, 1827.

In those days, and until about 1844, the ball was reckoned to be "dead" as soon as a "wide" had been called and an allowance of one run only was made to the batsman.

In 1835, however, it was decided that the ball would not become "dead" on the call of "wide" and the batting side was entitled to as many runs as they could make off such a ball.

The greatest number of "wides" recorded against an England bowler in a Test match with Australia is eight by B. J. Bosanquet, at Leeds, in 1905.

Most "wides" by an Australian bowler in a Test against England is six by M. A. Noble, also at Leeds in 1905.

WILTSHIRE C.C.C.

Founded: In the 1790's. Figured in Minor County Championship for the first time in 1896. Secretary: E. W. Minter, 29 Ridings Mead, Chippenham. Highest score for: 502 for 3 declared v. M.C.C., 1902; in Minor County Championship—491 v. Devon, 1901. Highest score against: 735 by M.C.C. and Ground, at Lord's, August 13, 1888; in Minor County Championship—504 by Berkshire, 1926. Highest individual score for: 219 by W. S. Medlicott, 1902. Highest individual score against: 282 by E. Garnett of Berkshire, at Reading, 1908. Lowest score for: 17 v. Gentlemen of Hampshire, 1835; in Minor County Championship—35 v. Surrey II, 1953. Lowest score against: 20 by Glamorgan, at Chippenham, 1905. Honours: Minor County Champions: 1902, 1909.

WINS

Most in a season

In the County Championship with at least 20 games played the following sides have secured the highest number of victories in a single season:

Yorkshire: Played 32, won 25; season 1923.

Surrey: Played 28, won 23; season 1955. Most wins by a touring team:

23 by the Australians who played 31 first-class matches in England in 1948. Captain: D. G. Bradman.

Most wins by an official M.C.C. touring team:

12 of 21 first-class matches played in Australia and New Zealand in 1954–55. Captain: L. Hutton.

No wins

After beating Somerset, at Taunton, in the opening game of the 1935 season, Northamptonshire did not win a County Championship match until they defeated Leicestershire, at Northampton in May 1939.

Winning runs

In 1954 and 1955 Surrey had a run of 16 successive County Championship victories. This run was halted with a defeat by Yorkshire, at Leeds, in June 1955.

Middlesex won 15 successive Championship matches in 1920–21.

In 1923 Yorkshire had 13 successive victories.

WISDEN, John (1826–1884)

The name John Wisden is immortalised in his cricketers' almanack which has become the most widely read reference book of the game and is accepted today as the most authentic record of cricketing events.

However, while everyone knows that John Wisden was responsible for the earliest issues of the "Cricketers' Bible" his name has become so closely associated with this publication and the sports outfitting business that some may be inclined to overlook the fact that John Wisden was himself a first-class cricketer of outstanding ability.

Born the son of a Brighton builder, John Wisden learnt his cricket with Tom Box the Sussex wicket-keeper with whom he lived after his father's death.

Wisden was only five feet four inches and weighed no more than seven stone, but he developed into the greatest fast bowler of his day and became known as the "Little Wonder".

He first appeared for Sussex in 1845 and played regularly for that county until 1863. In 1846 he accepted an invitation to join William Clarke's All-England XI and played many games with this famous side until, in 1852, he and Jem Dean rebelled against the leadership of Clarke and broke away to form a rival side, the United England XI.

When Clarke died in 1856 Wisden got together with the new captain of the All-England XI, George Parr, and in 1859 the pick of the two sides set sail for America on the first overseas cricketing tour.

As regards his prowess on the field,

during his best period he was taking well over 200 wickets a season. In the four years 1848–51 his total bag was 1,307. In 1851 alone he took 455 wickets in only 41 matches, 279 of them clean bowled.

His most notable success was that at Lord's in 1850 when he clean bowled all ten wickets in the second innings for the North v. South.

He was also a fine batsman and when the Bramall Lane Ground opened in 1855, with a match between Yorkshire and Sussex, Wisden's contribution to the historic occasion was an innings of 148.

John Wisden died of cancer at the age of 58 in 1884.

WISDEN CRICKETERS' ALMANACK

When John Wisden first published his *Cricketers' Almanack* in 1864, price one shilling, he cannot have imagined that he was laying the foundations of the most authoritative cricket book in the world. Neither could he have been so optimistic as to think that his almanack would still be an annual publication 90 years after his death.

Wisden's first almanack contained only 112 pages and not a great deal of detailed information apart from the results to date of the All England, United England, and Gentlemen v. Players matches.

The second edition included the scores of all first-class matches of the previous season and descriptions of matches appeared first in 1870.

The almanack has since increased in size to something over 1,000 pages including the complete results of the previous season's first-class matches, overseas tours of the penultimate season, and details of all the principal cricket records established.

WOMEN'S CRICKET

The first women's cricket match of which there is any record was that played between eleven maids of Bramley and eleven maids of Hambledon (Surrey) on Gosden Common, near Guildford, July 26, 1745. Hambledon won by eight notches. A return match was played 11 days later.

Apparently women cricketers were taken seriously even in those days for women's matches were first played on the famous Artillery Ground as early as 1747. There is, however, a report of one of these matches being abandoned after spectators had invaded the pitch and some of the players had been injured in an outbreak of hooliganism.

Nevertheless, there were many more women's cricket matches during the latter part of the 18th century.

The first women's "county" match was probably that played near Ball's Pond, Newington, Middlesex, on October 3, 1811, between Surrey and Hampshire. This game was played for 500 guineas and was won by Hampshire after three days.

The White Heather Club was the first women's cricket club to be founded and it included various famous women players among its members, the most eminent of these being Lady Baldwin. It was formed in 1887 and was not finally disbanded until 1958.

When women's cricket staged a revival in the 1920's it continued to be scorned for many years by the men. But after the formation of the Women's Cricket Association, in October 1926, the game, as played by the fairer sex, not only increased in popularity but reached such a high standard that many critics were forced to acknowledge that women could play cricket as well as the men.

The first representative game to be played under the auspices of the new association was London and District v. The Rest of England, at Beckenham, July 1929.

In 1933 an England XI met The Rest on the Leicester County Ground, and the following year saw the women's game established on the highest level when England played The Rest at Old Trafford and an England team left these shores for a tour of Australia and New Zealand.

Women's cricket had been thriving in Australia around the beginning of the 20th century and the Victoria W.C.A. had been founded in 1905. Although Australian women's cricket faded out at about the time of the First World War it was revived in the 1920's and the Australian W.C.A. was formed in 1931.

The first women's cricket match played in New Zealand was probably at Nelson in 1886. The New Zealand W.C.A. was formed in 1934.

The first women's Test matches of three days' duration were played during England's tour of 1934–35. England won the first two at Brisbane and Sydney, and the third, played at Melbourne, ended in a draw.

Since then the Women's Cricket Association, which is at it were the M.C.C. of women's cricket, has sent teams to Australia and New Zealand in 1948–49, 1957–58 and 1968–69. Australia has toured England in 1937, 1951, 1963, 1973 and 1976, while New Zealand visited England in 1954 and 1966. A tour of the West Indies was made in 1971.

The South African and Rhodesian W.C.A. was formed in 1952, the Jamaica W.C.A. in 1966, and Trinidad and Tobago W.C.A. in 1968.

The first tour of South Africa was made in 1960–61 when four Tests were played.

England have also toured Jamaica 1970, Bermuda and the West Indies in 1971.

A World Cup series, won by the hosts, was held in England in 1973, including representative teams from Australia, New Zealand, Trinidad & Tobago, and Jamaica.

The first women's cricket match to be played at Old Trafford took place in July 1934 and the first at the Oval in June 1935.

In 1949, for the first time, two representatives of the W.C.A. were included in the M.C.C. Cricket Enquiry Committee at Lord's. This was an outstanding event in the history of women's cricket which has since grown to such proportions that an International Women's Cricket Council was formed in 1958.

Women's cricket is strictly amateur and in 1972 there are 22 official Women's County Cricket Associations in the United Kingdom.

Women cricketers first appeared at Lord's when they played a one-day international—England v. Australia, August 4, 1976.

Over the years many women of exceptional ability have played international cricket. After seeing these ladies in action all prejudice against women cricketers has been swept away.

Notable women cricketers of the past and present include:

Peggy Antonio: Was one of the cleverest women spin bowlers of all time. Came to England with the Australian side in 1937 and took 50 wickets for less than 12 runs each. At Northampton that summer she captured nine England wickets (6 for 51 and 3 for 40).

Mary Duggan: One of England's finest all-rounders of the post-war era. Took 20 wickets in Test series v. Australia in 1951, including record of 5 for 5 in third Test at the Oval. Against Australia in 1963, she became the first woman to score a century at the Oval—101*.

Rachael Flint: An England Test player since 1960 and captain since 1966. A naturally talented player and the first to hit a six in Women's Test cricket. Scored 102* in 89 minutes. her highest score was 144. Awarded M.B.E. in 1972 for services to women's cricket. She also played hockey for England.

Molly Hide: Captained England both before and after World War II. A really stylish player and a hard hitter who scored a century before lunch on the first day for the South of England v. Australia, at Hove, in July 1937. That day her score of 145 included 18 fours.

She scored five centuries on the 1948–49 tour of Ceylon, Australia and New Zealand, when her Test match average was 57.

Myrtle MacLagan: Surrey and England opening batsman and medium-pace bowler. In 1934 she had an average of 63.25 in nine innings against the Australians, scoring the first century in women's Test cricket—119 at Sydney.

She scored 115 out of an England total of 222 v. Australia at Blackpool in 1937.

After World War II she got four centuries on the 1948–49 tour and also took 63 wickets (av. 12.06).

Majorie Pollard: A hard-hitting batsman and a player who also did much to publicise the women's game in other ways. She made several radio broadcasts, contributed regular articles to various journals, and started the official magazine of the W.C.A. She captained England and among her best scores are 72* at Worcester in 1932, and 54 for The Rest v. the departing Touring Team in 1934.

Hazel Pritchard: When she visited England in 1937 this Australian won the hearts of all cricketing enthusiasts at the Oval where she gave an astonishing display of well-timed hitting while scoring 66 out of 94 in 70 minutes. This lady was such an accomplished batsman that she became known as "The Australian Lady Bradman".

Cecilia Robinson: Former England opening bat, holds record of 64.00 average in Test series in Australia in 1957–58.

Betty Wilson: This Australian was one of the cleverest all-rounders in women's cricket. In 1949 at Adelaide she scored 111 and 29 against England and also took 9 wickets for 62 runs. On the same ground in 1958 she not only enjoyed an innings of 127 against England but also took 6 for 71

in England's first innings. She was also the first to claim a hat-trick in women's Test cricket—at Melbourne in 1958.

The record individual innings in a first-class women's cricket match is 200 (retired) by Pat Holmes for the Australians v. West, at Basingstoke, 1937. But Mabel Bryant scored 201 for the Visitors v. the Residents, at Eastbourne, 1901.

The highest individual score in women's Test cricket is 189 by Betty Snowball for England v. New Zealand, at Christchurch, 1935.

WOODFULL, William Maldon (1897–1965)

At one stage of his career this Australian batsman was known as "The Great Unbowlable". He played through two seasons without ever allowing a ball to hit his wicket and when he toured New Zealand with the Victoria XI he emerged with an average of 148.33 from 13 innings (being seven times not out).

Woodfull was not a stylish but a patient plodding type of batsman who was particularly strong in defence.

His 212* for Victoria v. Canterbury, at Christchurch, in 1924–25, attracted the attention of the Australian selectors, but it was his 236 v. South Australia at Melbourne in 1925–26 which prompted them to add his name to the list of players already booked to tour England.

It was a fortunate last-minute decision for Woodfull headed the batting averages on that tour with 1.672 runs (av 57.65). In the Tests his average of 51.00 placed him third behind Macartney and Bardsley, but it was Woodfull who enjoyed the distinction of making the highest score of the tour, 201 v. Essex at Leyton.

Woodfull made two other trips to England in 1930 (av. 57.36; highest score 216 v. Cambridge University) and in 1934 (av. 52.83; highest score 228* v. Glamorgan at Swansea).

Woodfull was at his stubborn best in the Brisbane Test of 1928–29 against the bowling of J. C. White, Tate and Larwood. His side's second innings score was 66, with one man absent hurt, but Woodfull batted right through to make 30*.

In 35 Test appearances he averaged 46.00. His highest score being 161 v. South Africa at Melbourne in 1931–32.

Woodfull captained Australia in 25 of those Tests, five rubbers of these he lost only one—the "Body-line" series of 1932–33.

WOOLLEY, Frank Edward (1887–   )

One of the greatest left-handed all-rounders in the history of English cricket, F. E. Woolley had a long and distinguished career which began with Kent in 1906 and continued for 33 years until he retired at the age of 51.

A remarkable feature of his career is that although it was such a long time from his first complete season in 1907 until his retirement he never failed to score 1,000 runs. His 1,000 runs in 28 seasons (World War I intervened) is a record equalled only by W. G. Grace.

Woolley nearly always made rungetting look easy and he was one of the fastest scorers in the history of the game. Many of his innings were rightly described as devastating and none more so than his 229 against Surrey, at the Oval in 1935. In compiling his score in only three hours at the wicket he drove one ball clear out of the ground and into a garden on the far side of Harleyford Road. His biggest display of six-hitting was at Gravesend in 1925 when his innings of 215 against Somerset included eight hits over the boundary.

Completing the double on eight occasions during his illustrious career, his best seasons were in the early 1920s when he exceeded 2,000 runs and 100 wickets in three consecutive campaigns, 1921–22–23.

In addition to his prowess with bat and ball Woolley is regarded as one of the finest first slips ever seen. He held six catches in one game against Warwickshire in 1920 and he shares the record in Test cricket by catching six men in one match against Australia, at Sydney in 1911–12. His career aggregate of 1,015 catches is a world record.

It is worth noting that there were more than 25 years between his first and last Test appearances, both of which were at the Oval against Australia. In all he played in 64 Test matches, including a run of 52 consecutive appearances which is a record shared by P. B. H. May and beaten only by J. R. Reid of New Zealand, and G. S. Sobers of the West Indies.

WORCESTERSHIRE C.C.C.

Founded: 1844. Reformed 1865. Admitted to the County Championship 1899. Secretary: M. Vockins, County Ground, Worcester WR2 4QQ. Highest score for: 633 v. Warwickshire, at Worcester, August 6–8, 1906. Highest score gainst: 701 for 4 declared by Leicestershire, at Worcester, July 19–21, 1906. Highest individual score for: 276 by F. L. Bowley v. Hampshire, at Dudley, 1914. Highest individual score against: 331* by J. D. Robertson of Middlesex, at Worcester, 1949. Lowest score for: 24 v. Yorkshire, at Huddersfield, July 16–18, 1903. Lowest score against: 30 by Hampshire, at Worcester, June 18–19, 1903. In a second-class game—19 by Herefordshire, 1846. Colours: Dark Green and Black. Badge: Shield, argent bearing fess between three pears sable. Honours: County Champions: 1964, 1965, 1974. Minor Counties Champions: 1895 (tie with Norfolk and Durham), 1896, 1897, 1898. Benson and Hedges Cup: Finalists, 1973. Gillette Cup: Finalists, 1963, 1966. John Player League Champions, 1971.

WORRELL, Sir Frank Mortimer Maglinne (1924–1967)

This brilliant all-rounder was only 18 when he made his debut for Barbados v. Trinidad in 1942–43 and scored 64*, and when he made 308* v. Trinidad in the following season, he was the youngest player ever to score a triple century in first-class cricket.

Worrell was a precise stroke player, a real artist with the bat, who began a four-year spell in League cricket in England before playing some of the most devastating cricket of his career in the Test series against England in 1950.

He headed the West Indies Test averages with 89.83 that summer, and at Nottingham, he gave one of the finest displays of exhilarating play seen on that ground for many years. His innings was 261, 239 of which was scored in a single day's play, and included 35 fours and 2 sixes.

This relaxed batsman was also a fine stock bowler, left-arm medium pace swingers, and against Australia at Adelaide in 1951–52 he took 6 for 38 in one innings.

He is the only batsman ever to share in two stands of over 500 runs in first-class cricket. Both were for Barbados v. Trinidad; the first 502* with J. D. C. Goddard v. Trinidad in 1943–44, and the second, 574*, with C. L. Walcott in 1945–46.

Captained West Indies in 15 of his 51 Tests and is ranked among the finest captains in the game's history.

Was only 42 when he died of leukaemia.

WRIGHT, Douglas Vivian Pawson (1914–   )

The former Kent medium-pace leg-break and googly bowler was sometimes expensive but he could also be devastating. He holds the record for having performed the "hat-trick" seven times during his career which extended from 1932 to the end of 1957. On one of those occasions, Kent v. Gloucestershire at Bristol in 1939, he went on to complete the innings with 9 for 47.

Wright, who had a 16-yard run-up, began his Test career by taking five wickets against the Australians at Nottingham in June 1938.

After that he played in 33 more Tests and his best performance in these matches was his 7 for 105 in the Australians' first innings at Sydney in 1947.

In addition to the occasion already mentioned he also took nine wickets in an innings against Leicestershire at Maidstone in 1949, 9 for 51, followed by 6 for 112.

The fact that he bowled leg breaks at a much faster pace than any other bowler of his type accounted for his inconsistency but also at times made him virtually unplayable.

WYATT, Robert Elliott Storey (1901–   )

R. E. S. Wyatt captained Warwickshire for eight seasons before World War II, and Worcestershire for three seasons after the war. He also led England in 16 Tests.

A reliable batsman, strong in defence, and a useful change bowler, Wyatt made his debut for Warwickshire in 1923, the first of his 40 Test appearances following in 1927–28, when he toured South Africa.

There was quite a stir when he displaced Percy Chapman as captain of England in the fifth Test against Australia in 1930 at the Oval, but although England lost the Test Wyatt played an important part by helping Sutcliffe to put on 170 for the sixth wicket in the first innings.

Wyatt scored 39,404 runs in first-class cricket. His highest being 232 for Warwickshire v. Derbyshire, at Birmingham, in 1937. In Test cricket his highest was 149 v. South Africa at Nottingham in 1935.

Before he retired from county cricket at the end of 1952, this serious minded player had topped 1,000 runs in a season 18 times. His best was 2,630 (av. 53.67) in 1929.

Y

YARDLEY, Norman Walter Dransfield (1915–   )

Stylish batsman and medium-pace bowler, N. W. D. Yardley was a Cambridge "Blue" 1935–36–37–38. In the last year he captained his University. He was also a hockey "Blue" and an outstanding rackets player.

Even before going up to University this Barnsley born Yorkshireman distinguished himself as a cricketer when he scored 189 for the Young Amateurs v. Young Professionals and 63 for Public Schools v. Army, at Lord's.

Yardley toured India with Lord Tennyson's team in 1937–38 and went with the M.C.C. to South Africa in the following winter, appearing in his first Test.

In all Yardley played in 20 Test matches, captaining England in 14 of them. His highest score in these games was 99 v. South Africa at Nottingham in 1947.

During the 1946–47 tour of Australia in which he first took over from Hammond as captain, Yardley had the satisfaction of taking Bradman's wicket in three successive innings and topped England's bowling averages for the rubber with 10 wickets (37.20).

His career with Yorkshire began in 1936 and but for the break during the war he played regularly for them until the end of 1955. He captained the county from 1948 until his retirement.

YORKSHIRE C.C.C.

Founded: 1861. Secretary: J. Lister Headingley Cricket Ground, Leeds LS6 3BU. Highest score for: 887 v. Warwickshire, at Birmingham, May 7–9, 1896. Highest score against: 630 by Somerset, at Leeds, July 15–17, 1901. Highest individual score for: 341 by G. H. Hirst v. Leicestershire, at Leicester, May 20, 1905. Highest individual score against: 318* by Dr. W. G. Grace of Gloucestershire, at Cheltenham, August 1876. Lowest score for: 23 v. Hampshire, at Middlesbrough, May 20, 1965. Lowest score against: 13 by Nottinghamshire (W. Rhodes 6 for 4), at Nottingham, June 20–21, 1901. Colours: Oxford Blue, Cambridge Blue and Gold. Badge: White Rose. Honours: County Champions: 1867, 1869 (with Nottinghamshire), 1870, 1893, 1896, 1898, 1900, 1901, 1902, 1905, 1908, 1912, 1919, 1922, 1923, 1924, 1925, 1931, 1932, 1933, 1935, 1937, 1938, 1939, 1946, 1949 (tie with Middlesex), 1959, 1960, 1962, 1963, 1966, 1967, 1968. Minor Counties Champions: (Second XI) 1947, 1957, 1958, 1968, 1971, 1972. Benson and Hedges Cup: Finalists, 1972. Gillette Cup: Winners, 1965, 1969.

INDEX